World Economic and Financial Surveys

World Economic Outlook
April 2016

Too Slow for Too Long

· ·

INTERNATIONAL MONETARY FUND

©2016 International Monetary Fund

Cover and Design: Luisa Menjivar and Jorge Salazar
Composition: AGS, An RR Donnelley Company

Cataloging-in-Publication Data

Joint Bank-Fund Library

Names: International Monetary Fund.
Title: World economic outlook (International Monetary Fund)
Other titles: WEO | Occasional paper (International Monetary Fund) | World economic and
   financial surveys.
Description: Washington, DC : International Monetary Fund, 1980- | Semiannual | Some
   issues also have thematic titles. | Began with issue for May 1980. | 1981-1984: Occasional
   paper / International Monetary Fund, 0251-6365 | 1986-: World economic and financial
   surveys, 0256-6877.
Identifiers: ISSN 0256-6877 (print) | ISSN 1564-5215 (online)
Subjects: LCSH: Economic development—Periodicals. | International economic relations—
   Periodicals. | Debts, External—Periodicals. | Balance of payments—Periodicals. |
   International finance—Periodicals. | Economic forecasting—Periodicals.
Classification: LCC HC10.W79

HC10.80

ISBN 978-1-49839-858-9 (paper)
      978-1-47554-372-8 (PDF)
      978-1-47556-199-9 (ePub)
      978-1-47556-264-4 (Mobi)

Publication orders may be placed online, by fax, or through the mail:
International Monetary Fund, Publication Services
P.O. Box 92780, Washington, DC 20090, U.S.A.
Tel.: (202) 623-7430 Fax: (202) 623-7201
E-mail: publications@imf.org
www.imfbookstore.org
www.elibrary.imf.org

CONTENTS

Tables

Online Tables

Figures

ASSUMPTIONS AND CONVENTIONS

A number of assumptions have been adopted for the projections presented in the *World Economic Outlook* (WEO). It has been assumed that real effective exchange rates remained constant at their average levels during February 2–March 1, 2016, except for those for the currencies participating in the European exchange rate mechanism II (ERM II), which are assumed to have remained constant in nominal terms relative to the euro; that established policies of national authorities will be maintained (for specific assumptions about fiscal and monetary policies for selected economies, see Box A1 in the Statistical Appendix); that the average price of oil will be $34.75 a barrel in 2016 and $40.99 a barrel in 2017 and will remain unchanged in real terms over the medium term; that the six-month London interbank offered rate (LIBOR) on U.S. dollar deposits will average 0.9 percent in 2016 and 1.5 percent in 2017; that the three-month euro deposit rate will average –0.3 percent in 2016 and –0.4 percent in 2017; and that the six-month Japanese yen deposit rate will yield on average –0.1 percent in 2016 and –0.3 percent in 2017. These are, of course, working hypotheses rather than forecasts, and the uncertainties surrounding them add to the margin of error that would in any event be involved in the projections. The estimates and projections are based on statistical information available through March 25, 2016.

The following conventions are used throughout the WEO:

- . . .   to indicate that data are not available or not applicable;
- –   between years or months (for example, 2015–16 or January–June) to indicate the years or months covered, including the beginning and ending years or months;
- /   between years or months (for example, 2015/16) to indicate a fiscal or financial year.

"Billion" means a thousand million; "trillion" means a thousand billion.

"Basis points" refers to hundredths of 1 percentage point (for example, 25 basis points are equivalent to ¼ of 1 percentage point).

Data refer to calendar years, except in the case of a few countries that use fiscal years. Please refer to Table F in the Statistical Appendix, which lists the economies with exceptional reporting periods for national accounts and government finance data for each country.

For some countries, the figures for 2015 and earlier are based on estimates rather than actual outturns. Please refer to Table G in the Statistical Appendix, which lists the latest actual outturns for the indicators in the national accounts, prices, government finance, and balance of payments indicators for each country.

- Data for Macao Special Administrative Region and the Commonwealth of Puerto Rico are included in data aggregated for the advanced economies. Macao is a Special Administrative Region of China, and Puerto Rico is a territory of the United States, but the WEO maintains statistical data for both economies on a separate and independent basis.
- Argentina's and Venezuela's consumer prices are excluded from all the WEO groups' aggregates.

In the tables and figures, the following conventions apply:

- If no source is listed on tables and figures, data are drawn from the WEO database.
- When countries are not listed alphabetically, they are ordered on the basis of economic size.
- Minor discrepancies between sums of constituent figures and totals shown reflect rounding.

As used in this report, the terms "country" and "economy" do not in all cases refer to a territorial entity that is a state as understood by international law and practice. As used here, the term also covers some territorial entities that are not states but for which statistical data are maintained on a separate and independent basis.

Composite data are provided for various groups of countries organized according to economic characteristics or region. Unless noted otherwise, country group composites represent calculations based on 90 percent or more of the weighted group data.

The boundaries, colors, denominations, and any other information shown on the maps do not imply, on the part of the International Monetary Fund, any judgment on the legal status of any territory or any endorsement or acceptance of such boundaries.

FURTHER INFORMATION AND DATA

This version of the *World Economic Outlook* (WEO) is available in full through the IMF eLibrary (www.elibrary.imf.org) and the IMF website (www.imf.org). Accompanying the publication on the IMF website is a larger compilation of data from the WEO database than is included in the report itself, including files containing the series most frequently requested by readers. These files may be downloaded for use in a variety of software packages.

The data appearing in the *World Economic Outlook* are compiled by the IMF staff at the time of the WEO exercises. The historical data and projections are based on the information gathered by the IMF country desk officers in the context of their missions to IMF member countries and through their ongoing analysis of the evolving situation in each country. Historical data are updated on a continual basis as more information becomes available, and structural breaks in data are often adjusted to produce smooth series with the use of splicing and other techniques. IMF staff estimates continue to serve as proxies for historical series when complete information is unavailable. As a result, WEO data can differ from those in other sources with official data, including the IMF's *International Financial Statistics*.

The WEO data and metadata provided are "as is" and "as available," and every effort is made to ensure their timeliness, accuracy, and completeness, but it cannot be guaranteed. When errors are discovered, there is a concerted effort to correct them as appropriate and feasible. Corrections and revisions made after publication are incorporated into the electronic editions available from the IMF eLibrary (www.elibrary.imf.org) and on the IMF website (www.imf.org). All substantive changes are listed in detail in the online tables of contents.

For details on the terms and conditions for usage of the WEO database, please refer to the IMF Copyright and Usage website (www.imf.org/external/terms.htm).

Inquiries about the content of the *World Economic Outlook* and the WEO database should be sent by mail, fax, or online forum (telephone inquiries cannot be accepted):

World Economic Studies Division
Research Department
International Monetary Fund
700 19th Street, N.W.
Washington, DC 20431, U.S.A.
Fax: (202) 623-6343
Online Forum: www.imf.org/weoforum

PREFACE

The analysis and projections contained in the *World Economic Outlook* are integral elements of the IMF's surveillance of economic developments and policies in its member countries, of developments in international financial markets, and of the global economic system. The survey of prospects and policies is the product of a comprehensive interdepartmental review of world economic developments, which draws primarily on information the IMF staff gathers through its consultations with member countries. These consultations are carried out in particular by the IMF's area departments—namely, the African Department, Asia and Pacific Department, European Department, Middle East and Central Asia Department, and Western Hemisphere Department—together with the Strategy, Policy, and Review Department, the Monetary and Capital Markets Department, and the Fiscal Affairs Department.

The analysis in this report was coordinated in the Research Department under the general direction of Maurice Obstfeld, Economic Counsellor and Director of Research. The project was directed by Gian Maria Milesi-Ferretti, Deputy Director, Research Department, and Oya Celasun, Division Chief, Research Department.

The primary contributors to this report were Rudolfs Bems, Luis Catão, Romain Duval, Davide Furceri, Alexander Hijzen, João Jalles, Sinem Kılıç Çelik, Zsóka Kóczán, Weicheng Lian, and Marcos Poplawski-Ribeiro.

Other contributors include Jaebin Ahn, Juliana Araujo, Rabah Arezki, Gavin Asdorian, Aqib Aslam, Samya Beidas-Strom, Christian Bogmans, Romain Bouis, Emine Boz, Matteo Cacciatore, Eugenio Cerutti, Vanessa Diaz Montelongo, Angela Espiritu, Johannes Eugster, Rachel Yuting Fan, Giuseppe Fiori, Emily Forrest, Peter Gal, Fabio Ghironi, Eric Gould, Mitko Grigorov, Mahnaz Hemmati, Bingjie Hu, Ben Hunt, Carla Intal, Hao Jiang, Maria Jovanović, Sung Eun Jung, Alimata Kini Kaboré, Toh Kuan, Douglas Laxton, Christina Yun Liu, Prakash Loungani, Olivia Ma, Pedro Martins, Akito Matsumoto, Trevor Meadows, Giovanni Melina, Jakob Miethe, Susanna Mursula, Futoshi Narita, Huy Nguyen, Emory Oakes, Andrea Presbitero, Frantisek Ricka, Rachel Szymanski, Nicholas Tong, Petia Topalova, Hou Wang, Jilun Xing, Hong Yang, Felipe Zanna, Yuan Zeng, Fan Zhang, and Hongyan Zhao. Michael Harrup from the Communications Department led the editorial team for the report, with production and editorial support from Christine Ebrahimzadeh and editorial assistance from Lucy Scott Morales, Linda Long, Lorraine Coffey, Gregg Forte, and EEI Communications.

The analysis has benefited from comments and suggestions by staff members from other IMF departments, as well as by Executive Directors following their discussion of the report on March 28, 2016. However, both projections and policy considerations are those of the IMF staff and should not be attributed to Executive Directors or to their national authorities.

FOREWORD

Global recovery continues, but at an ever-slowing and increasingly fragile pace. The months since the last *World Economic Outlook* have seen a renewed episode of global asset market volatility, some loss of growth momentum in the advanced economies, and continuing headwinds for emerging market economies and lower-income countries. In addition, several stresses of noneconomic origin threaten economic activity. Not only do these developments lead us to a further broad-based reduction in our baseline projections for economic growth in 2016 and 2017; they also suggest that possible nonbaseline outcomes are at the same time less favorable and more likely.

Notwithstanding this cloudier picture of economic fundamentals, financial markets in advanced economies have, at this writing, partially reversed their swoon of the first weeks of 2016. Some improved data releases, a firming of oil prices, lower capital outflows from China, and decisions by major central banks have all contributed to improved sentiment. These developments are consistent with our central projection that growth over the next two years, while lower than we believed likely just a few months ago, will still be slightly higher than in 2015. Yet that outcome is far from assured. Significant downside risks remain, and events that make those risks more salient may well trigger renewed financial turbulence.

What are the risks? Important among purely economic risks is a return of financial turmoil itself, impairing confidence and demand in a self-confirming negative feedback loop. Despite the recent rebound in asset prices, financial conditions in the United States, Europe, and Japan have been on a tightening trend since mid-2014, as the new *Global Financial Stability Report* documents.

Yet financial conditions have tightened even more outside the advanced economies. Increased net capital outflows from emerging markets—the subject of Chapter 2 of this *World Economic Outlook* report—could lead to further depreciation of their currencies, eventually triggering adverse balance sheet effects. Market perceptions of constrained macroeconomic

policy space added to the recent bout of pessimism. These worries remain and are especially relevant for emerging market and developing economies.

China, now the world's largest economy on a purchasing-power-parity basis, is navigating a momentous but complex transition toward more sustainable growth based on consumption and services. Ultimately, that process will benefit both China and the world. Given China's important role in global trade, however, bumps along the way could have substantial spillover effects, especially on emerging market and developing economies.

Another threat is that persistent slow growth has scarring effects that themselves reduce potential output and with it, consumption and investment. Consecutive downgrades of future economic prospects carry the risk of a world economy that reaches stalling speed and falls into widespread secular stagnation.

Adding to this list are several pressures with origins in political, geopolitical, or natural developments. In both the United States and Europe, the political discussion is turning increasingly inward. The causes are complex but certainly reflect growing income inequality as well as structural shifts, some connected with globalization, that are seen as having favored economic elites while leaving others behind. Fear of terrorism also plays a role. The result could be a turn toward more nationalistic policies, including protectionist ones.

In the United Kingdom, the planned June referendum on European Union membership has already created uncertainty for investors; a "Brexit" could do severe regional and global damage by disrupting established trading relationships. Adding to political strains in Europe is the tragedy of large-scale refugee inflows, especially from the Middle East. Of course, a sizable fraction of refugee flows originates in violent extremism or sectarian strife, factors that devastate source economies and threaten their neighbors. Yet there are also natural causes of population displacement, some linked to climate change. Extreme flooding and drought from the current El Niño is worsening poverty and displacement in a range of emerging markets and low-income developing countries.

Apart from these risks, the April *World Economic Outlook* also describes a further weakening of global growth under its baseline scenario. An important cause is that demand, notably investment demand, remains weak worldwide, but especially in commodity exporters, whose terms of trade have collapsed. China's rebalancing process has subtracted measurably from world investment growth, and generally higher uncertainty about global growth prospects is also a factor. Weak investment demand, in turn, has been associated with slower growth in international trade, given the important roles played by capital and intermediate goods.

Emerging market and especially low-income commodity exporters will struggle to restore growth until they have diversified their export bases, a process that will take time. While in principle terms-of-trade losses by commodity exporters should translate into symmetric gains for importers, in practice the negative effects on producers seem to have dominated so far. The situation is not without precedent. In his classic 1973 book *The World in Depression: 1929–1939*, Charles P. Kindleberger noted a similar dynamic in the commodity price deflation of the 1920s: "The view taken here is that symmetry may obtain in the scholar's study, but that it is hard to find in the real world. . . . The consuming countries might ultimately have realized that their real incomes had increased and permitted them to expand spending. Meanwhile the primary producers cannot wait." As Chapter 1 in this *World Economic Outlook* report points out, commodity importers with policy interest rates currently near zero will face an additional offset to the positive income effect of lower commodity prices.

A diminished economic outlook burdened with larger downside risks raises the premium on intensifying and extending sound policies that safeguard near-term growth and boost potential output. Monetary policy must remain accommodative in the face of deflationary pressures, including through additional unconventional measures if needed. But monetary policy cannot bear the entire burden of responding to current challenges; it must be supported by other policies that directly boost supply and demand.

Infrastructure investment is needed across a range of countries and should be attractive in a setting of very low real interest rates. Countries with fiscal space should not wait to take advantage of it. Public action to encourage research and development activity, as documented in the new *Fiscal Monitor*, can boost output. At the same time, as Chapter 3 in this *World Economic Outlook* report shows, structural reforms in product and labor markets can be effective in boosting output, even in the short term, and especially if coupled with fiscal support. Tax reform, even when budget neutral, can create demand if well targeted, while simultaneously improving labor force participation and enhancing social cohesion. Not only financial stability, but the transmission of monetary and fiscal policy, would be enhanced by further financial reforms, including the resolution of impaired assets still held on banks' books.

These measures should be taken now, but countries should also cooperate to design collective measures to be deployed in the future in case downside risks materialize. A range of demand- and supply-side policies can be more effective through positive output spillovers across countries; policymakers could already formulate contingent plans.

In addition, cooperation to enhance the global financial safety net and the global regulatory regime is central to a resilient international monetary and financial system. Some of the risks coming from noneconomic sources likewise present public goods problems solvable through international coordination, on the model of the December 2015 Paris climate agreement.

The current diminished outlook and associated downside possibilities warrant an immediate response. If national policymakers were to clearly recognize the risks they jointly face and act together to prepare for them, the positive effects on global confidence could be substantial. The result would be stronger growth under the baseline outcome as well as insurance against a derailed recovery.

Maurice Obstfeld
Economic Counsellor

EXECUTIVE SUMMARY

The baseline projection for global growth in 2016 is a modest 3.2 percent, broadly in line with last year, and a 0.2 percentage point downward revision relative to the January 2016 World Economic Outlook (WEO) Update. *The recovery is projected to strengthen in 2017 and beyond, driven primarily by emerging market and developing economies, as conditions in stressed economies start gradually to normalize. But uncertainty has increased, and risks of weaker growth scenarios are becoming more tangible. The fragile conjuncture increases the urgency of a broad-based policy response to raise growth and manage vulnerabilities.*

The global recovery has weakened further amid increasing financial turbulence. Activity softened toward the end of 2015 in advanced economies, and stresses in several large emerging market economies showed no signs of abating. Adding to these headwinds are concerns about the global impact of the unwinding of prior excesses in China's economy as it transitions to a more balanced growth path after a decade of strong credit and investment growth, along with signs of distress in other large emerging markets, including from falling commodity prices. With heightened risk aversion and increasing concerns about the lack of policy space, the valuation of risky assets as well as oil prices dropped sharply in early 2016. However, market sentiment began to improve in mid-February, and by the end of March market valuations had recovered most of or all the ground lost earlier in the year.

While growth in emerging market and developing economies still accounts for the lion's share of projected world growth in 2016, prospects across countries remain uneven and generally weaker than over the past two decades. In particular, a number of large emerging markets—including Brazil and Russia—are still mired in deep recessions. Others, including several oil-exporting countries, also face a difficult macroeconomic environment with sharply weaker terms of trade and tighter external financial conditions. Growth in China and India has been broadly in line with projections, but trade growth has slowed down noticeably. The trade slowdown is related to the

decline in investment growth across emerging market economies, which reflects rebalancing in China but also the sharp scaling down of investment in commodity exporters, particularly those facing difficult macroeconomic conditions.

Growth in advanced economies is projected to remain modest, in line with 2015 outcomes. Unfavorable demographic trends, low productivity growth, and legacies from the global financial crisis continue to hamper a more robust pickup in activity. While very accommodative monetary policy and lower oil prices will support domestic demand, still-weak external demand, further exchange rate appreciation—especially in the United States—and somewhat tighter financial conditions will weigh on the recovery. In the euro area, the risk of a deanchoring of inflation expectations is a concern amid large debt overhangs in several countries.

The projected pickup in growth in 2017 (3.5 percent) and over the rest of the forecast horizon hinges crucially on rising growth in emerging market and developing economies, as growth in advanced economies is expected to remain modest, in line with weakened potential growth. This outcome relies on a number of important assumptions:

- A gradual normalization of conditions in several economies currently under stress
- A successful rebalancing of China's economy with trend growth rates that—while lower than those of the past two decades—remain high
- A pickup in activity in commodity exporters, albeit at rates more modest than in the past
- Resilient growth in other emerging market and developing economies

In the current environment, the likelihood that this central scenario will materialize has weakened, as risks of weaker growth have become more salient.

- Across advanced economies, activity slowed during the second part of 2015, and asset price declines and widening spreads have tightened financial conditions. If sustained, these developments could further weaken growth, with risks of a stagnation scenario with persistent negative output gaps and excessively low inflation.

- Emerging market stress could rise further, also reflecting domestic vulnerabilities. For instance, an additional bout of exchange rate depreciations could further worsen corporate balance sheets, and a sharp decline in capital inflows could force a rapid compression of domestic demand.

- A protracted period of low oil prices could further destabilize the outlook for oil-exporting countries. While some countries still have sizable buffers, these are eroding, and some countries already face the need for sharp expenditure cuts.

- The rebalancing process in China may be less smooth than assumed in the baseline scenario. A sharper slowdown in China than currently projected could have strong international spillovers through trade, commodity prices, and confidence, and lead to a more generalized slowdown in the global economy, especially if it further curtailed expectations of future income.

- Shocks of a noneconomic origin—related to geopolitical conflicts, political discord, terrorism, refugee flows, or global epidemics—loom over some countries and regions, and, if left unchecked, could have significant spillovers on global economic activity.

On the upside, the recent decline in oil prices may boost demand in oil-importing countries more strongly than currently envisaged, including through consumers' possible perception that prices will remain lower for longer. More aggressive policy actions to lift demand and supply potential, as discussed in the following paragraph, could also foster stronger growth, in both the short and longer term. This could also help boost financial market confidence, and imply a recovery in equity prices and an unwinding of the recent tightening in financial conditions.

The fragile conjuncture increases the urgency of a broad-based policy response that safeguards near-term growth, while raising potential output, and manages vulnerabilities.

- *Strengthening growth.* In advanced economies, securing higher and sustainable growth requires a three-pronged approach consisting of mutually reinforcing (1) structural reforms, (2) continued monetary policy accommodation, and (3) fiscal support—in the form of growth-friendly fiscal policies where adjustment is needed and fiscal stimulus where space allows. On the supply side, implementing a credible and country-specific structural reform agenda that takes into account both the short- and

medium-term impact of reforms is a key element of the comprehensive strategy. Reforms that entail fiscal stimulus (for example, reducing labor tax wedges and increasing public spending on active labor market policies) and reforms that lower barriers to entry in product and services markets may be most valuable at this juncture, as they can provide some near-term demand support, not only through increased confidence and expectations of higher future income, but directly. On the demand side, accommodative monetary policy remains essential where output gaps are negative and inflation is too low. However, with interest rates at historic lows, a more comprehensive strategy is needed to ensure higher growth. Monetary policy must be complemented by concerted efforts to accelerate the repair of private sector balance sheets—especially in the euro area—to improve monetary policy transmission, ensure orderly deleveraging and bolster credit supply, and contain financial sector risks. Stronger near-term fiscal policy support, with a focus on boosting future productive capacity and financing demand-friendly structural reforms—where needed and where fiscal space is available—should provide a fillip to growth.

- *Securing resilience.* In emerging market and developing economies, policymakers should reduce macroeconomic and financial vulnerabilities and rebuild resilience, including by implementing productivity-enhancing reforms. In some commodity exporters, fiscal buffers can help smooth the adjustment to lower commodity prices, but it will be important to plan for fiscal adjustment to durably lower commodity revenues and new, more diverse growth models. In others, financial strains may limit the room to implement a gradual adjustment. Exchange rate flexibility, where feasible, should also be used to cushion the impact of adverse terms-of-trade shocks, although the effects of exchange rate depreciations on private and public sector balance sheets and on domestic inflation need to be closely monitored. Establishing fiscal policy frameworks that anchor longer-term plans will help build resilience by allowing smoother expenditure adjustment in response to adverse shocks. In commodity importers, whether all the gains should be saved depends on the extent of economic slack, the availability of fiscal space, and countries' needs. In particular, these gains may provide an opportunity to finance critical structural reforms or growth-enhancing spending.

The threat of synchronized slowdown, the increase in the already significant downside risks, and restricted policy space in many economies call for bold multilateral actions to boost growth and contain risks at this critical stage of the global recovery.

- *The international policy response.* Should a significant shortfall in growth threaten to push the global economy back into recession, a collective macroeconomic policy reaction would be needed. Policymakers in the larger economies should proactively identify additional policy actions that could be implemented quickly if there are signs that global downside risks are about to materialize.

- *Enhancing the global financial safety net and oversight.* To address the potentially protracted risks faced by commodity exporters and emerging markets with strong fundamentals but high susceptibility to shocks, there may be a need to consider reforms to the global financial safety net. There also remains a pressing need at the global level to complement and implement the regulatory reform agenda.

- *Ring-fencing spillovers from noneconomic shocks.* A few countries are currently bearing the brunt of the spillovers with often limited capacity and fiscal space. A coordinated worldwide initiative should support their efforts, with those at risk from spillovers contributing financial resources, and multilateral agencies, including the IMF, reassessing how they can best help channel those resources to areas in greatest need.

CHAPTER 1

RECENT DEVELOPMENTS AND PROSPECTS

Recent Developments and Prospects

Major macroeconomic realignments are affecting prospects differentially across countries and regions. These include the slowdown and rebalancing in China; a further decline in commodity prices, especially for oil, with sizable redistributive consequences across sectors and countries; a related slowdown in investment and trade; and declining capital flows to emerging market and developing economies. These realignments—together with a host of noneconomic factors, including geopolitical tensions and political discord—are generating substantial uncertainty. On the whole, they are consistent with a subdued outlook for the world economy—but risks of much weaker global growth have also risen.

The World Economy in Recent Months

Preliminary data suggest that global growth during the second half of 2015, at 2.8 percent, was weaker than previously forecast, with a sizable slowdown during the last quarter of the year (Figure 1.1). The unexpected weakness in late 2015 reflected to an important extent softer activity in advanced economies—especially in the United States, but also in Japan and other advanced Asian economies. The picture for emerging markets is quite diverse, with high growth rates in China and most of emerging Asia, but severe macroeconomic conditions in Brazil, Russia, and a number of other commodity exporters.

- Growth in the United States fell to 1.4 percent at a seasonally adjusted annual rate in the fourth quarter of 2015. While some of the reasons for this decline—including very weak exports—are likely to prove temporary, final domestic demand was weaker as well, with a decline in nonresidential investment, including outside the energy sector. Despite signs of weakening growth, labor market indicators continued to improve. In particular, employment growth was very strong, labor force participation rebounded, and the unemployment rate continued its downward trend, with a 4.5 percent reading in March.

- The recovery was broadly in line with the January forecast in the euro area, as strengthening domestic demand offset a weaker external impulse. Among countries, growth was weaker than expected in Italy but the recovery was stronger in Spain.

- In Japan, growth came out significantly lower than expected during the fourth quarter, reflecting in particular a sharp drop in private consumption.

- Economic activity in other Asian advanced economies closely integrated with China—such as Hong Kong Special Administrative Region and Taiwan Province of China—weakened sharply during the first half of 2015, owing in part to steep declines in exports. Activity picked up by less than expected during the second half of the year, as domestic demand remained subdued and the recovery in exports was relatively modest.

- Growth in China was in contrast slightly stronger than previously forecast, reflecting resilient domestic demand, especially consumption. Robust growth in the services sector offset recent weakness in manufacturing activity.

- In Latin America, the downturn in Brazil was deeper than expected, while activity for the remainder of the region was broadly in line with forecasts.

- The recession in Russia in 2015 was broadly in line with expectations, and conditions worsened in most other Commonwealth of Independent States (CIS) economies, affected by spillovers from Russia as well as the adverse impact of lower oil prices on net oil-exporting countries.

- Macroeconomic indicators suggest that economic activity in sub-Saharan Africa and the Middle East—for which quarterly GDP series are not broadly available—also fell short of expectations, a result of the drop in oil prices, declines in other commodity prices, and geopolitical and domestic strife in a few countries.

- More generally, geopolitical tensions have been weighing on global growth. Output contractions in three particularly affected countries—Ukraine, Libya, and Yemen, which accounted for about half a percentage point of global GDP in 2013—subtracted 0.1 percentage point from global output during 2014–15.

Table 1.1. Overview of the *World Economic Outlook* Projections
(Percent change, unless noted otherwise)

	2015	Projections		Difference from January 2016 *WEO* Update[1]		Difference from October 2015 WEO[1]	
		2016	2017	2016	2017	2016	2017
World Output	**3.1**	**3.2**	**3.5**	**−0.2**	**−0.1**	**−0.4**	**−0.3**
Advanced Economies	**1.9**	**1.9**	**2.0**	**−0.2**	**−0.1**	**−0.3**	**−0.2**
United States	2.4	2.4	2.5	−0.2	−0.1	−0.4	−0.3
Euro Area	1.6	1.5	1.6	−0.2	−0.1	−0.1	−0.1
Germany	1.5	1.5	1.6	−0.2	−0.1	−0.1	0.1
France	1.1	1.1	1.3	−0.2	−0.2	−0.4	−0.3
Italy	0.8	1.0	1.1	−0.3	−0.1	−0.3	−0.1
Spain	3.2	2.6	2.3	−0.1	0.0	0.1	0.1
Japan	0.5	0.5	−0.1	−0.5	−0.4	−0.5	−0.5
United Kingdom	2.2	1.9	2.2	−0.3	0.0	−0.3	0.0
Canada	1.2	1.5	1.9	−0.2	−0.2	−0.2	−0.5
Other Advanced Economies[2]	2.0	2.1	2.4	−0.3	−0.4	−0.6	−0.5
Emerging Market and Developing Economies	**4.0**	**4.1**	**4.6**	**−0.2**	**−0.1**	**−0.4**	**−0.3**
Commonwealth of Independent States	−2.8	−1.1	1.3	−1.1	−0.4	−1.6	−0.7
Russia	−3.7	−1.8	0.8	−0.8	−0.2	−1.2	−0.2
Excluding Russia	−0.6	0.9	2.3	−1.4	−0.9	−1.9	−1.7
Emerging and Developing Asia	6.6	6.4	6.3	0.1	0.1	0.0	0.0
China	6.9	6.5	6.2	0.2	0.2	0.2	0.2
India[3]	7.3	7.5	7.5	0.0	0.0	0.0	0.0
ASEAN-5[4]	4.7	4.8	5.1	0.0	0.0	−0.1	−0.2
Emerging and Developing Europe	3.5	3.5	3.3	0.4	−0.1	0.5	−0.1
Latin America and the Caribbean	−0.1	−0.5	1.5	−0.2	−0.1	−1.3	−0.8
Brazil	−3.8	−3.8	0.0	−0.3	0.0	−2.8	−2.3
Mexico	2.5	2.4	2.6	−0.2	−0.3	−0.4	−0.5
Middle East, North Africa, Afghanistan, and Pakistan	2.5	3.1	3.5	−0.5	−0.1	−0.8	−0.6
Saudi Arabia	3.4	1.2	1.9	0.0	0.0	−1.0	−1.0
Sub-Saharan Africa	3.4	3.0	4.0	−1.0	−0.7	−1.3	−0.9
Nigeria	2.7	2.3	3.5	−1.8	−0.7	−2.0	−1.0
South Africa	1.3	0.6	1.2	−0.1	−0.6	−0.7	−0.9
Memorandum							
European Union	2.0	1.8	1.9	−0.2	−0.1	−0.1	−0.1
Low-Income Developing Countries	4.5	4.7	5.5	−0.9	−0.4	−1.1	−0.6
Middle East and North Africa	2.3	2.9	3.3	−0.6	−0.2	−0.9	−0.8
World Growth Based on Market Exchange Rates	2.4	2.5	2.9	−0.2	−0.1	−0.5	−0.3
World Trade Volume (goods and services)	**2.8**	**3.1**	**3.8**	**−0.3**	**−0.3**	**−1.0**	**−0.8**
Imports							
Advanced Economies	4.3	3.4	4.1	−0.3	0.0	−0.8	−0.4
Emerging Market and Developing Economies	0.5	3.0	3.7	−0.4	−0.6	−1.4	−1.7
Exports							
Advanced Economies	3.4	2.5	3.5	−0.4	−0.1	−0.9	−0.4
Emerging Market and Developing Economies	1.7	3.8	3.9	0.0	−0.5	−1.0	−1.4
Commodity Prices (U.S. dollars)							
Oil[5]	−47.2	−31.6	17.9	−14.0	3.0	−29.2	7.8
Nonfuel (average based on world commodity export weights)	−17.5	−9.4	−0.7	0.1	−1.1	−4.3	−1.0
Consumer Prices							
Advanced Economies	0.3	0.7	1.5	−0.4	−0.2	−0.5	−0.2
Emerging Market and Developing Economies[6]	4.7	4.5	4.2	0.2	0.1	0.2	0.0
London Interbank Offered Rate (percent)							
On U.S. Dollar Deposits (six month)	0.5	0.9	1.5	−0.3	−0.7	−0.3	−0.7
On Euro Deposits (three month)	0.0	−0.3	−0.4	0.0	−0.2	−0.3	−0.5
On Japanese Yen Deposits (six month)	0.1	−0.1	−0.3	−0.2	−0.4	−0.2	−0.5

Note: Real effective exchange rates are assumed to remain constant at the levels prevailing during February 2–March 1, 2016. Economies are listed on the basis of economic size. The aggregated quarterly data are seasonally adjusted.

[1]Difference based on rounded figures for the current, January 2016 *World Economic Outlook Update*, and October 2015 *World Economic Outlook* forecasts.

[2]Excludes the G7 (Canada, France, Germany, Italy, Japan, United Kingdom, United States) and euro area countries.

[3]For India, data and forecasts are presented on a fiscal year basis and GDP from 2011 onward is based on GDP at market prices with fiscal year 2011/12 as a base year.

[4]Indonesia, Malaysia, Philippines, Thailand, Vietnam.

	Year over Year				Q4 over Q4[7]			
			Projections				Projections	
	2014	2015	2016	2017	2014	2015	2016	2017
World Output	**3.4**	**3.1**	**3.2**	**3.5**	**3.1**	**2.9**	**3.3**	**3.4**
Advanced Economies	**1.8**	**1.9**	**1.9**	**2.0**	**1.7**	**1.8**	**2.1**	**1.9**
United States	2.4	2.4	2.4	2.5	2.5	2.0	2.6	2.4
Euro Area	0.9	1.6	1.5	1.6	1.0	1.6	1.6	1.5
Germany	1.6	1.5	1.5	1.6	1.5	1.3	1.6	1.6
France	0.2	1.1	1.1	1.3	0.0	1.4	1.3	1.0
Italy	−0.3	0.8	1.0	1.1	−0.3	1.0	1.3	1.0
Spain	1.4	3.2	2.6	2.3	2.1	3.5	2.1	2.5
Japan	0.0	0.5	0.5	−0.1	−0.9	0.8	1.1	−0.8
United Kingdom	2.9	2.2	1.9	2.2	2.8	1.9	2.0	2.2
Canada	2.5	1.2	1.5	1.9	2.4	0.5	1.7	2.0
Other Advanced Economies[2]	2.8	2.0	2.1	2.4	2.6	2.1	2.2	2.6
Emerging Market and Developing Economies	**4.6**	**4.0**	**4.1**	**4.6**	**4.5**	**3.9**	**4.5**	**4.7**
Commonwealth of Independent States	1.1	−2.8	−1.1	1.3	−1.4	−4.0	0.2	1.2
Russia	0.7	−3.7	−1.8	0.8	−0.8	−4.7	0.4	1.1
Excluding Russia	1.9	−0.6	0.9	2.3	. . .	. . .	. . .	. . .
Emerging and Developing Asia	6.8	6.6	6.4	6.3	6.7	6.5	6.2	6.3
China	7.3	6.9	6.5	6.2	7.1	6.8	6.1	6.0
India[3]	7.2	7.3	7.5	7.5	7.3	7.2	7.8	7.6
ASEAN-5[4]	4.6	4.7	4.8	5.1	4.9	4.8	4.5	5.2
Emerging and Developing Europe	2.8	3.5	3.5	3.3	2.8	3.0	5.0	2.8
Latin America and the Caribbean	1.3	−0.1	−0.5	1.5	0.6	−1.6	0.4	1.4
Brazil	0.1	−3.8	−3.8	0.0	−0.7	−5.9	−1.6	0.5
Mexico	2.3	2.5	2.4	2.6	2.6	2.5	2.4	2.6
Middle East, North Africa, Afghanistan, and Pakistan	2.8	2.5	3.1	3.5	. . .	. . .	. . .	. . .
Saudi Arabia	3.6	3.4	1.2	1.9	2.5	3.6	0.5	2.3
Sub-Saharan Africa	5.1	3.4	3.0	4.0	. . .	. . .	. . .	. . .
Nigeria	6.3	2.7	2.3	3.5	. . .	. . .	. . .	. . .
South Africa	1.5	1.3	0.6	1.2	1.3	0.3	0.8	1.4
Memorandum								
European Union	1.4	2.0	1.8	1.9	1.5	2.0	1.9	1.8
Low-Income Developing Countries	6.1	4.5	4.7	5.5	. . .	. . .	. . .	. . .
Middle East and North Africa	2.6	2.3	2.9	3.3	. . .	. . .	. . .	. . .
World Growth Based on Market Exchange Rates	2.7	2.4	2.5	2.9	2.4	2.2	2.7	2.8
World Trade Volume (goods and services)	**3.5**	**2.8**	**3.1**	**3.8**	. . .	. . .	. . .	. . .
Imports								
Advanced Economies	3.5	4.3	3.4	4.1	. . .	. . .	. . .	. . .
Emerging Market and Developing Economies	3.7	0.5	3.0	3.7	. . .	. . .	. . .	. . .
Exports								
Advanced Economies	3.5	3.4	2.5	3.5	. . .	. . .	. . .	. . .
Emerging Market and Developing Economies	3.1	1.7	3.8	3.9	. . .	. . .	. . .	. . .
Commodity Prices (U.S. dollars)								
Oil[5]	−7.5	−47.2	−31.6	17.9	−28.7	−43.4	−10.3	12.2
Nonfuel (average based on world commodity export weights)	−4.0	−17.5	−9.4	−0.7	−7.4	−19.1	−2.9	0.5
Consumer Prices								
Advanced Economies	1.4	0.3	0.7	1.5	1.0	0.4	0.8	1.8
Emerging Market and Developing Economies[6]	4.7	4.7	4.5	4.2	4.2	4.6	4.1	3.8
London Interbank Offered Rate (percent)								
On U.S. Dollar Deposits (six month)	0.3	0.5	0.9	1.5	. . .	. . .	. . .	. . .
On Euro Deposits (three month)	0.2	0.0	−0.3	−0.4	. . .	. . .	. . .	. . .
On Japanese Yen Deposits (six month)	0.2	0.1	−0.1	−0.3	. . .	. . .	. . .	. . .

[5]Simple average of prices of U.K. Brent, Dubai Fateh, and West Texas Intermediate crude oil. The average price of oil in U.S. dollars a barrel was $50.79 in 2015; the assumed price based on futures markets is $34.75 in 2016 and $40.99 in 2017.
[6]Excludes Argentina and Venezuela. See country-specific notes for Argentina in the "Country Notes" section of the Statistical Appendix.
[7]For World Output, the quarterly estimates and projections account for approximately 90 percent of annual world output at purchasing-power-parity weights. For Emerging Market and Developing Economies, the quarterly estimates and projections account for approximately 80 percent of annual emerging market and developing economies' output at purchasing-power-parity weights.

Figure 1.1. Global Activity Indicators

Global trade volumes rebounded in the second half of 2015 after contracting sharply in the first half of the year. Global industrial production remained subdued throughout the year. Global growth slowed in the last quarter of 2015. In both advanced and emerging market and developing economies, the growth projections suggest some pickup in activity in 2016, but to generally weaker levels than projected in the October 2015 *World Economic Outlook*.

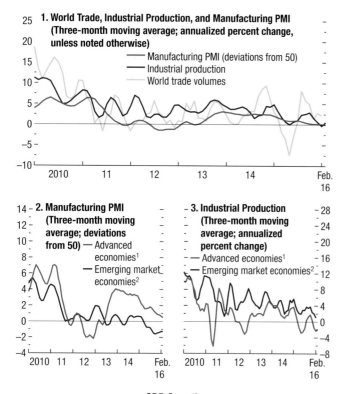

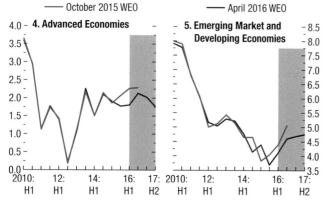

Sources: CPB Netherlands Bureau for Economic Policy Analysis; Haver Analytics; Markit Economics; and IMF staff estimates.
Note: IP = industrial production; PMI = purchasing managers' index.
[1]Australia, Canada, Czech Republic, Denmark, euro area, Hong Kong SAR (IP only), Israel, Japan, Korea, New Zealand, Norway (IP only), Singapore, Sweden (IP only), Switzerland, Taiwan Province of China, United Kingdom, United States.
[2]Argentina (IP only), Brazil, Bulgaria (IP only), Chile (IP only), China, Colombia (IP only), Hungary, India, Indonesia, Latvia (IP only), Lithuania (IP only), Malaysia (IP only), Mexico, Pakistan (IP only), Peru (IP only), Philippines (IP only), Poland, Romania (IP only), Russia, South Africa, Thailand (IP only), Turkey, Ukraine (IP only), Venezuela (IP only).

- Global industrial production, particularly of capital goods, remained subdued throughout 2015. This weakness is consistent with depressed investment worldwide—particularly in energy and mining—as well as the deceleration of China's manufacturing activity.

Low Inflation

Headline inflation in advanced economies in 2015, at 0.3 percent on average, was the lowest since the global financial crisis, mostly reflecting the sharp decline in commodity prices, with a pickup in the late part of 2015 (Figure 1.2). Core inflation remained broadly stable at 1.6–1.7 percent but was still well below central bank targets. In many emerging markets, lower prices for oil and other commodities (including food, which has a larger weight in the consumer price indices of emerging market and developing economies) have tended to reduce inflation, but in a number of countries, such as Brazil, Colombia, and Russia, sizable currency depreciations have offset to a large extent the effect of lower commodity prices, and inflation has risen.

Declining Commodity Prices

Oil prices decreased further by 32 percent between August 2015 and February 2016 (that is, between the reference period for the October *World Economic Outlook* [WEO] and that for the current WEO report) on account of strong supply from members of the Organization of the Petroleum Exporting Countries and Russia, expectations of higher supply from the Islamic Republic of Iran, and concerns about the resilience of global demand and medium-term growth prospects, as well as risk-off behavior in financial markets, leading investors to move away from commodities as well as stocks (Figure 1.3). Coal and natural gas prices also declined, as the latter are linked to oil prices, including through oil-indexed contract prices. Nonfuel commodity prices weakened as well, with metal and agricultural commodities prices declining by 9 percent and 4 percent, respectively. Excess oil supply pushed inventory levels in Organisation for Economic Co-operation and Development countries to record-high levels despite the strong oil demand that much lower prices spurred in 2015.[1] Oil prices recovered some ground in March, on the back of improved financial market sentiment.

---

[1]Global oil demand growth in 2015 is estimated to have been about 1.6 million barrels a day, significantly above earlier forecasts by the International Energy Agency.

Exchange Rates and Capital Flows

Between August 2015 and February 2016, the currencies of advanced economies tended to strengthen, and those of commodity exporters with floating exchange rates—especially oil-exporting countries—tended to weaken further (Figure 1.4, blue bars).

Across advanced economies, the Japanese yen's appreciation (about 10 percent in real effective terms) was particularly sharp, while the U.S. dollar and the euro strengthened by about 3 percent and 2 percent, respectively. In contrast, the British pound depreciated by 7 percent, driven by expectations of a later normalization of monetary policy in the United Kingdom and concerns about a potential exit from the European Union.

Among emerging market economies, depreciations were particularly sharp in South Africa, Mexico, Russia, and Colombia. The Chinese renminbi depreciated by about 2 percent, while the Indian rupee remained broadly stable.

Since February, the currencies of commodity-exporting advanced and emerging market economies have generally rebounded, reflecting a decline in global risk aversion and some recovery in commodity prices (Figure 1.4, red bars). Conversely, the dollar has depreciated by about 1½ percent and the euro by about 1 percent.

The decline in demand for emerging market assets was also reflected in a slowdown in capital inflows, as discussed extensively in Chapter 2. This decline was particularly steep during the second half of 2015, with net sales by foreign investors of portfolio holdings in emerging markets for the first time since the global financial crisis (Figure 1.5). Balance of payments developments in China loom large in explaining the dynamics of aggregate flows to and from emerging markets during this period. Motivated by changing expectations about the renminbi/dollar exchange rate since last summer, Chinese corporations undertook substantial repayments of dollar-denominated external debt (generating negative capital inflows), while Chinese residents increased their acquisitions of foreign assets (boosting capital outflows). With a tightly managed exchange rate, both developments have implied a substantial decline in China's foreign exchange reserves. Across emerging market and developing economies, reserves declined in a number of oil-exporting countries with exchange rate pegs, as sharply lower oil revenues weighed on current account balances.

Figure 1.2. Global Inflation
(Year-over-year percent change, unless noted otherwise)

Headline inflation has declined further in advanced economies, mostly reflecting the decline in the price of oil. In emerging market economies, lower commodity prices have also contributed to lowering headline inflation, but sizable currency depreciation has led to offsets on the upside in some economies.

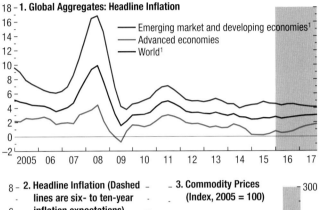

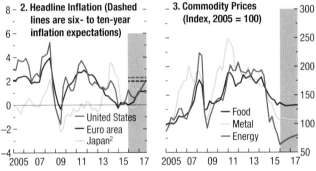

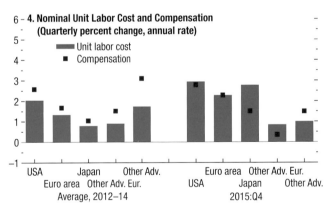

Sources: Consensus Economics; IMF, Primary Commodity Price System; and IMF staff estimates.
Note: Other Adv. = other advanced economies; Other Adv. Eur. = other advanced Europe; USA = United States.
[1]Excludes Venezuela.
[2]In Japan, the increase in inflation in 2014 reflects, to a large extent, the increase in the consumption tax.

Figure 1.3. Commodity and Oil Markets

In global oil markets, spot prices declined in late 2015 and early 2016. Resilient supply and the weakening in global growth projections were behind the renewed increases in oil inventories and downward pressures on prices.

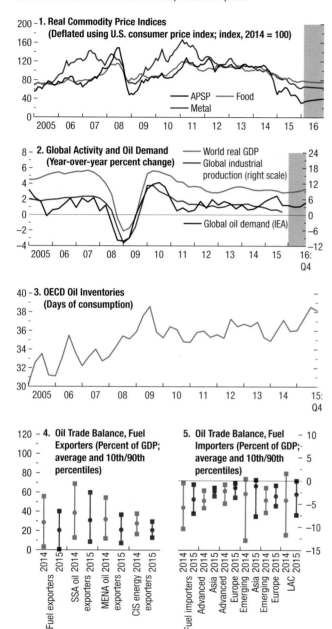

Sources: IMF, Primary Commodity Price System; International Energy Agency (IEA); Organisation for Economic Co-operation and Development (OECD); and IMF staff estimates.
Note: APSP = average petroleum spot price; CIS = Commonwealth of Independent States; LAC = Latin America and the Caribbean; MENA = Middle East and North Africa; SSA = sub-Saharan Africa.

Figure 1.4. Real Effective Exchange Rate Changes, August 2015–February 2016
(Percent)

Between August 2015 and February 2016, the currencies of advanced economies tended to strengthen. Currencies of commodity exporters with floating exchange rates—especially oil-exporting countries—tended to weaken further. Since February, the currencies of commodity-exporting economies have generally rebounded, and the U.S. dollar and euro have weakened.

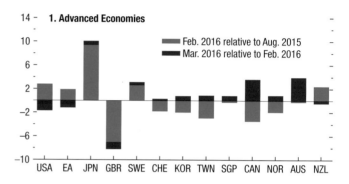

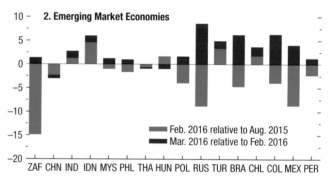

Source: IMF staff calculations.
Note: EA = euro area. Data labels in the figure use International Organization for Standardization (ISO) country codes.

Monetary Policy and Financial Conditions

Financial market volatility, which had subsided in October–November, increased again in December and especially in early 2016, amid rising global risk aversion, substantial declines in global equity markets, widening of credit spreads, and historically low yields for safe-haven government bonds (Figures 1.6–1.9). These developments were triggered by concerns about lack of policy space in advanced economies to respond to a potential worsening in the outlook, worries about the effects of very low oil prices, and questions about the speed at which China's economy is slowing as well as its authorities' policy intentions.

Since mid-February markets have rallied, recovering most or all of the ground lost earlier this year. Sovereign bond spreads, which had widened noticeably between September 2015 and February 2016 in Latin America—particularly in Brazil—narrowed again in March. Spreads broadly moved sideways in a number of other emerging markets in Asia and Europe and narrowed in Russia.

Financial conditions in advanced economies, while remaining accommodative overall, have seen some tightening associated with increasing yields in segments of corporate debt markets. Declining inflation expectations in the euro area are also contributing to tighter financial conditions by pushing up real interest rates. At the same time, long-term government bond yields in Germany, Japan, the United Kingdom, and the United States have declined sharply since September (30 to 60 basis points), reflecting both flight to safety and increased risk aversion, as well as actual and anticipated monetary policy responses to generally weaker inflation and growth expectations. Market turbulence had reflected to an important extent concerns regarding the prospects of financial sectors relating to fears of a persistent softening in global growth and its impact on already-weak profitability, unaddressed debt overhang legacies and changes in the regulatory environment in Europe, exposures to the commodity sector, and persistently low interest rates.

Monetary policy in advanced economies remains very accommodative, but with asymmetric shifts in the policy stance. In December the U.S. Federal Reserve raised policy rates above the zero lower bound for the first time since 2009, and it has communicated that any future policy actions will remain data dependent. On the other hand, the European Central Bank (ECB) announced a package of further easing measures in March, comprising an expansion of its asset purchase program, including purchases of corporate bonds, new longer-term refinancing operations, and a further reduction in all policy rates. And in late January the Bank of Japan introduced a negative interest rate on marginal excess reserves. In the United Kingdom, policy rates remain on hold at 50 basis points, and with a more subdued inflation outlook, expectations of interest rate increases have moved farther into the future.

The monetary policy stance has also moved in different directions across emerging markets. A number of commodity exporters have raised policy rates in response to currency depreciation and associated changes in inflation and inflation expectations (notably Mexico and South Africa, but also Chile, Colombia, and Peru). In contrast, policy rates have been eased in

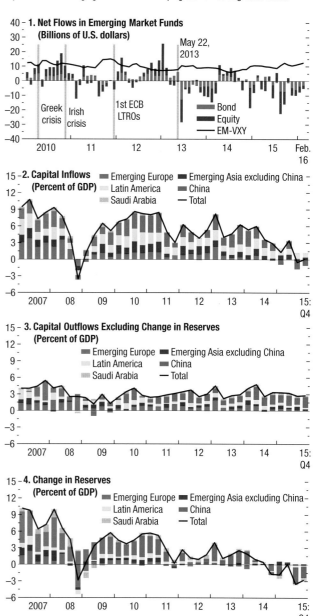

Figure 1.5. Emerging Market Economies: Capital Flows

Capital flows to emerging market and developing economies reached their lowest level since the global financial crisis in the second half of 2015. With capital outflows declining less than inflows, and with relatively little change in the aggregate current account balance, the change in reserves turned negative for these economies as a group in the last two quarters of 2015. Chapter 2 examines capital flows to emerging market and developing economies in greater detail.

Sources: Bloomberg, L.P.; EPFR Global; Haver Analytics; IMF, *International Financial Statistics;* and IMF staff calculations.
Note: Capital inflows are net purchases of domestic assets by nonresidents. Capital outflows are net purchases of foreign assets by domestic residents. Emerging Asia excluding China comprises India, Indonesia, Malaysia, the Philippines, and Thailand; emerging Europe comprises Poland, Romania, Russia, and Turkey; Latin America comprises Brazil, Chile, Colombia, Mexico, and Peru. ECB = European Central Bank; EM-VXY = J.P. Morgan Emerging Market Volatility Index; LTROs = longer-term refinancing operations.

Figure 1.6. Advanced Economies: Monetary and Financial Market Conditions

(Percent, unless noted otherwise)

Financial market volatility, which had subsided in October and November, increased again in December and especially in early 2016. Markets have rallied since mid-February, recovering most of the ground lost earlier in the year. Longer-term bond yields generally remain low.

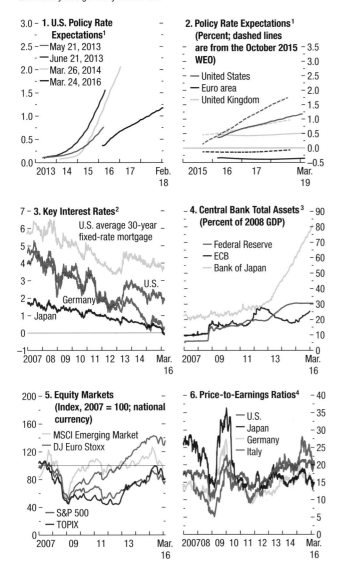

Figure 1.7. Advanced Economies: Credit, House Prices, and Balance Sheets

With accommodative monetary conditions in the euro area, credit growth has turned positive. In the United States, household net worth has broadly stabilized at a higher level, with a small downtick at the end of 2015 due to lower equity valuations. U.S. household debt continues to decline as a share of gross disposable income.

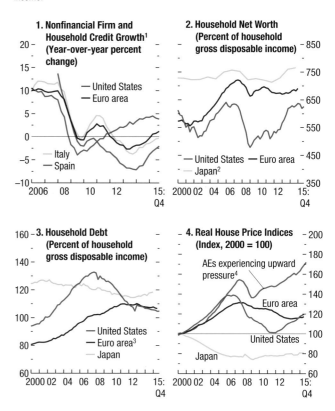

Sources: Bank of England; Bank of Spain; Bloomberg, L.P.; European Central Bank (ECB); Haver Analytics; Organisation for Economic Co-operation and Development; and IMF staff calculations.
[1]Flow-of-funds data are used for the euro area, Spain, and the United States. Italian bank loans to Italian residents are corrected for securitizations.
[2]Interpolated from annual net worth as a percentage of disposable income.
[3]Includes subsector employers (including self-employed workers).
[4]Upward-pressure countries are those with a residential real estate vulnerability index above the median for advanced economies (AEs): Australia, Austria, Belgium, Canada, France, Hong Kong SAR, Israel, Luxembourg, New Zealand, Norway, Portugal, Spain, Sweden, and the United Kingdom.

Sources: Bank of Spain; Bloomberg, L.P.; Haver Analytics; Thomson Reuters Datastream; and IMF staff calculations.
Note: DJ = Dow Jones; ECB = European Central Bank; MSCI = Morgan Stanley Capital International; S&P = Standard & Poor's; TOPIX = Tokyo Stock Price Index.
[1]Expectations are based on the federal funds rate futures for the United States, the sterling overnight interbank average rate for the United Kingdom, and the euro interbank offered forward rate for the euro area; updated March 24, 2016.
[2]Interest rates are 10-year government bond yields, unless noted otherwise. Data are through March 28, 2016.
[3]Data are through March 25, 2016. ECB calculations are based on the Eurosystem's weekly financial statement.
[4]Data are through March 24, 2016.

India and more recently in Indonesia, while reserve requirements were cut in China.

The Macroeconomic Implications of Global Realignments

Trade Spillovers from China

The current slowdown in China's growth has been driven mainly by investment and exports. The weakening in investment reflects a correction after an extended period of very rapid growth. Given China's

Figure 1.8. Emerging Market Economies: Interest Rates

Financial conditions in emerging market economies have continued to tighten in the face of these countries' diminished growth prospects, but developments across countries have been quite differentiated. Real policy rates are generally low.

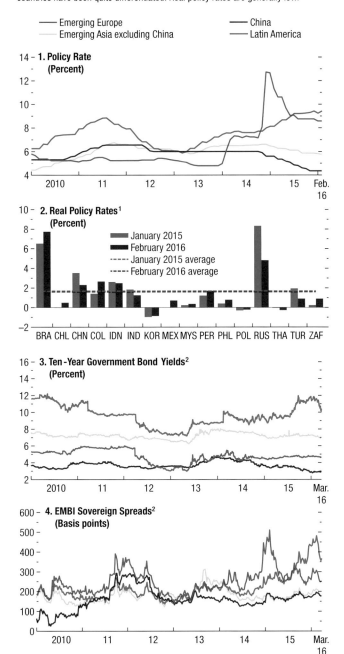

Figure 1.9. Emerging Market Economies: Equity Markets and Credit

Equity prices in most emerging market economies weakened in late 2015 and early 2016. Real credit growth has continued to decelerate in some emerging market economies but has picked up again in others. The credit-to-GDP ratio continues to increase in many emerging market economies.

Real Credit Growth[1]
(Year-over-year percent change)

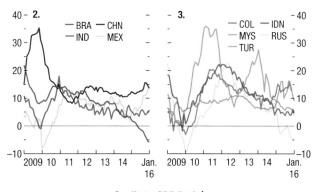

Credit-to-GDP Ratio[1]
(Percent)

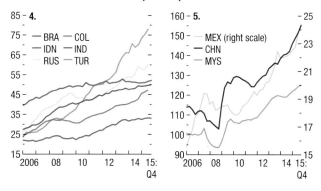

Sources: Bloomberg, L.P.; EPFR Global; Haver Analytics; IMF, *International Financial Statistics;* and IMF staff calculations.
Note: Emerging Asia excluding China comprises India, Indonesia, Malaysia, the Philippines, and Thailand; emerging Europe comprises Poland, Romania (capital inflows only), Russia, and Turkey; Latin America comprises Brazil, Chile, Colombia, Mexico, and Peru. EMBI = J.P. Morgan Emerging Market Bond Index. Data labels in the figure use International Organization for Standardization (ISO) country codes.
[1]Deflated by two-year-ahead *World Economic Outlook* inflation projections.
[2]Data are through March 25, 2016.

Sources: Haver Analytics; IMF, International Financial Statistics (IFS) database; and IMF staff calculations.
Note: Data labels in the figure use International Organization for Standardization (ISO) country codes.
[1]Credit is other depository corporations' claims on the private sector (from IFS), except in the case of Brazil, for which private sector credit is from the Monetary

Figure 1.10. China's Share of Value-Added Exports and Change in Export Volume Growth[1]

Countries where China accounts for a relatively high share of value-added exports tended to experience weaker export growth in 2015, but with some exceptions.

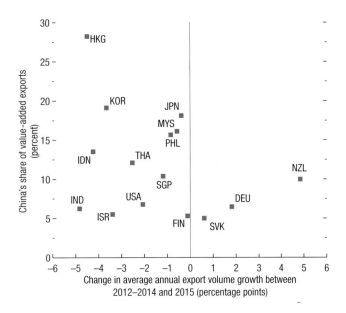

Sources: IMF, *Direction of Trade Statistics;* Organisation for Economic Co-operation and Development and World Trade Organization, Trade in Value Added database; and IMF staff calculations.
Note: China's share of value-added exports is calculated as value added absorbed in China divided by total foreign-absorbed value added. Data labels in the figure use International Organization for Standardization (ISO) country codes.
[1]Data for value-added exports are from the latest year available, as of 2011. Commodity exporters are excluded.

size, openness, and high investment rate and the high import content of its investment and exports, the slowdown has entailed sizable global spillovers through trade channels. These trade effects are both direct (reduced demand for trading partners' products) and indirect (impact on world prices for specific goods that China imports—for example, commodities), affecting other countries' exchange rates and asset markets.

- **Trade**—China is one of the main (top 10) trading partners of more than 100 economies that account for about 80 percent of world GDP. Given its key role in global and regional supply chains—importing intermediate and capital goods and exporting processed goods—China can also be a conduit for shocks that originate in other countries. Furthermore, over the past decade, China's role as a source of final demand has increased markedly: China's imports of final capital goods and consumption

goods from Europe and the United States are material. IMF staff analysis suggests that a 1 percentage point investment-driven drop in China's output growth would reduce Group of Twenty (G20) growth by ¼ percentage point. Indeed, Figure 1.10 suggests that among countries in which China accounts for a large share of exports of value added, those with the highest shares tended to experience larger declines of export growth in 2015 relative to 2012–14.

- **Commodities**—China is a major importer across a range of commodities, especially metals, for which it accounted for about 40 percent of total global demand in 2014. China's investment slowdown has had a significant impact on the demand for and prices of those commodities closely related to investment activities—indeed, metal prices have fallen steadily since early 2011 (by almost 60 percent on average). This has generated substantial excess capacity in mining sectors and forced exporters to adjust to lower revenues (see Chapter 2 of the October 2015 WEO). In contrast, China's demand for oil remained strong in 2015, also reflecting the accumulation of inventories.

- **Manufacturing**—Excess capacity in some segments of the Chinese manufacturing sector can contribute to lowering the prices of specific manufactured products (for example, steel) and hence affect China's competitors, reducing their profits and possibly investment rates.

Commodity Price Declines and Disposable Income

The recent further declines in prices of commodities, especially oil, have compounded sizable shifts in international relative prices since 2011. These shifts have generated sharp changes in disposable income across countries. A simple proxy for these changes can be constructed by calculating the impact of variations in terms of trade on a country's disposable income.[2] As shown in panel 1 of Figure 1.11, the steep declines in oil prices during the second half of 2014 and late 2015 triggered large income losses for oil-exporting countries and gains for oil-importing countries. Relative to GDP, the windfall losses for oil-exporting countries

[2]The proportional effect on disposable income for year t is calculated as the percentage change in export prices between years t and $t–1$ multiplied by nominal exports in year $t–1$, minus the percentage change in import prices between years t and $t–1$ multiplied by nominal imports in year $t–1$, with the preceding difference divided by nominal GDP in year $t–1$.

Figure 1.11. Terms-of-Trade Windfall Gains and Losses, Domestic Demand, Imports, and Output

The recent declines in commodity prices have generated sharp changes in disposable income across countries. Domestic demand has tended to strengthen in countries with terms-of-trade gains and weaken in those with losses. The responses of real output have typically been smaller, as net exports have tended to improve in countries with losses and weaken in those with gains, in some cases facilitated by exchange rate adjustments.

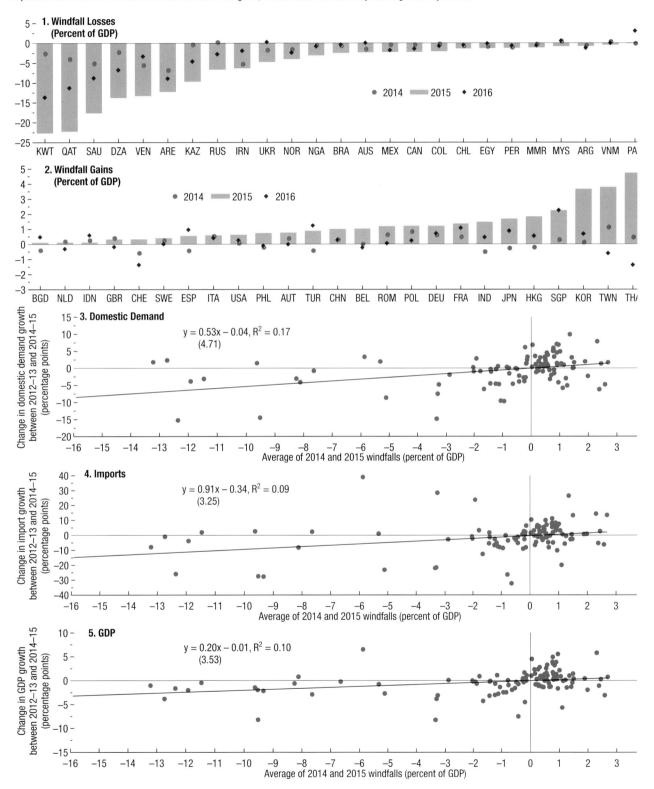

Source: IMF staff estimates.
Note: See note 2 in the chapter for the definition of windfall gains and losses. The change in growth is calculated as the difference between the average growth rate in 2014–15 and the average growth rate in 2012–13. The sample includes countries with populations above 1 million; the bottom 10 percent of countries (by GDP level, adding up to 0.5 percent of global output) are excluded. The numbers in parentheses in the equations represent t-statistics. Data labels use International Organization for Standardization (ISO) country codes.

were larger and more concentrated than the windfall benefits for oil-importing countries.[3]

These changes in disposable income have had sizable macroeconomic repercussions. Domestic demand has tended to strengthen in countries with terms-of-trade gains and weaken among those with losses, with dramatic contractions among some of the hardest hit (Figure 1.11, panels 2–4). On average, a 1 percentage point loss in income induced by weaker terms of trade subtracted about 0.6 percentage point from domestic demand growth in 2014–15 relative to 2012–13. Among the components of domestic demand, investment responded particularly strongly, as discussed in the following section. The response of real imports was larger than that of domestic demand: for instance, a country experiencing a windfall loss of 1 percent of GDP saw, on average, a 1 percentage point decline in real import growth. For countries experiencing terms-of-trade losses, weaker imports—together with a mild but positive response in export growth—cushioned the impact of the terms-of-trade decline on domestic output: for each percentage point loss in income, real GDP growth weakened on average by about 0.22 percentage point (Figure 1.11, panel 5).

Investment in Energy and Mining

One important channel through which changes in commodity prices affect aggregate demand is through their impact on investment, particularly in energy and mining, which are very capital-intensive activities. Investment was high during the commodity price boom but has declined sharply in recent years. For instance, estimates of investment spending in the oil and gas sector in major energy exporters indicate a fall of 24 percent in 2015 in dollar terms relative to a year earlier (Figure 1.12). The decline corresponds to 0.28 percent of 2014 global GDP measured at market exchange rates. While this may overstate the decline in real terms in light of the appreciation of the dollar (which reduces the dollar value of capital spending undertaken in different currencies), the direct drag on 2015 global GDP growth is still sizable.

As shown in the second panel of Figure 1.12, investment weakness appears to have extended to exporters of extractive products more broadly; coun-

tries where energy and mining products account for a larger share of GDP experienced large declines in domestic investment in 2015 relative to the previous three years. In turn, the weakness in investment has contributed to weakness in global manufacturing activity and trade.

Slowdown in Global Investment and Trade

Figure 1.13 provides further evidence on the global slowdown in investment and shows how declining real investment growth is mirrored by weakness in real import growth.[4] Trade growth was particularly weak in relation to GDP growth in 2015 in emerging market and developing economies (Figure 1.13, panel 3). Box 1.1 explores in more detail the weakness in trade.

The discussion earlier in this section suggests that the slowdown and rebalancing in China plays an important role in explaining these trends, given China's large share of global trade (more than 10 percent) and especially global investment (about 25 percent). Indeed, China's import growth declined by about 4 percentage points and its investment growth by about 2 percentage points between 2014 and 2015. But declining investment and imports in some commodity exporters also played a major role. Brazil, Russia, and a small group of other commodity-exporting countries facing macroeconomic difficulties, altogether accounting for about 5 percent of global trade and investment in 2014, experienced dramatic contractions in investment during 2015 of close to 20 percent and commensurate declines in imports. These developments reflect, in addition to the weakness in commodity-related investment, the significant exchange rate depreciation in many of these countries and the impact of sanctions in Russia, as well as the high sensitivity of capital spending and imports to aggregate demand during periods of economic turmoil. For the remaining emerging market and developing economies, the decline in trade and investment growth was more muted and broadly in line with the slowdown in aggregate economic activity (Figure 1.13, panel 4).

Global Implications of Lower Oil Prices

Scenarios outlining the global impact of a supply-driven oil price decline presented in the April 2015 WEO indicate that a positive oil supply shock should

---

[3]Emerging market and developing economies that are fuel exporters accounted for about 12 percent of global GDP measured at purchasing power parity in 2014–15.

[4]Indeed, the correlation between the two series over the past two decades is close to 0.9 for the various country groupings.

Figure 1.12. Energy and Mining Investment

Capital investment in the energy and mining sectors contracted sharply in 2015 amid weaker commodity prices. Countries where energy and mining exports accounted for a larger share of GDP tended to experience weaker investment growth during 2014–15.

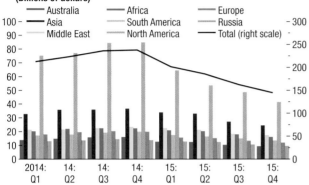

1. Quarterly Capital Expenditures in the Oil and Gas Sector in Major Producers (Billions of dollars)

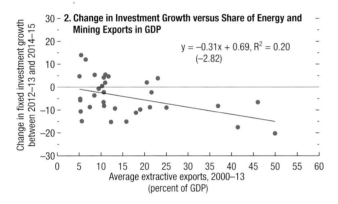

2. Change in Investment Growth versus Share of Energy and Mining Exports in GDP

$$y = -0.31x + 0.69, R^2 = 0.20$$
$$(-2.82)$$

Sources: Rystad Energy; and IMF staff estimates.
Note: In panel 2, the change in fixed investment growth is calculated as the difference between the average growth rate in 2014–15 and the average growth rate in 2012–13. The sample in panel 2 includes countries with populations above 1 million and with energy and mining exports above 5 percent of GDP. The numbers in parentheses in the equations represent *t*-statistics.

be expansionary for the global economy, primarily reflecting a higher marginal propensity to consume in countries receiving the windfall from oil compared to oil-exporting countries, as well as a boost to aggregate supply stemming from the decline in the cost of an input to production. The disappointing performance of the global economy over the past year has led some observers to question whether an oil price decline is truly "a shot in the arm" for world growth. Part of the explanation is that demand shocks have slowed global economic activity, while also contributing to the decline in oil prices. But at the same time, a number of factors have muted the positive impact of a

Figure 1.13. Global Investment and Trade Slowdown
(Percent change)

After bouncing back following the global financial crisis, global trade and investment have slowed notably, both in absolute terms and in relation to world GDP growth. This slowdown has been more pronounced in emerging market and developing economies. The slowdown and rebalancing in China play an important role in explaining these trends, but so do declining investment and imports in some commodity exporters facing macroeconomic difficulties. For the remainder of emerging market and developing economies, the decline in trade and investment growth is more muted.

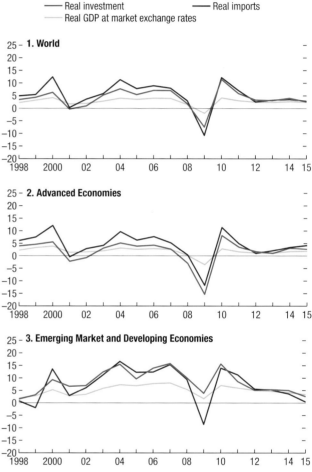

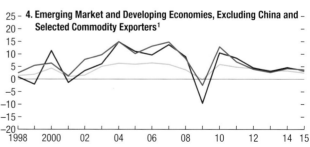

Source: IMF staff calculations.
[1]Selected commodity exporters = Angola, Bahrain, Belarus, Brazil, Ecuador, Kazakhstan, Russia, Ukraine, Venezuela.

supply-driven oil price decline—especially for the most recent period.

The first—and arguably the most important—of these factors concerns the ability of oil-exporting countries to smooth the negative shock, reducing expenditure by less than the amount of the loss in oil revenues. Expectations that oil prices may stay low for a protracted period of time reinforce pressures on oil-exporting countries to adjust spending downward. Furthermore, with oil prices already much lower when the latest decline started in the second half of 2015, a number of oil-exporting countries find themselves in much more difficult macroeconomic situations and with much tighter external financing conditions, circumstances that limit their ability to avoid sharp expenditure cuts. Indeed, downward revisions to domestic demand in fuel-exporting emerging market and developing economies have been sizable: the level of demand in 2015 was some 9 percentage points lower than in the April 2014 WEO forecasts, with the difference now expected to widen to 15 percentage points in 2016.

A second factor is the limited extent to which oil importers' private consumption levels have risen in response to their higher disposable incomes. While private consumption growth has picked up in most oil-importing advanced economies, it has done so less strongly than previous episodes of oil price declines would have suggested, possibly owing to continued deleveraging in some of these economies. For some oil-importing emerging market economies, the expansionary effects of lower oil prices have also been dampened by a low pass-through of global spot oil price changes to retail prices, owing to a con-comitant reduction in subsidies in some cases and increased taxation, higher profit margins for refiners or distributors, or the use of forward contracts in others.

A third factor is the impact of oil price declines on capital expenditure. Even in countries that are commodity importers, the sharp decline in cap-ital expenditure in the energy and mining sector worldwide has taken a toll on aggregate investment. This impact may in part reflect the fact that, at least in some advanced economies, such as the United States, firms operating in the energy sector were increasing leverage (with outlays exceeding cash flow) prior to the price decline. The redistribution of resources away from these firms—and the asso-ciated tightening of their access to credit—has led

them to cut spending substantially and thereby exert a drag on aggregate demand.

A fourth factor is that falling oil prices coincide with a period of slow economic growth characterized by exceptionally low inflation and policy interest rates in oil-importing advanced economies. Hence, major central banks have little or no capacity to lower their policy interest rates further to support growth and combat deflationary pressures, which have been exac-erbated by a falling oil price. But when central banks cannot lower the policy interest rate, even a decline in inflation owing to the positive supply effect of lower production costs raises the real rate of interest, with negative effects on demand.

The analysis presented in Scenario Box 1 pulls some of these threads together. In the scenario, the oil price decline reflects mostly higher oil supply, but also weaker global demand (consistent with weaker actual and expected global growth since the initial decline in prices in the second half of 2014) and a trend increase in energy efficiency. In addition, the scenario assumes an increase in financial distress in fuel exporters as oil prices decline, which raises their external borrowing costs.

The Forecast

Policy Assumptions

After a period of consolidation, fiscal policy is projected to be neutral in advanced economies as a whole in 2016—somewhat expansionary in some countries, such as Canada, Germany, Italy, and the United States, and somewhat contractionary in Japan, Spain, and the United Kingdom (Figure 1.14). The projected neutral policy stance in emerging markets masks a substantial diversity across countries and regions but for the group as a whole is tighter than projected in the October 2015 WEO, to an import-ant extent reflecting the sharper fiscal adjustment planned in oil-exporting countries (see the April 2016 *Fiscal Monitor*).

Turning to monetary policy, the forecast is based on the assumption that the policy interest rate in the United States increases gradually but steadily (Figure 1.6). Short-term interest rates stay negative in the euro area through part of 2017 and close to zero (in effec-tive terms) in Japan through 2018. Monetary policy stances across emerging market economies remain divergent, reflecting the variety in circumstances.

Scenario Box 1. The Estimated Impact of Lower Oil Prices

This scenario uses the IMF's G20 Model (G20MOD) to estimate the net macroeconomic impact of the decline in oil prices since 2014 based on estimates of the three components underlying that decline: higher oil supply, expectations of weaker global demand independent of oil prices, and improved energy efficiency. The latter two factors imply lower demand for oil. The model-based estimates indicate that the decline in oil prices associated with higher oil supply has a positive impact on global GDP. However, this positive impact is more than offset by the weakness in global economic activity, which underpins the demand-driven component of the oil price decline.

Factors Driving the Decline in Oil Prices

Oil prices fell by roughly 50 percent in 2015 relative to 2014 (in annual average terms). Prices in futures markets suggest a further 10 percent average decline in 2016 and only a very gradual recovery afterward. As detailed by Arezki, Toscani, and van der Ploeg (forthcoming) and shown in Scenario Figure 1, the decline in current and expected oil prices relative to the path expected at the time of the April 2014 WEO can be decomposed into three key factors: increases in oil supply, weaker global demand, and improved energy efficiency. This decomposition is done using historical and forecast data on oil supply from the International Energy Agency's (IEA's) *World Energy Outlook* and the oil model described by Benes and others (2015). As Scenario Figure 1 shows, higher oil supply is estimated to account for almost all the decline in oil prices in 2015 and the major, but diminishing, share in the decline in oil prices that futures markets suggest will persist for an extended period (blue-shaded area). Weaker actual and expected global demand, while accounting for very little of the decline in 2015, accounts for a growing share thereafter (red-shaded area). Improved energy efficiency is projected to account for a small, but increasing, share of the decline from 2016 onward (yellow-shaded area).

Estimating the Net Global Impact

To estimate the net impact of the decline in oil prices on global GDP, these three factors are combined in their respective proportions in G20MOD. In addition, the scenario also estimates the potential impact of the fiscal pressures and financial market stress that lower oil prices have caused in key oil-exporting countries and regions. The scenario presented in Scenario

Scenario Figure 1. Decomposition of the Change in Oil Prices: 2014 *World Economic Outlook* versus April 2016 *World Economic Outlook*
(2013 U.S. dollars)

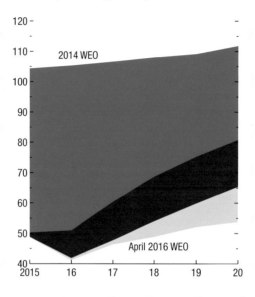

Figure 2 thus includes four layers: higher oil supply; weaker global demand; improved energy efficiency; and increased fiscal and financial stress in key oil-exporting countries.

Higher Oil Supply

The first layer (blue line in the figure) is the marginal impact of the reduction in oil prices driven solely by increases in the global supply of oil. This increase in supply reduces oil prices by roughly 50 percent in 2015 and 2016, and then gradually moderates, so that by 2021 oil prices are about 30 percent below the price expected in 2014. This decline in oil prices, driven by the supply increase, has a positive impact on global GDP that peaks at about 1 percent in 2016 and 2017 before it gradually moderates to about ¾ percent by 2021 as oil prices recover. Advanced economies, which are less dependent on oil exports, benefit the most, with a sustained improvement in GDP of more than 1 percent. Emerging market economies as a group, where more oil production is concentrated, benefit in the near term, but their combined GDP

Scenario Box 1. The Estimated Impact of Lower Oil Prices *(continued)*

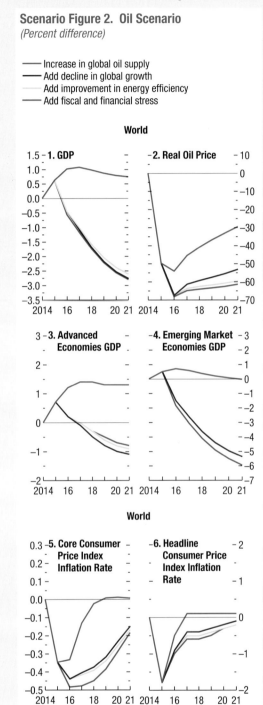

Scenario Figure 2. Oil Scenario
(Percent difference)

— Increase in global oil supply
— Add decline in global growth
— Add improvement in energy efficiency
— Add fiscal and financial stress

Source: IMF staff estimates.

returns to baseline by 2021 as the adjustment to the reduction in oil sector revenue is completed.

Weaker Global Demand

The second layer (red line) adds the decline in global aggregate demand that is required to account for the estimated share of the fall in oil prices presented in the decomposition in Figure 1. That is, this layer captures the weakness in global GDP growth that is independent of oil prices. Consistent with the evolution of WEO forecasts since 2014, the weakening in global demand is more heavily concentrated in emerging markets. The addition of the weakening in global demand results in global GDP that is now almost 3 percent below baseline by 2021. Hence adding the demand layer more than offsets the positive impact on advanced economies' GDP coming from the supply-induced decline in oil prices. For emerging market economies, output is well below baseline after the demand component is added.

Improved Energy Efficiency

The third layer (yellow line) adds the forecast improvement in energy efficiency, which is essentially a decline in the demand for oil that is independent of global GDP growth, leading to lower oil prices. This efficiency-related decline in the price of oil has a small positive impact on global GDP, with the benefits accruing largely to advanced economies.

Additional Stress in Key Oil-Exporting Countries

The final layer (green line) adds the additional fiscal and financial stress in key oil-exporting countries that could arise from the collapse in their oil export revenues. Although fiscal policy in oil-exporting countries adjusts endogenously to the worsening in revenue, the adjustment in the baseline version of the model takes place via reduced transfers to households, and these measures do not have large multiplier effects. However, given the magnitude of the fiscal adjustment in countries like Russia, Saudi Arabia, and other oil-exporting countries, public expenditure may also need to bear some of the burden. Hence it is assumed that public consumption and investment also need to be cut to maintain fiscal sustainability. In addition, it is assumed that risk premiums rise in a number of oil exporters with lower net external assets, by 100 basis points in 2016 and 2017. The result is a further reduction in global GDP of roughly ¼ percent, concentrated in emerging market economies.

Other Assumptions

Global financial conditions are assumed to remain broadly accommodative, but with some segments—notably commodities and related industries and oil-exporting countries—facing tighter financing conditions. The process of monetary policy normalization in the United States is assumed to proceed smoothly, without sharp movements in long-term interest rates. The tightening of financial conditions for some emerging market economies over the past few months, with rising interest rate spreads and declining equity prices, is expected to persist. Oil prices are projected to increase gradually over the forecast horizon, from an average of about $35 a barrel in 2016 to $41 a barrel in 2017. In contrast, nonfuel commodity prices are expected to stabilize around recent levels. Geopolitical tensions are assumed to stay elevated in 2016, with the situation in Russia and Ukraine remaining difficult and strife continuing in some countries in the Middle East. These tensions are generally assumed to ease, allowing for a gradual recovery in the most severely affected economies in 2017 and beyond.

Global Outlook for 2016 and 2017

Global output is estimated to have grown by 3.1 percent in 2015, with 1.9 percent growth for advanced economies and 4.0 percent growth for emerging market and developing economies. Global growth is projected to remain modest in 2016, at 3.2 percent, before picking up to 3.5 percent in 2017 (Table 1.1).

Emerging market and developing economies will still account for the lion's share of world growth in 2016, yet their growth rate is projected to increase only modestly relative to 2015, remaining 2 percentage points below the average of the past decade. This growth projection reflects a combination of factors: weakness in oil-exporting countries; a moderate slowdown in China (0.4 percentage point), where growth continues to shift away from manufacturing and investment; and a still-weak outlook for exporters of non-oil commodities, including in Latin America, following further price declines. Oil-importing emerging market economies are benefiting from terms-of-trade gains but in some instances are facing tighter financing conditions and weakness in external demand, which counter the positive terms-of-trade impact on domestic demand and growth. The modest acceleration of growth in advanced economies to a large extent reflects support from lower energy prices (Figure 1.3) and

Figure 1.14. Fiscal Policies
(Percent of GDP, unless noted otherwise)

After a period of consolidation, fiscal policy is projected to be neutral in 2016 in advanced economies. The projected broadly neutral fiscal policy stance inemerging market economies masks a substantial diversity across countries and regions.

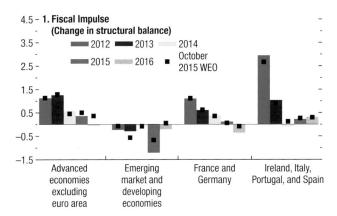

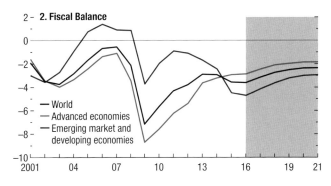

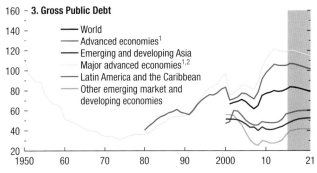

Source: IMF staff estimates.
[1]Data through 2000 exclude the United States.
[2]Canada, France, Germany, Italy, Japan, United Kingdom, United States.

accommodative monetary policies, notwithstanding the expected gradual Federal Reserve tightening in the United States.

The projected pickup in growth in 2017, in turn, reflects stronger performance in emerging market economies. In particular, growth in countries experiencing severe macroeconomic conditions in 2015–16 (including Brazil, Russia, and some countries in Latin America and in the Middle East), while remaining weak or negative, is projected to rise, with a return to positive growth in both Latin America and the CIS and a sizable pickup in growth in sub-Saharan Africa. These developments more than offset the projected continuation of the slowdown in China.

Among advanced economies, growth is again projected to increase marginally, as the projected decline in growth in Japan due to the planned consumption tax increase is more than offset by slightly stronger performance in most other advanced economies.

The outlook is weaker than that in the January 2016 *WEO Update* for both advanced economies and emerging markets. Relative to the October 2015 WEO, global growth has been revised downward by 0.4 percentage point in 2016 and 0.3 percentage point in 2017.

Global Outlook for the Medium Term

Global growth is projected to increase further beyond 2017, to just below 4 percent by the end of the forecast horizon in 2021, reflecting a further pickup in growth in emerging market and developing economies. This outcome relies on a number of important assumptions, which—as discussed in the following section—are subject to sizable downside risks:

- A gradual normalization of conditions in several economies currently under stress
- A successful rebalancing of China's economy, with trend growth rates that—while lower than those of the past two decades—remain high
- A pickup in activity in commodity exporters, albeit with growth rates more modest than in the past
- Resilient growth in other emerging market and developing economies

In this context, the gradual increase in the global weight of fast-growing countries such as China and India also plays a role in boosting global growth. Growth in advanced economies is projected to remain at about 2 percent as output gaps close and then slow owing to diminished growth in the labor force as populations continue to age.

Economic Outlook for Individual Countries and Regions

- Growth is projected to continue in the *United States* at a moderate pace, supported by strengthening balance sheets, no further fiscal drag in 2016, and an improving housing market. These forces are expected to offset the drag to net exports coming from the strengthening of the dollar and slower growth in trading partners, the additional decline in energy investment, weaker manufacturing, and tighter domestic financial conditions for some sectors of the economy (for example, oil and gas and related industries). As a result, growth is projected to level off at 2.4 percent in 2016, with a modest uptick in 2017. Longer-term growth prospects are weaker, with potential growth estimated to be only about 2 percent, weighed down by an aging population and low total factor productivity growth.

- The modest *euro area* recovery is projected to continue in 2016–17, with weakening external demand outweighed by the favorable effects of lower energy prices, a modest fiscal expansion, and supportive financial conditions. Potential growth is expected to remain weak, as a result of crisis legacies (high private and public debt, low investment, and eroding skills due to high long-term unemployment), aging effects, and slow total factor productivity growth. Output in the euro area is expected to grow at about 1.5 percent in 2016 and 1.6 percent in 2017 and remain around 1.5 percent in the medium term. Growth is expected to increase modestly in *Germany* (to 1.6 percent by 2017), *France* (to 1.1 percent in 2016 and 1.3 percent in 2017), and *Italy* (to 1 percent in 2016 and 1.1 percent in 2017). Growth in *Spain* is projected to soften (to 2.6 percent in 2016 and 2.3 percent in 2017) while remaining above the euro area average. Activity is expected to decelerate in *Portugal* (to 1.4 percent in 2016 and 1.3 percent in 2017), while *Greece* is expected to return to growth in 2017 after contracting further this year.

- In *Japan,* growth is projected to remain at 0.5 percent in 2016, before turning slightly negative to −0.1 percent in 2017 as the scheduled increase in the consumption tax rate (of 2 percentage points) goes into effect. The recent appreciation of the yen and weaker demand from emerging market economies are projected to restrain activity during the first half of 2016, but lower energy prices and fiscal measures adopted through the supplementary budget are expected to boost growth (with fiscal stimulus alone adding 0.5 percentage point to output). The Bank of Japan's quantitative and qualitative easing measures—including negative interest rates on marginal excess reserve deposits adopted in February—are expected to support private demand. Japan's medium- to long-term growth prospects remain weak, primarily reflecting a declining labor force.

- The picture for other advanced economies is more mixed, reflecting in part uneven effects from lower commodity prices, as well as different degrees of spillovers from the economic rebalancing in China.

  ○ In the *United Kingdom*, growth (forecast at 1.9 percent in 2016 and 2.2 percent in 2017) is expected to be driven by domestic private demand supported by lower energy prices and a buoyant property market, which help to offset headwinds from fiscal consolidation and heightened uncertainty ahead of the June referendum on European Union membership.

  ○ Strong growth projected for *Sweden* (about 3.7 percent in 2016, easing to 2.8 percent in 2017) is underpinned by expansionary monetary policy, higher residential investment in response to rising house prices, and higher public spending owing to large refugee inflows.

  ○ In *Switzerland*, growth is expected to increase modestly to 1.2 percent in 2016 and 1.5 percent in 2017, as the drag from last year's exchange rate appreciation wanes.

  ○ Commodity-exporting advanced economies continue to adjust to reduced income and resource-related investment. In *Norway*, GDP growth is projected to soften to 1.0 percent this year as the decline in oil prices weighs on investment and consumption and to recover gradually afterward. In *Canada*, growth is expected to recover to 1.5 percent in 2016, with the drag from the energy sector offset partially by a more competitive currency and an expected increase in public investment, before it accelerates to 1.9 percent in 2017. In *Australia*, growth is expected to remain below potential at 2.5 percent in 2016 but to rise above potential to 3 percent over the next two years, supported in part by a more competitive currency.

  ○ Among other advanced economies in Asia, the downturn in China's imports in 2015 has been an important drag. In 2016, growth will soften in *Singapore* (to 1.8 percent) and *Hong Kong Special Administrative Region* (to 2.2 percent) and pick up modestly in *Korea* (to 2.7 percent) and more noticeably in *Taiwan Province of China* (to 1.5 percent, after the sharp drop to 0.7 percent in 2015). Growth in all four of these economies is expected to pick up more robustly from 2017 onward, as China's import demand recovers. Population aging is increasingly weighing on potential growth in these economies, most notably in Korea and Singapore.

- Growth in *China* is projected to slow to 6.5 percent this year and 6.2 percent in 2017, slightly higher than the projections in the October 2015 WEO, reflecting announced policy stimulus. A further weakening is expected in the industrial sector, as excess capacity continues to unwind, especially in real estate and related upstream industries, as well as in manufacturing. Services sector growth should be robust as the economy continues to rebalance from investment to consumption. High income growth, a robust labor market, and structural reforms designed to support consumption are assumed to keep the rebalancing process on track over the forecast horizon.

- Elsewhere in emerging and developing Asia, activity remains robust. In *India*, growth is projected to notch up to 7.5 percent in 2016–17, as forecast in October. Growth will continue to be driven by private consumption, which has benefited from lower energy prices and higher real incomes. With the revival of sentiment and pickup in industrial activity, a recovery of private investment is expected to further strengthen growth. Among the ASEAN-5 economies (*Indonesia, Malaysia, Philippines, Thailand, Vietnam*), growth will ease in 2016 in Malaysia and Vietnam (to 4.4 percent and 6.3 percent, respectively) but increase moderately in Indonesia, the Philippines, and Thailand (to 4.9 percent, 6.0 percent, and 3.0 percent, respectively). Growth in the ASEAN-5 is envisaged to pick up further in 2017 and thereafter, underpinned by strong domestic demand and a gradual increase in exports.

- In *Latin America and the Caribbean*, overall growth in 2016 is expected to be negative for a second consecutive year (at –0.5 percent). However, across all countries in the region, economic activity is expected to strengthen in 2017, with growth picking up to 1.5 percent. There are substantial differences across regions and countries. While South America remains heavily affected by the decline in commodity prices, Mexico, Central America, and the Caribbean are beneficiaries of the U.S. recovery and, in most cases, lower oil prices. Indeed, most countries in the region continue to grow, even if modestly.

○ *Mexico* is expected to continue to grow at a moderate pace (2.4 percent in 2016 and 2.6 percent in 2017), supported by healthy private domestic demand and spillovers from a robust U.S. economy.

○ In *Brazil*, output is expected to contract by a further 3.8 percent in 2016 (following a contraction of 3.8 percent in 2015), as the recession takes its toll on employment and real incomes and domestic uncertainties continue to constrain the government's ability to formulate and execute policies. With many of the large shocks from 2015–16 expected to have run their course, and helped by a weaker currency, growth is projected to turn positive during 2017; nevertheless, output on average will likely remain unchanged from the previous year. These forecasts are subject to large uncertainty.

○ Among oil-exporting South American countries, the projected deceleration of activity in *Colombia* (with growth easing to 2.5 percent in 2016 from 3.1 percent in 2015) reflects low oil prices, as well as tightening macroeconomic policies and financial conditions. *Venezuela* is projected to remain in a deep recession in 2016 (with output projected to contract by 8 percent following the contraction of 5.7 percent in 2015), amid political uncertainty and as the renewed decline in the price of oil has deepened existing macroeconomic imbalances and pressures, including an average inflation rate projected to rise to close to 500 percent in 2016. *Ecuador*'s outlook is highly uncertain and depends on the availability of external financing. Under the baseline scenario, the country's output is expected to contract this year (by 4.5 percent) amid lower oil prices, a loss of competitiveness on the back of an appreciating dollar, fiscal consolidation, and tight financing conditions.

○ Elsewhere in South America, the ongoing push to correct macroeconomic imbalances and microeconomic distortions in *Argentina* has improved pros-

pects for growth over the medium term, but the adjustment is likely to generate a mild recession in 2016. The protracted decline in the price of copper and tighter financial conditions are weighing on *Chile*'s outlook (with growth declining to 1.5 percent in 2016 from 2.1 percent in 2015). *Peru*'s growth is expected to pick up in 2016 and 2017 (to 3.7 and 4.1 percent, respectively), mostly driven by stronger activity in the resource sector.

• The economic outlook for the *Commonwealth of Independent States* remains very weak, reflecting the recession in *Russia* and its regional spillovers, as well as the effect of lower oil prices on oil-exporting countries. Output in the region is projected to decline further by 1.1 percent in 2016. A recovery is expected to take hold in 2017, with growth forecast at 1.3 percent. In Russia, growth is projected at –1.8 percent in 2016 (following a contraction of 3.7 percent last year), as international sanctions compound the effects of lower oil prices and structural weaknesses. *Ukraine*'s economy is projected to return to positive growth in 2016, supported by improving consumer and investor confidence, gradually rising real incomes, and a gradual easing of credit conditions. The sustained decline in oil prices, Russia's recession, and the slowdown and rebalancing of China's economy are weighing on growth in the Central Asia and Caucasus region by suppressing exports, remittances, and investment. The region's growth forecast has been downgraded to 1.2 percent in 2016, reflecting weak external demand, lower oil production, and weak confidence in Kazakhstan, weaker public investment in Azerbaijan and Turkmenistan, and lower remittances in the oil-importing countries. Growth is expected to recover only modestly to 2.5 percent in 2017.

• Growth in *emerging and developing Europe* is projected to remain broadly stable at 3.5 percent in 2016 and 3.3 percent in 2017. Activity in the region has benefited from lower oil prices and the gradual recovery in the euro area, but elevated corporate debt is hindering private investment. In *Turkey*, growth is projected to remain stable at 3.8 percent in 2016, with a large minimum wage increase sustaining domestic demand in the face of geopolitical uncertainty, weak external demand, and slowing credit growth. Growth is expected to moderate in *Hungary* as the effects of the high absorption of European Union funds gradually dissipate, but to pick up slightly in southeastern Europe.

- Growth in *sub-Saharan Africa* is expected to remain weak this year at 3.0 percent, about ½ percentage point lower than in 2015, and 1.3 percentage points lower than forecast in the October 2015 WEO. Growth is projected to pick up to 4.0 percent in 2017, helped by a small rebound in commodity prices and timely policy implementation. The ongoing slowdown is primarily driven by unfavorable external conditions: resource-intensive countries have suffered from the decline in commodity prices, while the region's frontier markets are adversely affected by tighter global financing conditions.

  - Sub-Saharan Africa's oil-exporting countries are now projected to grow at 2.0 percent in 2016 (a downward revision of 2.1 percentage points relative to the October 2015 forecast) and 3.4 percent in 2017. Within this group, growth in 2016 is expected to ease to 2.5 percent in *Angola* (down from 3.0 percent in 2015) and 2.3 percent in *Nigeria* (from 2.7 percent growth last year), as the negative impact of lower oil prices is compounded by disruptions to private sector activity through exchange rate restrictions.

  - The effect of the decline in oil prices on the region's oil-importing countries has been smaller than expected, as many of these economies export other nonrenewable resources whose prices have also dropped. In *South Africa,* growth is expected to be halved to 0.6 percent in 2016 owing to lower export prices, elevated policy uncertainty, and tighter monetary and fiscal policy. In *Zambia,* the impact of the drought on electricity production is adding to downward pressure from low copper prices, and growth will remain subdued at 3.4 percent (slightly below the 3.6 percent achieved in 2015). In *Ghana,* growth is projected to increase in 2016 to 4.5 percent, from 3.5 percent last year, when it was hampered by power shortages and fiscal consolidation. In many other oil importers, inflationary pressures stemming from the pass-through of a strong U.S. dollar (which notably limited the decline of fuel prices in domestic-currency terms) and high food prices (due to the drought in eastern and southern Africa) have also offset to some extent the benefits of lower oil prices. Nonetheless, ongoing investment in infrastructure and strong consumption in countries such as *Côte d'Ivoire, Kenya, Rwanda, Senegal,* and *Tanzania* are expected to drive growth at rates of 6–7 percent or more this

year and next. By contrast, *Ethiopia*'s economy is held back by a drought, with growth projected to decline substantially to 4.5 percent (from 10.2 percent in 2015).

- The outlook across the *Middle East, North Africa, Afghanistan, and Pakistan* (MENAP) region has weakened considerably because of further declines in oil prices and intensifying conflicts and security risks. Growth in the region overall is projected at 3.1 percent in 2016 and 3.5 percent in 2017, 0.8 percentage point and 0.7 percentage point weaker, respectively, than projected in the October 2015 WEO.

  - With oil prices now expected to remain low for longer, oil-exporting MENAP countries have taken substantial further steps to restrain government spending, cut subsidies, and raise revenues. Even with these measures, fiscal deficits are projected to widen this year. Growth in the member countries of the Cooperation Council for the Arab States of the Gulf (GCC) is now expected to decline from 3.3 percent in 2015 to 1.8 percent in 2016 and pick up to more than 2 percent over the medium term. However, increased oil production in the postsanctions *Islamic Republic of Iran* and in *Iraq,* as well as the bottoming out of activity in *Yemen* as the conflict is assumed to ease gradually, is projected to raise the aggregate growth rate of oil-exporting MENAP countries to 2.9 percent in 2016 and 3.1 percent in 2017 from 1.9 percent last year.

  - Growth in oil-importing MENAP countries is expected to remain subdued as gains from greater political stability, economic reforms, reduced drag from fiscal consolidation, and lower oil prices are offset by spillovers from security disruptions, social tensions, and spillovers from regional conflicts, and, more recently, slowdowns in member countries of the GCC.

Global Inflation

With the December 2015 declines in oil prices mostly expected to persist this year, consumer price inflation has been revised downward across almost all advanced economies and is projected to remain below central bank targets in 2016. Excluding Venezuela (where average inflation is projected to rise to close to 500 percent this year and even further next year), inflation in emerging market and developing economies is projected to fall to 4.5 percent in 2016, from 4.7

percent in 2015, reflecting the decline in commodity prices and the dissipating effects of last year's currency depreciations.

- In the euro area, headline inflation is projected to reach 0.4 percent in 2016 (from about zero in 2015) and to increase further to 1.1 percent in 2017 with support from monetary policy easing by the ECB. Inflation is thereafter expected to rise only very gradually over the medium term.
- In Japan, inflation is expected to be negative at –0.2 percent in 2016 because of lower energy prices and the strengthening of the yen in recent months. Over the medium term, inflation is projected to rise to 1.0–1.5 percent, as accommodative monetary policy conditions and the closing of the output gap apply upward pressure on prices.
- In the United States, inflation in 2016 is projected to rise to 0.8 percent from 0.1 percent in 2015 amid a tightening labor market, even though dollar appreciation and pass-through from lower oil prices are exerting downward pressure on prices. Consumer price index inflation is projected to rise over the medium term to about 2¼ percent, with inflation measured with the personal consumption expenditure deflator—the Federal Reserve's preferred inflation measure—reaching 2 percent.
- Average inflation in other advanced economies will also remain below central bank targets, mostly as a result of the decline in oil prices. Inflation is projected to return to target next year in Korea (partly because the Bank of Korea recently reduced its inflation target), but only over the medium term in Singapore and Sweden. Consumer prices in Switzerland are projected to decline in 2016 and 2017 given the appreciation of the currency last year.

In emerging market economies, the downward pressure from lower oil prices is offset to varying degrees by the pass-through of nominal exchange rate depreciations to domestic prices, especially in countries with strong depreciations, such as Brazil, Colombia, Russia, and more recently, Kazakhstan. In subsequent years, inflation is expected to ease gradually toward official targets.

- In China, inflation is forecast to remain low at about 1.8 percent in 2016, reflecting lower commodity prices, the real appreciation of the renminbi, and somewhat weaker domestic demand.
- In India, monetary conditions remain consistent with achieving the inflation target of 5 percent in the first half of 2017, although an unfavorable monsoon and an expected public sector wage increase pose upside risks. In Brazil, average inflation is expected to fall slightly to 8.7 percent this year from 9.0 percent last year, as the effects of the large administered price adjustments and currency depreciation in 2015 diminish. In Russia, inflation is projected to decline from 15.5 percent in 2015 to 8.4 percent in 2016. In Turkey, inflation for 2016 is projected at 9.8 percent, almost 5 percentage points above target.
- A few other emerging markets, especially in central and southeastern Europe, such as Hungary and Poland, are projected to experience headline consumer price inflation well below target in 2016.

External Sector Outlook

Global trade growth is projected to remain moderate but to pick up gradually from 2016 onward, primarily reflecting stronger growth in domestic demand in emerging market and developing economies.

The main factor affecting the evolution of global current account balances in 2015 has once again been the decline in oil prices. As a result of this decline, the aggregate current account balance of oil-exporting emerging market and developing economies has turned into a deficit for the first time since 1998 (Figure 1.15, panel 1). Among oil-importing surplus regions, more than half of the $370 billion worsening of the current account balance in oil-exporting countries was offset by higher surpluses in China and other oil-importing advanced Asian economies, particularly Japan. Across oil-importing countries and regions with current account deficits, changes were roughly offsetting, with some worsening of the current account balance in the United States offset by improving current account balances in European deficit countries. And the global current account discrepancy (an apparent surplus in the world current account), which had reached $378 billion in 2014, shrank by about 40 percent in 2015.

Similar factors are expected to be at play in 2016, in light of the further decline in average oil prices relative to their 2015 levels, albeit on a more modest scale. In subsequent years imbalances are forecast to narrow as China rebalances and the surpluses of advanced European economies gradually decline as a share of world GDP, more than offsetting the return to surplus of oil-exporting countries given the forecast of higher oil prices. This rebalancing notwithstanding, net external creditor and debtor positions are projected to expand further as a share of both domestic and global GDP, with a particularly sharp increase in the net international investment position of creditor countries in advanced Europe, such as Germany and the Netherlands, reflecting projections of continued large current account surpluses (Figure 1.15, panel 2).

Exchange rate movements over the past year have reflected important shifts in underlying economic fundamentals, such as changes in commodity prices, trading partners' growth prospects, and external vulnerabilities. In particular, as shown in panel 3 of Figure 1.15 for a sample of countries without exchange rate pegs, real effective exchange rates have tended to appreciate in countries with terms-of-trade gains and depreciate in those with losses. Indeed, the measure of income gains and losses from terms-of-trade changes described earlier in the chapter can by itself explain more than half of the variation in real effective exchange rate movements since 2014.

Growth rates in creditor countries have continued to exceed those in debtor countries (Figure 1.16), reflecting primarily strong growth in China, a pattern that is expected to persist in 2016.[5] The growth differential is mostly explained by different growth rates of domestic demand, but also by some reliance on net external demand on the part of creditors. For 2015–16, such reliance on net external demand reflects primarily developments in creditor countries that are oil exporters, where import demand has declined sharply following the collapse in oil prices. Stronger reliance on domestic demand in a number of creditor countries would help facilitate global rebalancing while sustaining world growth.

A Pronounced Increase in Downside Risks

WEO growth forecasts form a central, or modal, scenario—growth rates that the IMF staff estimates to be the most likely in each year of the forecast horizon. The weakening in global growth in late 2015 and the escalation of threats to global economic activity since the start of this year have led the staff to reduce the projected growth rates under the central scenario.

---

[5]Creditor countries and regions include China, advanced Asia, and creditor countries in advanced Europe (such as Germany and the Netherlands), as well as most oil-exporting countries. Debtor countries and regions include the United States, debtor nations in advanced and developing Europe (such as Italy, Spain, Turkey, and the United Kingdom), Latin America, India and some other economies in emerging Asia, and Australia and New Zealand.

Figure 1.15. External Sector

Global current account imbalances have declined in recent years, mostly reflecting the reduced balances of oil exporters. Nonetheless, net creditor and debtor positions continue to widen. In countries with flexible exchange rates, exchange rate movements over the past year have been correlated with terms-of-trade movements.

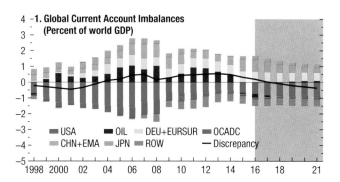

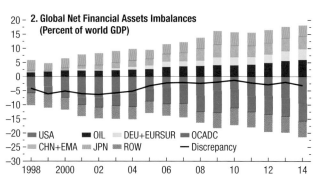

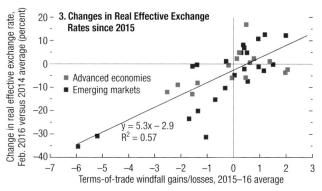

Source: IMF staff estimates.
Note: CHN+EMA = China and emerging Asia (Hong Kong SAR, Indonesia, Korea, Malaysia, Philippines, Singapore, Taiwan Province of China,Thailand); DEU+EUR-SUR = Germany and other European advanced surplus economies (Austria, Denmark, Luxembourg, Netherlands, Sweden, Switzerland); OCADC = other European countries with precrisis current account deficits (Greece, Ireland, Italy, Portugal, Spain, United Kingdom, WEO group of emerging and developing Europe); OIL = Norway and WEO group of emerging market and developing economy fuel exporters; ROW = rest of the world. Data labels in the figure use International Organization for Standardization (ISO) country codes.

Figure 1.16. Creditors versus Debtors

Growth rates in creditor countries have continued to exceed those in debtor countries, reflecting primarily strong growth in China. The growth differential is mostly explained by different growth rates of domestic demand, but also some reliance on net external demand by creditors, especially by oil exporters in 2015 and 2016.

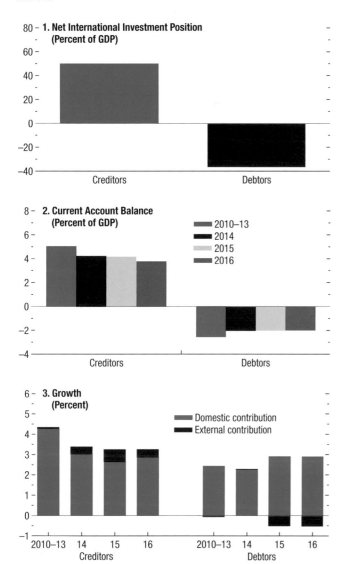

Source: IMF staff estimates.
Note: In panel 1, data on the net international investment position are the latest available (2015:Q3 for most countries).

Alongside these reduced central projections, the staff views the likelihood of outcomes worse than those in the central scenario as having increased. Put differently, not only is the central WEO scenario now less favorable and less likely; in addition, the even weaker downside outcomes have become more likely.

Heightened downside risks stem from both an intensification of the hazards highlighted in the January 2016 *WEO Update* and further bouts of financial turbulence leading to a tightening in financial conditions, including in advanced economies. Over the near term, the main risks to the outlook revolve around (1) the threat of a disorderly pullback of capital flows and growing risks to financial stability in emerging market economies, (2) the international ramifications of the economic transition in China, (3) growing strains in countries that are heavily reliant on oil exports, (4) the possible impact of tighter financial conditions and bouts of financial market volatility on confidence and growth if they persist, (5) more protracted recessions in emerging market economies that are currently experiencing distress, (6) geopolitical risks, and (7) the United Kingdom's potential exit from the European Union. Materialization of any of these risks could raise the likelihood of other adverse developments. Perceptions of limited policy space to respond to negative shocks, in both advanced and emerging market economies, are exacerbating concerns about these adverse scenarios. In the euro area, the persistence of low inflation and its interaction with the debt overhang is also a growing concern.

Beyond the immediate juncture, the danger of secular stagnation and an entrenchment of excessively low inflation in advanced economies, as well as of lower-than-anticipated potential growth worldwide, has become more tangible.

Financial Stability Risks in Emerging Markets

After five years of declining economic growth and a downward shift in capital inflows that gained momentum in 2015, emerging market economies are increasingly vulnerable to a change in investor sentiment. As highlighted in Chapter 3 of the October 2015 *Global Financial Stability Report* (GFSR), sizable currency depreciations over the past two to two and a half years have eroded the financial buffers of companies that have high dollar-denominated debt but limited claims or earnings in dollars. Fiscal buffers have also diminished; public-debt-to-GDP ratios of most emerging market economies are now noticeably above their 2007 levels (April 2016 *Fiscal Monitor*). The once-rapid accumulation of international reserves has given way to reserve losses in some economies.

A stronger pullback of capital flows could tighten financial conditions in emerging market economies and put additional downward pressure on their currencies, leading to adverse balance sheet effects and possibly funding challenges. The trigger for such a development could take a variety of forms: increased investor concerns about stressed emerging market economies and commodity sectors, idiosyncratic events in the larger emerging market economies, or the materialization of other risks to the outlook, such as a weakening in global demand due to protracted financial market turbulence. Regardless of the trigger, a flight from riskier asset classes could spark disruptive declines in asset prices and currency values, generating contagion effects and harming growth further. The countries that are potentially more vulnerable to a discrete change in investor sentiment are those with larger external financing needs, weaker net international investment positions, and higher yield spreads.

International Ramifications of Developments in China

China's transition to a new growth model and a more market-based economy is inherently challenging and has been bumpy at times. Corporate profitability in China has eroded over the past few years, as growth has declined toward a more sustainable pace following a period of rapid credit growth and investment. Lower corporate earnings, in turn, are hindering the ability of Chinese firms to service their debt obligations, raising banks' levels of nonperforming loans (Chapter 1 of the April 2016 GFSR). As bank lending capacity is increasingly constrained, Chinese firms are turning to capital markets. The combination of corporate balance sheet weakness, a high level of nonperforming loans, and inefficiencies in bond and equity markets is posing risks to financial stability, complicating the authorities' task of achieving a smooth rebalancing of the economy while reducing vulnerabilities from excess leverage. Limited progress on key reforms and increasing risks in the corporate and financial sectors have led to medium-term growth concerns, triggering turbulence in Chinese and global financial markets. Policy actions to dampen market volatility have, at times, been ineffective and poorly communicated.

A sharper-than-forecast slowdown in China could have strong international spillovers through trade, commodity prices, and confidence, with attendant effects on global financial markets and currency valuations as discussed in Chapter 2 of the April 2016 *Regional Economic Outlook: Asia and Pacific*. That outcome could lead to a more generalized slowdown in both emerging market and advanced economies,

especially if it should further compromise investment, potential growth, and expectations of future income.

Risks of Further Strains in Oil-Exporting Countries

With diminishing fiscal buffers, the renewed declines in oil prices in late 2015 and early 2016 could force oil-exporting countries to cut spending more significantly than envisaged in the WEO forecast. Additional retrenchment in spending could be motivated by a tightening of global financial conditions and market perceptions of heightened sovereign risk, as discussed in Scenario Box 1.

These risks would be exacerbated if oil prices were to decline even further. And in the current low-inflation environment, a scenario of even lower oil prices comes with a risk of a further reduction in inflation expectations and possibly also core inflation rates in advanced economies, raising real interest rates and deflation risks. At the same time, further declines in oil prices could bolster the perception that prices will stay low for long, boosting oil-importing countries' spending out of the windfall and thereby cushioning some of these adverse effects.

Recent Turbulence in Financial Markets and Losses in Equity Wealth

Equity markets worldwide posted large losses in early 2016, with price declines in advanced economies especially large for banking sector stocks. From the end of December 2015 to mid-February 2016, stock price indices in advanced economies fell by more than 12 percent and those in emerging market economies by about 9 percent. Markets have since rebounded, bringing the year-to-date changes to about –2 percent for advanced economies and into positive territory for emerging market economies as of the end of March. Nevertheless, stock price indices remain well below the peaks reached in the spring of 2015, especially for emerging market economies. As discussed in the April 2016 GFSR, a lasting increase in financial market turbulence and persistent declines in equity valuations could tighten financial conditions, by increasing risk premiums and some interest rates, while reducing capital availability for firms, further depressing investment levels, which have yet to fully recover (Chapter 3 of the April 2015 WEO). Such asset market disruptions could also generate adverse wealth and confidence effects that harm private consumption, especially in those advanced economies in which equity holdings are an important part of household wealth. Though the global equity valuation losses so far in 2016 are likely to have a very small adverse impact on consumption, the decline follows larger losses in the second half of 2015 that, if increasingly seen as persistent by households, would weaken consumer demand and growth in advanced economies and, ultimately, in the global economy. Weaker growth would leave the global economy vulnerable to further shocks and raise recession risks, feeding back into weaker investor risk appetite.

Possible Delays in Normalization of Conditions in Economies in Recession

The economies of Brazil and Russia, which together account for about 6 percent of world output based on purchasing-power-parity exchange rates, have been contracting since mid-2014. Lower-than-expected growth in Brazil was a major contributor to the downward revisions to estimated 2015 growth in the January 2016 *WEO Update*. The baseline WEO forecast factors in a very gradual normalization of conditions in these two economies, with a somewhat reduced pace of contraction in 2016 and zero or mildly positive growth in 2017. The outlook for Brazil and Russia remains uncertain, however, and possible delays in their return to more normal conditions could once again push global growth below the current forecast.

Geopolitical Tensions and Strife

The incidence of armed conflicts and terrorist acts has increased in the last couple of years. Ongoing events in parts of Africa and the Middle East, as well as in Ukraine, could further heighten domestic and international tensions, with increased disruptions in trade, tourism, and financial flows. In Europe, the surge of refugees is presenting major challenges to the absorptive capacity of EU labor markets and testing political systems, fueling skepticism about economic integration, as well as EU governance, and potentially hindering policymakers' ability to respond to both legacy and emergent economic challenges.

Potential Exit of the United Kingdom from the European Union

A British exit from the European Union could pose major challenges for both the United Kingdom and the rest of Europe. Negotiations on postexit arrangements would likely be protracted, resulting in an extended period of heightened uncertainty that could weigh heavily on confidence and investment, all the while increasing financial market volatility. A U.K. exit from Europe's single market would also likely disrupt and reduce mutual trade and financial flows, curtailing key benefits from economic cooperation and integration, such as those resulting from economies of scale and efficient specialization.

Secular Stagnation, Hysteresis, and Lower Potential Output

In advanced economies, the risk of a protracted shortfall in domestic demand and a further weakening of potential output due to hysteresis effects remains a concern, especially in view of heightened risks to near-term activity. In some economies, especially in vulnerable euro area countries, demand remains particularly sluggish, and slack in labor markets remains sizable. The declines in the price of oil and other commodities since December 2015 raise the risk of deflation in advanced economies. The scenario presented later, in the "Policy Priorities" section, provides an illustration of how secular stagnation could affect global economic activity.

A rising likelihood of lower potential output due to a protracted demand shortfall is increasingly a worry for emerging market economies as well, in particular for economies experiencing deep and prolonged recessions. A combination of ongoing supply-side constraints, persistently weak investment, and in some cases, high unemployment rates and skill losses could weigh on medium-term supply potential in these economies, especially where structural reform momentum is weak. Last but not least, economies facing domestic strife and surging refugee outflows are facing a massive loss of future economic potential.

The Fan Chart: Risks around the Global GDP Forecast

With a lower baseline forecast for global growth and a slightly wider confidence band around the baseline forecast, the fan chart documents a moderate but noticeable increase in the probability of global growth declining below 2 percent as compared to a year ago (Figure 1.17).[6] Analysis based on the IMF's Global

---

[6]The indicators used in the construction of the fan chart are based on prices of derivatives or on the distribution of forecasts of

Projection Model similarly suggests an increase in the probability of a recession in major advanced economies over a four-quarter horizon relative to the probabilities computed in April and October 2015 (Figure 1.18). That increase reflects a combination of lower growth in the baseline and a negative shift in the distribution of future shocks to demand and financial variables, consistent with adverse confidence effects given heightened perceptions of limited policy space. The simulations also suggest an increase in the risk of deflation in the euro area, Japan, and the United States for the last quarter of 2016, consistent with heightened downside risks to growth and the recent decline in oil prices. Deflation probabilities would decline in subsequent quarters if oil and other commodity prices evolve as assumed under the current WEO baseline.

Policy Priorities

In qualitative terms, the policy challenges currently facing most countries are similar to those highlighted in recent WEO reports. The main priorities are to lift both actual and potential output in advanced economies and to contain vulnerabilities and build resilience in emerging market and developing economies as they adjust to diminished growth prospects. Yet with expectations of global growth once again scaled down and a manifest increase in the downside risks facing most economies, the urgency of policy action to safeguard near-term growth—and of planning timely policy responses should downside risks materialize—has increased further.

Advanced Economies: Tackling Demand and Supply Weaknesses amid Growing Headwinds

Growth in advanced economies is expected to be modest under the baseline, reflecting subdued demand and a broad-based weakening of potential growth. The main factors underlying the weakening in potential growth are population aging, which would reduce trend employment at current rates of labor market participation; sluggish investment, held back in part by weak demand and impaired balance sheets; and a weakening of total factor productivity growth

the underlying variables. The chart compares the current confidence intervals with those in the April 2015 WEO to ensure that a forecast horizon of equal length is used; the horizon for current- and next-year forecasts are longer in April than in October, when more data affecting current- and next-year outcomes are known.

Figure 1.17. Risks to the Global Outlook

With a lower baseline forecast for global growth and a slightly wider confidence band around the baseline forecast, the fan chart shows that risks of weaker growth outcomes have increased.

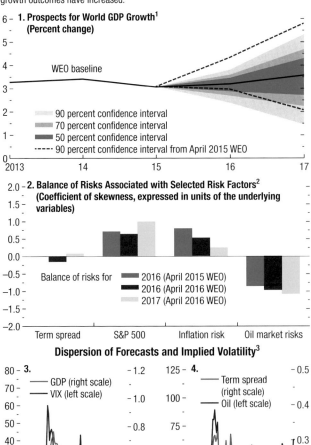

Sources: Bloomberg, L.P.; Chicago Board Options Exchange (CBOE); Consensus Economics; Haver Analytics; and IMF staff estimates.
[1]The fan chart shows the uncertainty around the WEO central forecast with 50, 70, and 90 percent confidence intervals. As shown, the 70 percent confidence interval includes the 50 percent interval, and the 90 percent confidence interval includes the 50 and 70 percent intervals. See Appendix 1.2 of the April 2009 WEO for details. The 90 percent intervals for the current-year and one-year-ahead forecasts from the April 2015 WEO are shown relative to the April 2015 baseline.
[2]The bars depict the coefficient of skewness expressed in units of the underlying variables. The values for inflation risks and oil price risks enter with the opposite sign since they represent downside risks to growth.
[3]GDP measures the purchasing-power-parity-weighted average dispersion of GDP growth forecasts for the G7 economies (Canada, France, Germany, Italy, Japan, United Kingdom, United States), Brazil, China, India, and Mexico. VIX is the CBOE Volatility Index. Term spread measures the average dispersion ofterm spreads implicit in interest rate forecasts for Germany, Japan, the UnitedKingdom, and the United States. Oil is the CBOE crude oil volatility index. Forecastsare from Consensus Economics surveys. Dashed lines represent the averagevalues from 2000 to the present.

Figure 1.18. Recession and Deflation Risks
(Percent)

Analysis based on the IMF's Global Projection Model suggests an increase in the probability of a recession in major advanced economies over a four-quarter horizon relative to the probabilities computed in April and October 2015. The model's simulations also suggest an increase in the risk of deflation in the euro area, Japan, and the United States, consistent with heightened downside risks to growth and weaker commodity prices.

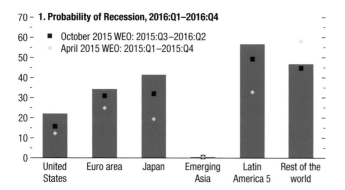

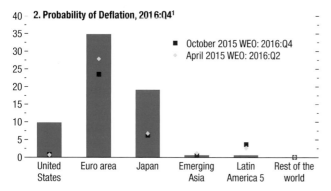

Source: IMF staff estimates.
Note: Emerging Asia comprises China, Hong Kong SAR, India, Indonesia, Korea, Malaysia, the Philippines, Singapore, Taiwan Province of China, and Thailand; Latin America 5 comprises Brazil, Chile, Colombia, Mexico, and Peru; Rest of the world comprises Argentina, Australia, Bulgaria, Canada, Czech Republic, Denmark, Israel, New Zealand, Norway, Russia, South Africa, Sweden, Switzerland, Turkey, United Kingdom, and Venezuela.
[1]Deflation is defined as a fall in the price level on a year-over-year basis in the quarter indicated in the figure.

that predates the crisis (see Chapter 3 of the April 2015 WEO). Increasing headwinds from the growth slowdown in emerging market economies and the recent tightening in financial conditions are threatening to further weaken near-term demand in advanced economies.

Securing higher and sustainable growth in advanced economies requires a three-pronged approach consisting of mutually reinforcing (1) structural reforms, (2) continued monetary policy accommodation, and (3) fiscal support—in the form of growth-friendly fiscal policies where adjustment is needed and fiscal

stimulus where space allows. In practice, fiscal space should be assessed using a risk management approach, comparing the evolution of public debt and GDP along a trajectory with no policy response, accounting for risks of a further slowdown and stagnation, with that under a forceful policy response that boosts the trajectory of output and mitigates downside risks. On the supply side, Chapter 3 documents that structural reforms—tailored to country needs—can make important contributions to potential output and employment in many advanced economies over the medium term. Yet as discussed in that chapter, certain types of structural reform can also boost demand in the short term, whereas others require supportive macroeconomic policies to accelerate their benefits and minimize their possible contractionary and deflationary short-term side effects. Comprehensive strategies that take into account both the short- and medium-term impacts are therefore needed to maximize the credibility of reforms and the likelihood that they will build confidence and stimulate near-term investment and consumption.

Reforms that entail fiscal stimulus are the most valuable at this juncture, including those that reduce labor tax wedges and increase public spending on active labor market policies. Such measures nonetheless remain effective when implemented in a budget-neutral way, for example, as part of broad reforms of tax and spending policies.

Product market reforms aimed at reducing anticompetitive barriers to firm entry—such as those in certain network industries, retail trade, and professional services—can rapidly buoy output by boosting investment and hiring as new firms expand. Nonetheless, complementary policies aimed at addressing the weak bank and corporate balance sheets that are currently inhibiting investment are key to enhancing the short-term investment impact of these reforms.

Other labor market reforms, including reforms of unemployment benefits and—especially—employment protection rules, boost productivity in the medium term but could be contractionary in the short term under the current weak economic conditions. These measures therefore require supportive macroeconomic policies to avoid a drag on demand and deflationary side effects.

Country-specific structural reform priorities continue to differ to some extent.

• In the *United States*, boosting the labor supply will require an expansion of the earned income tax credit; an increase in the federal minimum wage; stronger family benefits (including child care assistance); and a comprehensive, skills-based immigration reform. Enhanced infrastructure spending and innovation incentives are critical to fostering investment in the short term and productivity in the medium term.

- In the *euro area*, priorities vary across countries. With persistently high youth unemployment rates in many countries, skill erosion and its effect on trend employment are palpable concerns. Lowering disincentives to employment—including the labor tax wedge—and putting in place better-targeted active labor market policies would be important to boost demand and minimize the scarring effect of long-term unemployment. Reforms of product, services, and labor markets, public administration, and insolvency regimes would help improve firms' productivity, competitiveness, and investment prospects. Such reforms could also help expedite the disbursement of pan–European Union investment funds to support investment and innovation at the national level. At the regional level, a strong push to complete the single markets in services, capital, transport, energy, and digital technologies would promote productivity-enhancing economic integration. The European Union also needs a more effective economic governance framework—including outcome-based structural reform benchmarks, effective use of EU legislation, and full use of Stability and Growth Pact flexibility for structural reforms.
- In *Japan*, structural reforms that raise productivity are vital for tackling medium-term risks and raising potential output, while income policies are needed to bolster wage-price dynamics and increase monetary policy effectiveness. Structural reforms should focus on boosting the supply of labor (including of women), reforming labor markets to remove duality, further deregulating product and services markets, and supporting investment through corporate governance reform, as well as improving the provision of risk capital by the financial system.
- In *Europe* more broadly, policy actions to support the integration of migrants into the labor force are crucial to allay concerns about social exclusion and long-term fiscal costs, while unlocking the potential long-term economic benefits of refugee inflows. Policies that can help facilitate integration include minimizing restrictions that prevent refugees from taking up work during the asylum application phase,

strengthening active labor market policies specifically targeted to refugees, and providing wage subsidies to private employers that hire immigrants. Initiatives to make self-employment easier and facilitate skill recognition could also help refugees succeed. Finally, reducing restrictions on refugees' geographical mobility, including those linked to housing, would allow them to move to locations where the probability of good job matches is high.

On the demand side, macroeconomic policy support can raise actual output while enhancing the benefits of structural reforms. Monetary policy should remain accommodative where output gaps are negative and inflation is too low. In addition, given the uncertain effects of product and labor market reforms on prices, and amid persistent low inflation in many countries, strong and credible monetary policy frameworks are essential. Specifically, such frameworks—including quantitative easing or negative deposit rates, where relevant—can keep medium-term inflation expectations anchored and ease the zero-lower-bound constraint on policy interest rates, thus preempting risks that structural reforms will create deflation, increase the real interest rate, and weigh on aggregate demand in the short term.

- In the *United States*, the mid-December increase in the federal funds rate reflected a stronger U.S. economy. At present, a broad range of indicators suggest a notable improvement in the labor market, accompanied by signs of firming wage and price pressures. The pace of further rate increases should therefore be gradual. An effective monetary policy communication strategy will remain essential, particularly in an environment of higher financial market volatility in which spillovers through financial channels could be material.
- In the *euro area*, the ECB's asset purchase program has supported the recovery by improving confidence and financial conditions. But persistently low inflation and subdued growth point to the need for policy to remain accommodative for an extended period. The wide range of mutually reinforcing policy measures taken recently by the ECB are appropriate, in view of the increased downside risks to the outlook. They strengthen its forward guidance and signal a strong commitment to meet its price stability objective over the medium term. They will also facilitate the pass-through of improved bank funding conditions to the real economy by encouraging greater lending

while reducing the impact of negative deposit rates on bank profitability. The ECB should continue to signal strongly its willingness to use all available instruments until its price stability objective is met. These monetary policy efforts should be supported by measures to strengthen bank balance sheets, which would help improve monetary policy transmission, bolster credit supply, and reduce banking sector vulnerabilities. Enhanced prudential oversight to provide banks with incentives to clean up balance sheets, reforms to enhance debt enforcement regimes and insolvency frameworks, and the development of distressed debt markets (including through asset management vehicles) are priorities in this regard (see Aiyar and others 2015).

- In *Japan*, the introduction of a negative rate on marginal reserve deposits by the Bank of Japan underscores its commitment to maintaining inflation momentum. Building on recent achievements, the authorities should consider adopting a (softly enforceable) wage growth target, supported by higher public sector and minimum wages. The central bank should also consider providing stronger guidance to markets by moving toward more forecast-oriented monetary policy communication. The latter would increase the transparency of the bank's assessment of inflation prospects and signal its commitment to the inflation target by facilitating the communication of envisaged policy changes when inflation gets off track.

In addition to an accomodative monetary policy stance, fiscal support is also essential. Fiscal policy should be growth friendly, especially in countries where fiscal consolidation is necessary. Specifically, it should support demand in the short run, protecting the most vulnerable, and increase potential output over the medium term by encouraging job creation and fostering productivity, including through innovation (see Chapter 2 of the April 2016 *Fiscal Monitor*). Where public debt is high or financing conditions are unfavorable, commitments to credible medium-term consolidation plans can create policy space. Fiscal stimulus should be implemented where space is available and should focus on boosting future productive capacity, such as through infrastructure investment. Such a fiscal policy stance would raise demand, improve productivity, offset the short-term economic costs of some structural reforms (for example, to employment protection legislation and unemployment benefit systems in some euro area countries), and amplify the gains from others (for example, labor

tax wedge reductions or increased spending on active labor market policies).

- In the *United States*, the bipartisan budget agreement of December 2015 reduced immediate risks related to fiscal brinkmanship, but further fiscal efforts are needed to stabilize the debt-to-GDP ratio over the medium term as interest rates gradually increase and the country's demographic transition intensifies. Building on the 2013 and 2015 bipartisan budget arrangements, a further agreement on a credible medium-term deficit reduction plan would provide the space to fund much-needed investments in infrastructure, raise productivity and innovation, and enhance workers' skills.
- In the *euro area*, countries with fiscal space under the Stability and Growth Pact should do more to support demand—for example, by expanding public investment. Prompt and effective implementation—and possibly expansion—of the EU scheme to provide public and private investment would raise growth in the short and medium term, including through positive spillovers within the region. Expenditures necessary to absorb and integrate refugees should be considered on a case-by-case basis when assessing fiscal efforts to attain Stability and Growth Pact targets.
- In *Japan*, a commitment to fiscal consolidation centered on a preannounced path of gradual consumption tax hikes and a strengthening of fiscal institutions would create near-term policy space to maintain growth momentum.

The importance of timely policy actions in the event of a downside scenario and their implications for global output are illustrated in Scenario Box 2. The scenario assumes that secular-stagnation forces give rise to a persistent output shortfall, with a widening of the negative output gap, but also an erosion of potential output due to persistently deficient aggregate demand. The scenario then assumes a concerted policy response relying on both demand-side and supply-side measures (a temporary fiscal expansion consisting of measures with large short-term multipliers and targeted to raise long-term potential output, accompanied by product and labor market reform commitments). This policy response can fully offset the initial negative shocks and raise output above the initial baseline.

Emerging Market and Developing Economies: Managing Vulnerabilities and Bolstering Potential Output

The challenges facing policymakers in emerging market and developing economies are diverse, reflect-

Scenario Box 2. Responding to Secular Stagnation Forces

This scenario uses the IMF's G20 Model (G20MOD) to illustrate the importance of policymakers' responding quickly to the negative self-reinforcing growth dynamics that could be unleashed should secular stagnation develop in advanced economies. The scenario also illustrates the additional benefits to Group of Twenty (G20) countries of following through on their remaining Brisbane Growth Strategies structural reform commitments, which will further add to sustainable output.

The first layer of the scenario (blue line in Scenario Figure 3) considers the implications of secular stagnation's appearing in advanced economies (see also the second risk scenario in the October 2014 WEO). The layer embodies lower-than-expected private investment and higher-than-expected private saving, leading to weaker domestic demand that in turn harms these economies' supply potential. One hysteresis mechanism is capital-embodied technology, which implies that lower investment results in slower productivity growth. In addition, overall weak demand leads to higher unemployment that results in a reduced labor supply as (1) skill depreciation generates a higher natural rate of unemployment and (2) discouraged workers withdraw from the labor force. Taken together, these scarring effects on productivity growth and the labor force push the path of output progressively below the baseline over time.

In the second layer (red line), it is assumed that in year 2, after seeing weaker activity in the first year, many advanced economies and a few large emerging market economies launch a collective expansionary fiscal response.

For illustrative purposes, the fiscal response is assumed to amount to 2 percent of GDP in the second and third years in those countries that have the fiscal space to participate. Assumptions on which advanced economies implement the coordinated fiscal response are guided by the considerations in Chapter 1 of the April 2016 *Fiscal Monitor* (see in particular Figure 1.6). For advanced economies as a group, this collective policy implies a fiscal impulse of roughly 1.5 percent of GDP, and for emerging market economies, about 1 percent of GDP.

The fiscal response is designed both to have large short-term multipliers and to raise long-term potential output; it includes measures such as infrastructure investment, active labor market policies, and investments in research and development, as well as

Scenario Figure 3. Secular Stagnation and Reform
(Percent difference, unless noted otherwise)

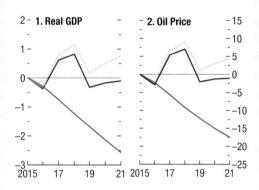
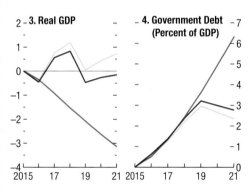
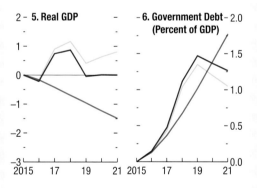

Source: IMF staff estimates.

Scenario Box 2. Responding to Secular Stagnation Forces *(continued)*

transfers targeted to households that would be hardest hit by a reduction in activity. It is also assumed that monetary authorities worldwide fully accommodate the fiscal response to further amplify the benefits.

In the final layer (yellow line), G20 countries are assumed to follow through on those product and labor market reforms from their Brisbane Growth Strategies that have not yet been fully implemented. Their Brisbane Growth Strategies commitments in terms of higher infrastructure spending are already incorporated in the fiscal response.

In the secular stagnation layer (blue line), global growth is roughly 0.4 percentage point below baseline, with inflation falling roughly ½ percentage point below baseline by the end of the WEO horizon. The ½-percentage-point-lower advanced economy growth has significant spillovers to emerging market economies, both directly through lower external demand and indirectly via commodity prices and equity prices (as emerging market equity

markets are assumed to reflect some of the weakness in advanced economy equity markets). When policymakers respond in the second year with collective and well-targeted fiscal measures, the negative growth spiral starts to quickly reverse (red line). However, some of the scarring effects on supply are slow to dissipate and are not fully offset by the supply-friendly measures in the fiscal response; output is therefore still below baseline at the end of the WEO horizon. However, if policymakers take advantage of the robust aggregate demand conditions when the fiscal measures are first introduced to press ahead with other product and labor market reform commitments (yellow line), then the medium-term scarring effects can be more than fully offset, and global output is above baseline by the end of the WEO horizon, with even more benefits to come beyond. Of course, an additional boost to potential output could come from the adoption of structural reforms that go beyond the commitments in the Brisbane Growth Strategies.

---

ing the heterogeneity in circumstances and the way in which individual countries are being affected by the various realignments in the global economy. Common challenges center on dealing with slowing growth and increased vulnerabilities after a decade or so of buoyant activity, facilitated in many cases by rapid credit expansion. Priorities range from ensuring a successful rebalancing of the Chinese economy and managing the cross-border spillovers of the slowdown in China to containing the vulnerabilities associated with tighter financial conditions and declining capital inflows as growth softens, and adjusting to lower commodity prices. Countries that are enjoying terms-of-trade gains from lower commodity prices should use the windfall to rebuild buffers. These near-term challenges notwithstanding, policymakers in emerging market economies also should act to lift medium-term growth, to safeguard hard-won gains in living standards and ensure continued convergence toward advanced economy income levels.

Supporting a Smooth Transition to More Balanced Growth in China

As discussed in the previous sections, the slowdown and rebalancing of the Chinese economy have

substantial international ramifications. Even countries that have few direct trade linkages with China are being affected through the Chinese slowdown's impact on prices of commodities and manufactured goods, and on global confidence and risk sentiment. Yet a well-managed rebalancing of China's growth model would ultimately lift global growth and reduce tail risks. The international community should therefore support China's efforts to reform and rebalance its economy.

The main challenge faced by the Chinese authorities is to transit to a more consumption- and service-oriented growth model while reducing the vulnerabilities from excess leverage bequeathed by the prior investment boom. Strengthening the influence of market forces in the Chinese economy, including in the foreign exchange market, is also a key objective.

Further structural measures, such as social security reform, will be needed to ensure that consumption increasingly and durably takes up the baton from investment. Any further policy support to secure a gradual growth slowdown should take the form of on-budget fiscal stimulus that supports the rebalancing process. Broader reforms should give market mechanisms a more decisive role in the economy and eliminate distortions, with emphasis on state enterprise reforms, ending implicit guarantees, reforms to strengthen financial regulation and supervision, and increased reliance on interest rates as an instrument of monetary policy. Good progress has been made in financial liberalization and laying the foundations for stronger local-government finances. However, the reform strategy for state-owned enterprises needs to be more ambitious. Specifically, it should provide a clearer road map to a substantially greater role for the private sector and to hard budget constraints—and at an accelerated pace. The authorities should also communicate their policies, including exchange rate policies, clearly and be willing to accept the moderately lower growth that is consistent with rebalancing.

Policies to Manage Vulnerabilities

As discussed in Chapter 2, emerging market economies have so far withstood the slowdown in capital flows generally well, with fewer adverse effects compared to past episodes of generalized capital flow retraction. That chapter finds that the ongoing slowdown is tightly linked to the decline in the growth rates of emerging market economies relative to advanced economies and that swings in capital flows have tended to be smaller in countries with more flexible exchange rates, lower public debt levels, and higher levels of foreign exchange reserves.

Although exchange rate flexibility has so far helped insulate countries' capital inflows from global factors and their own diminishing growth prospects, policymakers need to stay vigilant in regard to the possible adverse balance sheet effects of large currency depreciations, especially given the buildup of dollar-denominated corporate debt in emerging markets in the aftermath of the global financial crisis. Adjustments to large depreciations so far have been orderly, with little signs of systemic stress among corporate borrowers. Yet some companies' financial buffers are likely to have diminished as a result of the large depreciations, especially in a context of sluggish earnings. Exchange rate flexibility should remain the first line of defense against adverse shocks in countries with floating rates, but foreign exchange intervention may become necessary when pressures become acute and signs of disorderly markets emerge.

Keeping financial stability risks in check gains importance in an environment of reduced global risk appetite.

Strong supervision and macroprudential frameworks and close monitoring of the possible vulnerabilities of both borrowers and lenders are essential. As financial conditions tighten, policymakers face a delicate balancing act: they need to prevent a further buildup of vulnerabilities in domestic financial institutions, while taking care not to exacerbate the tightening of credit conditions in a context of subdued activity.

Managing the Adjustment to Lower Commodity Prices

With renewed declines in commodity prices, emerging market and developing economies that are heavily reliant on commodity exports are confronting a significant deterioration in their fiscal and external positions. Given that commodity prices are projected to stay low over an extended period, these countries will need to make sizable adjustments to domestic spending. Exchange rate flexibility will be important for cushioning the impact of adverse terms-of-trade shocks in many of these economies, although the effects of exchange rate depreciations on private and public sector balance sheets and on domestic inflation rates need to be closely monitored. In many cases, fiscal adjustments—based on a combination of spending cuts and revenue increases—will also be needed. Making public sector expenditures more efficient and broadening the revenue base toward noncommodity activities would make the adjustment less painful. Establishing transparent fiscal policy frameworks that provide anchors for longer-term policy objectives would bolster credibility and help keep financing conditions more favorable. The latter would allow expenditures to reflect medium- rather than short-term price developments and thus help avoid excessive procyclicality during the adjustments.

Oil-importing emerging market and developing economies, on the other hand, have enjoyed significant terms-of-trade windfall gains from the sharp drop in oil prices. Lower oil prices have alleviated inflation pressures and reduced external vulnerabilities. In some importing countries with oil-related subsidies, the windfall gains from lower oil prices have been used to increase public sector savings and strengthen fiscal positions. Whether all the gains should be saved depends on the extent of economic slack, the availability of fiscal space, and country-specific needs. In particular, terms-of-trade gains may provide an opportunity to finance critical structural reforms or growth-enhancing spending.

Policy Requirements for Individual Emerging Market Economies

- In response to the oil price collapse, policymakers in *Russia* will need to implement an ambitious medium-term fiscal consolidation, anchored in a rules-based framework. In addition, boosting potential growth will require stronger governance and protection of property rights, lower administrative barriers and regulation, and greater competition and efficiency in capital allocation.
- In *India,* lower commodity prices, a range of supply-side measures, and a relatively tight monetary stance have resulted in a faster-than-expected fall in inflation, making room for nominal interest rate cuts, but upside risks to inflation could necessitate a tightening of monetary policy. Fiscal consolidation should continue, underpinned by revenue reforms and further reductions in subsidies. Sustaining strong growth over the medium term will require labor market reforms and dismantling of infrastructure bottlenecks, especially in the power sector.
- In *Brazil*, the government should persevere with its fiscal consolidation efforts to foster a turnaround in confidence and investment. With the scope for cutting discretionary spending severely limited, tax measures are necessary in the short term, but the most important challenge is to address rigidities and unsustainable mandates on the spending side. A reduction in inflation toward the 4.5 percent target by 2017 will require a tight monetary policy stance. Structural reforms to raise productivity and competitiveness—including the infrastructure concessions program—are essential to reinvigorate potential growth.
- The steep decline in oil prices is weighing heavily on the macroeconomic outlook in *Saudi Arabia.* Despite the significant fiscal consolidation in 2015, further spending restraint and revenue measures—including energy price reforms, containing the wage bill, prioritizing capital spending, and expanding non-oil tax revenues—will be necessary, in addition to a credible and well-communicated medium-term fiscal consolidation plan. Structural reforms to rebalance the economy toward non-oil activities and the private sector are essential. Adequate buffers support the maintenance of the pegged exchange rate regime, and further fiscal consolidation will help support the regime over the long term.

Policy Priorities for Low-Income Countries

Economic activity in low-income countries has weakened (Box 1.2). In 2015, growth was the lowest in the past two decades, falling short of the October WEO forecast. Near-term growth expectations have also been marked down significantly. Economic weakness in advanced economies, slower growth in emerging market economies, and the sharp retreat in commodity prices are all partly responsible for the subdued outlook for low-income countries. In addition, greater access to foreign-market financing has increased some low-income countries' exposure to more demanding global financial conditions.

Policies must respond to the heightened challenges and vulnerabilities. As low-income countries face a similarly unfavorable external environment—lower commodity prices, lower external demand, and tighter financial conditions—many of their policy priorities are similar to those of emerging markets:

- Given the subdued outlook for commodity prices, policies for *commodity-exporting low-income countries* will need to be recalibrated. Exchange rate flexibility has allowed many of these countries to cope better with terms-of-trade shocks; further flexibility could still help with the adjustment in some countries. However, some tightening of the macroeconomic policy stance and a strengthening of monetary policy frameworks may be also required to limit second-round effects of depreciation on inflation, which runs substantially higher than in emerging markets. Enhanced financial sector regulation and supervision will also be necessary to manage foreign-currency exposures in balance sheets. To preserve hard-won macroeconomic stability with commodity prices projected to remain low, there is an urgent need for more fiscal adjustment where policy buffers are running low and debt levels have already risen. To improve economic resilience over the medium term, fiscal buffers should be rebuilt as commodity prices recover, and structural reforms should be implemented to achieve economic diversification and higher productivity.
- *Low-income countries that are less resource dependent* and continue to enjoy strong economic growth should focus on rebuilding eroded policy buffers. Strong macroeconomic policies and prudent debt management will also help some low-income countries that are exposed to global financial markets and the related volatility in capital inflows.

Low-income countries should not lose sight of the Sustainable Development Goals.[7] In achieving these goals, a key priority is to create necessary fiscal space by enhancing domestic resource mobilization and improving the efficiency of government spending, while protecting the vulnerable and fostering inclusive growth. These efforts should also help alleviate the pressures on public finances that some commodity-exporting low-income countries are currently facing. Deeper domestic financial markets could also increase the scope for domestic financing of the Sustainable Development Goals. More efficient public investment management can help ensure that infrastructure investment raises productive capacity without jeopardizing public debt sustainability.

Low-income countries also need to act now to build resilience to the challenges of climate change by identifying key risks and investing in targeted infrastructure and disaster management capacity. In that regard, the international community could help by providing needed financing, capacity-building support, and policy advice.

Multilateral Actions to Boost Growth and Resilience

In the current environment, policymakers across the globe face a particularly challenging task. With the threat of a synchronized slowdown, and an even higher salience of significant downside risks, short-term domestic macroeconomic policies need to remain supportive of activity and confidence. Yet policy space is restricted in many economies. Despite this limitation, a more proactive multilateral approach to containing downside risks would be desirable.

---

[7]The Sustainable Development Goals, which replaced the Millennium Development Goals in September 2015, focus on economically, socially, and environmentally sustainable development and include ending poverty and hunger, providing inclusive and equitable education, ensuring access to energy and water, and promoting full employment, among others. See Fabrizio and others 2015.

- Should a significant shortfall in growth threaten to push the global economy back into recession, a collective macroeconomic policy reaction would be needed. Policymakers in the larger economies should proactively identify additional policy actions that could be implemented quickly and in a concerted fashion if there are signs that global downside risks are materializing. The simulations in Scenario Box 2 emphasize the global benefits of prompt and collective policy action in a downside scenario.

- Collective efforts are also urgently needed to enhance the global financial safety net. At a time of higher risks of financial turmoil and contagion, progress on this front would help mitigate the risks faced by commodity exporters and emerging market and developing economies that are susceptible to shocks despite strong medium-term fundamentals. There also remains a pressing need at the global level to complete and implement the regulatory reform agenda. In addition, advanced and emerging market economies should continue to strengthen the regulation and supervision of rapidly expanding financial activities outside the banking system.

- There are solid grounds for the international community to support countries that are bearing the brunt of geopolitical or other noneconomic spillovers. The world economy lacks mechanisms to handle externalities due to such shocks—for example, global epidemics and refugee flows triggered by geopolitical conflicts. Many of the affected countries are shouldering a burden for others, often with limited absorptive capacity and fiscal space. In light of the global-public-good nature of their efforts, a concerted worldwide initiative to provide support is amply justified, with those at risk from the spillovers contributing financial resources and multilateral agencies, including the IMF, assessing how they can best help channel those resources to the areas in greatest need.

Annex 1.1. Regional Projections

Annex Table 1.1.1. European Economies: Real GDP, Consumer Prices, Current Account Balance, and Unemployment

(Annual percent change, unless noted otherwise)

	Real GDP			Consumer Prices[1]			Current Account Balance[2]			Unemployment[3]		
		Projections			Projections			Projections			Projections	
	2015	2016	2017	2015	2016	2017	2015	2016	2017	2015	2016	2017
Europe	**2.1**	**2.0**	**2.1**	**0.6**	**1.1**	**1.9**	**2.5**	**2.5**	**2.3**	...	...	...
Advanced Europe	**1.8**	**1.6**	**1.8**	**0.1**	**0.5**	**1.3**	**3.0**	**3.0**	**2.8**	**9.5**	**8.9**	**8.6**
Euro Area[4]	1.6	1.5	1.6	0.0	0.4	1.1	3.0	3.5	3.2	10.9	10.3	9.9
Germany	1.5	1.5	1.6	0.1	0.5	1.4	8.5	8.4	8.0	4.6	4.6	4.8
France	1.1	1.1	1.3	0.1	0.4	1.1	−0.1	0.6	0.3	10.4	10.1	10.0
Italy	0.8	1.0	1.1	0.1	0.2	0.7	2.1	2.3	2.0	11.9	11.4	10.9
Spain	3.2	2.6	2.3	−0.5	−0.4	1.0	1.4	1.9	2.0	22.1	19.7	18.3
Netherlands	1.9	1.8	1.9	0.2	0.3	0.7	11.0	10.6	10.2	6.9	6.4	6.2
Belgium	1.4	1.2	1.4	0.6	1.2	1.1	0.5	0.5	0.1	8.3	8.3	8.2
Austria	0.9	1.2	1.4	0.8	1.4	1.8	3.6	3.6	3.5	5.7	6.2	6.4
Greece	−0.2	−0.6	2.7	−1.1	0.0	0.6	0.0	−0.2	−0.3	25.0	25.0	23.4
Portugal	1.5	1.4	1.3	0.5	0.7	1.2	0.5	0.9	0.4	12.4	11.6	11.1
Ireland	7.8	5.0	3.6	0.0	0.9	1.4	4.5	4.0	3.5	9.4	8.3	7.5
Finland	0.4	0.9	1.1	−0.2	0.4	1.4	0.1	0.0	−0.1	9.3	9.3	9.0
Slovak Republic	3.6	3.3	3.4	−0.3	0.2	1.4	−1.1	−1.0	−1.0	11.5	10.4	9.6
Lithuania	1.6	2.7	3.1	−0.7	0.6	1.9	−2.3	−3.0	−2.9	9.1	8.6	8.5
Slovenia	2.9	1.9	2.0	−0.5	0.1	1.0	7.3	7.6	7.1	9.1	7.9	7.6
Luxembourg	4.5	3.5	3.4	0.1	0.5	1.3	5.2	5.1	5.0	6.9	6.4	6.3
Latvia	2.7	3.2	3.6	0.2	0.5	1.5	−1.6	−2.0	−2.2	9.9	9.5	9.1
Estonia	1.1	2.2	2.8	0.1	2.0	2.9	1.9	1.2	0.5	6.8	6.5	6.5
Cyprus	1.6	1.6	2.0	−1.5	0.6	1.3	−5.1	−4.8	−4.7	15.3	14.2	13.0
Malta	5.4	3.5	3.0	1.2	1.6	1.8	4.1	5.3	5.3	5.3	5.4	5.3
United Kingdom[5]	2.2	1.9	2.2	0.1	0.8	1.9	−4.3	−4.3	−4.0	5.4	5.0	5.0
Switzerland	0.9	1.2	1.5	−1.1	−0.6	−0.1	11.4	9.3	8.8	3.3	3.5	3.3
Sweden	4.1	3.7	2.8	0.7	1.1	1.4	5.9	5.8	5.7	7.4	6.8	7.0
Norway	1.6	1.0	1.5	2.2	2.8	2.5	9.0	6.5	7.3	4.4	4.6	4.4
Czech Republic	4.2	2.5	2.4	0.3	1.0	2.2	0.9	0.6	0.6	5.0	4.7	4.6
Denmark	1.2	1.6	1.8	0.5	0.8	1.4	6.9	6.6	6.5	6.2	6.0	5.8
Iceland	4.0	4.2	3.2	1.6	2.6	3.9	4.2	4.1	2.4	4.0	3.8	3.7
San Marino	1.0	1.1	1.2	0.4	0.9	1.1	...	...	...	8.4	7.9	7.3
Emerging and Developing Europe[6]	**3.5**	**3.5**	**3.3**	**2.9**	**4.1**	**4.8**	**−1.9**	**−2.1**	**−2.6**	...	...	...
Turkey	3.8	3.8	3.4	7.7	9.8	8.8	−4.4	−3.6	−4.1	10.2	10.8	10.5
Poland	3.6	3.6	3.6	−0.9	−0.2	1.3	−0.5	−1.8	−2.1	7.5	6.9	6.9
Romania	3.7	4.2	3.6	−0.6	−0.4	3.1	−1.1	−1.7	−2.5	6.8	6.4	6.2
Hungary	2.9	2.3	2.5	−0.1	0.5	2.4	5.1	5.4	5.2	6.9	6.7	6.5
Bulgaria[5]	3.0	2.3	2.3	−1.1	0.2	1.2	2.1	1.7	0.8	9.2	8.6	7.9
Serbia	0.7	1.8	2.3	1.4	1.7	3.1	−4.8	−4.4	−4.3	18.5	18.7	18.9
Croatia	1.6	1.9	2.1	−0.5	0.4	1.3	4.4	2.7	2.1	16.9	16.4	15.9

Note: Data for some countries are based on fiscal years. Please refer to Table F in the Statistical Appendix for a list of economies with exceptional reporting periods.
[1]Movements in consumer prices are shown as annual averages. Year-end to year-end changes can be found in Tables A6 and A7 in the Statistical Appendix.
[2]Percent of GDP.
[3]Percent. National definitions of unemployment may differ.
[4]Current account position corrected for reporting discrepancies in intra-area transactions.
[5]Based on Eurostat's harmonized index of consumer prices.
[6]Includes Albania, Bosnia and Herzegovina, Kosovo, FYR Macedonia, and Montenegro.

Annex Table 1.1.2. Asian and Pacific Economies: Real GDP, Consumer Prices, Current Account Balance, and Unemployment
(Annual percent change, unless noted otherwise)

	Real GDP			Consumer Prices[1]			Current Account Balance[2]			Unemployment[3]		
		Projections			Projections			Projections			Projections	
	2015	2016	2017	2015	2016	2017	2015	2016	2017	2015	2016	2017
Asia	**5.4**	**5.3**	**5.3**	**2.3**	**2.4**	**2.9**	**2.7**	**2.7**	**2.2**	. . .	. . .	. . .
Advanced Asia	**1.2**	**1.3**	**1.4**	**0.8**	**0.6**	**1.6**	**4.2**	**4.6**	**4.4**	**3.7**	**3.6**	**3.6**
Japan	0.5	0.5	−0.1	0.8	−0.2	1.2	3.3	3.8	3.7	3.4	3.3	3.3
Korea	2.6	2.7	2.9	0.7	1.3	2.2	7.7	8.2	7.4	3.6	3.5	3.3
Australia	2.5	2.5	3.0	1.5	2.1	2.4	−4.6	−3.6	−3.5	6.1	5.9	5.8
Taiwan Province of China	0.7	1.5	2.2	−0.3	0.7	1.1	14.5	15.0	14.4	3.8	3.8	3.9
Singapore	2.0	1.8	2.2	−0.5	0.2	1.3	19.7	21.2	20.5	1.9	2.0	2.0
Hong Kong SAR	2.4	2.2	2.4	3.0	2.5	2.6	3.0	3.1	3.2	3.3	3.2	3.1
New Zealand	3.4	2.0	2.5	0.3	1.5	1.9	−3.0	−3.7	−3.7	5.8	5.9	5.8
Macao SAR[4]	−20.3	−7.2	0.7	4.6	3.0	3.0	26.2	20.0	17.2	1.8	2.0	2.0
Emerging and Developing Asia	**6.6**	**6.4**	**6.3**	**2.7**	**2.9**	**3.2**	**1.9**	**1.7**	**1.1**	. . .	. . .	. . .
China	6.9	6.5	6.2	1.4	1.8	2.0	2.7	2.6	2.1	4.1	4.1	4.1
India	7.3	7.5	7.5	4.9	5.3	5.3	−1.3	−1.5	−2.1	. . .	. . .	. . .
ASEAN-5	**4.7**	**4.8**	**5.1**	**3.3**	**2.8**	**3.5**	**1.8**	**1.1**	**0.5**	. . .	. . .	. . .
Indonesia	4.8	4.9	5.3	6.4	4.3	4.5	−2.1	−2.6	−2.8	6.2	5.9	5.7
Thailand	2.8	3.0	3.2	−0.9	0.2	2.0	8.8	8.0	5.7	0.9	0.8	0.7
Malaysia	5.0	4.4	4.8	2.1	3.1	2.9	2.9	2.3	1.9	3.2	3.2	3.2
Philippines	5.8	6.0	6.2	1.4	2.0	3.4	2.9	2.6	2.4	6.3	6.0	5.9
Vietnam	6.7	6.3	6.2	0.6	1.3	2.3	1.4	0.6	0.2	2.4	2.4	2.4
Other Emerging and Developing Asia[5]	**5.9**	**6.0**	**6.3**	**6.1**	**6.3**	**6.4**	**−2.9**	**−3.3**	**−3.7**	. . .	. . .	. . .
Memorandum												
Emerging Asia[6]	6.6	6.4	6.3	2.6	2.8	3.1	2.0	1.8	1.2	. . .	. . .	. . .

Note: Data for some countries are based on fiscal years. Please refer to Table F in the Statistical Appendix for a list of economies with exceptional reporting periods.
[1]Movements in consumer prices are shown as annual averages. Year-end to year-end changes can be found in Tables A6 and A7 in the Statistical Appendix.
[2]Percent of GDP.
[3]Percent. National definitions of unemployment may differ.
[4]Macao SAR is classified as an advanced economy. It is a Special Administrative Region of China, but its statistical data are maintained on a separate and independent basis.
[5]Other Emerging and Developing Asia comprises Bangladesh, Bhutan, Brunei Darussalam, Cambodia, Fiji, Kiribati, Lao P.D.R., Maldives, Marshall Islands, Micronesia, Mongolia, Myanmar, Nepal, Palau, Papua New Guinea, Samoa, Solomon Islands, Sri Lanka, Timor-Leste, Tonga, Tuvalu, and Vanuatu.
[6]Emerging Asia comprises the ASEAN-5 (Indonesia, Malaysia, Philippines, Thailand, Vietnam) economies, China, and India.

Annex Table 1.1.3. Western Hemisphere Economies: Real GDP, Consumer Prices, Current Account Balance, and Unemployment

(Annual percent change, unless noted otherwise)

| | Real GDP | | | Consumer Prices[1] | | | Current Account Balance[2] | | | Unemployment[3] | | |
| | | Projections | | | Projections | | | Projections | | | Projections | |
	2015	2016	2017	2015	2016	2017	2015	2016	2017	2015	2016	2017
North America	**2.3**	**2.3**	**2.4**	**0.4**	**1.1**	**1.7**	**−2.8**	**−2.9**	**−3.3**	...	...	...
United States	2.4	2.4	2.5	0.1	0.8	1.5	−2.7	−2.9	−3.3	5.3	4.9	4.8
Canada	1.2	1.5	1.9	1.1	1.3	1.9	−3.3	−3.5	−3.0	6.9	7.3	7.4
Mexico	2.5	2.4	2.6	2.7	2.9	3.0	−2.8	−2.6	−2.6	4.3	4.0	3.9
Puerto Rico[4]	−1.3	−1.3	−1.4	−0.8	−0.6	1.2	...	...	...	12.0	12.0	11.9
South America[5]	**−1.4**	**−2.0**	**0.8**	...	...	...	**−3.8**	**−2.8**	**−2.2**	...	...	...
Brazil	−3.8	−3.8	0.0	9.0	8.7	6.1	−3.3	−2.0	−1.5	6.8	9.2	10.2
Argentina[6]	1.2	−1.0	2.8	...	...	19.9	−2.8	−1.7	−2.2	6.5	7.8	7.4
Colombia	3.1	2.5	3.0	5.0	7.3	3.4	−6.5	−6.0	−4.3	8.9	9.8	9.4
Venezuela	−5.7	−8.0	−4.5	121.7	481.5	1,642.8	−7.6	−6.6	−2.5	7.4	17.4	20.7
Chile	2.1	1.5	2.1	4.3	4.1	3.0	−2.0	−2.1	−2.7	6.2	6.8	7.5
Peru	3.3	3.7	4.1	3.5	3.1	2.5	−4.4	−3.9	−3.3	6.0	6.0	6.0
Ecuador	0.0	−4.5	−4.3	4.0	1.6	0.2	−2.9	−2.3	−0.2	4.8	5.7	6.5
Bolivia	4.8	3.8	3.5	4.1	4.0	5.0	−6.9	−8.3	−7.1	4.0	4.0	4.0
Uruguay	1.5	1.4	2.6	8.7	9.4	8.4	−3.9	−3.9	−3.7	7.6	7.8	7.6
Paraguay	3.0	2.9	3.2	2.9	3.8	4.5	−1.8	−1.2	−1.1	6.1	6.2	6.1
Central America[7]	**4.1**	**4.3**	**4.3**	**1.4**	**2.7**	**3.2**	**−4.0**	**−3.9**	**−4.0**	...	...	...
Caribbean[8]	**4.0**	**3.5**	**3.6**	**2.3**	**4.1**	**4.3**	**−4.1**	**−3.4**	**−3.5**	...	...	...
Memorandum												
Latin America and the Caribbean[9]	−0.1	−0.5	1.5	5.5	5.7	4.3	−3.6	−2.8	−2.4	...	...	...
East Caribbean Currency Union[10]	2.2	2.6	2.5	−0.6	−0.1	1.3	−12.2	−11.7	−12.5	...	...	...

Note: Data for some countries are based on fiscal years. Please refer to Table F in the Statistical Appendix for a list of economies with exceptional reporting periods.
[1]Movements in consumer prices are shown as annual averages. Year-end to year-end changes can be found in Tables A6 and A7 in the Statistical Appendix.
[2]Percent of GDP.
[3]Percent. National definitions of unemployment may differ.
[4]The Commonwealth of Puerto Rico is classified as an advanced economy. It is a territory of the United States, but its statistical data are maintained on a separate and independent basis.
[5]Includes Guyana and Suriname. Data for Argentina's and Venezuela's consumer prices are excluded. See country-specific notes for Argentina in the "Country Notes" section of the Statistical Appendix.
[6]See country-specific notes for Argentina in the "Country Notes" section of the Statistical Appendix.
[7]Central America comprises Belize, Costa Rica, El Salvador, Guatemala, Honduras, Nicaragua, and Panama.
[8]The Caribbean comprises Antigua and Barbuda, The Bahamas, Barbados, Dominica, the Dominican Republic, Grenada, Haiti, Jamaica, St. Kitts and Nevis, St. Lucia, St. Vincent and the Grenadines, and Trinidad and Tobago.
[9]Latin America and the Caribbean comprises Mexico and economies from the Caribbean, Central America, and South America. Data for Argentina's and Venezuela's consumer prices are excluded. See country-specific notes for Argentina in the "Country Notes" section of the Statistical Appendix.
[10]Eastern Caribbean Currency Union comprises Antigua and Barbuda, Dominica, Grenada, St. Kitts and Nevis, St. Lucia, and St. Vincent and the Grenadines as well as Anguilla and Montserrat, which are not IMF members.

Annex Table 1.1.4. Commonwealth of Independent States Economies: Real GDP, Consumer Prices, Current Account Balance, and Unemployment

(Annual percent change, unless noted otherwise)

	Real GDP			Consumer Prices[1]			Current Account Balance[2]			Unemployment[3]		
		Projections			Projections			Projections			Projections	
	2015	2016	2017	2015	2016	2017	2015	2016	2017	2015	2016	2017
Commonwealth of Independent States[4]	−2.8	**−1.1**	**1.3**	15.5	**9.4**	**7.4**	2.8	**2.0**	**3.0**	...	...	...
Net Energy Exporters	−2.4	**−1.3**	**1.1**	13.7	**8.9**	**7.0**	3.4	**2.8**	**3.8**	...	...	...
Russia	−3.7	−1.8	0.8	15.5	8.4	6.5	5.0	4.2	5.1	5.6	6.5	6.3
Kazakhstan	1.2	0.1	1.0	6.5	13.1	9.3	−2.6	−4.0	−1.5	5.0	5.0	5.0
Uzbekistan	8.0	5.0	5.5	8.5	8.5	9.4	0.0	0.2	0.5	...	...	...
Azerbaijan	1.1	−3.0	1.0	4.0	12.8	9.5	0.2	−0.2	0.2	6.0	6.0	6.0
Turkmenistan	6.5	4.3	4.5	5.5	5.4	4.4	−12.7	−15.4	−11.6	...	...	...
Net Energy Importers	−5.9	**0.6**	**2.1**	29.5	**12.8**	**10.2**	−2.9	**−4.4**	**−3.9**	...	...	...
Ukraine	−9.9	1.5	2.5	48.7	15.1	11.0	−0.3	−2.6	−2.3	9.5	9.2	8.8
Belarus	−3.9	−2.7	0.4	13.5	13.6	12.1	−1.9	−3.5	−3.1	1.0	2.0	2.5
Georgia	2.8	2.5	4.5	4.0	4.3	4.5	−11.6	−10.3	−9.1	...	...	...
Armenia	3.0	1.9	2.5	3.7	2.6	4.0	−3.2	−4.3	−5.1	17.7	18.2	18.3
Tajikistan	3.0	3.0	3.5	5.8	9.2	8.5	−10.2	−8.4	−7.3	...	...	...
Kyrgyz Republic	3.5	3.5	2.7	6.5	5.5	6.9	−14.7	−18.4	−15.4	7.5	7.4	7.3
Moldova	−1.1	0.5	2.5	9.6	9.8	7.4	−6.6	−4.0	−4.4	4.9	4.8	4.7
Memorandum												
Caucasus and Central Asia[5]	3.1	1.2	2.5	6.1	10.5	8.5	−3.4	−4.7	−3.0	...	...	...
Low-Income CIS Countries[6]	5.8	4.0	4.7	7.3	7.5	8.1	−3.8	−3.5	−3.1	...	...	...
Net Energy Exporters Excluding Russia	3.2	1.1	2.4	6.3	11.2	8.8	−2.7	−4.0	−2.2	...	...	...

Note: Data for some countries are based on fiscal years. Please refer to Table F in the Statistical Appendix for a list of economies with exceptional reporting periods.
[1]Movements in consumer prices are shown as annual averages. Year-end to year-end changes can be found in Table A7 in the Statistical Appendix.
[2]Percent of GDP.
[3]Percent. National definitions of unemployment may differ.
[4]Georgia, Turkmenistan, and Ukraine, which are not members of the Commonwealth of Independent States (CIS), are included in this group for reasons of geography and similarity in economic structure.
[5]Caucasus and Central Asia comprises Armenia, Azerbaijan, Georgia, Kazakhstan, the Kyrgyz Republic, Tajikistan, Turkmenistan, and Uzbekistan.
[6]Low-Income CIS Countries comprise Armenia, Georgia, the Kyrgyz Republic, Moldova, Tajikistan, and Uzbekistan.

Annex Table 1.1.5. Middle East and North African Economies, Afghanistan, and Pakistan: Real GDP, Consumer Prices, Current Account Balance, and Unemployment

(Annual percent change, unless noted otherwise)

	Real GDP			Consumer Prices[1]			Current Account Balance[2]			Unemployment[3]		
		Projections			Projections			Projections			Projections	
	2015	2016	2017	2015	2016	2017	2015	2016	2017	2015	2016	2017
Middle East, North Africa, Afghanistan, and Pakistan	**2.5**	**3.1**	**3.5**	**5.7**	**5.2**	**4.8**	**−3.6**	**−6.9**	**−5.2**	...	...	...
Oil Exporters[4]	**1.9**	**2.9**	**3.1**	**5.2**	**4.9**	**3.9**	**−3.1**	**−8.0**	**−5.6**	...	...	...
Saudi Arabia	3.4	1.2	1.9	2.2	3.8	1.0	−6.3	−10.2	−6.1	...	...	...
Iran[5]	0.0	4.0	3.7	12.0	8.9	8.2	0.4	−0.8	0.0	10.8	11.3	11.6
United Arab Emirates	3.9	2.4	2.6	4.1	3.2	2.7	3.9	−1.0	0.1	...	...	...
Algeria	3.7	3.4	2.9	4.8	4.3	4.0	−15.7	−17.1	−16.2	11.3	11.6	12.1
Iraq	2.4	7.2	3.3	1.4	2.0	2.0	−6.4	−14.4	−11.0	...	...	...
Qatar	3.3	3.4	3.4	1.7	2.4	2.7	4.9	−5.0	−4.9	...	...	...
Kuwait	0.9	2.4	2.6	3.4	3.4	3.5	11.5	−1.0	3.3	2.1	2.1	2.1
Oil Importers[6]	**3.8**	**3.5**	**4.2**	**6.7**	**5.8**	**6.5**	**−4.6**	**−4.5**	**−4.6**	...	...	...
Egypt	4.2	3.3	4.3	11.0	9.6	9.5	−3.7	−5.3	−5.3	12.9	13.0	12.4
Pakistan	4.2	4.5	4.7	4.5	3.3	5.0	−1.0	−1.1	−1.6	6.0	6.1	6.1
Morocco	4.5	2.3	4.1	1.6	1.5	2.0	−1.4	0.4	0.1	9.8	9.7	9.6
Sudan	3.5	3.7	4.0	16.9	13.0	12.3	−7.7	−6.3	−5.5	21.6	20.6	19.6
Tunisia	0.8	2.0	3.0	4.9	4.0	3.9	−8.9	−7.7	−7.0	15.0	14.0	13.0
Lebanon	1.0	1.0	2.0	−3.7	−0.7	2.0	−25.0	−21.3	−21.2	...	...	...
Jordan	2.5	3.2	3.7	−0.9	0.2	2.1	−8.8	−6.4	−5.6	...	...	...
Memorandum												
Middle East and North Africa	2.3	2.9	3.3	5.9	5.5	4.7	−3.9	−7.5	−5.6	...	...	...
Israel[7]	2.6	2.8	3.0	−0.6	−0.1	0.9	4.1	4.0	3.5	5.3	5.3	5.3
Maghreb[8]	2.7	2.5	4.1	4.2	3.9	3.7	−13.8	−14.1	−13.2	...	...	...
Mashreq[9]	3.9	3.1	4.1	9.1	8.2	8.4	−6.7	−7.3	−7.1	...	...	...

Note: Data for some countries are based on fiscal years. Please refer to Table F in the Statistical Appendix for a list of economies with exceptional reporting periods.

[1]Movements in consumer prices are shown as annual averages. Year-end to year-end changes can be found in Tables A6 and A7 in the Statistical Appendix.

[2]Percent of GDP.

[3]Percent. National definitions of unemployment may differ.

[4]Includes Bahrain, Libya, Oman, and Yemen.

[5]For Iran, data and forecasts are based on GDP at market prices. Corresponding data used by the IMF staff for GDP growth at factor prices are 0.0 percent for 2015/16, 4.0 percent for 2016/17, and 3.7 percent for 2017/18.

[6]Includes Afghanistan, Djibouti, and Mauritania. Syria is excluded because of the uncertain political situation.

[7]Israel, which is not a member of the economic region, is included for reasons of geography. Note that Israel is not included in the regional aggregates.

[8]The Maghreb comprises Algeria, Libya, Mauritania, Morocco, and Tunisia.

[9]The Mashreq comprises Egypt, Jordan, and Lebanon. Syria is excluded because of the uncertain political situation.

Annex Table 1.1.6. Sub-Saharan African Economies: Real GDP, Consumer Prices, Current Account Balance, and Unemployment

(Annual percent change, unless noted otherwise)

	Real GDP			Consumer Prices[1]			Current Account Balance[2]			Unemployment[3]		
		Projections			Projections			Projections			Projections	
	2015	2016	2017	2015	2016	2017	2015	2016	2017	2015	2016	2017
Sub-Saharan Africa	3.4	3.0	4.0	7.0	9.0	8.3	−5.9	−6.2	−5.5	...	...	...
Oil Exporters [4]	**2.4**	**2.0**	**3.4**	**9.2**	**12.5**	**12.1**	**−3.9**	**−4.5**	**−2.9**	...	...	...
Nigeria	2.7	2.3	3.5	9.0	10.4	12.4	−2.4	−2.8	−1.8	9.9	...	...
Angola	3.0	2.5	2.7	10.3	19.1	15.2	−8.5	−11.6	−8.8	...	...	...
Gabon	4.0	3.2	4.5	0.1	2.5	2.5	−2.8	−7.2	−5.8	...	...	...
Chad	1.8	−0.4	1.6	3.6	3.2	3.1	−12.8	−13.0	−8.8	...	...	...
Republic of Congo	2.5	4.4	4.3	2.0	2.3	2.4	−14.2	−23.1	−10.8	...	...	...
Middle-Income Countries[5]	**2.6**	**2.4**	**3.2**	**5.4**	**7.1**	**5.8**	**−4.4**	**−4.7**	**−4.6**	...	...	...
South Africa	1.3	0.6	1.2	4.6	6.5	6.3	−4.4	−4.4	−4.9	25.4	26.1	26.7
Ghana	3.5	4.5	7.7	17.2	15.7	8.9	−8.3	−7.2	−5.4	...	...	...
Côte d'Ivoire	8.6	8.5	8.0	1.2	2.1	2.0	−1.7	−1.8	−2.7	...	...	...
Cameroon	5.9	4.9	4.6	2.7	2.2	2.2	−5.8	−5.7	−5.5	...	...	...
Zambia	3.6	3.4	4.8	10.1	22.5	9.9	−3.5	−3.8	−1.7	...	...	...
Senegal	6.5	6.6	6.8	0.1	1.2	1.2	−7.6	−6.0	−5.8	...	...	...
Low-Income Countries[6]	**5.9**	**5.2**	**5.9**	**5.7**	**6.2**	**6.1**	**−11.8**	**−11.0**	**−11.3**	...	...	...
Ethiopia	10.2	4.5	7.0	10.1	10.6	11.6	−12.8	−10.7	−9.7	...	...	...
Kenya	5.6	6.0	6.1	6.6	6.3	6.0	−8.2	−8.3	−6.9	...	...	...
Tanzania	7.0	6.9	6.8	5.6	6.1	5.1	−8.7	−7.7	−7.4	...	...	...
Uganda	5.0	5.3	5.7	5.8	6.7	5.9	−8.9	−8.4	−8.5	...	...	...
Madagascar	3.0	4.1	4.5	7.4	7.2	7.0	−2.2	−3.0	−4.4	...	...	...
Democratic Republic of the Congo	7.7	4.9	5.1	1.0	1.7	2.5	−12.2	−14.2	−12.3	...	...	...
Memorandum												
Sub-Saharan Africa Excluding South Sudan	3.4	3.1	4.0	6.7	8.3	8.2	−5.9	−6.2	−5.5	...	...	...

Note: Data for some countries are based on fiscal years. Please refer to Table F in the Statistical Appendix for a list of economies with exceptional reporting periods.
[1]Movements in consumer prices are shown as annual averages. Year-end to year-end changes can be found in Table A7 in the Statistical Appendix.
[2]Percent of GDP.
[3]Percent. National definitions of unemployment may differ.
[4]Includes Equatorial Guinea and South Sudan.
[5]Includes Botswana, Cabo Verde, Lesotho, Mauritius, Namibia, Seychelles, and Swaziland.
[6]Includes Benin, Burkina Faso, Burundi, the Central African Republic, Comoros, Eritrea, The Gambia, Guinea, Guinea-Bissau, Liberia, Malawi, Mali, Mozambique, Niger, Rwanda, São Tomé and Príncipe, Sierra Leone, Togo, and Zimbabwe.

Special Feature: Commodity Market Developments and Forecasts, with a Focus on the Energy Transition in an Era of Low Fossil Fuel Prices

Commodity prices have declined since the release of the October 2015 World Economic Outlook *(WEO). Diminishing growth prospects for emerging market economies, especially China, combined with abundant supply are putting downward pressure on the prices of most commodities, although the relative importance of each force differs across commodities. Oil prices have declined mostly on account of news about strong supply magnified by risk-off behavior in financial markets. Metal prices have fallen owing to slower demand growth from China. Food prices have also declined as the result of a record-high harvest, although prices of selected food items have rebounded from unfavorable weather triggered by El Niño. This special feature includes an in-depth analysis of the energy transition in an era of low fossil fuel prices.*

The IMF's Primary Commodities Price Index has declined 19 percent since August 2015, the reference period for the October WEO (Figure 1.SF.1, panel 1). Oil prices have decreased further, by 32 percent, on account of strong supply from members of the Organization of the Petroleum Exporting Countries (OPEC) and risk-off behavior in financial markets, with investors moving away from what they perceive to be riskier assets, including commodities and stocks. The further collapse in oil prices has proceeded in spite of geopolitical tensions in the Middle East, suggesting that market expectations are firmly anchored in "low for long" oil prices. Natural gas and coal prices have also declined, as the former are linked to oil prices, including through oil-indexed contract prices, albeit with a lag. Nonfuel commodity prices have weakened as well, with metal and agricultural commodities prices declining by 9 percent and 4 percent, respectively, over the period.

Excess oil supply has pushed inventory levels in the Organisation for Economic Co-operation and Development (OECD) to record-high levels in spite of strong oil demand. Global oil demand growth in 2015 is estimated to have been about 1.6 million barrels a day (mbd), the largest increase in five years, and significantly higher than earlier forecast by the International Energy Agency (IEA). Oil supply has been quite resilient in spite of low prices, mostly on account of strong OPEC and Russian production, as well as the Islamic Republic of Iran's return

to world oil markets. However, there have been signs of a slowdown in shale oil production in the United States recently, driven by record low oil prices since 2003. This suggests an inflection point in the relative resilience of shale oil production owing to the dramatic operational efficiency gains that have prevailed during the past year. Turmoil in financial markets, as well as a strong U.S. dollar, have also been putting downward pressure on oil prices (Figure 1.SF.1, panel 2).

For the next year, world oil demand is expected to grow at the much slower pace of 1.2 mbd, according to the IEA, although the global economy is expected to grow slightly faster than in 2015. The expected slower pace is partly because the decline in oil prices has temporarily stimulated consumption of oil over the past year. Non-OPEC supply is expected to shrink for the first time in eight years, although only by a small margin. OPEC maintained its supply target at its last meeting in December 2015. In practice, however, OPEC members have been producing well above their target levels. Some OPEC countries have a strong incentive to increase production, considering the dire state of their public finances. The Islamic Republic of Iran is eager to increase production to regain market share lost during the sanctions era. At a meeting in Doha on February 16, 2016, oil ministers from Qatar, Russia, Saudi Arabia, and Venezuela agreed to freeze output, and the Islamic Republic of Iran and Iraq subsequently welcomed the initiative, but without any commitment to stop or slow their scheduled production increases. A credible agreement that would significantly reduce the OPEC production target to support higher oil prices appears unlikely.

Natural gas prices are also declining, with one leading natural gas price index (the average of prices in Europe, Japan, and the United States) down by 22 percent since August 2015. Falling oil prices and a relatively warm winter as a result of El Niño have contributed to this decline. An important coal price index (the average of Australian and South African prices) has also declined 12 percent since August 2015, in tandem with oil prices.

Oil futures contracts point to rising prices (Figure 1.SF.1, panel 3). Baseline assumptions for the IMF's average petroleum spot prices, which are based on futures prices, suggest average annual prices of $34.75 a barrel in 2016—a decline of 32 percent from 2015—and $40.99 a barrel in 2017 (Figure 1.SF.1, panel 4). There remains substantial uncertainty around the baseline assumptions for oil prices. While geopolitical tensions in the Middle East could potentially cause oil market disruptions, high

The authors of this feature are Rabah Arezki (team leader), Christian Bogmans, and Akito Matsumoto, with research assistance from Rachel Yuting Fan and Vanessa Diaz Montelongo.

Figure 1.SF.1. Commodity Market Developments

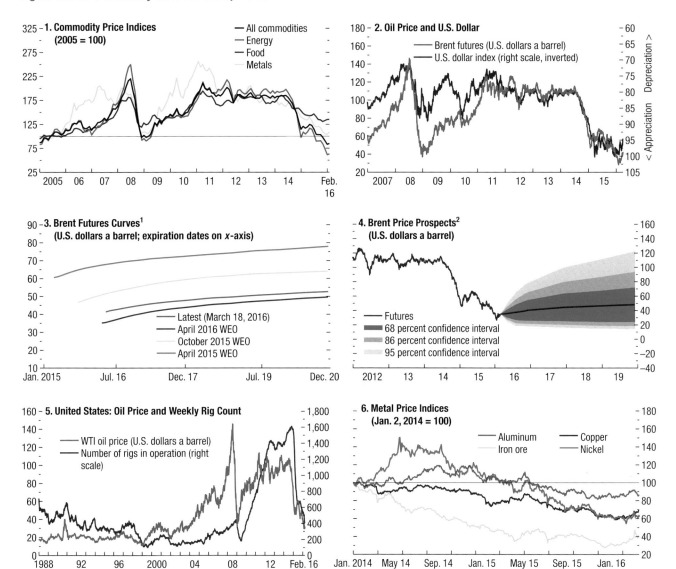

Sources: Baker Hughes Inc.; Bloomberg, L.P.; IMF, Primary Commodity Price System; Thomson Reuters Datastream; and IMF staff estimates.
Note: WTI = West Texas Intermediate.
[1]*World Economic Outlook* (WEO) futures prices are baseline assumptions for each WEO report and derived from futures prices. April 2016 WEO prices are based on February 26, 2016, closing.
[2]Derived from prices of futures options on February 26, 2016.

inventory levels and a rapid response from U.S. shale producers should limit the scope for a sharp price adjustment in the near future. That said, sustained oil prices of about $30 a barrel might lead to significant price recovery farther down the road, as many relatively high-cost producers could end up halting production in response to the prolonged lower prices, and declining oil prices have already dramatically reduced investment in extraction activities (Figure 1.SF.1, panel 5).

Metal prices have declined 9 percent since August 2015 (Figure 1.SF.1, panel 6). Prices have been gradually declining because of a slowdown and a shift away from commodity-intensive investment in China, which consumes roughly half of global metals. Metal prices are projected to decline by 14 percent in 2016 and 1 percent in 2017. Futures prices point to continued low prices, but with rising uncertainty on account of both demand (especially from China) and stronger supply. Iron ore prices have declined

17 percent since August in spite of a major mine accident in Samarco, Brazil.[1]

Prices of agricultural commodities have declined by 4 percent overall relative to August 2015. Food prices have decreased by 4 percent, with declines in most food items, except sugar and a few oilseeds. Sugar and palm oil prices have increased because of a drought in India and Malaysia, likely caused by El Niño. El Niño has also taken a toll on East Africa. International prices do not fully reflect the adverse weather shock, however, because of high prior inventory levels. For example, Ethiopia is suffering from its worst drought in 30 years. Unusually dry weather in North Africa is also likely to reduce harvests significantly, including those for cereals. The beverage price index has stagnated as a cocoa price increase has offset a decline in coffee prices.

Annual food prices are projected to languish over the next two years owing to ample supply—supported by high levels of stocks—and slower demand. Food prices are projected to decline by 6 percent in 2016 from the previous year; current price levels are already 5 percent below 2015 levels. However, over the next two years, prices for major food products, such as wheat, corn, and soybeans, are expected to increase slightly from current levels. Risks to food prices are associated with weather variability, particularly concerns over El Niño conditions, which are expected to strengthen throughout the Northern Hemisphere and persist beyond the first quarter of 2016.

The Energy Transition in an Era of Low Fossil Fuel Prices

The human influence on the climate system is clear and is evident from the increasing greenhouse gas concentrations in the atmosphere, positive radiative forcing, observed warming, and understanding of the climate system.

—Intergovernmental Panel on Climate Change,
Fifth Assessment Report

The United Nations' 2015 Climate Change Conference (COP21) was by all accounts a success. Nearly all countries around the globe have now firmly committed to reducing their greenhouse gas emissions through the Intended Nationally Determined Contributions (INDCs). The post-COP21 agenda now focuses on the implementation of these INDCs. At the heart of that implementation is the so-called energy transition, which consists of moving away from using fossil fuels (petroleum products, natural gas, and coal) and toward clean energies to power the global economy. While the energy

transition is arguably at an early stage, with important differences across countries, it is at a critical juncture. Indeed, to avoid the irreversible consequences of climate change induced by greenhouse gas emissions, the energy transition must firmly take root at a time when fossil fuel prices are likely to stay low for long. It involves significant opportunities and risks, which energy policies will need to tackle.

This section provides answers to four key questions about the energy transition:
- Where do we stand on fossil fuels?
- What is the status of clean energy?
- What opportunities and risks are associated with the energy transition?
- What is the way forward?

Where Do We Stand on Fossil Fuels?

Oil prices have dropped by more than 70 percent since June 2014 and are expected to remain low for a long time owing to a variety of factors (see Arezki and Obstfeld 2015). On the supply side, the advent and relative resilience of shale oil production and increased oil production by OPEC members play an important role. On the demand side, lower GDP growth in emerging markets has tended to reduce oil demand growth, especially in light of the secular increase in global oil efficiency (Figure 1.SF.2), and is expected to continue to do so. That said, the expansion of the middle class in emerging giants is expected to increase dramatically the demand for transport services and the level of car ownership and, in turn, to support oil demand growth (Figure 1.SF.3). The balance among these forces will determine the strength of demand growth.

Natural gas and coal have similarly seen price declines that look to be long lived. The North American shale gas boom has resulted in record-low prices there. Recent discoveries of vast gas fields in developing countries add to the pool of available reserves.[2] The resumption of nuclear-powered electricity generation in Japan is a permanent factor contributing to lower natural gas prices in Asia. Coal prices also are low, owing to oversupply and the scaling down of demand because of environmental concerns and slower economic activity, especially from China, which burns half of the world's coal.

The share of oil in global primary energy consumption has declined rapidly, from 50 percent in 1970 to about 30 percent today (Figure 1.SF.4). The share of coal, now

[1]Samarco accounts for between 8 percent and 10 percent of iron ore production in Brazil.

[2]The recent discovery of the giant Zohr gas field off the Egyptian coast and, more recently, the discovery of natural gas off the coast of Senegal will eventually have repercussions for pricing in Europe, the Mediterranean region, and western Africa. In addition, many other locales, especially in developing countries, that are opening up for resource exploration offer significant potential (see Arezki, Toscani, and van der Ploeg, forthcoming).

Figure 1.SF.2. World Energy Intensity

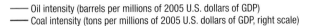

—— Oil intensity (barrels per millions of 2005 U.S. dollars of GDP)
—— Coal intensity (tons per millions of 2005 U.S. dollars of GDP, right scale)

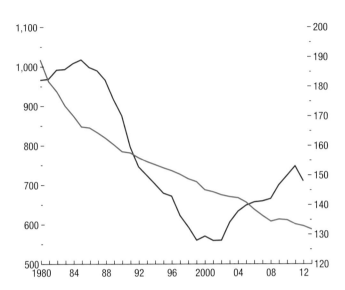

Sources: U.S. Energy Information Administration; World Bank, *World Development Indicators*; and IMF staff calculations.

Figure 1.SF.3. Car Ownership and GDP per Capita, 2013

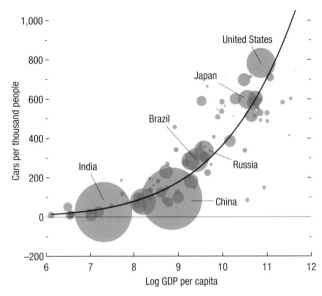

Sources: International Road Federation, *World Road Statistics*; and IMF staff calculations.
Note: Size of bubble represents population in 2013. Cars per thousand people for India is from 2012.

reaching 30 percent of global energy consumption, has been increasing since the early 2000s, mostly on account of rising demand from China, and recently also from India. In contrast with the case of oil, more coal per unit of global GDP is now burned relative to the early 2000s (Figure 1.SF.2). Natural gas consumption has increased steadily since the 1970s, now accounting for nearly 25 percent of global primary energy consumption. Global demand for natural gas is projected to increase strongly over the medium term (IEA 2015), with emerging market and developing economies accounting for the bulk of the growth. The outlook for oil and coal demand growth falls short of that for total energy demand, partly because advanced economies are expected to drastically reduce their demand for coal and oil, in contrast with emerging markets. According to the IEA, the shares of oil and coal are expected to drop from 36 percent and 19 percent, respectively, in 2013 to 26 percent and 12 percent, respectively, in 2040.

Oil is used mostly to fuel transportation, whereas coal and natural gas are used mainly as inputs into the power sector, consisting of electricity and heat generation, which accounts for more than one-third of total primary energy consumption (Table 1.SF.1). For electricity generation alone, the biggest source of energy is coal, but renewables, including hydropower, are second, followed by natural gas.[3]

[3]The share of natural gas in total primary energy demand is expected to rise, but it faces competition from substitutes for gas in

Figure 1.SF.4. World Energy Consumption Share by Fuel Type
(Percent)

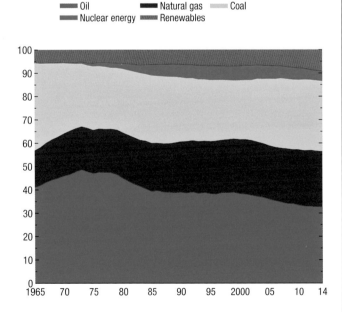

Source: BP, *Statistical Review of World Energy 2015*.
Note: Consumption of renewables is based on gross primary hydroelectric generation and gross generation from other renewable sources, including wind, geothermal, solar, biomass, and waste.

Table 1.SF.1. World Energy Usage, 2013
(Millions of tons of oil equivalent)

Energy Source	Power Generation (electricity and heat)	Final Consumption			Total Primary Energy Demand
		Industry	Transportation	Buildings	
Coal	2,404	768	3	128	3,929
Oil	284	302	2,357	317	4,219
Gas	1,172	557	96	627	2,901
Nuclear	646	–	–	–	646
Hydro	326	–	–	–	326
Bioenergy/Biofuels	155	194	65	861	1,376
Other Renewables	127	1	–	32	161
Electricity and Heat	–	842	26	1,040	...
Total	5,115	2,664	2,547	3,004	13,559

Sources: International Energy Agency, *World Energy Outlook* and *World Energy Balance*; and IMF staff calculations.
Note: Because of statistical discrepancies, individual data in each row do not sum exactly to total primary energy demand. – = negligible.

Figure 1.SF.5. Carbon Emissions for Various Fuels

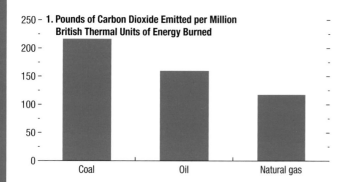

1. Pounds of Carbon Dioxide Emitted per Million British Thermal Units of Energy Burned

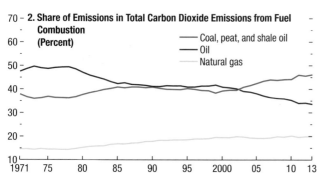

2. Share of Emissions in Total Carbon Dioxide Emissions from Fuel Combustion (Percent)

Sources: International Energy Agency; and IMF staff calculations.

Roughly equal, and substantial, amounts of energy are also consumed in the industry, transport, and building construction sectors. The transport sector accounts for roughly two-thirds of oil use in the world. The industry, transport, and building construction sectors also consume electricity and heat that are generated by primary energy.

Natural gas is the cleanest energy source among fossil fuels in terms of carbon dioxide emissions. Oil is second to natural gas in this respect, and coal is the dirtiest source, especially when used by older, low-efficiency plants (Figure 1.SF.5, panel 1). Besides carbon dioxide, old plants tend to emit more air pollutants such as nitrogen oxides and sulfur oxides. While China, the world's largest coal consumer, is shifting toward renewable energy resources, demand from other developing countries, especially India, is expected to increase, especially if coal prices stay low (Figure 1.SF.6). In fact, global carbon intensity per unit of energy has increased since the beginning of the 1990s owing to the rising consumption of coal, especially in Asia (see Steckel, Edenhofer, and Jakob 2015). In spite of the increased use of renewables and the decreased use of oil as fuel, total greenhouse gas emissions have increased because of the increase in demand for coal (Figure 1.SF.5, panel 2). This increase has resulted from higher growth in emerging market economies, where coal intensity has risen.

If the energy intensity of economic activity does not fall or if countries in the developing world do not adopt state-of-the-art technology for coal-powered plants to lower the carbon intensity of their electricity generation,

many sectors, especially from renewables and coal in power generation—in part because of subsidies and gas-pricing regimes. Natural gas is expected to make further inroads into the transportation sector in particular, in which its use is still very limited. This development,

along with the eventual use of liquefied natural gas as shipping fuel, will contribute to the displacement of oil.

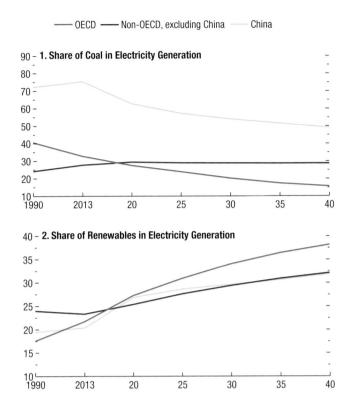

Figure 1.SF.6. Electricity Generation
(Percent)

— OECD — Non-OECD, excluding China — China

1. Share of Coal in Electricity Generation

2. Share of Renewables in Electricity Generation

Sources: International Energy Agency; and IMF staff calculations.
Note: These shares relate to electricity generation only and exclude the heating sector. OECD = Organisation for Economic Co-operation and Development.

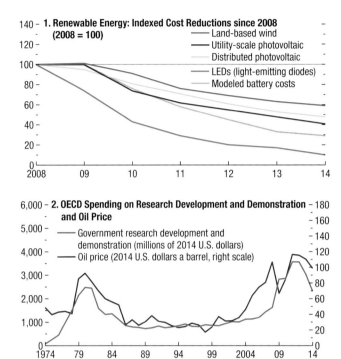

Figure 1.SF.7. Cost of Renewables and Research and Development Efforts

1. Renewable Energy: Indexed Cost Reductions since 2008 (2008 = 100)

Land-based wind
Utility-scale photovoltaic
Distributed photovoltaic
LEDs (light-emitting diodes)
Modeled battery costs

2. OECD Spending on Research Development and Demonstration and Oil Price

Government research development and demonstration (millions of 2014 U.S. dollars)
Oil price (2014 U.S. dollars a barrel, right scale)

Sources: International Energy Agency, *Energy Technology Research Development and Demonstration 2015*; and U.S. Department of Energy.
Note: OECD = Organisation for Economic Co-operation and Development.

economic development in most regions of the world will continue to drive global emissions upward. Emissions will reach dramatic levels and, in turn, accelerate global warming. Poorly designed regulations for the use of coal in developing countries could also discourage technological change in the electricity sector. As a result, the world might not benefit, in terms of lower global emissions, from the downward trend in coal use in developed countries.

Considering its relative cleanliness and abundance, natural gas can play a key role as a bridge in the transition from coal to renewables. Growth in shale gas production in the United States is expected to make natural gas the energy of choice there. There is also potential for growth in the use of shale gas and conventional natural gas in China and many other locales around the globe (see Chakravorty, Fischer, and Hubert 2015).

What Is the Status of Clean Energy?

One of the most notable trends in energy consumption is the increase in the use of renewable energy resources (Figure 1.SF.4), which has been supported by a formidable reduction in the costs of various renewables, including solar and wind (Figure 1.SF.7, panel 1). These cost reductions are the result of research and development (R&D) efforts to promote clean energy and energy efficiency ("grey" technology) (Figure 1.SF.7, panel 2). Early R&D investment dates to the 1970s, an era of record-high fossil fuel prices, and was mostly government financed. This is no surprise, as the private sector typically does not internalize the positive externalities associated with an increase in R&D. Public R&D spending early on, however, paved the way for corporate R&D spending during the 2000s, another period of high fossil fuel prices. The result has been a flow of technological innovations across sectors, including the development of electric cars, although they (notably plug-in hybrid vehicles) still have a low penetration rate, accounting for less than 1 percent of car sales in the United States. Unsurprisingly, electric car sales have decreased with the recent drop in gasoline prices (Figure 1.SF.8).

Among primary energy sources, renewables (including hydropower) are the least carbon intensive. The IEA fore-

Figure 1.SF.8. U.S. Sales of Electric Vehicles and Gasoline Price

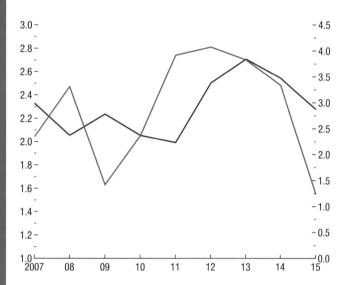

Sources: Electric Drive Transportation Association; and IMF, Primary Commodity Price System.
Note: Total electric drive market share includes hybrid vehicles.

Figure 1.SF.9. Duck Curve: Illustrative Change in Projections of Net Load Curve
(Megawatts)

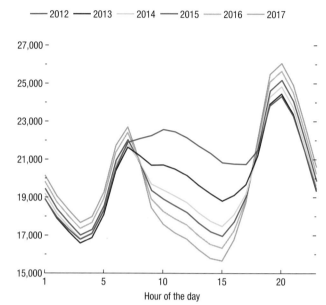

Source: California Energy Commission staff, Energy Assessments Division.
Note: Projections are based on load shapes and production profiles from actual data of California Independent System Operator on March 22, 2013.

casts that the share of renewables in global total primary energy consumption will increase from 14 percent in 2013 to 19 percent in 2040 in light of expected energy policy changes. The electricity sector, in which the share of renewables is projected to increase from 22 percent to 34 percent over the same period, will be one of the sectors to change most dramatically.

One potential difficulty with depending on renewable energy in the power sector is intermittency, and hence reliability. Unstable supply patterns of wind, sun, and rainfall can trigger supply-demand mismatches. The increasing reliance on renewables, including solar and wind, as sources of power generation will require much steeper ramping up of supply during daily peaks to achieve load balancing.[4] In other words, the intermittencies associated with the increased usage of renewables trigger spikes in demand for "controllable" power, for example, from natural gas (Figure 1.SF.9). For renewables to overcome this problem, the power sector needs to develop economical battery backup technology and foster

electricity exchange. Battery technology has shown steady progress, suggesting that eventually electricity storage technology will facilitate a more widespread reliance on renewables.

Bioenergy has long been employed for power generation in the electricity sector. Biosolids are relatively cheap sources of energy, as they are residuals from other processes or simply waste. Power plants fired by biomass also have the flexibility to compensate for generation lapses associated with other renewables, as they can operate at any time of the day. Both advanced economies and developing countries are expected to develop more bioenergy-based facilities. In the transportation sector, biofuels are usually blended with conventional gasoline or diesel, sometimes following government regulation. As a result, the share of biofuels in transportation fuels has doubled over the past decade. While biofuels can reduce carbon emissions, some types also put pressure on food markets and have been blamed for food price increases (see Chakravorty and others 2015).

Nuclear energy makes up only a small share of global energy consumption. Carbon emissions associated with nuclear energy generation are limited, but in the aftermath of the March 2011 Fukushima disaster, several countries have imposed moratoriums on nuclear energy use on account of environmental liabilities and safety

---

[4]The net load curve represents the variable portion of the load that integrated system operators must meet in real time. The net load is calculated by taking the forecast load and subtracting the forecast of electricity generation from variable generation resources, wind, and solar (see California ISO 2013).

Table 1.SF.2. Summary of Severe Accidents in the Energy Sector, 1970–2008

Energy Chain	OECD		Non-OECD	
	Accidents	Immediate Fatalities	Accidents	Immediate Fatalities
Coal	87	2,259	2,394	38,672
Oil	187	3,495	358	19,516
Natural gas	109	1,258	78	1,556
Liquefied petroleum gas	58	1,856	70	2,789
Hydro	1	14	9	30,069
Nuclear	–	–	1	31
Biofuel	–	–	–	–
Biogas	–	–	2	18
Geothermal	–	–	1	21

Source: Burgherr and Hirschberg 2014.
Note: Accidents with more than five fatalities are considered severe. Accidents in Organisation for Economic Co-operation and Development (OECD) countries from hydro power refer to the U.S. Teton Dam failure in 1976. For nuclear accidents, only immediate fatalities of the Chernobyl accident are shown. – = negligible.

concerns. In addition to human health risks, the overall impact on the environment is hard to judge, as waste management of used nuclear fuel is still at an early stage. There are also concerns about the diversion of materials involved in nuclear power generation to military use. There are, however, important benefits of nuclear energy. For example, and in contrast with renewable energy, nuclear power is not plagued by the problem of intermittency. Also, immediate fatalities associated with nuclear power plant accidents—as opposed to long-term health consequences related to radiation and pollution exposure—are historically much lower than for any other type of power plant, including coal-fired plants (Table 1.SF.2). The potential for using nuclear energy as a source of clean energy is relatively high. Some countries, such as China and the United States, are using more nuclear energy to curb their greenhouse gas emissions. While there are serious issues that need to be solved in terms of safety and waste management, many scientists argue that it will be hard to achieve INDC targets without greater use of nuclear energy.

What Opportunities and Risks Are Associated with the Energy Transition?

The current low fossil fuel price environment will certainly delay the energy transition. Indeed, progress in the development of renewables could prove fragile if fossil fuel prices remain low for long (see Arezki and Obstfeld 2015).[5] While renewables account for only a small share of global primary energy consumption, renewable energy will need to displace fossil fuels to a much greater extent to forestall further significant climate risks. The current low prices for oil, gas, and coal may provide scant economic incentive for research to find even cheaper substitutes for those fuels. Lower prices have already raised demand in some countries, such as Germany, boosting the use of coal (the dirtiest fossil fuel) at the expense of natural gas (the cleanest).[6] Evidence indicates that higher fossil fuel prices strongly encourage both innovation and adoption of cleaner technology (see Aghion and others 2012 and Busse, Knittel, and Zettelmeyer 2013). For example, lower gasoline prices reduce the incentive to purchase fuel-efficient or electric cars (Figure 1.SF.8). Similarly, the number of clean- or grey-energy patents correlates positively with the price of fossil fuels (Figure 1.SF.10). Finally, low prices for energy in general may hamper the decoupling of economic growth and overall energy consumption if consumers substitute energy for other commodities.

A few countries have committed to reducing coal-powered generation. Because coal is currently relatively cheap, however, it is tempting for a country to use coal for power generation, especially if it cannot afford cleaner alternatives, which are typically more expensive. As mentioned earlier, even advanced economies in Europe increased their use of coal when the shale revolution in

[5]Low oil prices may in part reflect, in addition to the factors discussed earlier in the chapter, an independent process of structural transformation that is taking place in China and is diminishing (or slowing down the growth of) the oil intensity of GDP (see Stefanski 2014).

[6]As the relative price of coal to natural gas in Europe declined in recent years, the share of coal in electricity generation increased in Germany, from 43.1 percent in 2010 to 46.3 percent in 2013. Over the same time period, the share of natural gas fell from 14.3 percent to 10.9 percent.

Figure 1.SF.10. World Patents
(Number of patents)

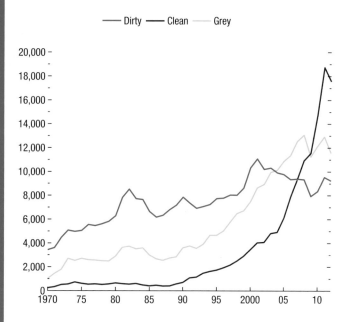

Source: Aghion and others 2012.
Note: Calculations are based on the European Patent Office's World Patent Statistical Database. Dirty = auto technology affecting internal combustion engines; Clean = auto technology in electric and hybrid vehicles and fuel cells for hydrogen vehicles, among others; Grey = innovations in fuel efficiency.

the United States displaced coal there and international coal prices dropped.[7] In addition to these short-term effects of low coal prices, low prices may boost capacity investment in coal power plants but reduce efforts to develop more efficient technology.

Efficiency and pollution intensity differ significantly across coal power plants. With the prospects of lower demand for coal plants over environmental concerns, power plant manufacturers that have up to this point improved plant efficiency and reduced emissions might now moderate their development efforts. This could leave emerging market economies with less efficient and more pollution-intensive coal power plants. Another key technology that can potentially salvage the coal industry in regard to its poor emissions profile is carbon capture and storage, which will be useful not only for power plants but also in other carbon-emitting industries, such as steel production. At this point, carbon capture and

[7]The share of coal as an input in power plants among European OECD members increased from 23.7 percent in 2010 to 26.0 percent in 2012 (with the increase in coal use largely arising from displacement of natural gas use), although the share of renewable energy increased as well. Japan increased its share of natural gas and coal significantly after it stopped nuclear power plant operations following the Fukushima accident.

storage and clean coal technologies are not considered to be main global-warming mitigation tools, but it may still be important for coal and oil producers to pursue these technologies to some degree.

In the long term, if and when the energy transition is successful, fossil fuels could become "stranded assets" (that is, assets that either lose value unexpectedly or prematurely or become liabilities) without proper carbon capture and storage. In the case of fossil fuel industries, stranded assets might involve "stranded reserves," that is, fossil fuel reserves that are no longer recoverable, and "stranded or underutilized capital," that is, sunk capital investments that would become obsolete (for example, an oil platform that will never be used). Because it remains to be seen how rapidly the energy transition might take place, however, there is significant uncertainty regarding the time horizon over which fossil fuel assets would become stranded. One important lesson from earlier energy transitions—which include the transition from wood and biomass to coal in the eighteenth and nineteenth centuries and the transition from coal to oil in the nineteenth and twentieth centuries—is that these transitions take time to complete. History may not repeat itself in that regard, however, in that the technological forces unleashed by the anticipated public and private response to climate change seem much more potent than the factors driving earlier energy transitions and may lead to a relatively swifter transition this time, notwithstanding the potential delay implied by the current low-for-long fossil fuel price environment. Considering the industry's carbon emissions intensity, coal-related assets are more exposed to the risk of becoming stranded than are oil and natural gas assets.

The consequences of stranded assets would be dramatic for coal and oil companies and exporting countries that rely heavily on fossil fuel exports, which would face heavy losses. Many major oil companies have long diversified across fossil fuels by investing more heavily in the production of natural gas and have also started to invest in so-called breakthrough renewable technologies in an effort to adapt to emerging realities. Oil-exporting countries have also attempted to diversify their economies away from oil, but this has proven challenging. Nevertheless, opportunities exist. For example, the United Arab Emirates has endorsed an ambitious target to draw 24 percent of its primary energy consumption from renewable sources by 2021.

Solar power concentration is highest in the Middle East and Africa and parts of Asia and the United States, according to the U.S. National Aeronautics and Space Administration (Figure 1.SF.11). Interestingly, Morocco, the host of the next United Nations Conference on Climate Change (COP22), has recently unveiled the first

Figure 1.SF.11. Direct Normal Irradiation

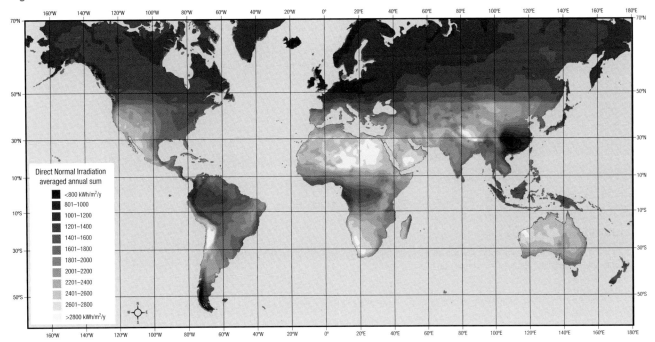

Source: U.S. National Aeronautics and Space Administration.

phase of a massive solar power plant in the Sahara Desert that is expected to have a combined capacity of two giga-watts by 2020, making it the single largest solar power production facility in the world.

What Is the Way Forward?

Large economies tend to be the biggest emitters of greenhouse gases. Indeed, the 10 largest emitters are responsible for more than 60 percent of global greenhouse gas emissions (Table 1.SF.3). Any effort to address global warming should therefore encompass all of the largest economies (see Arezki and Matsumoto 2015). While high-income countries are big greenhouse gas emitters in per capita terms, energy efficiency has been gaining ground rapidly in these countries. Many high-income countries are reducing greenhouse gas emissions already and are committed to continue doing so. Consumption of fossil fuels by advanced econo-mies can therefore be expected to continue to decrease. Though large economies account for the bulk of current emissions, emerging markets will continue to drive the growth of future emissions. In contrast to the falling emissions intensity of the advanced economies, emerg-ing market and developing economies remain heavily reliant on coal, and their consumption of fossil fuels will continue to rise.

There are important variations across countries in efforts to shift their energy mixes at least partly toward renewables and away from fossil fuels, especially coal and oil. Today, the European Union and Sweden, respectively, get 13 percent and more than 38 percent of their energy from renewables. Sweden in 1991 was the first country to adopt a carbon tax. Pressured by very high pollution levels, China has adopted an ambitious plan to derive a significant fraction of its future energy needs from renewables.

As noted earlier, the COP21 was by all accounts a success, with nearly all countries around the globe having firmly committed to reducing their greenhouse gas emissions through the INDCs (Table 1.SF.4). Well before Paris, in 1997, the Kyoto Protocol aimed to achieve inter-nationally coordinated reductions in carbon dioxide emis-sions, but a few major countries, such as China, India, and the United States, did not agree to legally binding targets. The 2009 Copenhagen climate change conference did not yield any agreement, and real progress had to await the 2015 Paris conference. As mentioned previously, the challenge following the COP21 is, however, one of implementation. As such, setting the right incentives for achieving the INDCs is essential.

The IEA (2015) and most scientists also note that the INDCs, in their current form, are not sufficient,

Table 1.SF.3. Global Share of Greenhouse Gas Emissions by Country
(CO$_2$ emissions from fuel combustion, 2013)

Country	Share (of global)	CO$_2$/Population (tons of CO$_2$ per capita)	CO$_2$/GDP PPP (kilograms of CO$_2$ per current international dollar)	GDP per capita (current PPP)
China	28.0	6.65	0.55	12,196
United States	15.9	16.18	0.31	52,980
India	5.8	1.49	0.28	5,418
Russia	4.8	10.75	0.43	25,033
Japan	3.8	9.70	0.27	36,223
Germany	2.4	9.42	0.21	43,887
Korea	1.8	11.39	0.34	33,089
Canada	1.7	15.25	0.35	43,033
Iran	1.6	6.79	0.42	16,067
Saudi Arabia	1.5	16.39	0.31	52,993
Total share (top 10 countries)	67.3			

Sources: International Energy Agency; World Bank, *World Development Indicators*; and IMF staff calculations.
Note: CO$_2$ = carbon dioxide; PPP = purchasing power parity.

Table 1.SF.4. Greenhouse Gas Emissions Target Reductions, Paris Agreement, December 2015

Country	Target Reductions
United States[1]	Between 26 percent and 28 percent below 2005 levels by 2025
European Union[1]	40 percent below 1990 levels by 2030
Japan[1]	26 percent below 2013 levels by 2030
Canada[1]	30 percent below 2005 levels by 2030
China[1]	60 percent to 65 percent below 2005 levels by 2030 (CO$_2$ emissions intensity)
India[2]	33 percent to 35 percent below 2005 levels by 2030 (CO$_2$ emissions intensity)
Russia[1]	25 percent to 30 percent below 1990 levels by 2030
Brazil[1]	37 percent below national baseline scenario by 2025
South Africa[2]	Between 398 and 614 million tons of CO$_2$ emissions by 2025 and 2030

Source: Admiraal and others 2015.
Note: By November 29, 2015, 184 parties (including the European Union) had submitted their Intended Nationally Determined Contributions (INDCs) in preparation for the adoption of the Paris Agreement in December 2015.
[1] Unconditional INDC.
[2] Conditional INDC.

and more is needed to avoid the worst effects of climate change. In addition to implementing mitigation efforts, countries will need to adapt to global warming, which calls for adjusting to the new reality of a warmer planet. This implies population displacements from exposed areas, or new infrastructure and housing better suited to withstand new climate risks. But adaption alone is neither fully acceptable nor sufficient, considering that global warming can cause irreversible damage. For instance, some ecosystems will be unable to adapt to rising temperatures and thus will experience substantially reduced biodiversity.

Short of pervasive and economically viable carbon capture and storage technologies, the planet will be exposed to potentially catastrophic climate risks (see Meehl and others 2007) unless renewables become cheap enough to guarantee that substantial fossil fuel deposits are left underground for a very long time, if not forever. The price of fossil fuels should reflect the negative externality that the consumption of the latter inflicts. The price of carbon should equal the social cost of carbon, which is the present discounted value of marginal global warming damages from burning one ton of carbon today.[8] In this regard, a global carbon tax would be the most efficient way to reduce emissions.

[8]See D'Autume, Schubert, and Withagen 2011, Golosov and others 2014, and Rezai and van der Ploeg 2014 for useful references on the design of carbon taxes.

Politically, low fossil fuel prices may provide an opportune moment to eliminate energy subsidies and introduce carbon prices that could gradually rise over time toward efficient levels. However, it is probably unrealistic to aim for implementation of the full optimal price all at once. Global carbon pricing will have important redistributive implications, both across and within countries, and these call for gradual implementation, complemented by mitigating and adaptive measures that shield the most vulnerable.[9] The hope is that the success of the Paris conference opens the door to future international agreement on carbon prices. Agreement on an international carbon price floor would be a good starting point in that process. Failure to address comprehensively the problem of greenhouse gas emissions, however, exposes this generation and future generations to incalculable risks (see Stern 2015).[10]

For developing countries in particular, aid may be necessary to facilitate the clean technology imports necessary to ensure that these countries participate in the energy transition.[11] This aid would help offset the countries' transitional costs associated with removing carbon subsidies and levying positive carbon taxes. In this vein, the Green Climate Fund—a fund within the framework of the United Nations—was founded as a mechanism to assist developing countries in putting in place adaptation and mitigation practices. It is intended to be the centerpiece of efforts to raise climate finance to $100 billion a year by 2020. The IMF is also supporting its members in dealing with the macroeconomic challenges of climate change.[12]

As noted previously, shifting away from fossil fuels to clean, renewable energy resources or nuclear energy can help reduce greenhouse gas emissions. In addition, shifting from coal to gas in electricity generation can help significantly in this regard. Development of the renewable energy sector will require an overhaul of the existing energy infrastructure and involve the need to train and retool the labor force. These transformations will be a source of jobs and cleaner, more sustainable growth. Indeed, the investment needs associated with the energy transition come at an opportune time, when interest rates are at historic lows and the world economy needs infrastructure spending both to support demand and to spur future potential growth.

[9]Farid and others (2016) discuss macro and financial policies to address climate change.

[10]Li, Narajabad, and Temzelides (2014) show that, even when some degree of uncertainty is accounted for, taking into account the damage from climate change can cause a significant drop in optimal energy extraction.

[11]Collier and Venables (2012) discuss Africa's needs to achieve its potential in hydro and solar power.

[12]See "The Managing Director's Statement on the Role of the Fund in Addressing Climate Change" (IMF 2015b).

Box 1.1. Dissecting the Global Trade Slowdown

Since the rebound from the great trade collapse of 2008–09, when world trade fell by much more than GDP, global trade growth has slowed notably, both in absolute terms and relative to world GDP growth. This slowdown has been more pronounced in emerging market and developing economies, where it intensified in 2015. This box lays out some facts about the distribution of the slowdown across countries and types of products.[1]

In the two decades leading up to the global financial crisis, international trade expanded rapidly, at a pace roughly double that of world GDP. World trade volume growth, however, has moderated notably in recent years, both in its level and relative to GDP growth. As a result, the increase in trade as a share of global GDP has decelerated (Figure 1.1.1).

The slowdown in trade has been remarkably widespread. An analysis of recent trade patterns of 174 individual countries reveals that trade growth has

The authors of this box are Emine Boz, Eugenio Cerutti, and Sung Eun Jung.

[1]See Hoekman 2015 for a compilation of studies analyzing the drivers behind the recent trade slowdown.

weakened in an overwhelming majority of countries. This holds true even after the weak growth in income and the decline in trade prices are taken into account. As depicted in Figure 1.1.2, most countries have been importing less, relative to their incomes during 2012–15, than in the years leading up to the global financial crisis. For 65 percent of the countries, accounting for 74 percent of global imports, the ratio of average import volume growth to GDP growth (a simple measure of the income elasticity of import demand) observed during 2012–15 was below that during 2003–06.

The observed slowdown in import income elasticity has been more pronounced in emerging market and developing economies than in advanced economies.

Figure 1.1.2. Import Elasticity

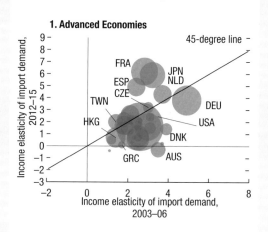

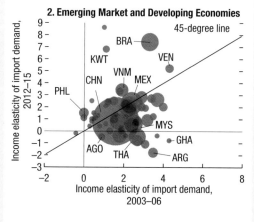

Source: IMF staff calculations.
Note: Data labels in the figure use International Organization for Standardization (ISO) country codes.

Figure 1.1.1. Trade and Output Growth
(Year-over-year percent change)

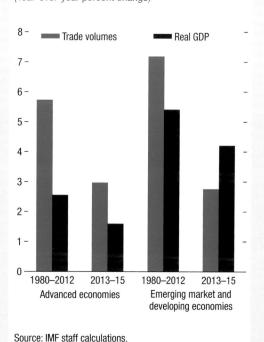

Source: IMF staff calculations.

Box 1.1 *(continued)*

Most emerging market and developing economies are tightly clustered below the 45-degree line in Figure 1.1.2, while advanced economies' experience has been more varied. A comparison of import income elasticities computed using aggregated GDP and trade data across advanced and emerging market and developing economies supports this finding. For the advanced economy aggregate, the elasticity of imports with respect to GDP fell from 2.77 during 2003–06 to 2.09 during 2012–15, while for emerging market and developing economies, import income elasticity fell more sharply—from 1.9 to 0.7—over the same period.

Trade weakness was particularly noticeable in emerging and developing Asia, including China. For the region as a whole, export volumes declined slightly in 2015—a striking development in light of the region's high income growth and historically strong trade performance relative to other regions.

Which Types of Goods Are Traded Less?

Documenting differences in trade volume trends across various types of goods helps explain potential drivers of the trade slowdown. For instance, particularly weak growth in capital goods imports may signal weak investment and an associated shift in the composition of domestic absorption as a driver of the trade slowdown. Similarly, the dynamics of intermediate goods imports may shed light on the behavior of global value chains. Consistent analysis of the global trade slowdown through the lens of disaggregated trade flows across a large number of countries has, however, been difficult because of limited comparable data on trade volumes and price indices by product type. This limitation is especially relevant for recent years, given the sharp relative price shifts as a result of commodity price declines.

Using highly disaggregated trade data on import volume and values through 2014, Boz and Cerutti (2016) construct import volume indices for four different types of goods by end use: consumer, capital, primary intermediate, and other intermediate goods. Figures 1.1.3 and 1.1.4 plot the growth rates of these indices for selected advanced and emerging market economies.[2]

---

[2]2015 data are available only for a small subset of countries. Chained Fisher price indices are constructed using Harmonized System six-digit product-level data (for both quantity and value) from the UN Comtrade and World Bank World Integrated Trade

Figure 1.1.3. Import Volume Index by End Use
(Year-over-year percent change)

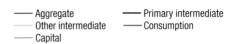

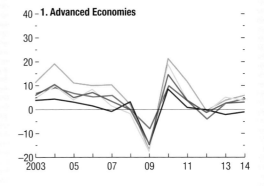

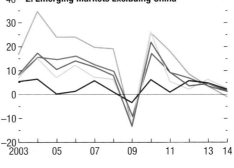

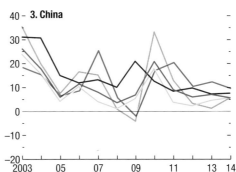

Sources: United Nations Comtrade database; World Bank, World Integration Trade Solution database; and IMF staff estimates.

Box 1.1 *(continued)*

Figure 1.1.4. Capital Goods Import Volume Index
(Year-over-year percent change)

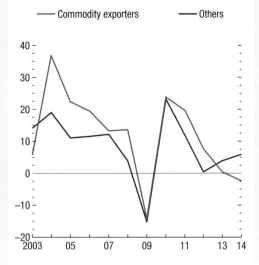

Sources: United Nations Comtrade database; World Bank World Integration Trade Solution database; and IMF staff calculations.

• In advanced economies, the drop in imports of primary intermediate goods stood out in recent years. As a result, the share of primary intermediate goods imports in advanced economies'

Solution (WITS) databases. End-use categorization is based on UN Broad Economic Categories. Motor spirits and passenger cars, along with other unclassified Broad Economic Categories groupings, are excluded. Countries included in the sample are 28 advanced economies (Australia, Austria, Belgium, Canada, Czech Republic, Denmark, Finland, France, Germany, Greece, Hong Kong Special Administrative Region, Ireland, Israel, Italy, Japan, Korea, Luxembourg, Netherlands, Norway, Portugal, Singapore, Slovak Republic, Spain, Sweden, Switzerland, Taiwan Province of China, United Kingdom, United States) and 21 emerging market economies (Algeria, Argentina, Brazil, Chile, China, Colombia, Hungary, India, Indonesia, Kazakhstan, Malaysia, Mexico, Philippines, Poland, Romania, Russia, South Africa, Thailand, Turkey, Ukraine, Vietnam).

total imports dropped from 16 percent in 2012 to 13.6 percent in 2014. This was partly driven by the increase in domestic production of oil in the United States, leading to a decline in its oil imports.

• Consistent with its rebalancing process, China's imports of consumer goods held up relatively strongly. Consumer goods, however, constituted only about 5 percent of China's total imports as of 2014. Other intermediate goods (including parts and accessories), at 76 percent of total imports, accounted for the lion's share. The slowdowns in nonprimary intermediate and capital goods imports were the most prominent and may have been a reflection of declines in China's manufacturing production and investment.

• Emerging markets, excluding China, varied less in regard to the behavior of imports across end-use categories. Still, imports of capital goods shrank in 2014, faring worse than the remaining categories, which continued to grow at low, but positive, rates.

The weakness in emerging markets' capital goods imports may have been partially driven by commodity exporters in this country group. A split of the sample based on whether a country was classified as a commodity exporter in Chapter 2 of the October 2015 *World Economic Outlook* supports this conjecture.[3] More specifically, as Figure 1.1.4 shows, after a protracted period of robust growth in imports of capital goods before the global financial crisis, commodity exporters faced a marked decline in their capital goods imports in 2014, reflecting retrenchment in their energy sector and mining investment. These countries' capital goods imports constituted a nonnegligible share of the world's capital goods imports—about 15 percent in 2014.

[3]This classification is based on countries' gross and net exports of commodities. Out of 12 commodity-exporting countries in the sample (Algeria, Argentina, Australia, Brazil, Canada, Chile, Colombia, Indonesia, Kazakhstan, Malaysia, Russia, Norway), 9 are emerging market economies.

Box 1.2. Macroeconomic Developments and Outlook in Low-Income Developing Countries: The Role of External Factors

After more than a decade of growth averaging more than 6 percent, low-income developing countries saw their economic activity slow sharply in 2015. The slowdown reflects, in part, a less favorable external environment: sharply lower commodity prices, lower growth in trading partners, and tighter financing conditions. Domestic factors and the policy environment also played a role.[1]

Oil-exporting low-income developing countries were hit hardest, followed by other commodity-dependent countries (Figure 1.2.1). Growth in oil exporters—which account for one-third of low-income developing countries' aggregate output in purchasing-power-parity terms (Figure 1.2.2) and 1¼ percent of global output—fell by half, from over 6 percent in 2014 to less than 3 percent in 2015. Growth in non-oil commodity exporters, which account for about one-fifth of low-income developing country output, declined from 5½ percent in 2014 to 4½ percent in 2015. Countries that depend relatively less on commodity exports (*diversified exporters,* for simplicity), which account for slightly more than half of low-income developing country output, fared better, with growth still above 6 percent, although some were affected by conflicts and natural disasters (for example, Haiti, Liberia, and Nepal). Growth in 2016 is projected to be weaker than in 2015 for all three groups, although with significant differences in prospects and risks within each group.

A measure of the income gains and losses from the sharp fall in international commodity prices confirms that the impact on low-income developing countries' economic prospects varied (see Gruss 2014 and IMF 2015a). Income in oil exporters fell by about 7–8 percent of GDP in 2015 (Figure 1.2.3). In contrast, low-income developing countries that are less dependent on commodity exports saw a slight gain, in part because these countries import oil. As shown in model simulations later in this box, the decline in commodity prices in 2016 is likely to play a role in further con-

The authors of this box are Giovanni Melina, Futoshi Narita, Andrea Presbitero, and Felipe Zanna.
[1]See the October 2015 *Regional Economic Outlook: Sub-Saharan Africa* and IMF 2015a. Also see the April 2016 *Fiscal Monitor* for discussions of other key drivers of the growth slowdown in low-income developing countries and Chapter 2 of the April 2016 *Regional Economic Outlook: Sub-Saharan Africa* for discussions of the role of exchange rate flexibility in terms-of-trade shocks for sub-Saharan African countries.

Figure 1.2.1. Low-Income Developing Countries: Real GDP Growth
(Percent; averages weighted by GDP at purchasing power parity)

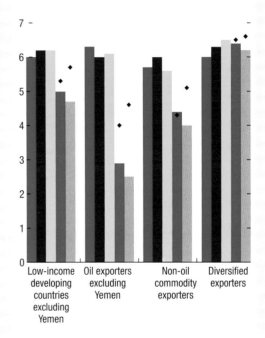

Source: IMF staff calculations.
Note: The figure excludes Yemen (where activity collapsed by 28 percent in 2015 and is projected to increase by 1 percent in 2016) as an outlier.

straining growth in oil exporters, where income losses have typically been larger.

Low-income developing countries were also affected by lower growth in their trading partners. During 2015, trading partners' growth declined more sharply for non-oil commodity-dependent low-income developing countries than for other low-income developing countries—reflecting weaker growth in emerging markets (Figure 1.2.4, panel 1). In 2016, the drag from slower growth in trading partners is expected to continue for most low-income developing countries (Figure 1.2.4, panel 2).

Tighter external financial conditions will also dampen low-income developing country growth. Since mid-

Box 1.2 *(continued)*

Figure 1.2.2. Low-Income Developing Countries: Purchasing-Power-Parity GDP Shares
(Percent of total)

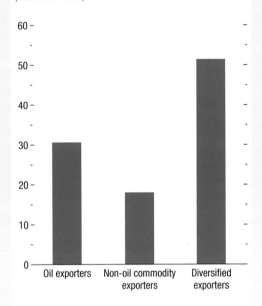

Source: IMF staff calculations.
Note: The definition of low-income developing country subgroups follows IMF 2015a, except that Cameroon and Ghana are classified only as oil exporters and excluded from diversified exporters to make the subgroups mutually exclusive.

Figure 1.2.3. Terms-of-Trade Windfall Gains and Losses
(Percent of GDP; averages weighted by GDP at purchasing power parity)

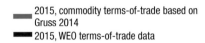

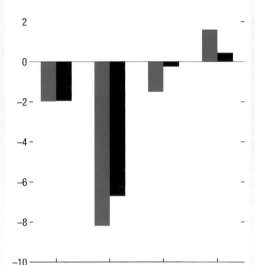

Sources: Gruss 2014; and IMF staff calculations.

2015, sovereign bond spreads in frontier low-income developing countries have increased more sharply than those in emerging markets (Figure 1.2.5). In 2015, the number of sovereign bond issuances was almost halved compared to 2014; in 2016 that number is likely to be even lower. Some of the increase in sovereign bond spreads may reflect a weaker growth outlook, but higher spreads may mean that these countries will be less able or willing to access markets. There could be some rollover risk as well, reflecting the sizable share of nonconcessional debt in public external debt in many low-income developing countries (for example, more than one-third in Côte d'Ivoire and Ghana). Historically, higher interest rates have tended to be associated with a lower ratio of public investment to GDP in low-income developing countries.

Against this backdrop, oil-exporting low-income developing countries face considerable downside risks

to their near-term growth and fiscal prospects. Model simulations reveal that unlike diversified low-income developing countries, oil exporters could, absent mitigating policies, experience growth rates lower than current baseline projections, along with rapid surges in total public debt (Figure 1.2.6, panels 1 and 2).[2] For an average oil-exporting low-income developing coun-

[2]This box uses the Debt, Investment, Growth and Natural Resources (DIGNAR) model developed by Melina, Yang, and Zanna (2016) and calibrated to capture aspects pertinent to oil-exporting and diversified low-income developing countries. The model is a neoclassical growth model that captures several of the transmission channels from lower commodity prices to growth, as well as the implications for fiscal adjustment and public debt. These include mechanisms related to resource allocation, private investment and returns, private and public saving, fiscal reaction functions, and debt accumulation. The oil price changes growth temporarily, in line with the empirical evidence. The simulations assume no tax or spending adjustments and that the only shock affecting low-income developing countries is the

Box 1.2 *(continued)*

Figure 1.2.4. Trading Partners' GDP Growth Changes
(Percentage points)

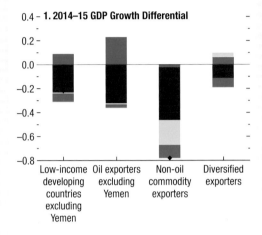

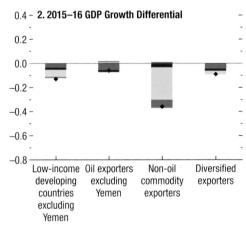

Source: IMF staff estimates.
Note: The figure excludes Yemen (where activity collapsed by 28 percent in 2015 and is projected to increase by 1 percent in 2016) as an outlier. Trading partners' growth rates are constructed as the average of real GDP growth rates of all trading partners for each low-income developing country (LIDC) weighted by LIDCs' average exports in total exports (of goods) to trading partners during 2012–14. The growth rates are then averaged across LIDC-subgroup countries using purchasing-power-parity GDP weights. AEs = advanced economies; BRICS = Brazil, Russia, India, China, South Africa; EMs = emerging markets.

Figure 1.2.5. Sovereign Bond Spreads in Low-Income Developing Countries
(Basis points)

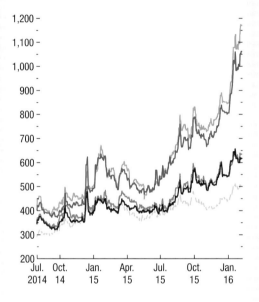

Source: Bloomberg, L.P.
Note: The sample of low-income developing countries comprises Bolivia, Ghana, Mongolia, Mozambique, Nigeria, and Zambia (oil and other commodity exporters), Côte d'Ivoire, Honduras, Kenya, Rwanda, Senegal, Tanzania, and Vietnam (diversified exporters).

try, the decline in growth—from about 3 percent in 2015 to about 2 percent in 2016—is driven mainly by the impact of lower oil revenues on output and their spillovers on aggregate demand. The increase in total public debt, from an average of 37 percent of GDP in 2015 to about 55 percent in 2017, reflects declines both in oil-related government revenues and in other non-oil tax revenues as a result of a diminished non-oil tax base. Moreover, in the simulations, the speed of debt buildup is intensified by depreciation of the real exchange rate, a higher sovereign risk premium, and

sharp fall in oil prices. On the importance of diversification to mitigate external shocks, see Callen and others 2014.

Box 1.2 *(continued)*

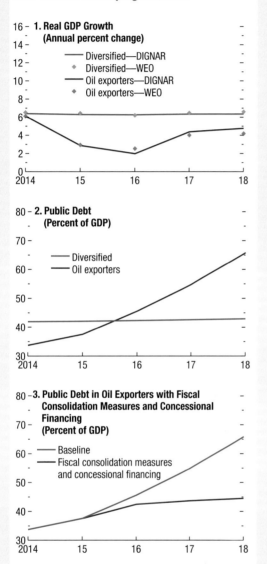

Figure 1.2.6. Simulated Effects of Lower Oil Prices on Growth and Public Debt in Low-Income Developing Countries

Sources: Simulations using the DIGNAR (Debt, Investment, Growth, and Natural Resources) model (Melina, Yang, and Zanna 2016); and IMF staff estimates.
Note: Oil exporters exclude Yemen (where activity collapsed by 28 percent in 2015 and is projected to increase by 1 percent in 2016) as an outlier.

pervasive inefficient non-oil tax revenue mobilization (IMF 2011).

Growth-friendly fiscal consolidation measures and additional concessional financing can help contain the debt buildup. Improved revenue mobilization, through better tax administration and a broader tax base, as well as measures such as prioritizing current expenditures and reducing subsidies on fuel products, could mitigate the effect of reduced oil-related government revenues on fiscal balances. That said, historical evidence suggests that achieving sizable improvements in fiscal positions over a short period is challenging. Concessional financing could help address the remaining fiscal gap and contain increases in sovereign risk premiums. This would lighten the debt interest burden, although securing such financing in an environment of low global growth could be very difficult. An illustrative scenario for a typical oil-exporting low-income developing country combines an increase in tax collection efficiency, which raises non-oil tax revenue by 2 percent of GDP; a decline in government current expenditures of 2.5 percent of GDP; and a cumulative increase in concessional financing of about 4 percent of GDP over the simulation horizon. This policy package slows the accumulation of public debt and stabilizes debt-to-GDP ratios over the medium term at below 45 percent (Figure 1.2.6, panel 3).

References

Admiraal, Annemiek, Michel den Elzen, Nicklas Forsell, Olga Turkovska, Mark Roelfsema, and Heleen van Soest. 2015. *Assessing Intended Nationally Determined Contributions to the Paris Climate Agreement—What Are the Projected Global and National Emission Levels for 2025–2030?* Bilthoven, Netherlands: PBL Netherlands Environmental Assessment Agency. http://www.pbl.nl/sites/default/files/cms/publicaties/pbl-2015-assessing-intended-nationally-determined-contributions-to-the-paris-climate-agreement_1879.pdf.

Aghion, Philippe, Antoine Dechezleprêtre, David Hemous, Ralf Martin, and John van Reenen. 2012. "Carbon Taxes, Path Dependency and Directed Technical Change: Evidence from the Auto Industry." NBER Working Paper 18596, National Bureau of Economic Research, Cambridge, Massachusetts.

Aiyar, Shekhar, Wolfgang Bergthaler, Jose M. Garrido, Anna Ilyina, Andreas Jobst, Kenneth Kang, Dmitriy Kovtun, Yan Liu, Dermot Monaghan, and Marina Moretti. 2015. "A Strategy for Resolving Europe's Problem Loans." IMF Staff Discussion Note 15/19, International Monetary Fund, Washington.

Arezki, Rabah, and Akito Matsumoto. 2015. "Q&A: Seven Questions about Climate Change." *IMF Research Bulletin* 16 (4): 1–5.

Arezki, Rabah, and Maurice Obstfeld. 2015. "The Price of Oil and the Price of Carbon." *iMFdirect*, December 2.

Arezki, Rabah, Frederik Toscani, and Frederick van der Ploeg. Forthcoming. "Shifting Frontiers of Global Resource Extraction: The Role of Institutions." IMF Working Paper, International Monetary Fund, Washington.

Benes, Jaromir, Marcelle Chauvet, Ondra Kamenik, Michael Kumhof, Douglas Laxton, Susanna Mursula, and Jack Selody. 2015. "The Future of Oil: Geology versus Technology." *International Journal of Forecasting* 31 (1): 207–21.

Boz, Emine, and Eugenio Cerutti. 2016. "Global Trade Slowdown: A Cross-Country Analysis." Unpublished.

Burgherr, Peter, and Stefan Hirschberg. 2014. Comparative Risk Assessment of Severe Accidents in the Energy Sector. Energy Policy 74 (Suppl. 1): S45–S56.

Busse, Meghan, Christopher Knittel, and Florian Zettelmeyer. 2013. "Are Consumers Myopic? Evidence from New and Used Car Purchases." *American Economic Review* 103 (1): 220–56.

California ISO. 2013. "Fast Facts: What the Duck Curve Tells Us about Managing a Green Grid." http://www.caiso.com/Documents/FlexibleResourcesHelpRenewables_FastFacts.pdf.

Callen, Tim, Reda Cherif, Fuad Hasanov, Amgad Hegazy, and Padamja Khandelwal. 2014. "Economic Diversification in the GCC: Past, Present, and Future." IMF Staff Discussion Note 14/12, International Monetary Fund, Washington.

Chakravorty, Ujjayant, Carolyn Fischer, and Marie-Hélène Hubert. 2015. "Will Shale Gas Reduce Carbon Emissions from China?" Unpublished, Resources for the Future, Washington.

Chakravorty, Ujjayant, Marie-Hélène Hubert, Michel Moreaux, and Linda Nøstbakken. 2015. "The Long-Run Impact of Biofuels on Food Prices." RFF Discussion Paper 15-48, Resources for the Future, Washington.

Collier, Paul, and Anthony J. Venables. 2012. "Greening Africa? Technologies, Endowments and the Latecomer Effect." *Energy Economics* 34 (Suppl. 1): S75–S84.

D'Autume, Antoine, Katheline Schubert, and Cees Withagen. 2011. "Should the Carbon Price Be the Same in All Countries?" Documents de travail du Centre d'Economie de la Sorbonne 11076, Université Panthéon–Sorbonne (Paris 1), Paris.

Fabrizio, Stefania, Rodrigo Garcia-Verdu, Catherine A. Pattillo, Adrian Peralta-Alva, Andrea Presbitero, Baoping Shang, Geneviève Verdier, Marie-Thérèse Camilleri, Kazuaki Washimi, Lisa Kolovich, Monique Newiak, Martin Cihak, Inci Otker-Robe, Luis-Felipe Zanna, and Carol L. Baker. 2015. "Policies in Support of Selected Sustainable Development Goals." IMF Staff Discussion Note 15/18, International Monetary Fund, Washington.

Farid, Mai, Michael Keen, Michael Papaioannou, Ian Parry, Catherine Pattillo, Anna Ter-Martirosyan, and IMF staff. 2016. "Fiscal, Macroeconomic and Financial Aspects of Global Warming." IMF Staff Discussion Note 16/01, International Monetary Fund, Washington.

Golosov, Mikhail, John Hassler, Per Krusell, and Aleh Tsyvinski. 2014. "Optimal Taxes on Fossil Fuel in General Equilibrium." *Econometrica* 82 (1): 41–88.

Gruss, Bertrand. 2014. "After the Boom—Commodity Prices and Economic Growth in Latin America and the Caribbean." IMF Working Paper 14/154, International Monetary Fund, Washington.

Hoekman, Bernard, editor. 2015. *The Global Trade Slowdown: A New Normal?* Washington: Center for Economic and Policy Research Press. http://www.voxeu.org/sites/default/files/file/Global%20Trade%20Slowdown_nocover.pdf.

International Energy Agency (IEA). 2015. *World Energy Outlook 2015.* Vienna.

International Monetary Fund (IMF). 2011. "Revenue Mobilization in Developing Countries." International Monetary Fund, Washington.

———. 2015a. "Macroeconomic Developments and Prospects in Low-Income Developing Countries: 2015." IMF Policy Paper, International Monetary Fund, Washington.

———. 2015b. "The Managing Director's Statement on the Role of the Fund in Addressing Climate Change." Washington. https://www.imf.org/external/np/pp/eng/2015/112515.pdf.

Li, Xin, Borghan Narajabad, and Ted Temzelides. 2014. "Robust Dynamic Optimal Taxation and Environmental Externalities." Finance and Economics Discussion Series 2014-75, Federal Reserve Board, Washington.

Meehl, Gerald A., Thomas F. Stocker, William D. Collins, Pierre Friedlingstein, Amadou T. Gaye, Jonathan M. Gregory, Akio Kitoh, Reto Knutti, James M. Murphy, Akira Noda, Sarah C. B. Raper, Ian G. Watterson, Andrew J. Weaver, and Zong-Ci Zhao. 2007. "Global Climate Projections." In *Climate Change 2007: The Physical Science Basis.* Contribution of Working Group I to the Fourth Assessment Report of the Intergovernmental Panel on Climate Change, edited by S. Solomon, D. Qin, M. Manning, Z. Chen, M. Marquis, K. B. Averyt, M. Tignor and H. L. Miller, 747–846. New York: Cambridge University Press.

Melina, Giovanni, Shu-Chun Yang, and Luis-Felipe Zanna. 2016. "Debt Sustainability, Public Investment and Natural Resources in Developing Countries: The DIGNAR Model." *Economic Modelling* 52 (Part B): 630–49.

Rezai, Armon, and Frederick van der Ploeg. 2014. "Intergenerational Inequality Aversion, Growth, and the Role of Damages: Occam's Rule for the Global Carbon Tax."

Discussion Paper 10292, Centre for Economic and Policy Research, London.

Steckel, Jan Christoph, Ottmar Edenhofer, and Michael Jakob. 2015. "Drivers for the Renaissance of Coal." *Proceedings of the National Academy of Sciences of the United States of America* 112 (29): E3775–81.

Stefanski, Radoslaw. 2014. "Structural Transformation and the Oil Price." *Review of Economic Dynamics* 17 (3): 484–504.

Stern, Nicholas. 2015. *Why Are We Waiting? The Logic, Urgency, and Promise of Tackling Climate Change.* Lionel Robbins Lectures. Cambridge, Massachusetts: MIT Press.

CHAPTER 2

UNDERSTANDING THE SLOWDOWN IN CAPITAL FLOWS TO EMERGING MARKETS

Net capital flows to emerging market economies have slowed since 2010, affecting all regions. This chapter shows that both weaker inflows and stronger outflows have contributed to the slowdown and that much of the decline in inflows can be explained by the narrowing differential in growth prospects between emerging market and advanced economies. The chapter also highlights that the incidence of external debt crises in the ongoing episode has so far been much lower, although the slowdown in net capital inflows has been comparable in breadth and size to the major slowdowns of the 1980s and 1990s. Improved policy frameworks have contributed greatly to this difference. Crucially, more flexible exchange rate regimes have facilitated orderly currency depreciations that have mitigated the effects of the global capital flow cycle on many emerging market economies. Higher levels of foreign asset holdings by emerging market economies, in particular higher levels of foreign reserves, as well as lower shares of external liabilities denominated in foreign currency (that is, less of the so-called original sin) have also been instrumental.

After a peak in 2010, net nonreserve capital inflows into emerging market economies have slowed considerably over the course of the past several years (Figure 2.1).[1] The slowdown in capital flows has occurred against a backdrop of a protracted growth slowdown in emerging market economies and, more recently, the first steps toward a tightening of monetary policy in the United States.

A historical perspective offers cause for concern. Capital inflow slowdowns after sustained expansions have been associated with costly economic crises and linked to turning points in monetary policy in advanced economies (Calvo, Leiderman, and Reinhart 1996; Kaminsky and Reinhart 1999). Moreover, two factors—emerging market economies' increased inte-

The authors of this chapter are Rudolfs Bems (lead author), Luis Catão (lead author), Zsóka Kóczán, Weicheng Lian, and Marcos Poplawski-Ribeiro, with support from Hao Jiang, Yun Liu, and Hong Yang.

[1]Throughout the chapter *net capital inflows* denotes net capital inflows, excluding reserve assets.

gration into global financial markets and higher share in global output—imply that a capital flow downturn that disrupts these economies' investment and growth prospects can also have more powerful international spillovers than in the past.[2]

Against this backdrop, this chapter examines the following questions:

- What are the main characteristics of the recent slowdown in capital flows to emerging markets? Has it been broad based across regions and types of flows? How have exchange rates and the cost of capital evolved?

- How does the recent slowdown compare with past slowdowns in capital flows? Has the composition of flows changed?

- What is driving the recent slowdown? Can changes in emerging market growth prospects, monetary policy in advanced economies, global risk appetite, or decreasing commodity prices explain most or all of the decline?

- Have policy-controlled variables, such as exchange rate flexibility, the level of reserves, and the level of debt, played a significant role? In particular, is there evidence that exchange rate flexibility has provided some insulation from the global capital flow cycle?[3]

---

[2]In 1980 emerging market economies accounted for 21 percent of world GDP and 27 percent of world trade, both measured in current dollars. By 2014, these shares had risen to 36 percent and 44 percent, respectively.

[3]A well-known theory attributed to Mundell (1963) postulates the existence of a "trilemma" in monetary policy, according to which a country, once it decides to have an open capital account, can independently pursue countercyclical monetary policies only if its exchange rate is flexible. Rey (forthcoming) argues that the insulation power of flexible exchange rates turns out to be very limited in practice and that only capital controls can provide effective insulation from the global financial cycle. As such, policymakers in financially open economies effectively face a dilemma between higher capital controls (which, in principle, lower the benefits of international financial integration) and lower or no capital controls (which then make economies more vulnerable to the global capital flow cycle). Obstfeld (2015) provides evidence, however, that exchange rate flexibility is still instrumental in decoupling short-term interest rates in emerging markets from interest rate changes in global financial centers (notably the United States), thus helping provide some insulation from the global financial cycle.

Figure 2.1. Net Capital Inflows to Emerging Market Economies and Number of Debt Crises, 1980–2015:Q3
(Percent of GDP, unless noted otherwise)

Net capital inflows in emerging markets over the past four decades have exhibited cycles. A slowdown phase of one such cycle has been taking place since 2010. Past net capital inflow slowdowns have been associated with external debt crises.

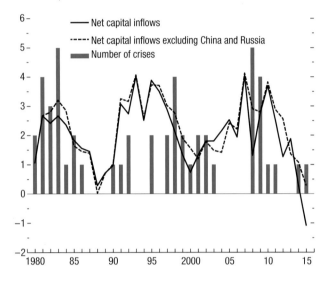

Sources: Catão and Milesi-Ferretti 2014; CEIC Asia database; CEIC China database; Haver Analytics; IMF, *Balance of Payments Statistics*; IMF, *International Financial Statistics*; World Bank, World Development Indicators database; and IMF staff calculations.
Note: Calculations are based on a sample of 45 emerging market economies. The observation for 2015 refers to the first three quarters of 2015. Data on the number of crises refer to the external crisis variable in Catão and Milesi-Ferretti 2014, updated to the third quarter of 2015. See Annex 2.1 for the complete list of sample countries and external crisis episodes.

The analysis employs a variety of approaches, including accounting decompositions, event analyses, and panel regression methodologies. The models extend the set of possible explanatory variables and data coverage to capture regularities that may be more specific to the recent slowdown.

The chapter's main findings regarding the 2010–15 slowdown in net capital inflows are as follows:

- The slowdown affected three-quarters of the 45 sampled emerging market economies with available data. Both lower inflows and higher outflows contributed to the slowdown in net inflows. Countries that had relatively flexible exchange rate regimes in 2010 experienced large currency depreciations over the period.
- The current slowdown is similar in size and breadth to episodes in the 1980s and 1990s, but the contexts then and now are marked by several key differences:

  ○ Emerging market economies in the current episode have larger holdings of external liabilities and assets, including foreign reserve assets.
  ○ Capital outflows have become increasingly important for the dynamics of net capital inflows.
  ○ Exchange rates are now more flexible, and domestic prices seem better anchored, perhaps partly because of the widespread use of inflation-targeting regimes.

- Diminished prospects for growth in emerging markets relative to advanced economies can explain most of the slowdown in total capital flows to emerging markets since 2010, while national policies affect the cross-country distribution of those flows.
- In particular, flexible exchange rates appear to have helped some emerging markets mitigate the slowdown in capital flows so far by dampening the effects of global factors, as well as the effects of these economies' own slowing growth prospects.
- Swings in capital flows are also smaller in emerging markets with lower public debt, tighter capital controls, and higher foreign exchange reserves.

These findings have significant implications for both outlook and policy. On the positive side, they (1) corroborate that policy frameworks in emerging market economies have improved and (2) highlight these economies' reduced vulnerability due to a combination of much higher central bank reserves and lessened balance sheet exposure to currency risk (that is, less of the so-called original sin).

On the negative side, they point to two additional sources of risk. One is the narrowed growth differentials relative to advanced economies; the other is the dynamics of gross outflows. The narrowed growth differentials, which appear to be connected to much weaker gross capital inflows, may not be reversed anytime soon. Their persistence reinforces the need for prudent fiscal policies (as a diminished supply of external funds raises the cost of borrowing and servicing public debt), currency flexibility, and active reserve management policy as appropriate.

The second risk is more speculative and novel: in recent years, more sizable gross outflows contributed to the slowdown in net inflows, rather than mitigating it. This is because, in contrast to previous episodes, which featured a tight positive comovement between gross capital inflows and gross capital outflows (Broner and others 2013), such comovement has been much looser this time, including some negative comovement between gross inflows and gross outflows in some countries and during some quarters. Whether this is a long-lasting feature of the dynamics of gross capital flows remains to be seen, but the analysis draws attention to the possibility.

The chapter begins by analyzing capital flow developments, including on the price side, in the context of developments since 2000. Next, it compares the recent slowdown with two similar episodes, one in the early 1980s and the second in the late 1990s, highlighting differences in the structure of external portfolios and exchange rate behavior. It then uses econometric tools to analyze the drivers of the recent slowdown. The chapter's conclusion summarizes the main findings.

Anatomy of the Slowdown in Net Capital Inflows

This section presents detailed statistics on the evolution of net capital inflows and their components for emerging market economies. The presentation focuses on capital flow dynamics in the aftermath of the global financial crisis and puts the findings in the context of the net capital inflow cycles prior to the crisis.[4] The section also looks at the cost of financing, as captured by exchange rates and sovereign yields, which evolve in tandem with capital flows.

Preliminaries

Detailed data sources, as well as the emerging market economy sample and variable definitions as used in this chapter, are presented in Annex 2.1. The country sample consists of 45 emerging market economies. To utilize the most recent balance of payments capital flow data, while at the same time avoiding the large seasonal fluctuations in the quarterly data, this section's findings are based on annual data, combined with data for the first three quarters of 2015.

Definitions of key variables used in this chapter are as follows: *capital inflows* are defined as net acquisition of domestic assets by nonresidents; *capital outflows* are defined as net acquisition of foreign assets by residents, excluding reserve assets; and *net capital inflows* are defined as the difference between capital inflows and

outflows. Net capital inflows and changes in reserve assets together constitute the *financial account balance*, as defined in the IMF's *Balance of Payments Manual*.

Capital Flows

Net capital inflows to emerging market economies have shown a sizable decline since 2010 (Figure 2.2). A decline of comparable magnitude is present in all quartiles of the 45-country sample, as well as for the weighted mean of capital inflows.[5] The behavior of the weighted mean is similar regardless of whether it includes China and Russia, but with those two countries included, the measure declines more sharply in 2014–15.[6]

The overall size of the 2010–15 slowdown, measured as the change in net capital inflows between 2010 and the year ending in the third quarter of 2015 (that is, from the fourth quarter of 2014 through the third quarter of 2015), was $1.123 trillion for the full sample of 45 emerging market economies and $448 billion when China and Russia are excluded. Expressed relative to economic activity, the aggregate decline in net capital inflows was 4.9 percent of the sample's GDP—reflecting that the weighted mean of net capital inflows swung from an inflow of 3.7 percent of GDP in 2010 to an outflow of 1.2 percent during the most recent four quarters (the fourth quarter of 2014 through the third quarter of 2015). The slowdown occurred in three-quarters of the 45 emerging market economies.[7] Net inflows in the third quarter of 2015 were particularly weak, and preliminary data suggest that the weakness continued in the fourth quarter.

To document the role of key capital flow components in the 2010–15 slowdown, the analysis next decomposes net capital inflows by direction of flow, type of flow, and recipient region. Starting with the direction of flow, the results show that, over the entire 2010–15 period, the slowdown is explained

---

[4]Comparable statistics for the evolution of capital flows in low-income developing countries are discussed in Box 2.1. Results for low-income developing countries reveal notably different capital flow dynamics, with increasing net capital inflows until 2013 and a sharp reversal thereafter.

[5]The *weighted mean of capital flows* is defined throughout the chapter as the GDP-weighted mean of the capital-flow-to-GDP ratio, which is equivalent to the sum of capital inflows divided by the sum of GDP for the countries in the sample.

[6]China is singled out because of its large size relative to other sample countries, Russia because of the sanctions imposed since 2014.

[7]The chapter's sample of 45 countries leaves out several large fuel exporters, such as Algeria, Angola, Kuwait, Nigeria, and Qatar, whose capital flow data do not cover the entire 2000–15 period, but are available more recently. In contrast to most of the countries in the main sample, these fuel exporters exhibited net capital outflows during 2011–15, although, with lower oil prices and trade balances, such net outflows diminished over time.

Figure 2.2. Net Capital Inflows to Emerging Market Economies, 2000–15:Q3
(Percent of GDP)

Net capital inflows to emerging market economies have shown a persistent and sizable decline since 2010.

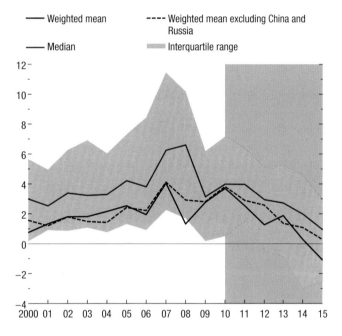

Sources: CEIC Asia database; CEIC China database; Haver Analytics; IMF, *Balance of Payments Statistics*; IMF, *International Financial Statistics*; World Bank, World Development Indicators database; and IMF staff calculations.
Note: Balanced sample of 45 emerging market economies. See Annex 2.1 for the complete list of sample countries. The observation for 2015 refers to the first three quarters.

Figure 2.3. Capital Inflows and Outflows for Emerging Market Economies, 2000–15:Q3
(Percent of GDP)

A fall in gross capital inflows explains the net capital inflow slowdown over the entire 2010–15 period. At the same time, a rise in gross capital outflows was the main contributor to the slowdown during 2012–14.

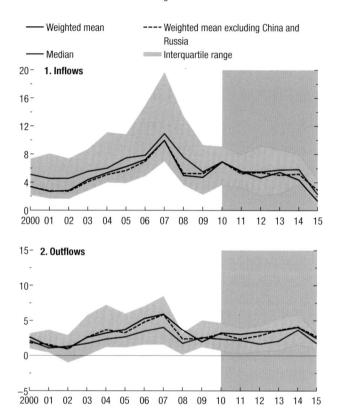

Sources: CEIC Asia database; CEIC China database; Haver Analytics; IMF, *Balance of Payments Statistics*; IMF, *International Financial Statistics*; World Bank, World Development Indicators database; and IMF staff calculations.
Note: Balanced sample of 45 emerging market economies. See Annex 2.1 for the complete list of sample countries. The observation for 2015 refers to the first three quarters.

by a fall in inflows (Figure 2.3). At the same time, the decomposition reveals that, behind the sustained decline in net capital inflows, the contributions from inflows and from outflows vary sizably over time. A rise in outflows was the main driver of the slowdown during 2012–14, whereas a decline in inflows was the chief contributor in 2011 and even more so in the first three quarters of 2015. During the latter episode, capital outflows fell as well, mitigating the slowdown in net inflows. Hence, a focus on the flows in only one direction will bias the dating of the slowdown. For example, if only gross inflows are considered, an uninterrupted slowdown starts in 2014 and accelerates in 2015.

The 2010–15 slowdown reflects some combination of a decline in inflows and a rise in outflows for all four asset types shown in the balance of payments data: foreign direct investment (FDI), portfolio equity, portfolio debt, and "other investments" (including

bank flows), although the rise in outflows was reversed in 2015. The decline in inflows, which appears in both the weighted-mean and median measures (Figure 2.4, panels 1–4), is somewhat more pronounced for debt-generating inflows than for equity-like[8] inflows (including FDI).[9]

---

[8] *Equity-like inflows* are defined as FDI and portfolio equity inflows.
[9] Several recent papers focus on the composition of gross capital flows. Cerutti, Claessens, and Puy (2015) find significant heterogeneity in gross inflows across asset types, with bank-related and portfolio flows comoving more strongly across countries than other types of flows. These authors also find that the role of global push factors varies by the type of flow. Blanchard and others (forthcoming) differ-

Figure 2.4 also highlights distinct time profiles for the four asset types. FDI and "other investment"—the two largest gross inflow components—exhibit marked declines relative to the peaks attained before the global financial crisis, with the decline for "other investment" being driven by the retrenchment of global banks following the crisis. In contrast, portfolio debt inflows increased considerably compared with the trough of the crisis, peaking in 2010–12 and declining thereafter.[10] Last, as revealed by the median in panel 2 of Figure 2.4, portfolio equity inflows remained negligible throughout the 2000–15 period for the majority of the sample. This comparison of inflows by type highlights an important point: that the surge in portfolio inflows after the global financial crisis was not matched by a surge in aggregate gross inflows, which remained below the peak reached in 2007 (Figure 2.3, panel 1).

As in the case of inflows, all asset types contribute to the increase in capital outflows during 2010–14, but with more pronounced contributions for debt-generating flows than for equity-like flows (Figure 2.4, panels 5–8). During 2015, outflows for all asset types contracted. Similar to inflows, FDI and "other investment" were the largest components of outflows. The surge in portfolio debt inflows following the global financial crisis was not coupled with a similar pickup in portfolio debt outflows (panels 3 and 7).

The slowdown in net capital inflows has been broad based across regions (Figure 2.5). Further results (not shown here to save space) also reveal that both commodity exporters and non–commodity exporters exhibited a similar slowdown.

Yet there have been significant interregional differences in the slowdown. It has been more pronounced and persistent in eastern Europe, while in Latin America and "other emerging markets" it was concentrated in 2014–15 (Figure 2.5, panels 1, 3, and 4). These differences reflect both the composition of capital flows (notably the sharper decline in bank-based flows in eastern Europe following large inflows before the global financial crisis) and, as documented later in the chapter, greater exchange rate flexibility in Latin America, which appears to have mitigated the slowdown. One can also note sizable differences in the average

---

entiate between bond and nonbond capital inflows and find the two types of flows to have a different impact on the economy.

[10]The surge and heightened volatility in emerging markets' portfolio inflows during 2009–13 and their possible implications have been studied in detail by Sahay and others (2014) as well as in Chapter 3 of the October 2015 *Global Financial Stability Report*.

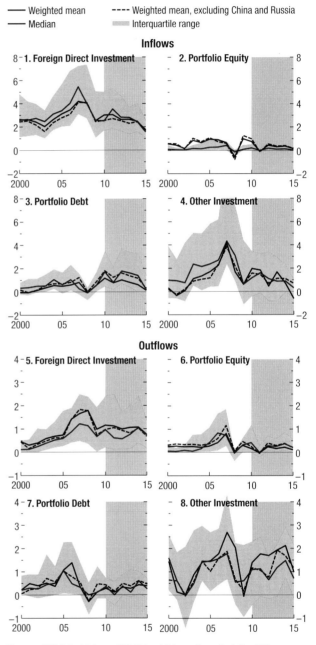

Figure 2.4. Capital Inflows and Outflows for Emerging Market Economies by Asset Type, 2000–15:Q3
(Percent of GDP)

There was a broad-based decrease in gross capital inflows across asset types during the 2010–15 slowdown. At the same time, gross outflows across all asset types increased, except for the sharp reversal in 2015. Changes in gross capital inflows and outflows were more pronounced for debt-generating flows than for equity-like flows.

Sources: CEIC Asia database; CEIC China database; Haver Analytics; IMF, *Balance of Payments Statistics*; IMF, *International Financial Statistics*; World Bank, World Development Indicators database; and IMF staff calculations.
Note: Balanced sample of 45 emerging market economies. See Annex 2.1 for the complete list of sample countries. The observation for 2015 refers to the first three quarters.

Figure 2.5. Net Capital Inflows by Region, 2000–15:Q3
(Percent of GDP)

The 2010–15 slowdown in net capital inflows was broad based across regions.

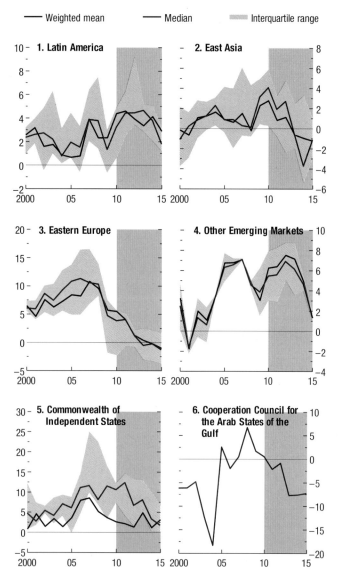

Sources: CEIC Asia database; CEIC China database; Haver Analytics; IMF, *Balance of Payments Statistics*; IMF, *International Financial Statistics*; World Bank, World Development Indicators database; and IMF staff calculations.
Note: Balanced sample of 45 emerging market economies. See Annex 2.1 for the complete list of sample countries. The observation for 2015 refers to the first three quarters.

level of net capital inflows by region. In net terms, capital has been flowing out of east Asia,[11] member states of the Cooperation Council for the Arab States

of the Gulf,[12] and eastern Europe (Figure 2.5, panels 2, 3, and 6). Meanwhile, Latin America, the Commonwealth of Independent States, and "other emerging markets" have continued to receive inflows (Figure 2.5, panels 1, 4, and 5).

The discussion of capital flows so far has excluded the change in foreign reserve assets, which in this chapter is treated as a separate component of the financial account. The behavior of foreign reserve assets in emerging markets shows a striking similarity to the 2010–15 slowdown in net capital inflows (Figure 2.6). After peaking in 2007, the pace of accumulation of foreign reserve assets gradually slowed, and in the first three quarters of 2015, reserves in the median emerging market economy were reduced by 0.03 percent of GDP.[13] To the extent that the 2010–15 slowdown in net capital inflows was matched by a deceleration in the pace at which reserve assets were built up, the adjustment to the slowdown took place within the balance of payments financial account and, hence, did not require an accompanying adjustment in the current account. This observation is explored in more detail in a later section.

How robust is the preceding interpretation of recent capital flow developments in emerging markets? Several tests suggest the findings are not sensitive to a range of potential measurement issues. First, results pertaining to the 2010–15 slowdown remain broadly unchanged if constant exchange rates are used. In some emerging markets, exchange rates have depreciated sizably against the dollar. The depreciation has driven down the value of emerging market economies' GDPs measured in dollar terms and could, therefore, have increased the measured capital-flow-to-GDP ratio. The calculations show that using current exchange rates generates an upward bias in the ratio of capital flows to GDP but has a limited quantitative impact on this chapter's capital flow statistics.

Second, the documented findings are robust to using alternative samples. The results in Figures 2.2–2.6 remain broadly similar if the full sample (which includes 45 countries) is replaced with a subset consisting of the 20 largest emerging market economies. The findings in Figure 2.4 are not sensitive to the balanced-sample

---

[11]Throughout the chapter, *east Asia* is used to denote a region that includes both east and south Asian economies. See Annex 2.1 for details.

[12]Among the member states of the Cooperation Council for the Arab States of the Gulf, full 2000–15 sample coverage is available only for Saudi Arabia.

[13]The pattern of a decline in net reserve asset accumulation is considerably more pronounced when Russia and, especially, China are included in the sample; both countries witnessed a reduction in their reserves in the first half of 2015.

Figure 2.6. Net Reserve Assets of Emerging Market Economies, 2000–15:Q3
(Percent of GDP)

The pace of reserve accumulation decreased in tandem with the slowdown in net capital inflows.

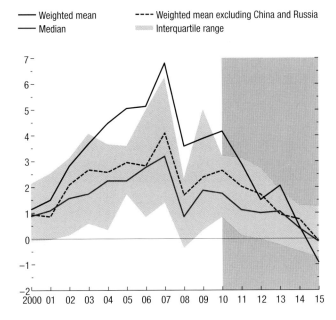

Sources: CEIC Asia database; CEIC China database; Haver Analytics; IMF, *Balance of Payments Statistics*; IMF, *International Financial Statistics*; World Bank, World Development Indicators database; and IMF staff calculations.
Note: Balanced sample of 45 emerging market economies. See Annex 2.1 for the complete list of sample countries. The observation for 2015 refers to the first three quarters.

Figure 2.7. Exchange Rates of Emerging Market Economies, 2010–15:Q3
(Percent change)

Exchange rates of emerging market economies depreciated against the dollar in recent years. The depreciation was particularly pronounced in 2015.

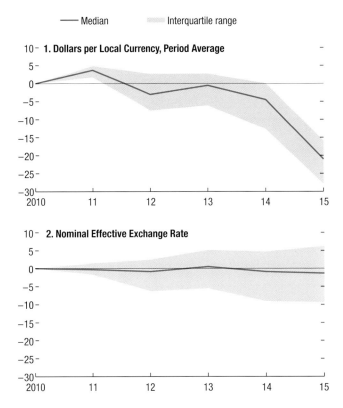

Sources: IMF, Information Notice System; IMF, International Financial Statistics database; and IMF staff calculations.
Note: Balanced sample of 40 emerging market economies. See Annex 2.1 for the complete list of sample countries. Economic and Monetary Union members—Estonia, Latvia, Lithuania, the Slovak Republic, and Slovenia—are excluded from the sample.

assumption and remain broadly unchanged if unbalanced data are used instead. Also, the results are robust to the exclusion of China and Russia from the full sample. The latter finding can be seen in Figures 2.2–2.5 by comparing the weighted mean for the full sample of 45 countries with the weighted mean that excludes China and Russia. While China is a dominant emerging market in terms of the size of both its GDP and its capital flows, its capital flows as a share of its GDP are broadly in line with those of other emerging markets. However, China's international reserves are well above the average for other emerging markets, both in level terms and in terms of the average pace of accumulation over 2000–15 as well.

Exchange Rates and the Cost of Capital

The exchange rates of emerging market economies, taken as a group, depreciated notably, particularly with

respect to the dollar, during the 2010–15 slowdown, with the bulk of the adjustment taking place in 2014–15 (Figure 2.7, panel 1). The currency depreciations were considerably less pronounced in effective terms (Figure 2.7, panel 2), as most currencies depreciated against the dollar over the same period.[14]

However, there was considerable cross-country heterogeneity in exchange rate behavior over the period (Figure 2.8). The exchange rates of several large emerging market economies, including Brazil, South Africa, and Turkey, depreciated by about 40 percent in nomi-

[14]For a discussion of the dollar cycle see the IMF's *2015 Spillover Report* (IMF 2015b).

Figure 2.8. Net Capital Inflow Slowdown and Exchange Rate Changes, 2010–15:Q3

Currency depreciation and the decline in net capital inflows exhibit no systematic association. Yet among the largest emerging markets, such as Brazil, China, and India, the association appears to be negative.

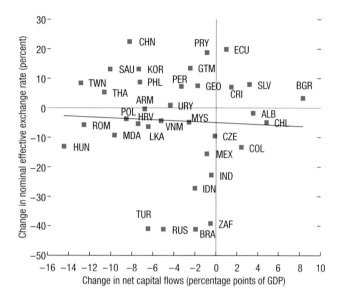

Sources: CEIC Asia database; CEIC China database; Haver Analytics; IMF, *Balance of Payments Statistics*; IMF, *International Financial Statistics*; IMF, Information Notice System; World Bank, World Development Indicators database; and IMF staff calculations.
Note: Changes in nominal effective exchange rate and in net capital inflows are defined as the difference between 2010 and the first three quarters of 2015. Economic and Monetary Union members—Estonia, Latvia, Lithuania, the Slovak Republic, and Slovenia—are excluded from the sample. Argentina, Belarus, Kazakhstan, and Ukraine are excluded as outliers. Data labels in the figure use International Organization for Standardization (ISO) country codes.

nal effective terms during 2010–15. At the same time, nominal effective exchange rates appreciated in more than two-fifths of the emerging market economies in the sample, including in China, Korea, the Philippines, and Thailand.

For the cross section of the sample's emerging market economies there is no systematic correlation (–0.04) between the slowdown in net capital inflows and changes in nominal effective exchange rates. However, countries with the largest depreciations (20 percent or more) on average saw a smaller slowdown (2.3 percent of GDP) than did the rest of the sample (4.5 percent of GDP).[15] At the same time, several key emerging market economies with large nominal

[15]The group of countries with the largest depreciations includes Brazil, India, Indonesia, South Africa, and Turkey but excludes Russia, given that Russia's capital flows were affected by an idiosyncratic factor (international sanctions).

effective exchange rate appreciations had above-average slowdowns. China is the leading case among such economies, with the sample's largest exchange rate appreciation in nominal effective terms (22.5 percent) and an above-average fall in net capital inflows (8.2 percent of GDP). This evidence suggests that flexible exchange rates might have mitigated the slowdown in net capital inflows.

The overall cost of borrowing in emerging market economies is well below levels observed prior to the global financial crisis. The main contributor to the historically low level of borrowing costs is the declining trend in bond yields in advanced economies over the past two decades. For example, 10-year U.S. Treasury bond yields decreased from 640 basis points to 200 basis points between 2000 and 2015. Over the same period, emerging market sovereign spreads—as captured by the J.P. Morgan Emerging Market Bond Index—decreased for the median country by 170 basis points (Figure 2.9, panel 1).

However, sovereign spreads have increased in recent quarters. The fall in net capital flows during the 2010–15 slowdown was associated with rising sovereign spreads in emerging market economies (Figure 2.9, panel 2). At the same time, countries with larger depreciations in nominal effective exchange rates faced higher spreads (Figure 2.9, panel 3).

Historical Comparisons: What Is Different This Time?

To put the 2010–15 slowdown in historical perspective, this section compares it with two similar past episodes (in the early 1980s and late 1990s) and examines shifts in the structural characteristics and policies of emerging market economies in the intervening years.

The three major capital flow slowdown episodes, as measured from the peak to the bottom of the ratio of total net capital inflows to GDP, are 1981–88, 1995–2000, and 2010 through the third quarter of 2015 (Figure 2.10).[16] The first of these episodes covers the

[16]A strand of research starting in the 1990s focuses on unexpected and abrupt reversals in net capital flows—the so-called sudden stops (see Dornbusch and others 1994 and Calvo 1998). Subsequently assembled historical evidence shows that boom-bust cycles in cross-border capital flows are not new: capital flows displayed long-lasting swings of up to several percentage points of GDP in the first globalization period, which started in the late nineteenth century and ended with the Great Depression of the 1930s (see Catão 2007; Bordo and Haubrich 2010; Reinhart and Rogoff 2011; and Accominotti and Eichengreen, forthcoming).

Figure 2.9. Cost of Financing, Sovereign Spreads, and Capital Flows in Emerging Market Economies

The cost of financing, defined as the sum of the 10-year U.S. Treasury bond yield and EMBI spreads, remains well below historical peaks, but has increased in recent quarters. Recent increases in sovereign spreads are positively associated with (1) net capital inflow slowdowns and (2) exchange rate depreciations.

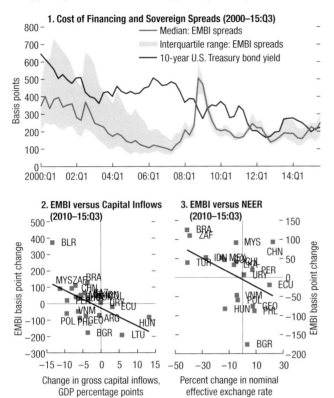

Sources: Bloomberg L.P.; CEIC Asia database; CEIC China database; Haver Analytics; IMF, *Balance of Payments Statistics*; IMF, *International Financial Statistics*; World Bank, World Development Indicators database; and IMF staff calculations.
Note: See Annex 2.1 for the complete list of sample countries included in each panel. EMBI = J.P. Morgan Emerging Market Bond Index; NEER = nominal effective exchange rate. Data labels in the figure use International Organization for Standardization (ISO) country codes.

Figure 2.10. Three Major Net Capital Inflow Slowdown Episodes
(Percent of GDP)

The recent net capital inflow slowdown episode was similar to previous episodes in terms of the magnitude and breadth of the slowdown.

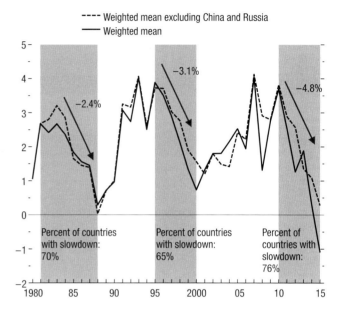

Sources: CEIC Asia database; CEIC China database; Haver Analytics; IMF, *Balance of Payments Statistics*; IMF, *International Financial Statistics*; World Bank, World Development Indicators database; and IMF staff calculations.
Note: Calculations are based on a sample of 45 emerging market economies. The observation for 2015 refers to the first three quarters. See Annex 2.1 for the complete list of sample countries.

developing country debt crisis of the 1980s, while the second one overlaps with the Asian crisis of 1997–98 and other major emerging market crises. All three episodes were preceded by a prolonged surge in capital inflows, and all three are similar both in the aggregate size of the slowdown (ranging from 2.4 percent to 4.8 percent) and in the fraction of the economies with declining ratios of net capital inflows to GDP (65 percent to 76 percent).[17]

[17]In terms of the aggregate size of the slowdown, the 2010–15 episode is more comparable with earlier episodes when China is excluded from the sample, decreasing the size of the slowdown from –4.8 percent to –3.3 percent of GDP.

Changing Structure of External Portfolios

Capital flows to and from emerging market economies affect those economies' external portfolios, and the external portfolio structures, in turn, affect capital flows. After each of the previous two slowdowns, emerging market economies saw a surge in cross-border capital flows; as a result, over time they accumulated external assets and liabilities and became increasingly integrated into global financial markets. This has meant more asset trade with other countries, especially with advanced economies, but potentially also more cross-border spillovers.[18]

Between 1980 and 2014, external equity liabilities of emerging market economies surged, from below 10

[18]The IMF's Coordinated Portfolio Investment Survey shows that advanced economies are the main source of, and destination for, the increased capital flows involving emerging market economies. Flows among emerging market economies have also increased, but from a low base.

Figure 2.11. External Balance Sheets of Emerging Market Economies, 1980–2014
(Percent of GDP)

Emerging market economies are increasingly integrated into global financial markets. The increase in the external liabilities of these economies has been mostly driven by equity liabilities, while on the external asset side, both equity and debt assets have contributed. Growth in reserve assets has broadly kept pace with nonreserve assets and has been particularly pronounced in east Asia.

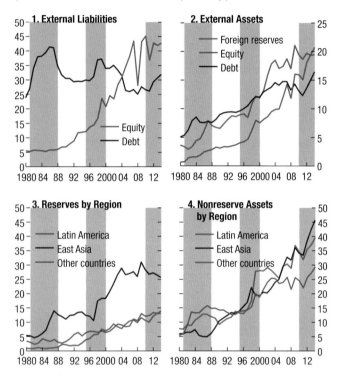

Sources: External Wealth of Nations Mark II database; and IMF staff calculations.
Note: Balanced sample of 22 countries from the full sample of 45 emerging market economies. See Annex 2.1 for the complete list of sample countries. All variables are GDP weighted.

percent of GDP to more than 40 percent of GDP,[19] while external debt liabilities remained broadly trendless (Figure 2.11, panel 1).[20] On the external asset side, both equity and debt assets as a share of GDP rose over the period, from about 5 percent to almost 40 percent in 2014.[21]

[19]This finding is documented by Lane and Milesi-Ferretti (2007).
[20]Within debt liabilities, the share of portfolio debt in external debt liabilities rose from about 30 percent in 2008 to more than 40 percent in 2014. In the aggregate, the increase in portfolio debt is largely offset by a decline in banks' debt liabilities, reflecting the postcrisis deleveraging of global banks.
[21]Avdjiev, Chui, and Shin (2014) show that the split of assets into equity and debt is not clear-cut, as much of FDI is actually not equity, but intrafirm debt.

In the three decades leading up to 2009, the increase in the ratio of foreign reserves to GDP largely kept pace with the rise in the rest of external portfolio assets (Figure 2.11, panel 2). The increase in foreign reserves was most pronounced in east Asia, especially after the Asian crisis of 1997–98 (Figure 2.11, panel 3), whereas the increase in the stock of nonreserve assets was more uniform across regions (Figure 2.11, panel 4).[22]

These structural changes in external portfolios have several immediate and important implications for the episodes of slowdowns in net capital inflows, which are discussed next.

Increasing Role of Capital Outflows

The flip side of the increasing external assets of emerging markets is that gross capital outflows have gradually increased in size and are playing an increasingly important role in net capital flow dynamics. One way to see this is by comparing the contributions of capital inflows and outflows to the three slowdown episodes shown in Figure 2.12. In the 1980s, the slowdown was driven entirely by a decline in capital inflows. The same explanation broadly holds for the 1995–2000 slowdown episode. In contrast, capital outflows are contributing sizably to the most recent emerging market capital flow cycle.[23]

The growing role for capital outflows can at least partly be linked to income growth and the accompanying increase in outward FDI from emerging markets, as well as to institutional shifts, such as the emergence of pension funds and sovereign wealth funds. These developments open a possibility for gross outflows to play a role in the dynamics of net capital flows for emerging market economies. Chapter 4 of the October 2013 *World Economic Outlook* argues that emerging markets can improve their capital flow management through development of their financial markets, which fosters private sector outflows that can help stabilize net capital flows. Indeed, the overall strong positive correlation between capital inflows and outflows in emerging markets over 2000–10, shown in Figure 2.12, supports the

[22]For a comparative discussion on the links between capital flows and trends in reserve accumulation in emerging markets and advanced economies, see Choi, Sharma, and Strömqvist 2009.
[23]A significant part of the increased importance of gross capital outflows likely reflects improvements in the measurement of capital outflows over time. A number of studies (see, for example, Claessens and Naude 1993) argue that data for 1980–90 were marked by a severe underreporting of outflows, as capital flight was not captured in the balance of payments statistics.

Figure 2.12. Gross Capital Inflows and Outflows of Emerging Market Economies, 1980–2014
(Percent of GDP)

Gross capital inflows played a dominant role in net capital inflow slowdown episodes in the 1980s and 1990s. However, the role of gross capital outflows increased in the 2010–15 slowdown.

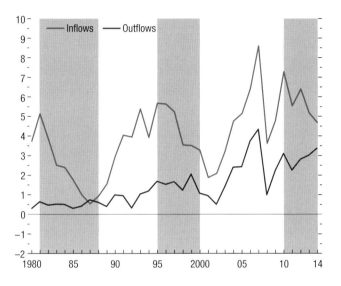

Sources: CEIC Asia database; CEIC China database; Haver Analytics; IMF, *Balance of Payments Statistics*; IMF, *International Financial Statistics*; World Bank, World Development Indicators database; and IMF staff calculations.
Note: Balanced sample of 22 economies from the full sample of 45 emerging market economies. See Annex 2.1 for a complete list of the sample countries.

Figure 2.13. Net External Debt Liabilities of Emerging Market Economies, 1980–2014
(Percent of GDP)

Overall, emerging markets' currency mismatches, as proxied by net external debt liabilities, have declined considerably over the past three decades. An increase in both external nonreserve assets and reserve assets has contributed to the decline.

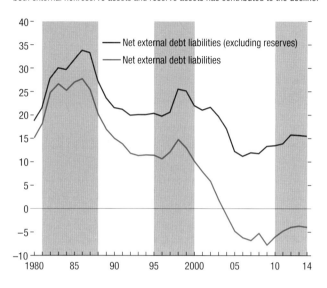

Sources: External Wealth of Nations Mark II database; and IMF staff calculations.
Note: Balanced sample of 22 economies from the full sample of 45 emerging market economies. See Annex 2.1 for the complete list of sample countries. All variables are GDP weighted.

notion that outflows played the role of a buffer during that period. Yet over 2012–14, outflows exacerbated the decline in net inflows, suggesting that a potentially destabilizing role cannot be ruled out.

Decline in Currency Mismatches

A large literature has documented the propensity of emerging markets to acquire foreign-currency debt liabilities and the attendant risks of doing so, stemming mainly from adverse balance sheet effects in case of a currency devaluation. Indeed, as discussed later, almost the entire stock of emerging market debt until the early 2000s was denominated in foreign currencies. By increasing their holdings of external assets by more than the increase in their external debt liabilities, emerging market economies as a whole have therefore considerably reduced the currency mismatch in their overall net external portfolios. When only external debt assets are considered, the overall improvement in the

net external position since the 1980s is about 20 percent of emerging market GDP. When foreign reserve assets are added, the decline in the net external position goes up to 30 percent of GDP (Figure 2.13).[24] The improvement is even more remarkable if external portfolio equity assets and the stock of FDI abroad are taken into account.

A second and more direct force reducing the currency mismatch has been the rise of debt liabilities denominated in domestic currency. The "original sin" of emerging market economies—the propensity to issue debt denominated in foreign currency (documented by Eichengreen and Hausmann 1998 and Eichengreen, Hausmann, and Panizza 2002)—has been substantially alleviated in both international and domestic markets.

The domestic-currency share of outstanding government debt rose substantially between 1995 and

---

[24]These trends in emerging market currency exposures have been documented in more detail by Lane and Shambaugh (2010) and Benetrix, Shambaugh, and Lane (2015).

Figure 2.14. Outstanding Debt of Emerging Market Economies Denominated in Domestic Currency, 1995–2015
(Percent of total)

Since 1995 both the government and the private sector in emerging market economies have increasingly been able to issue domestic-currency-denominated debt, which has further contributed to the reduction in currency mismatches.

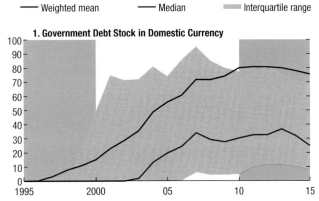

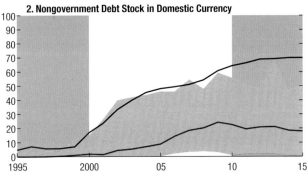

Sources: IMF, Vulnerability Exercise Securities Database; and IMF staff calculations.
Note: Calculations for government and private sectors are based on a balanced sample of 43 and 42 economies, respectively, within the 45 economies in the sample. See Annex 2.1 for the complete list of sample countries.

2010 (Figure 2.14, panel 1). Given the finding that the share of total government debt held by nonresidents was stable between 2004 and 2012 (Arslanalp and Tsuda 2014), the decline in original sin in public debt appears to have occurred both domestically and internationally. Original sin also declined in the nongovernment sector (Figure 2.14, panel 2). The much stronger increases for the weighted average share issued in domestic currency than for the median share suggest that original sin declined more in larger emerging market economies.

Despite the documented decline in currency mismatches, substantial vulnerabilities related to exchange rate movements remain. First, the net external debt position shown in Figure 2.13 abstracts from differences in maturity and liquidity of assets and liabilities

as well as from sectoral mismatches within economies. Second, as documented in Chapter 3 of the October 2015 *Global Financial Stability Report*, the stock of emerging market corporate debt has grown substantially over the past decade, even as the share of foreign-currency-denominated debt in total debt has declined. Finally, the majority of indicators of foreign-currency mismatches in Figures 2.13 and 2.14 peaked prior to 2010 and have remained stable or declined since.[25]

Shifts in Policy

Under the balance of payments identity, the sum of net nonreserve capital inflows and the current account balance equals the change in foreign reserves.[26] Hence, slowdowns in net nonreserve capital inflows are countered by some combination of a slower accumulation (or a faster decumulation) of foreign reserves and a higher current account balance. The three components of the identity are jointly determined. For example, during the years leading up to the global financial crisis, many commodity-exporting emerging market economies received strong capital inflows amid rising investment opportunities and accumulated reserves, with strong terms-of-trade gains offsetting the impact of rapid import growth on the current account. With the decline in commodity prices and more subdued growth prospects from 2011 onward, the process began to reverse. The following analysis uses the balance of payments identity as a guiding framework and discusses three relevant dimensions of the macro adjustment across episodes: exchange rates, foreign reserves, and the current account.

Foreign Reserves as a Buffer

Relative to previous slowdown episodes, in 2010–15 reserves played an important buffer role. To document this, based on the balance of payments identity, this subsection examines the extent to which the recent slowdown in emerging market net capital inflows has been countered by an increase in the current account balance—with potentially negative consequences for

[25]Only a part of the decline can be attributed to recent exchange rate depreciations in emerging markets.

[26]Two other items in the identity, typically small, are the capital account balance and errors and omissions. Here these terms are included in capital flows. Inclusion of errors and omissions in capital flows improves the measurement of changes in the current account and foreign reserves.

Table 2.1. Foreign Reserves and the Current Account in Balance of Payments Adjustments
(Dollars per dollar change in net capital inflows)

Episode	Δ Net Nonreserve Inflows + Δ Current Account Balance + Δ Change in Reserves = 0		
	Δ Net Nonreserve Inflows	Δ Current Account Balance	Δ Change in Reserves
1995–2000 Net Capital Inflow Slowdown	−1	**0.88**	0.12
2001–07 Net Capital Inflow Surge	1	0.11	**−1.11**
2010–15 Net Capital Inflow Slowdown	−1	0.07	**0.93**
Memorandum			
2013–15 Net Capital Inflow Slowdown	−1	0.18	**0.82**
2013–15 Net Capital Inflow Slowdown Excluding China	−1	0.30	**0.70**

Sources: CEIC Asia database; CEIC China database; Haver Analytics; IMF, *Balance of Payments Statistics*; IMF, *International Financial Statistics*; World Bank, World Development Indicators database; and IMF staff calculations.
Note: Δ denotes "change." A positive value of Δ change in reserves is defined as a decrease in the rate of increase of the stock of reserves. See Annex 2.1 for the complete list of sample countries. Net nonreserve inflows include errors and omissions and the capital account. The 2015 numbers refer to the first three quarters, annualized through a multiplier of 4/3.

domestic activity—or by a decrease in the pace of foreign reserve accumulation (or, alternatively, an increase in the pace of reserve decumulation, depending on whether at the start of the slowdown episode reserves were accumulated or decumulated).

Table 2.1 shows that for emerging markets as a whole, for each dollar decline in net capital inflows from 2010 through the third quarter of 2015, the current account balance increased by only 7 cents, while 93 cents came from the change in the pace of reserve accumulation. This change in pace reflects the fact that, while in 2010 the sample emerging markets as a group were accumulating foreign reserves, by 2015 the accumulation had stopped, and some countries are now decumulating foreign reserves (Figure 2.6). In contrast, during 1995–2000 the main counterpart to the capital inflow slowdown was an increase in current account balances amid a typically lower level of reserves.

As noted earlier, changes in net inflows and reserve accumulation during this period were substantial—close to 5 percent of countries' GDP. Most of the decline occurred from 2013 onward, a period during which China accounted for more than 80 percent of the change in net capital inflows and reserves. During this more recent period, the share of adjustment coming from the current account was higher in the overall sample, at 18 cents. The number is even higher once China is excluded, at 30 cents.

Table 2.1 also shows that during the capital flow surge episode of 2001–07, reserves played the role of a buffer. In fact, as a group, sample emerging markets even had an increase in current account balances (in some instances reflecting improved terms of trade), and the increased pace of reserve accumulation more than offset the surge in net capital inflows. One implica-

tion of this increased pace of reserve accumulation is that only in 2015 did emerging markets start to run down the liquidity buffers they had accumulated during the capital inflow boom episode that preceded the global financial crisis. During the 2010–14 period of the current slowdown, reserves continued to be accumulated, albeit at a decreasing pace (Figure 2.15). Furthermore, while in the initial years of the 2010–15 slowdown, the current account balances of emerging markets decreased—so that the decrease in the pace of reserve accumulation more than compensated for the slowdown in net capital inflows—during 2014–15, the current account balances increased, thus countering part of the slowdown.

The fact that reserve accumulation slowed down in tandem with diminished capital inflows (or turned into reserve losses in some countries seeing outflows) also has a positive side: by facilitating the repayment of residents' foreign-currency liabilities, the sale of foreign assets could reduce balance sheet fragilities and curtail the risk of default in the event that a currency depreciation eventually occurs. With strengthened domestic balance sheets, a currency depreciation can play its traditional role in switching demand toward domestic production and thus smooth the adjustment of output. Indeed, currency depreciation in 2014–15 coincides with the increase in the current account balance over the same period (Figure 2.15).

Increased Exchange Rate Flexibility and More Orderly Currency Depreciations

Flexible exchange rates cushion economic shocks and thus reduce the required amount of adjustment in capital flows. The main reason is that an immediate currency depreciation following an adverse shock raises

Figure 2.15. Net Capital Outflows and the Current Account during the 2010–15 Slowdown
(Percent of GDP)

Despite the slowdown in net capital inflows, emerging markets continued to accumulate foreign reserves until 2015, albeit at a decreasing pace. Meanwhile, the current account balance, after a prolonged decline, increased in 2014–15, countering part of the net capital inflow slowdown.

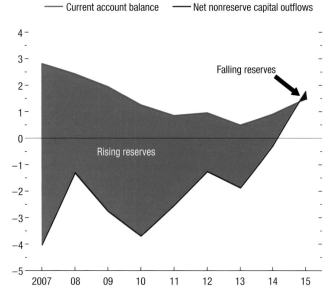

Sources: CEIC Asia database; CEIC China database; Haver Analytics; IMF, *Balance of Payments Statistics*; IMF, *International Financial Statistics*; World Bank, World Development Indicators database; and IMF staff calculations.
Note: Balanced sample of 45 emerging market economies. See Annex 2.1 for the complete list of sample economies. The observation for 2015 refers to the first three quarters. All variables are GDP weighted.

the cost of selling domestic assets and purchasing foreign currencies.[27] Put another way, immediate depreciations following negative shocks help hold capital in, while fears of future depreciations can drive capital out. Emerging market economies have been moving toward more flexible exchange rate regimes over the past two decades.[28]

Though exchange rates in many emerging market economies weakened in 2010–15, the depreciations

[27]Likewise, immediate appreciations in response to positive shocks deter capital inflows, as domestic assets become more expensive.

[28]Excluding countries that joined the euro area, 10 of the 45 economies in the sample saw an increase in their Reinhart-Rogoff flexibility indices from 1995 to 2010 (Argentina, Brazil, Czech Republic, Hungary, India, Indonesia, Korea, Malaysia, Moldova, Thailand). Furthermore, 7 economies that were classified as having freely falling exchange rate regimes in 1995 had flexible exchange rate regimes in 2010 (Armenia, Belarus, Mexico, Romania, Russia, Turkey, Uruguay). Over the same period the Reinhart-Rogoff flexibility index decreased for 4 of the sample's emerging markets (Albania, Costa Rica, Ecuador, Paraguay).

were less abrupt than they were in 1995–2000, and the overall size of the depreciation was smaller. Countries with relatively fixed exchange rate regimes[29] in 1995–2000 experienced sudden adjustments, in part reflecting pegs abandoned during currency crises. Several countries experienced an abrupt decline in their nominal effective exchange rates beginning in the third year of the episode, in 1998. For the 35 economies in the sample with relatively fixed exchange rate regimes in 1995, five fell into what Reinhart and Rogoff (2004) call "a freely falling exchange rate regime"[30] in one of the years between 1995 and 2000. In contrast, through the 2010–15 slowdown, countries with relatively fixed exchange rates maintained a stable nominal effective exchange rate (Figure 2.16, panel 1).

For countries with flexible exchange rate regimes,[31] the nominal effective exchange rate was stable in the first two years of the 1995–2000 episode and abruptly declined afterward, while in the 2010–15 episode, such countries saw a wide range of adjustments in their nominal effective exchange rates (Figure 2.16, panel 2). That pattern is consistent with the notion that exchange rate adjustments act as shock absorbers, and varying adjustments indicate that the shocks themselves were diverse (such as terms-of-trade declines in some countries and improvements in others).

The large currency depreciations in 2010–15 were more orderly than those in 1995–2000, in the sense that there were fewer large depreciations over a short period of time, and a much lower share of large depreciation episodes was associated with episodes of banking sector stress and external crises (Table 2.2, columns 4–6). The reduction in the incidence of crisis events is likely a consequence of a combination of factors. In addition to the less abrupt nature of exchange rate depreciations and more resilient balance sheets (with diminished currency mismatches), the external environment has been more favorable to emerging markets in the recent episode. First, the cost of financing in emerging markets during the current slowdown remains significantly lower than during 1995–2000 (Table 2.2, column 1). Although emerging market spreads have increased in recent quarters, they remain close to historical lows amid accommodative monetary conditions in advanced economies. Second, output growth rates in emerging markets during the current

[29]Categories 1 or 2 in the Reinhart-Rogoff coarse index.
[30]Category 5 in the Reinhart-Rogoff coarse index.
[31]Categories 3 or 4 in the Reinhart-Rogoff coarse index.

slowdown, relative to those in advanced economies, are significantly higher than in 1995–2000, owing to higher real growth in emerging markets as well as lower real growth in advanced economies (Table 2.2, columns 2 and 3). This favorable growth differential has helped emerging market economies continue to attract capital.

What Is Driving the Recent Slowdown in Capital Flows to Emerging Market Economies?

The drivers of the recent slowdown in net capital flows to emerging market economies are the subject of ongoing debate. While some analysts have argued that the slowdown is a consequence of diminished growth prospects in emerging market economies (including through lower commodity prices), others have highlighted the role of prospective shifts in monetary policy in the United States following several years of near-zero interest rates and quantitative easing.

Against this backdrop, the goals of this section are twofold. The first goal is to link the recent slowdown in capital inflows to emerging market economies (and the pickup in capital outflows) to a set of potential contributing factors such as diminished growth and interest rate differentials, the exit from extraordinarily accommodative monetary policy in the United States, and changes in investors' risk appetite and commodity prices. Given evidence that gross inflows and gross outflows have in their own right—rather than just in terms of the net gap between them—a distinct importance in determining systemic risk (Avdjiev, McCauley, and Shin 2015), the following econometric analysis provides separate regressions seeking to explain the individual behaviors of gross inflows and outflows. The section's second goal is to examine how the structural characteristics and policy frameworks of emerging market economies shape the dynamics of capital flows, such as whether flexible exchange rates have helped mitigate the slowdown in capital flows.

Methodology

Empirical Strategy

To achieve these goals, two complementary estimation strategies are used, each tailored to a specific purpose:[32]

[32]The macroeconomic variables used in the regressions, such as GDP and capital flows, influence each other in complex ways, mak-

Figure 2.16. Nominal Effective Exchange Rate Adjustment in 1995–2000 and 2010–15:Q3
(Percent change, years on x-axis)

Exchange rate adjustments during the 2010–15 slowdown were less abrupt than in 1995–2000. Countries with fixed exchange rate regimes managed to maintain their pegs, and countries with flexible exchange rate regimes avoided the broad-based abrupt declines observed during 1995–2000.

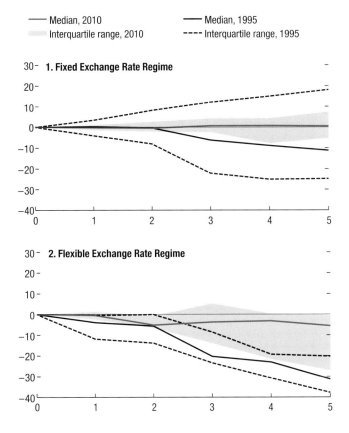

Sources: IMF, Information Notice System; and IMF staff calculations.
Note: Calculations are based on a balanced sample of 45 emerging market economies. See Annex 2.1 for the complete list of sample countries included in each panel. Flexible exchange rate regimes include those classified in categories 3 or 4 in the Reinhart and Rogoff (2004) "coarse" index, and fixed exchange rate regimes those in categories 1 or 2.

- To understand the drivers of the slowdown in capital flows to emerging market economies, the average of capital flows to a broad sample of emerging market economies is regressed on key economic explanatory factors such as differentials in the growth rates and interest rates between emerging market and advanced economies, measures of global investors' risk appetite, the gap between

ing it difficult to obtain clear causal estimates. The main goal of the analysis is therefore to establish robust correlations, examining which variables track the evolution of capital flows more strongly.

Table 2.2. Large Depreciations, Banking Sector Stress, and External Crises during Slowdown Episodes

Episode	Funding Costs (Percent)	Advanced Economy Growth (Percent)	Emerging Market Growth (Percent)	Number of Large Depreciations	Number of Large Depreciations Associated with Banking Sector Stress	Number of External Crises
1995–2000	13.0	3.0	4.7	18	14	11
2010–15	5.8	1.6	5.3	8	3	4

Sources: IMF, *International Financial Statistics*; IMF, Information Notice System; J.P. Morgan Emerging Market Bond Index (EMBI) Global; and IMF staff calculations.
Note: Funding costs are calculated as the sum of EMBI sovereign spreads and 10-year U.S. Treasury bond yields. Advanced economy growth refers to the aggregated real GDP growth rate of Canada, France, Germany, Italy, Japan, the United Kingdom, and the United States. Emerging market growth refers to the aggregated real GDP growth rate of the 45 emerging market economies listed in Annex 2.1. External crises are defined as by Catão and Milesi-Ferretti (2014), based on sovereign default or rescheduling events and IMF borrowing in excess of 200 percent of quota. Large depreciations are defined in the same way as in Chapter 3 of the October 2015 *World Economic Outlook*, with the details described in Annex 2.1. Banking sector stress is defined based on the Laeven and Valencia (2013) data set and includes borderline cases. A large depreciation is associated with banking sector stress if the stress occurs within a window from three years prior to three years subsequent to the year of the large depreciation. Funding costs in the first column are calculated for a sample consisting of Argentina, Brazil, Bulgaria, China, Ecuador, Mexico, Poland, and South Africa. The event counts in the last three columns are based on the full sample of 45 emerging market economies. A complete list of counted events in each column is provided in Annex 2.1.

long- and short-maturity bond yields in the United States (henceforth the *U.S. yield gap*), spreads on U.S. high-yield corporate bonds, and percentage changes in oil prices. The advantage of this specification is that it can be used to track the drivers of the slowdown in aggregate flows documented in previous sections.[33]

- To zoom in on how structural characteristics and policies of recipient countries shape the dynamics of capital flows (during the recent slowdown in particular), the relationship of capital flows to growth and interest rate differentials for each country (measured relative to a weighted basket of advanced economies' growth and interest rates, respectively), as well as to emerging market structural characteristics and policies on capital flows, is explored.[34]

Within each step, inflows and outflows are examined separately given the earlier finding that both components have contributed to the recent slowdown in net flows.

Relationship to Existing Literature

In general terms, the empirical specifications used in this section can be motivated by international investors' optimal portfolio allocation decisions. Cross-border capital flows reflect decisions by residents and nonresidents to allocate investments across countries. Investments in a particular country are more desirable the higher the risk-adjusted returns relative to those from investing in other countries. Expected returns from investing in a particular

country can be related to factors such as growth and interest rate differentials, the risk appetite of investors, and the quality of domestic policymaking and institutions.

An extensive empirical literature has sought to explain determinants of cross-border capital flows, focusing on gross inflows or net flows. Ahmed and Zlate (2013) estimate a panel regression for 12 emerging market economies to examine determinants of net capital inflows during 2002–12. Key country-specific and global explanatory variables that these authors consider are emerging market–advanced economy growth rate differentials, emerging market–U.S. interest rate differentials, and global risk aversion, as well as capital controls as a policy variable. In another recent paper, Nier, Sedik, and Mondino (2014) estimate a similar panel regression for gross non-FDI capital inflows of 29 emerging market economies with the same key explanatory variables and add market capitalization and public debt as country-specific structural characteristics and policy variables. In both of these studies, GDP growth rate differentials and global risk aversion emerge as the most robust statistically significant determinants of aggregate capital flows to emerging market economies. In an extensive survey of the empirical capital flow literature, Koepke (2015) similarly lists emerging market economic performance and global risk aversion among the most important determinants of capital flows to emerging market economies.

The empirical specifications used in this section are broadly consistent with these earlier studies. The chapter's findings in terms of the significance of various

---

[33]For a detailed description of the methodology, see Annex 2.3.
[34]For a detailed description of the methodology, see Annex 2.3.

explanatory factors are also broadly similar to those in the literature. The key addition of the chapter's analysis to the existing literature is to use the regression model to estimate the contribution of specific economic factors to the 2010–15 slowdown in net capital inflows to emerging market economies. A further contribution is to use an augmented panel regression specification to study the impact of emerging market structural characteristics and policies on capital inflows in general, and during the 2010–15 slowdown in particular.

Data

The sample of 22 countries included in the analysis was selected on the basis of quarterly data availability for the first quarter of 2000 through the second quarter of 2015 (see Annex 2.1 for the list of countries).[35] The starting point for the time period is motivated by data coverage for some of the explanatory variables and helps to mitigate econometric issues associated with structural breaks in capital flow dynamics during the 1980s and 1990s. For a detailed description of included variables and their sources, see Annex 2.2.

Estimation Results

Linking the Overall Emerging Market Slowdown to Contributing Economic Factors

Average growth and interest rate differentials between emerging markets and advanced economies, global investor risk appetite, the U.S. yield gap, and spreads on U.S. high-yield bonds are estimated to be statistically significant determinants of average capital inflows to emerging market economies. The regression results for average capital inflows to emerging market economies are presented in Annex Table 2.3.1.

To gauge the economic significance of the explanatory variables, panels 1 and 2 of Figure 2.17 compare actual average capital inflows with predictions from this regression. Panel 1 points to a tight empirical link between the actual and predicted capital inflows—for the estimation period as a whole as well as during 2010–15. Predictions from this regression model can match almost the entire slowdown in capital inflows between 2010 and 2015. Panel 2 breaks down the

---

[35]The sample includes China and Russia (before 2014), but the results are qualitatively similar when these two countries are excluded. The results are also robust to the inclusion of Russia's post-2014 data and the introduction of an intervention dummy for the effect of sanctions on capital flows.

Figure 2.17. Role of Global Factors in the Recent Slowdown
(Percent of GDP)

The decline in gross capital inflows to emerging markets during 2010–15 shows a strong association with the shrinking growth differential between emerging markets and advanced economies. The behavior of gross capital outflows remains, however, more difficult to track.

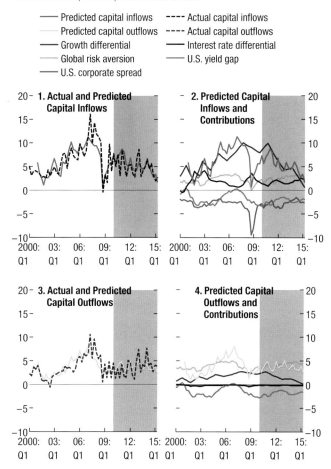

Sources: CEIC Asia database; CEIC China database; Fernández and others 2015; Haver Analytics; IMF, *Balance of Payments Statistics*; IMF, *International Financial Statistics*; Standard & Poor's; World Bank, World Development Indicators database; World Bank, World Governance Indicators; and IMF staff calculations.
Note: Average gross capital inflows (outflows) are regressed on overall emerging market economy–advanced economy growth and interest rate differentials, global risk aversion, the change in the oil price, the U.S. yield gap, the U.S. corporate spread, and seasonal dummies. Contributions of the change in the oil price are very small and thus not reported. Predicted capital flows refer to the predicted values from these regressions. See Annex 2.1 for a description of the sample, Annex 2.2 for a detailed description of included variables and sources, and Annex 2.3 for details on the estimation methodology.

predicted capital inflows series into contributions from each explanatory variable. The decline in inflows during 2010–15 shows a strong association with the shrinking real GDP growth differential between emerging markets and advanced economies. Diminished emerging market growth prospects relative to advanced economies counterbalance the effect of decreasing risk aversion, which would predict an increase in capital inflows to emerging market economies during this period. Other factors, such as global risk appetite, commodity prices, and accommodative monetary policy in advanced economies, contribute, but substantially less.[36] Overall, the strong association between capital flows and real GDP growth stands out as very robust to alternative sets of explanatory variables and sample breakdowns.[37]

Panels 3 and 4 in Figure 2.17 present symmetric results for overall emerging market capital outflows, with the regression results reported in Annex Table 2.3.2. The model does not perform that differently in regard to its predictions for outflows before the global financial crisis than it does in regard to its predictions for inflows. After 2010, however, the model does fall short of explaining the large outflows associated with the 2013 "taper tantrum" and the very recent pickup in outflows (Figure 2.17, panel 3). As discussed in Box 2.2, this deficiency is partly due to large temporary shifts in market expectations regarding the course of monetary policy in the United States, which are difficult to control for in a relatively parsimonious regression specification using quarterly data. This change in the correlation pattern between inflows and outflows is a relatively new phenomenon; Broner and others (2013) show that in earlier episodes, rising inflows were typically accompanied by pickups in outflows. Karolyi, Ng, and Prasad (2013) highlight that outflows are increasingly driven by new, structural factors, notably portfolio rebalancing by domestic institutional investors facilitated by greater access to information. Such structural drivers of outflows are not easily picked up by regression analysis based on macroeconomic data.

Role of Country Characteristics and Policies

The second step of the analysis focuses on the role of structural characteristics and policies in shaping the dynamics of capital flows to emerging

market economies. To this end, the section uses a panel data specification that relates country-specific capital flows to country-specific growth and interest rate differentials and to country characteristics, as well as country and time fixed effects.[38] The regression, shown in the first column of Annex Table 2.3.3, results in a positive and statistically significant coefficient on the growth differential, while the estimated coefficients on the real interest rate differential and other country characteristics are not statistically significant.

The time fixed effects included in this specification are highly correlated with average capital inflows to emerging market economies used in the previous analysis (Figure 2.18) and are thus capturing, by and large, the effects of global variables fleshed out previously—namely, the emerging market–advanced economy growth and interest rate differentials, as well as global financial conditions, including changes in the U.S. monetary policy stance and global risk appetite.

The extent to which the estimated common trend in capital inflows (that is, the estimated time effects) accounts for the total variation in capital inflows depends on policy characteristics that are country specific (Figure 2.19).[39] This in turn indicates that individual emerging market economies are not simply bystanders—their policy choices matter for how they

[36]When total capital inflows are broken up into debt and equity components, the growth differential still shows a very strong association with both components, and a stronger slowdown is predicted for debt than for equity, in line with the behavior of actual flows. The strong association between debt flows and real GDP growth is consistent with well-established evidence of the beneficial effects of growth in lowering default risk.

[37]This includes separating commodity exporters from non–commodity exporters in the sample. Evidence on the significance of commodity price changes and associated effects on country-specific terms of trade and capital flows is provided later in the chapter.

[38]The methodology is explained in greater detail in Annex 2.3. The initial regression included not only expected growth and interest rate differentials, but also changes in the country's terms of trade, an indicator of its institutional quality, whether the country is participating in a large IMF-sponsored adjustment program, whether the country is in default with creditors, and the degree to which capital inflows to the country are restricted by law. The sample excludes some quarterly observations of very high interest rates (Argentina, Brazil, and Turkey in the early 2000s). All variables except the growth differential were determined to be nonsignificant and were therefore dropped from the regression. The statistically nonsignificant and negatively signed coefficient on changes in a country's terms of trade is noteworthy. To the extent that lower real GDP growth picks up the effects of lower commodity prices among commodity exporters, the statistical nonsignificance of the terms-of-trade variable is partly due to its collinearity with GDP growth. The negative sign of the coefficient on that variable (albeit statistically nonsignificant) can be rationalized by the fact that weaker terms of trade tend to reduce the current account balance (all other factors held constant), necessitating higher external financing. Results are robust to the use of different measures of institutions and capital controls.

[39]Indeed, recent work by Aizenman, Chinn, and Ito (2015) shows that interactions between global liquidity trends and global growth are critical for understanding the exposure of individual emerging markets to swings in international capital flows.

Figure 2.18. Estimated Time Fixed Effects and Average Gross Capital Inflows to Emerging Market Economies
(Percent of GDP)

Estimated time fixed effects, which are common to all countries, are highly correlated with the simple and GDP-weighted averages of gross capital inflows to emerging markets and broadly capture the effects of global growth and interest rate differentials, global risk aversion, and global liquidity on capital flows.

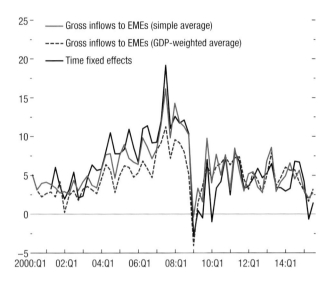

Sources: CEIC Asia database; CEIC China database; Haver Analytics; IMF, *Balance of Payments Statistics*; IMF, *International Financial Statistics*; World Bank, World Development Indicators database; and IMF staff calculations.
Note: Time fixed effects are estimated from a regression of gross capital inflows to emerging market economies (EMEs) on country characteristics and country and time fixed effects. See Annex 2.1 for a description of the sample, Annex 2.2 for a detailed description of included variables and sources, and Annex 2.3 for details on the methodology.

Figure 2.19. Share of Variation in Gross Capital Inflows Explained by Global Factors

Over the 2000–15 period, global factors had a smaller correlation with gross capital inflows in countries with less open capital accounts, more flexible exchange rates, higher reserves, and lower public debt.

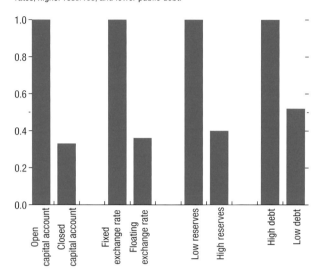

Sources: CEIC Asia database; CEIC China database; Fernández and others 2015; Haver Analytics; IMF, *Annual Report on Exchange Arrangements and Exchange Restrictions* (AREAER); IMF, *Balance of Payments Statistics*; IMF, *International Financial Statistics*; World Bank, World Development Indicators database; and IMF staff calculations.
Note: *R*-squared values are from a regression of country-specific gross capital inflows on average gross capital inflows, normalized using within-group standard deviations of flows, with the base group set to 1. Capital account openness is measured using Fernández and others' (2015) measure for controls on capital inflows, split at 0.5. Fixed and floating exchange rates are defined using the IMF's AREAER classification. High and low reserves are measured in months of imports, split at the sample median. High and low government debt are split at the sample median. See Annex 2.1 for a description of the sample, Annex 2.2 for a detailed description of included variables and sources, and Annex 2.3 for details on the methodology.

mitigate the volatility of their own capital inflows relative to global volatility:

- Emerging market economies that are financially more open appear more exposed to the common trend in capital inflows to emerging markets. This is evident in Figure 2.19 from the fact that a higher share of the total variance of capital inflows is explained by the common time effect (with differences in countries' expected growth performance controlled for) in countries with more open capital accounts. While this evidence may seem tautological at first, it does suggest that capital control regulations can have a real impact without implying, however, that they can be as effective (and certainly not as desirable) as other policy tools.
- More flexible exchange rates also reduce the share of the total variance of capital inflows explained by common global factors. This effect appears to be

quantitatively very important and is further elaborated on in the discussion later in this section.[40]

- By contrast, countries that have higher reserves and lower public debt tend to have a lower percentage of the fluctuations in their capital inflows attributable to global factors.

The findings for most of these characteristics seem intuitive. For instance, countries that have flexible exchange rate regimes would tend to see immedi-

[40]Aside from the discussion on the existence of a monetary policy trilemma referred to earlier, a large literature has studied the effectiveness of the exchange rate as a shock absorber. There is scarce evidence, however, on its role in smoothing the global capital flow cycle. Magud, Reinhart, and Vesperoni (2014) provide evidence that exchange rate flexibility smoothens the domestic credit cycle but find no evidence, in their regression analysis, that it dampens capital flows in itself (see Magud, Reinhart, and Vesperoni 2014, Table 4).

Figure 2.20. 2010–15 Gross Capital Inflow Slowdown and Country-Specific Characteristics
(Percent of GDP)

During 2010–15, in particular, countries with more open capital accounts, less flexible exchange rates, lower reserves, and higher public debt experienced substantially larger declines in their gross capital inflows.

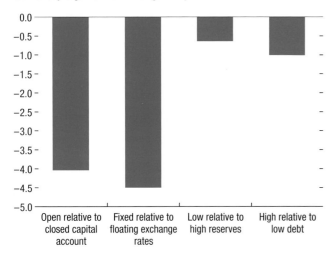

Sources: CEIC Asia database; CEIC China database; Fernández and others 2015; Haver Analytics; IMF, *Annual Report on Exchange Arrangements and Exchange Restrictions* (AREAER); IMF, *Balance of Payments Statistics*; IMF, *International Financial Statistics*; World Bank, World Development Indicators database; and IMF staff calculations.
Note: The figure shows estimated coefficients from a regression of gross capital inflows on the country-specific forecast growth differential, time fixed effects, and interactions of capital account openness, exchange rate flexibility, level of reserves, and level of public debt with the time fixed effects. See Annex 2.1 for a description of the sample, Annex 2.2 for a detailed description of included variables and sources, and Annex 2.3 for details on the methodology.

ate currency depreciations in response to a broader downward trend in the supply of capital to emerging market economies. By making domestic assets cheaper, a weaker currency would tend to attract capital into a country. Thus, exchange rate flexibility would reduce the sensitivity of capital inflows to global factors.

Likewise, because higher levels of reserves and lower public debt levels reduce country risk, foreign investors would be less tempted to pull out from countries with those characteristics, making their capital inflows more resilient to shifts in the global factors affecting all emerging market economies.

In light of these findings, the common time effects are interacted with dummy variables that split countries with low and high levels of capital controls, countries with less or more flexible exchange rates, countries with lower and higher levels of reserves, and countries with higher and lower debt levels. *F*-statistics confirm that the resulting interaction terms are

highly statistically significant (see Annex Table 2.3.5). The relevance of these interaction terms is corroborated by a sizable increase in the regression's fit: once such interactions of country-specific characteristics with the global trend are allowed for, the regression can explain an extra 31 percent of fluctuations in inflows (as gauged by the adjusted *R*-squared values rising from 0.12 to 0.43).

Policy-controlled variables, including the degree of capital account openness, exchange rate flexibility, and the level of reserves and public debt, also help explain the diversity of experiences across countries during the 2010–15 slowdown more specifically. All else being constant, economies that had an above-average degree of openness in their capital accounts lost 4 percentage points of GDP in capital inflows compared with those that had below-average degrees of openness (Figure 2.20). More generally, economies that were more open to inflows received far more inflows in the upswing of the global cycle (2002–07), and they tended to receive far less in the downswing phase. Regarding differences in the domain of reserves and fiscal variables, for countries with below-average levels of reserves or above-average ratios of public debt to GDP, the decline in inflows was 0.6–1 percentage point of GDP larger than was the case for countries with higher levels of reserves or lower debt levels.

Yet the biggest difference stems from exchange rate flexibility. Consistent with the foregoing discussion about the insulation properties of a floating exchange rate, the second bar in Figure 2.20 shows that countries with less flexible exchange rate arrangements lost about 4.5 percent of GDP in capital inflows during 2010–15 compared with those with more flexible exchange rates.

This finding can be elaborated further by delving into how exchange rate flexibility interacts with each of the main global factors highlighted in Figure 2.17—that is, the overall growth and interest rate differentials between emerging markets and advanced economies, as well as global risk aversion. As illustrated in Figure 2.21, a 75 basis point narrowing in the expected growth differential between emerging markets and advanced economies (which was roughly the annual average change in that differential during 2010–15) reduces capital flows by more than 4 percent of GDP, all else being constant, if a country has a fixed exchange rate regime. But if a country has a more flexible exchange rate, the expected drop declines to about 1.5 percent of GDP.

More dramatically, an increase in global risk aversion from 2015 levels to its historical average can reduce capital inflows by about 6.5 percent of GDP for countries with fixed exchange rate regimes, but by less than 2 percent of GDP for those with more flexible exchange rates.[41]

Finally, there is some—albeit more subtle—evidence that a country's degree of exchange rate flexibility also affects the sensitivity of capital inflows to changes in the country's own growth. Extending the panel specifications reported in Annex Table 2.3.3 by adding terms for the interaction between the degree of exchange rate flexibility and growth differentials suggests that in countries with more flexible exchange rates, inflows are less sensitive to changes in the country's own growth differential relative to advanced economies. Though the econometric precision of such estimates is not as high as that for other estimates reported elsewhere in this chapter, this is an effect that seems important to bear in mind when evaluating the effects on capital flows of differences in growth performance across emerging markets.

Conclusions

This chapter documents a sizable slowdown in net capital inflows to emerging market economies during 2010–15, to which both inflows and outflows contributed. The slowdown during the period is observed in about three-quarters of emerging market economies, and it is broad based across regions.

Capital flows to emerging market economies over the last several decades have exhibited distinct cycles, with previous slowdowns in the early 1980s and late 1990s showing a size and breadth that are broadly comparable to those of the current episode. As such, the current slowdown is not unprecedented. Nevertheless, the current episode is distinct in that substantial structural changes and policy shifts have taken place in emerging market economies since the late 1990s. Emerging market economies are now far more financially integrated into global financial markets, and currency mismatches (notably in public sector

[41]In a sample spanning 2000–15, such a historical average may be more elevated than that in a longer sample, because of the big spikes in global risk aversion in 2008 and 2009. This makes the comparison exercise embodied in Figure 2.21 more extreme than might seem likely, but it does deliver the important point that countries with floating and fixed exchange rates can differ substantially in regard to their resilience to "pushes" in global risk aversion.

Figure 2.21. Differences in the Contribution of Global Factors between More and Less Flexible Exchange Rate Regimes
(Percent of GDP)

Exchange rate flexibility also weakens the link between key global factors (such as aggregate growth differentials, short-term interest rate differentials, and global risk aversion) and gross capital inflows.

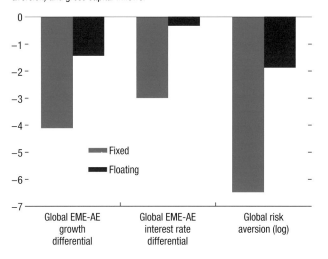

Source: IMF staff calculations.
Note: The figure shows the effect of a 0.75 percentage point decrease in the growth and interest rate differentials, respectively, and an increase of 3 in the Chicago Board Options Exchange Volatility Index (VIX), based on coefficients reported in Annex Table 2.3.6, column 3. See Annex 2.1 for a description of the sample, Annex 2.2 for a detailed description of included variables and sources, and Annex 2.3 for details on the methodology. AE = advanced economy; EME = emerging market economy.

borrowing) have been reduced. As emerging market residents now face lower capital controls than they did in the 1980s and 1990s and are wealthier—especially after years of brisk growth prior to the global financial crisis of 2008–09—they seek to diversify their portfolios internationally. This turns capital outflows into an increasingly important component of the overall dynamics of capital flows. Also in contrast with the past, emerging market economies now have much higher foreign reserves, which can be deployed as a buffer. As documented in this chapter, changes in the pace of reserve accumulation, including some decumulation, have counterbalanced much of the 2010–15 slowdown in net capital inflows. Moreover, exchange rates have become more flexible and are adjusting in a more orderly way in the current slowdown than in previous episodes.

The chapter's regression-based analysis shows that the emerging market–advanced economy growth differential is the economic factor most tightly associated with capital inflows to emerging market economies and can explain the bulk of the 2010–15 slowdown. Nevertheless, flexible exchange rates have helped mitigate the slowdown associated with a declining growth differential. Such insulation effects are consistent with the existence of the classical trilemma in monetary policy choices, rather than a mere dilemma between more or fewer capital controls. While the chapter's estimation results are less robust and harder to interpret for the determinants of capital outflows, its contribution on this count is to highlight the increasing importance of such outflows and to point out the need for more research on what drives them.

In terms of policy implications, the chapter documents that policy frameworks have played a role in mitigating the individual-country effects of global factors, implying that countries are not simply bystanders to the global financial cycle. Policy frameworks have generally improved over time, reducing the vulnerabilities stemming from a potentially disorderly retrenchment of capital flows and the balance sheet effects that accompany exchange rate adjustments. These improvements notwithstanding, a persistent narrowing of growth differentials in relation to advanced economies and the accompanying slowdown in capital inflows reinforce the need for a continued policy upgrade in emerging market economies to ensure an orderly external sector adjustment. The necessary policies include prudent fiscal policies (as the slowdown can raise the cost to an economy of servicing its debt), proactive macroprudential policies (to limit currency mismatches), exchange rate flexibility (which can work as a shock absorber), and foreign reserve management (which can insulate the domestic economy from shocks, though not indefinitely). The chapter's analysis also highlights the need for increased vigilance with regard to capital outflow dynamics, which can pose substantial risks, but are not yet sufficiently well understood.

Annex 2.1. Sample of Emerging Market Economies

The broadest sample of emerging market economies used for the analysis in this chapter comprises 45 emerging market economies. Countries were selected for the sample based on the availability of key capital flow data—capital inflows, capital outflows, and net capital inflows—based on annual balance of payments statistics for the 2000–14 period and quarterly balance of payments statistics for the first three quarters of

2015. The complete list of countries, grouped by region, is shown in Annex Table 2.1.1.

The country sample for the regression analysis includes the following subset of 22 emerging market economies: Argentina, Brazil, Bulgaria, Chile, China, Colombia, the Czech Republic, Hungary, India, Indonesia, Korea, Malaysia, Mexico, the Philippines, Poland, Romania, Russia, the Slovak Republic, South Africa, Taiwan Province of China, Thailand, and Turkey. The country sample for the regression analysis is more restricted, given the more limited availability of (1) explanatory variables used in the regressions and (2) balance of payments data at quarterly frequency (relative to annual data), including for breakdowns into equity and debt flows.

The remainder of this annex provides additional details on selected figures and tables in the chapter.

- Figure 2.1: Unbalanced sample including all 45 economies. External crisis episodes are shown in Annex Table 2.1.2.
- Figure 2.4: Panel 1: 45 economies. Panel 2: 33 economies, with Albania, Costa Rica, El Salvador, Georgia, Guatemala, the Kyrgyz Republic, Malaysia, Paraguay, Saudi Arabia, Sri Lanka, Uruguay, and Vietnam excluded. Panel 3: 34 economies, with Albania, China, Georgia, India, the Kyrgyz Republic, Malaysia, Moldova, Paraguay, Saudi Arabia, Sri Lanka, and Vietnam excluded. Panel 4: 44 economies, with Malaysia excluded. Panel 5: 35 economies, with Albania, Armenia, Ecuador, Indonesia, the Kyrgyz Republic, Mexico, Peru, Saudi Arabia, Sri Lanka, and Vietnam excluded. Panel 6: 22 economies (Armenia, Brazil, Bulgaria, Chile, Costa Rica, Croatia, the Czech Republic, Estonia, Georgia, Hungary, Kazakhstan, Korea, Latvia, Lithuania, Peru, the Philippines, Poland, Russia, the Slovak Republic, Slovenia, South Africa, and Taiwan Province of China). Panel 7: 31 economies, with Ecuador, Georgia, India, Indonesia, the Kyrgyz Republic, Malaysia, Moldova, Paraguay, Peru, Romania, Saudi Arabia, Sri Lanka, Ukraine, and Vietnam excluded. Panel 8: 44 economies, with Malaysia excluded.
- Figure 2.9: Panel 1: 12 economies (Brazil, Bulgaria, Chile, Colombia, Hungary, Indonesia, Malaysia, Mexico, the Philippines, Poland, South Africa, and Turkey). Panel 2: 23 economies (Argentina, Bulgaria, Belarus, Brazil, Chile, China, Colombia, Ecuador, Georgia, Hungary, Indonesia, Kazakhstan, Lithuania, Mexico, Malaysia, Peru, the Philippines, Poland, South Africa, Sri Lanka, Turkey, Uruguay, and Vietnam). Panel 3: 21 economies (Argentina,

Annex Table 2.1.1. Countries in the Chapter's Emerging Market Economies Sample

Region (Number of Countries)	Countries
Commonwealth of Independent States (8)	Armenia, Belarus, Georgia, Kazakhstan, Kyrgyz Republic, Moldova, Russia, Ukraine
Cooperation Council for the Arab States of the Gulf (1)	Saudi Arabia
East Asia (10)	China, India, Indonesia, Korea, Malaysia, Philippines, Sri Lanka, Taiwan Province of China, Thailand, Vietnam
Eastern Europe (12)	Albania, Bulgaria, Croatia, Czech Republic, Estonia, Hungary, Latvia, Lithuania, Poland, Romania, Slovak Republic, Slovenia
Latin America (12)	Argentina, Brazil, Chile, Colombia, Costa Rica, Ecuador, El Salvador, Guatemala, Mexico, Paraguay, Peru, Uruguay
Other Emerging Markets (2)	South Africa, Turkey

Annex Table 2.1.2. External Crisis Episodes, 1980–2015

1980–89		1990–2007		2008–15	
Country	Year of External Crisis	Country	Year of External Crisis	Country	Year of External Crisis
Korea	1980	Bulgaria	1990	Ecuador	2008
Philippines	1980	Albania	1991	Hungary	2008
Costa Rica	1981	Croatia	1992	Latvia	2008
Poland	1981	Slovenia	1992	Turkey[1]	2008
Sri Lanka	1981	Argentina	1995	Ukraine	2008
Thailand	1981	Mexico	1995	Armenia	2009
Argentina	1982	Korea	1997	Belarus	2009
Mexico	1982	Thailand	1997	Georgia	2009
Romania	1982	Armenia	1998	Romania	2009
Brazil	1983	Indonesia	1998	Sri Lanka	2010
Chile	1983	Moldova	1998	Moldova	2011
Ecuador	1983	Ukraine	1998	Ukraine	2014
Philippines	1983	Brazil	1999	Albania	2015
Uruguay	1983	Ecuador	1999		
India	1984	Turkey	2000		
South Africa	1985	Argentina	2001		
Thailand	1985	Brazil	2001		
Paraguay	1986	Moldova	2002		
		Uruguay	2002		
		Paraguay	2003		

Sources: Catão and Milesi-Ferretti 2014; IMF, *International Financial Statistics*; and IMF staff calculations.
[1]Turkey in 2008 is a special case. Because the disbursement of the preapproved final tranche under the ongoing IMF program at the time brought Turkey's IMF exposure to more than 200 percent of quota, the chapter's coding classifies it as a crisis event, even though Turkey's country risk was clearly dropping and the country did not experience an external crisis.

Bulgaria, Brazil, Chile, China, Colombia, Ecuador, Georgia, Hungary, Indonesia, Kazakhstan, Malaysia, Mexico, Peru, the Philippines, Poland, South Africa, Sri Lanka, Turkey, Uruguay, and Vietnam).
• Figure 2.11: 22 economies (Argentina, Brazil, Chile, Colombia, Costa Rica, Ecuador, El Salvador, Guatemala, India, Indonesia, Korea, Malaysia, Mexico, Paraguay, the Philippines, Poland, South Africa, Sri Lanka, Taiwan Province of China, Thailand, Turkey, and Uruguay).

• Figure 2.12: Balanced sample with 22 economies (Albania, Argentina, Bulgaria, Chile, Colombia, Costa Rica, El Salvador, Guatemala, India, Korea, Malaysia, Mexico, Paraguay, Peru, the Philippines, Poland, Romania, South Africa, Sri Lanka, Thailand, Turkey, and Uruguay).
• Figure 2.13: 22 economies (Argentina, Brazil, Chile, Colombia, Costa Rica, Ecuador, El Salvador, Guatemala, India, Indonesia, Korea, Malaysia, Mexico, Paraguay, the Philippines, Poland, South Africa, Sri

Annex Table 2.1.3. Large Depreciation Episodes, 1995–2000

Country	Year	Banking Sector Stress
Albania	1997	X
Belarus	1997	X
Brazil	1999	X
Georgia	1999	
Indonesia	1998	X
Kazakhstan	1999	
Korea	1998	X
Kyrgyz Republic	1997	X
Kyrgyz Republic	1999	X
Malaysia	1998	X
Mexico	1995	X
Moldova	1999	
Paraguay	1998	X
Philippines	1998	X
Romania	1996	X
Romania	1999	
Russia	1998	X
Ukraine	1998	X
Number	18	14

Sources: IMF, Information Notice System; and IMF staff calculations.
Note: For the definition of these episodes, see Table 2.2.

Annex Table 2.1.4. Large Depreciation Episodes, 2010–15

Country	Year	Banking Sector Stress
Belarus	2011	
Belarus	2015	
Brazil	2015	
Colombia	2015	
Georgia	2015	
Moldova	2015	X
Russia	2015	X
Ukraine	2014	X
Number	8	3

Sources: IMF, Information Notice System; and IMF staff calculations.
Note: For the definition of these episodes, see Table 2.2.

Lanka, Taiwan Province of China, Thailand, Turkey, and Uruguay).

- Figure 2.14: Panel 1 (government): Balanced sample, with Estonia and India excluded. Panel 2 (nongovernment): Balanced sample, with Albania, Moldova, and the Slovak Republic excluded.

- Figure 2.16: Panel 1: 25 economies with fixed exchange rate regimes (Albania, China, Costa Rica, Croatia, the Czech Republic, Ecuador, El Salvador, Estonia, Georgia, Guatemala, Hungary, India, Kazakhstan, Latvia, Lithuania, Moldova, Peru, the Philippines, Russia, Saudi Arabia, the Slovak Republic, Slovenia, Sri Lanka, Uruguay, and Vietnam). Panel 2: 13 economies with flexible exchange rate regimes as classified by Reinhart and Rogoff (2004) (Armenia, Brazil, Chile, Colombia, Indonesia, Korea, Mexico, Paraguay, Poland, Romania, South Africa, Thailand, and Turkey).

- Table 2.1: Episode 1995–2000: Balanced sample with 13 economies (Albania, Armenia, the Czech Republic, Estonia, Guatemala, Hungary, Lithuania, Peru, Romania, Russia, the Slovak Republic, Slovenia, and Sri Lanka). Episode 2001–07: Balanced sample with 20 economies (Albania, Armenia, Brazil, Bulgaria, Croatia, the Czech Republic, Ecuador, Estonia, Hungary, Kazakhstan, Korea, Latvia, Lithuania, Paraguay, Peru, the Philippines, Romania, Russia, Sri Lanka, and Ukraine). Episode 2010–15: Balanced sample with 33

economies (Albania, Armenia, Belarus, Brazil, Chile, China, Colombia, Costa Rica, Croatia, the Czech Republic, El Salvador, Georgia, Guatemala, Hungary, India, Indonesia, Kazakhstan, Korea, Malaysia, Mexico, Moldova, the Philippines, Poland, Russia, Saudi Arabia, South Africa, Sri Lanka, Taiwan Province of China, Thailand, Turkey, Ukraine, Uruguay, and Vietnam).

- Table 2.2: Large depreciations are defined based on two numerical thresholds: (1) a threshold set at the 90th percentile of all annual depreciations with respect to the dollar among emerging market and developing economies between 1970 and 2015 and (2) a threshold requiring the change in the depreciation rate compared with the previous year to be unusually large (greater than the 90th percentile of all changes), so that the same large exchange rate depreciation episode is not captured more than once. To ensure that the results are not unduly influenced by high-inflation episodes, the analysis considers only large depreciations that occur when the inflation rate is less than 50 percent. Episode 1995–2000: Large depreciations and large depreciations associated with banking sector stress are listed in Annex Table 2.1.3. Episode 2010–15: Large depreciations and large depreciations associated with banking sector stress are listed in Annex Table 2.1.4. External crises are listed in Annex Table 2.1.2.

Annex 2.2. Data

Capital flow data are from the IMF's Financial Flows Analytics database. Total gross inflows and outflows exclude derivatives flows; equity flows refer to the sum of foreign direct investment (FDI) and portfolio equity; and debt flows refer to the sum of portfolio debt and other flows. All flows are measured as shares of GDP.

Annex Table 2.3.1. Role of Global Factors in Explaining Gross Capital Inflows

	Total	Equity	Debt
Global Emerging Market Economy–Advanced Economy Growth Differential	2.404***	0.555	1.443***
	(0.633)	(0.440)	(0.321)
Global Emerging Market Economy–Advanced Economy Interest Rate Differential	0.707*	0.462	0.216
	(0.405)	(0.366)	(0.254)
Global Risk Aversion (log)	−1.981*	−1.135	−1.836**
	(1.019)	(0.788)	(0.850)
Change in Oil Price	0.000	0.002	0.009
	(0.018)	(0.011)	(0.012)
U.S. Yield Gap	−0.950**	−1.072***	−0.204
	(0.407)	(0.256)	(0.208)
U.S. Corporate Spread	−2.772**	0.119	−3.144**
	(1.214)	(0.831)	(1.275)
Number of Observations	58	58	58
Adjusted R^2	0.56	0.41	0.74

Source: IMF staff estimates.
Note: The dependent variable is mean inflows to emerging markets as a percent of GDP. Seasonal dummy variables are included but not reported. See Annex 2.1 for a description of the sample, Annex 2.2 for a detailed description of included variables and sources, and Annex 2.3 for details on the methodology.
*p <.10; **p < .05; ***p < .01.

Country-specific forecast growth and interest rate differentials are measured as the difference between a particular emerging market's rate and a weighted average of rates in advanced economies (with the latter group consisting of Canada, France, Germany, Italy, Japan, the United Kingdom, and the United States), with country-specific weights depending on average portfolio exposures during 2001–12 based on data from the IMF's Coordinated Portfolio Investment Survey (see Annex 2.3). Forecast growth is measured using one-year-ahead *World Economic Outlook* growth forecasts. Interest rate differentials are based on policy rates, deflated using one-year-ahead *World Economic Outlook* inflation forecasts. Institutional quality is measured using the rule of law measure from the World Bank's Worldwide Governance Indicators. Capital controls on inflows and outflows are based on Fernández and others 2015. A country is defined as having a large IMF-supported adjustment program if its IMF borrowing is more than 100 percent of its quota and growing. Default is measured following Standard & Poor's (S&P) definition (see Catão and Mano 2015). Fixed and floating exchange rates are defined using the IMF's *Annual Report on Exchange Arrangements and Exchange Restrictions* classification, as this measure is available through 2015.

Global growth differentials are based on weighted averages of the growth rates of 20 emerging markets and the advanced economies listed previously, with weights depending on average portfolio exposures using Coordinated Portfolio Investment Survey data (see Annex 2.3). Global risk aversion is measured

using the logarithm of the Chicago Board Options Exchange's Volatility Index (VIX). The change in the oil price refers to the year-over-year change in the West Texas Intermediate oil price.

Annex 2.3. Methodology

Overall Slowdown

The overall slowdown of capital flows to emerging market economies is studied in this chapter using a time series regression of average gross capital inflows to emerging markets (that is, the average gross-capital-inflow-to-GDP ratio across countries) on key economic explanatory factors: emerging market–advanced economy growth and interest rate differentials, investor risk aversion (measured using the logarithm of the Chicago Board Options Exchange's Volatility Index [VIX]), the U.S. yield gap, the U.S. corporate bond spread, and the percentage change in the oil price (with seasonal dummy variables also controlled for):

$$\overline{Kflows}_t = \gamma_0 + \gamma_1 \left(\bar{g}_t^{EM} - \bar{g}_t^{AE} \right) + \gamma_2 \left(\bar{ir}_t^{EM} - \bar{ir}_t^{AE} \right) + \gamma_3 riskaversion_t + \gamma_4 yield\,gap_t^{U.S.} + \gamma_5 corp.bond\,spread_t^{U.S.} + \gamma_6 \Delta P_t^{oil} + \varphi S_t + u_t,$$

in which $\left(\bar{g}_t^{EM} - \bar{g}_t^{AE} \right)$ and $\left(\bar{ir}_t^{EM} - \bar{ir}_t^{AE} \right)$ are average growth and interest rate differentials, as defined later in this annex. These results are reported in Annex Table 2.3.1 for inflows and Annex Table 2.3.2 for outflows. Results are robust to using a GDP-weighted average instead of a simple average of capital-flow-to-GDP ratios across countries.

Annex Table 2.3.2. Role of Global Factors in Explaining Gross Capital Outflows

	Total	Equity	Debt
Global Emerging Market Economy–Advanced Economy Growth Differential	0.676	0.378	0.484**
	(0.464)	(0.539)	(0.214)
Global Emerging Market Economy–Advanced Economy Interest Rate Differential	−0.066	0.072	0.076
	(0.316)	(0.290)	(0.139)
Global Risk Aversion (log)	−1.781*	−0.801	−0.888*
	(0.909)	(0.917)	(0.474)
Change in Oil Price	−0.002	−0.000	−0.004
	(0.012)	(0.014)	(0.006)
U.S. Yield Gap	−0.764***	−0.503**	−0.296***
	(0.295)	(0.227)	(0.108)
U.S. Corporate Spread	−0.137	0.774	−1.196**
	(0.967)	(1.018)	(0.561)
Number of Observations	58	58	58
Adjusted R^2	0.40	0.15	0.52

Source: IMF staff estimates.

Note: The dependent variable is mean outflows from emerging markets as a percent of GDP. Seasonal dummy variables are included but not reported. See Annex 2.1 for a description of the sample, Annex 2.2 for a detailed description of included variables and sources, and Annex 2.3 for details on the methodology.
$*p < .10; **p < .05; ***p < .01.$

Cross-Country Distribution

The cross-country distribution of gross capital inflows is modeled using a panel regression (with country fixed effects) of capital inflows on country-specific economic factors, such as country-specific forecast growth differentials relative to advanced economies, interest rate differentials, institutions, capital controls, whether the country has a large IMF loan, whether the country is in default, and percentage changes in the terms of trade (with time fixed effects controlled for):

$$Kflows_{it} = \theta_0 + \theta_1 \left(g_{it} - \bar{g}_{it}^{AE}\right) + \theta_2 \left(ir_{it} - \bar{ir}_{it}^{AE}\right) +$$
$$\theta_3 institutional\ quality_{it} + \theta_4 capital\ controls_{it} +$$
$$\theta_5 IMF\ loan_{it} + \theta_6 default_{it} +$$
$$\theta_7 \Delta termsoftrade_{it} + \tau T_t + \varepsilon_{it},$$

in which $\left(g_{it} - \bar{g}_{it}^{AE}\right)$ and $\left(ir_{it} - \bar{ir}_{it}^{AE}\right)$ are growth and interest rate differentials, as defined later in this annex, and T_t are a set of quarter dummy variables. These results are reported in the first columns of Annex Table 2.3.3 for inflows and Annex Table 2.3.4 for outflows.

As only the forecast growth differential is found to be statistically significant in this general regression, the specification is subsequently restricted to

$$Kflows_{it} = \alpha_0 + \alpha_1 \left(g_{it} - \bar{g}_{it}^{AE}\right) + \beta T_t + e_{it}.$$

These results are reported in the second columns of Annex Table 2.3.3 for inflows and Annex Table 2.3.4 for outflows.

Regressing gross capital inflows on the predicted values $\widehat{\beta T_t}$ from this regression yields the R-squared values used in Figure 2.19.

This specification is also used to examine how country characteristics affect the impact of the common trend for various types of countries using terms for the interactions between the time dummies and dummies for exchange rate regime, reserves, and public debt (reported in Annex Table 2.3.5 and Figure 2.20, adding also interactions for capital controls), and the differential impact of global factors, such as global growth and interest rate differentials and global risk aversion, for countries with fixed/flexible exchange rates, high/low levels of reserves, and high/low public debt levels (as reported in Annex Table 2.3.6 and Figure 2.21).

Weighting

In the country-specific regressions, the (growth or interest rate) differential for emerging market i ($i = 1, \ldots, 20$) at time t is given by the difference between the emerging market's own growth rate and a weighted average of advanced economy growth rates ($j = 1, \ldots, 7$):

$$g_{it} - \bar{g}_{it}^{AE} = g_{it} - \sum_{j=1}^{7} w_{ij} g_{jt},$$

with weights (varying by emerging market)

$$w_{ij} = \frac{PF_{ij}}{\sum_{j=1}^{7} PF_{ij}},$$

in which PF_{ij} is the average portfolio flow from advanced economy j to emerging market i over the years 2001–12 from the IMF's Coordinated Portfolio Investment Survey.

Annex Table 2.3.3. Role of Country Characteristics in Explaining Gross Capital Inflows

Growth Differential (forecast)	2.480***	2.634***	2.301***
	(0.750)	(0.801)	(0.725)
Real Interest Rate Differential	−0.217		
	(0.139)		
Institutional Quality	5.346		
	(7.884)		
Capital Controls (inflows)	4.668		
	(3.008)		
Large IMF Loan	4.349		
	(2.826)		
Default	0.099		
	(2.531)		
Change in Terms of Trade	−0.078		
	(0.080)		
Global Emerging Market Economy–Advanced Economy Growth Differential			2.284***
			(0.485)
Global Emerging Market Economy–Advanced Economy Interest Rate Differential			1.243*
			(0.608)
Global Risk Aversion (log)			−3.050***
			(0.880)
Change in Oil Price			−0.000
			(0.013)
U.S. Yield Gap			−1.775*
			(0.880)
U.S. Corporate Spread			−3.670**
			(1.416)
Time Fixed Effects	Yes	Yes	No
Country Fixed Effects	Yes	Yes	Yes
Number of Observations	1,111	1,111	1,111
Adjusted R^2	0.161	0.150	0.135

Source: IMF staff estimates.
Note: Based on a sample of 22 emerging market economies. See Annex 2.1 for a description of the sample, Annex 2.2 for a detailed description of included variables and sources, and Annex 2.3 for details on the methodology.
*$p <.10$; **$p < .05$; ***$p < .01$.

In the global regressions, the differential for emerging market i is given by the difference between a weighted average of emerging market growth rates and a weighted average of advanced economy growth rates:

In the global regressions, the differential for emerging market i is given by the difference between a weighted average of emerging market growth rates and a weighted average of advanced economy growth rates:

$$\bar{g}_t^{EM} - \bar{g}_t^{AE} = \sum_{i=1}^{20} w_{it} g_{it} - \sum_{j=1}^{7} w_{jt} g_{jt}$$

with weights (that do not vary by emerging market)

$$w_i = \frac{\sum_{j=1}^{7} PF_{ij}}{\sum_{i=1}^{20} \sum_{j=1}^{7} PF_{ij}},$$

$$w_j = \frac{1}{20} \sum_{i=1}^{20} w_{ijt}.$$

This differential does not vary across emerging markets.

Annex Table 2.3.4. Role of Country Characteristics in Explaining Gross Capital Outflows

Growth Differential (forecast)	0.502	0.584	0.657*
	(0.335)	(0.417)	(0.362)
Real Interest Rate Differential	0.0750		
	(0.076)		
Institutional Quality	3.972		
	(5.201)		
Capital Controls (outflows)	2.587		
	(3.199)		
Large IMF Loan	2.042***		
	(0.422)		
Default	1.052		
	(1.562)		
Change in Terms of Trade	0.0530		
	(0.062)		
Global Emerging Market Economy–Advanced Economy Growth Differential			0.656**
			(0.265)
Global Emerging Market Economy–Advanced Economy Interest Rate Differential			0.132
			(0.420)
Global Risk Aversion (log)			−1.918***
			(0.541)
Change in Oil Price			0.000829
			(0.010)
U.S. Yield Gap			−0.955
			(0.693)
U.S. Corporate Spread			−0.283
			(0.888)
Time Fixed Effects	Yes	Yes	No
Country Fixed Effects	Yes	Yes	Yes
Number of Observations	1,111	1,111	1,111
Adjusted R^2	0.049	0.046	0.047

Source: IMF staff estimates.
Note: Based on a sample of 22 emerging market economies. See Annex 2.1 for a description of the sample, Annex 2.2 for a detailed description of included variables and sources, and Annex 2.3 for details on the methodology.
$^*p <.10$; $^{**}p < .05$; $^{***}p < .01$.

Annex Table 2.3.5. Role of Interaction Terms in Explaining Gross Capital Inflows

	2.275***	1.738***	1.760***
Growth Differential (forecast)	(0.606)	(0.607)	(0.541)
Time Fixed Effects	Yes	Yes	No
Time Fixed Effects × Dummies (exchange rate regime, debt, reserves)	No	Yes	No
Global Variables	No	No	Yes
Global Variables × Dummies (exchange rate regime, debt, reserves)	No	No	Yes
Number of Observations	1,328	1,164	1,167
Adjusted R^2	0.12	0.43	0.19
		F-statistic (p-value)	
Capital Account Openness		5.72 (0.000)	
Exchange Rate Regime		35.72 (0.000)	
Reserves		4.90 (0.001)	
Debt		7.84 (0.000)	

Source: IMF staff estimates.
Note: F-statistics (and corresponding p-values) refer to the null hypotheses that respective interaction terms are jointly zero. See Annex 2.1 for a description of the sample, Annex 2.2 for a detailed description of included variables and sources, and Annex 2.3 for details on the methodology.
$^{***}p < .01$.

Annex Table 2.3.6. Role of Country Characteristics and Global Factors in Explaining Gross Capital Inflows

Growth Differential (forecast)	2.634***	2.842***	2.153***
	(0.801)	(0.868)	(0.539)
Capital Account Openness		−2.473**	
		(1.145)	
Floating Exchange Rate		−4.931***	
		(1.415)	
Low Reserves		−1.449	
		(1.164)	
High Debt		1.152	
		(0.921)	
Global Emerging Market Economy–Advanced Economy Growth Differential			5.492***
			(1.224)
Global Emerging Market Economy–Advanced Economy Interest Rate Differential			4.001**
			(1.509)
Global Risk Aversion (log)			−5.909***
			(1.538)
Change in Oil Price			0.047
			(0.030)
U.S. Yield Gap			−6.442**
			(2.450)
U.S. Corporate Spread			0.917
			(4.700)
Global Emerging Market Economy–Advanced Economy Growth Differential × Floating			−3.549**
			(1.280)
Global Emerging Market Economy–Advanced Economy Growth Differential × Low Reserves			−1.220
			(0.941)
Global Emerging Market Economy–Advanced Economy Growth Differential × High Debt			0.287
			(0.607)
Global Emerging Market Economy–Advanced Economy Interest Rate Differential × Floating			−3.542*
			(1.757)
Global Emerging Market Economy–Advanced Economy Interest Rate Differential × Low Reserves			−0.751
			(1.000)
Global Emerging Market Economy–Advanced Economy Interest Rate Differential × High Debt			0.408
			(0.729)
Global Risk Aversion (log) × Floating			4.184*
			(2.348)
Global Risk Aversion (log) × Low Reserves			−0.349
			(1.427)
Global Risk Aversion (log) × High Debt			−1.216
			(0.776)
Change in Oil Price × Floating			−0.074*
			(0.036)
Change in Oil Price × Low Reserves			0.046**
			(0.019)
Change in Oil Price × High Debt			−0.002
			(0.017)
U.S. Yield Gap × Floating			5.754*
			(2.807)
U.S. Yield Gap × Low Reserves			0.306
			(1.022)
U.S. Yield Gap × High Debt			−0.558
			(1.205)
U.S. Corporate Spread × Floating			−8.457
			(5.240)
U.S. Corporate Spread × Low Reserves			4.753*
			(2.657)
U.S. Corporate Spread × High Debt			3.266
			(2.082)
Number of Observations	1,111	1,096	1,096***
Adjusted R^2	0.15	0.16	−0.24

Source: IMF staff estimates.
Note: Based on a sample of 22 emerging market economies. See Annex 2.1 for a description of the sample, Annex 2.2 for a detailed description of included variables and sources, and Annex 2.3 for details on the methodology.
*$p < .10$; **$p < .05$; ***$p < .01$.

Box 2.1. Capital Flows to Low-Income Developing Countries

Low-income developing countries have typically been characterized by modest access to private external financing. Since the mid-2000s however, low-income developing countries have relied more on nonofficial inflows and increasingly have gained market access. Historical experience in other countries has emphasized not just the benefits of inflows—for instance, in providing financing for investment—but also the risks of inflow reversals that induce macroeconomic and financial volatility. This box documents recent experience with capital flows in 23 low-income developing countries, contrasting it with the 2010–15 slowdown in net capital inflows in emerging market economies.[1] The box extends the data set and analysis in Araujo and others 2015 and also draws on IMF 2015a.

Net capital inflows to low-income developing countries were broadly flat in the first half of the 2000s, with median net inflows fluctuating around 2 percent of GDP (Figure 2.1.1).[2] In line with improved growth prospects in a majority of low-income developing countries, inflows picked up in the second half of the 2000s, with median net inflows peaking at 5½ percent of GDP in 2008, before retrenching during the global financial crisis. After the crisis, median net capital inflows increased sizably, from 3¼ percent of GDP in 2009 to nearly 7½ percent of GDP in 2013. However, this increasing trend was reversed sharply in 2014, with median net capital inflows to low-income developing countries falling back to the 2010 level.

Thus, in contrast to the persistent 2010–15 net capital inflow slowdown in emerging market economies (as documented in this chapter), net capital inflows in low-income developing countries continued to expand strongly through much of the period, with a slowdown starting only in 2014. While this box does not identify the drivers behind the different capital

The author of this box is Juliana D. Araujo.

[1] The analysis imposes a balanced-sample requirement, which limits the low-income developing country sample to 23 nonsmall and nonfragile countries, with frontier markets representing more than half of the sample: Bangladesh*, Bolivia*, Cambodia, Ghana*, Honduras, Kenya*, the Kyrgyz Republic, Lesotho, Mauritania, Moldova, Mongolia*, Mozambique*, Nepal, Nicaragua, Nigeria*, Papua New Guinea*, Rwanda, Senegal*, Tanzania*, Uganda*, Uzbekistan, Vietnam*, and Zambia*, where asterisks denote frontier markets as defined in IMF 2015a. Country samples in each figure may vary depending on data availability.

[2] The data exclude other investment flows to the official sector (the general government and monetary authorities), whether or not they originate from official or private sources (the underlying data source provides a breakdown by debtor but not by creditor).

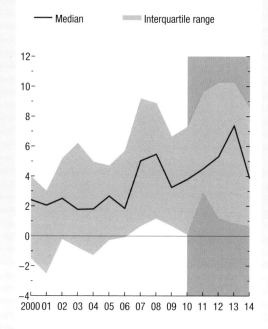

Figure 2.1.1. Net Capital Inflows to Low-Income Developing Countries, 2000–14
(Percent of GDP)

Sources: Araujo and others 2015; and IMF staff calculations.

inflow experience of the two groups of countries, differences in their growth experiences likely played an important role. Unlike in emerging market economies, which experienced a relatively persistent growth slowdown after 2010, growth in low-income developing countries remained stronger, averaging 6 percent in 2013–14. The strong growth performance was aided in part by improved macroeconomic frameworks but also by favorable external conditions (see Box 1.2).[3] Since mid-2014, many commodity-dependent low-income developing countries have also seen sharply lower global commodity prices, particularly that of oil, and decelerating growth.

The documented 2009–14 net capital inflow trends in low-income developing countries closely followed gross capital inflows, with outflows remaining broadly

[3] Several low-income developing countries also went through debt reduction programs, which started in the 1990s with bilateral creditor debt reduction negotiations and culminated in the mid-2000s with the Heavily Indebted Poor Countries Initiative and later the Multilateral Debt Relief Initiative.

Box 2.1 *(continued)*

stable (Figure 2.1.2, panels 1 and 2). Growth in net
inflows after 2009 was broad based—nearly two-thirds
of low-income developing countries received higher
net capital inflows in 2013 relative to 2009. Turning
to inflows by asset type, the post-2009 rise in gross
capital inflows to low-income developing countries
included both foreign direct investment (FDI) and
non-FDI inflows (the latter comprising portfolio—
debt and equity—inflows and other nonofficial
investment—for example, bank deposits, corporate
and bank loans, and trade credit).

Furthermore, by 2012–13, the size of both FDI
and non-FDI inflows, relative to GDP, for low-income
developing countries exceeded inflows in emerging
market economies, especially for FDI (Figure 2.1.3,
panels 1 and 2, and Figure 2.1.4). Meanwhile, within
non-FDI inflows, portfolio flows to low-income
developing countries were very limited until 2013,
with the recent increases largely driven by frontier
low-income developing countries (Figure 2.1.3, panel
3). Examples of recent sovereign bond issuers include
Mongolia (with a 2012 issue equivalent to 20 percent
of GDP) and Kenya (with a debut issue of more than
3 percent of GDP in 2014). Côte d'Ivoire, Ethiopia,
Ghana, Senegal, Vietnam, and Zambia also issued
sovereign bonds in 2014. Finally, net capital inflows
in low-income developing countries followed similar
trends in sub-Saharan Africa (corresponding to nearly
half of the sample) and Asia (about a quarter of the
sample), despite some recent deceleration in net capital
inflows to Asian low-income developing countries
(Figure 2.1.3, panel 4).[4]

Trends in reserve accumulation indicate that during
the post-2009 period, foreign reserves have played less
of a buffer role for low-income developing countries,
compared with emerging market economies, with the
current account counterbalancing the bulk of the net
capital inflow movement. Despite the surge in net capital inflows, the pace of foreign reserve accumulation
in low-income developing countries during 2009–13
remained broadly unchanged at about 2.6 percent
of GDP (Figure 2.1.4, panel 1). During the same
period, the current account balance for the median
low-income developing country decreased markedly—
from –6.5 to –10 percent of GDP (Figure 2.1.4, panel
2). Furthermore, in tandem with the sharp net capital

[4]See the April 2011 and October 2013 *Regional Economic
Outlook: Sub-Saharan Africa* reports for an examination of capital
flows to sub-Saharan Africa.

**Figure 2.1.2. Capital Inflows and Outflows of
Low-Income Developing Countries, 2000–14**
(Percent of GDP)

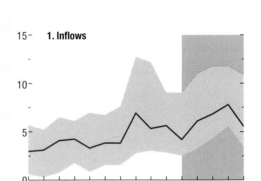

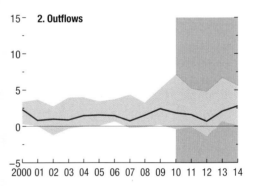

Sources: Araujo and others 2015; and IMF staff
calculations.

inflow reversal in 2014, the current account balance for the median low-income developing country
improved.[5]

In contrast, reserves played a more important buffer
role prior to the global financial crisis. Net reserve
accumulation peaked in 2007, with a median and
top-quartile accumulation of 3¼ percent of GDP and

[5]Nonetheless, the interpretation of current account developments in countries with large investment projects financed exter-
nally could be more challenging. More generally, FDI-related
imports could create a direct link between capital inflows and
the current account balance. During 2009–14 the remaining components (median and interquartile) of the balance of
payments identity—other investment flows to the official sector,
capital account balance, and net errors and omissions—remained
broadly stable.

Box 2.1 *(continued)*

Figure 2.1.3. Capital Inflows to Low-Income Developing Countries by Asset Type and Net Capital Inflows by Region, 2000–14
(Percent of GDP)

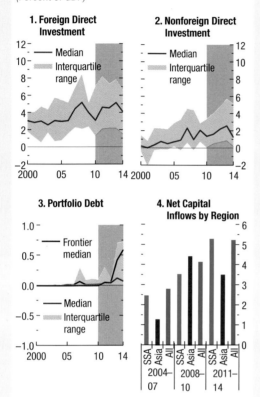

Sources: Araujo and others 2015; and IMF staff calculations.
Note: SSA = Sub-Saharan Africa.

Figure 2.1.4. Net Reserve Assets and Current Account Balance, 2000–14
(Percent of GDP)

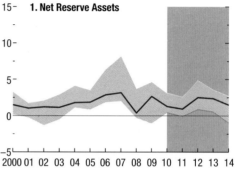

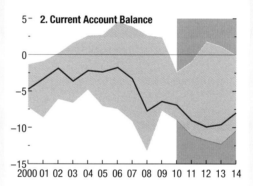

Sources: CEIC Asia database; CEIC China database; Haver Analytics; IMF, *Balance of Payments Statistics*; IMF, *International Financial Statistics*; World Bank, World Development Indicators database; and IMF staff calculations.

8¼ percent of GDP, respectively. The median current account was broadly flat during that period.

How have net capital inflows in low-income developing countries evolved since 2014? Preliminary evidence for the first half of 2015 for a limited sample of eight countries with available balance of payments data suggests that the reversal in net inflows continued in 2015 (Figure 2.1.5). After decreasing by 1.6 percentage points of GDP in 2014 relative to 2013, median net capital inflows decreased by a further 1.8 percentage points in the first half of 2015.[6] Low-income developing countries' exchange rates fell sharply with respect to the dollar during 2014–15, although

[6]This most recent subsample has a limited coverage of sub-Saharan African countries.

less so compared with emerging market exchange rates (Figure 2.1.6). Moreover, depreciation was negligible in nominal effective terms. As also discussed in Box 1.2, since mid-2015, sovereign bond spreads in frontier low-income developing countries rose more sharply than those in emerging market economies.

Overall, low-income developing countries have displayed strong economic resilience in the aftermath of the global financial crisis, helping insulate them from the net capital inflow slowdown observed in emerging market economies. More recently, the deterioration of domestic conditions (such as lower growth and wider fiscal deficits) and external conditions have

Box 2.1 *(continued)*

Figure 2.1.5. Net Capital Inflows to Low-Income Developing Countries, 2012–15, Restricted Sample
(Percent of GDP)

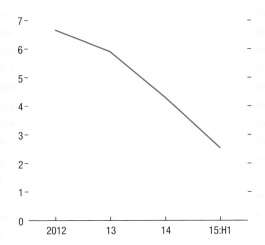

Sources: CEIC Asia database; CEIC China database; Haver Analytics; IMF, *Balance of Payments Statistics*; IMF, *International Financial Statistics*; World Bank, World Development Indicators database; and IMF staff calculations.
Note: Country sample comprises Bangladesh, Honduras, Lesotho, Moldova, Mongolia, Nicaragua, Uganda, and Vietnam.

Figure 2.1.6. Exchange Rates of Low-Income Developing Countries, 2009–15:Q3
(Percent change)

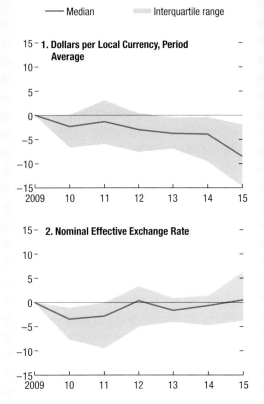

Sources: IMF, Information Notice System; IMF, International Financial Statistics database; and IMF staff calculations.

played an important role in driving down the level of capital inflows and driving up the price of capital (for example, sovereign spreads; see also the October 2013 *Regional Economic Outlook: Sub-Saharan Africa* and IMF 2015a). Amid external conditions, lower commodity prices and lower growth among trading partners have likely had a substantial impact on

low-income developing countries' economic prospects (see Box 1.2), coinciding with the recent period of capital flow slowdown in these countries.

Box 2.2. U.S. Monetary Policy and Capital Flows to Emerging Markets

In the immediate aftermath of the global financial crisis, capital flows to emerging market economies were buoyed by accommodative monetary policy conditions in Europe, in Japan, and especially in the United States, as well as by substantially better growth prospects than those in the slowly recovering advanced economies. Portfolio flows represented a large part of the increase.

Although this tide began to turn shortly after 2010, as documented in this chapter, a marked inflection point for many countries relates to the May 22, 2013, announcement by Federal Reserve Chairman Ben Bernanke of a gradual tapering of the Federal Reserve's quantitative easing program, possibly later that year. That surprise gave rise to the so-called taper tantrum—a period of several weeks during which large volumes of portfolio funds appeared to flee emerging markets, according to the emerging markets fund flows data collected by Emerging Portfolio Fund Research (EPFR) Global.[1] Emerging market currencies depreciated and emerging market asset prices generally fell. In contrast, following the actual rate liftoff on December 16, 2015, emerging market asset prices barely responded, and emerging market fund flows during the subsequent week, while negative, were not lower than the average in the previous six months.[2]

These two events point to the importance of changes in expectations regarding future U.S. policy interest rates in driving emerging market asset prices and asset flows in and out of emerging markets. They also illustrate how expectations of policy shifts can have distinct effects along the yield curve for U.S. Treasury bonds. The short-maturity end of the U.S. yield curve increased when the increase in the federal funds rate finally materialized in December 2015, whereas it did not move substantially during the taper tantrum (when market participants brought forward their expectations of the first rate hike, but did not

expect an imminent one). The difference in changes in the higher-maturity end of the yield curve during the two episodes, however, was far more striking. In the three weeks following May 22, 2013, 2-year and 10-year U.S. yields rose by 10 basis points and 25 basis points, respectively (they were up 20 basis points and more than 60 basis points, respectively, within five weeks after May 22, 2013). By contrast, 2-year U.S. yields were unchanged and 10-year yields were actually down 4 basis points three weeks after the December 2015 rate hike. This suggests that the anticipated policy move in December 2015 did not change the markets' expectations regarding slow and gradual further rate increases in the coming years.

Econometric analysis points to the importance of expected changes in U.S. interest rates in driving capital flows. Regression analysis reported in Table 2.2.1 helps explain the observation that the large shift in expectations of future interest rates during the taper tantrum, even in the absence of actual policy change, triggered outflows from emerging market investment funds whereas, with stable expectations around December 2015, the eventual rate hike did not have a meaningful short-term effect. The regression of EPFR weekly data on gross fund flows to emerging markets since the beginning of 2013 on the Chicago Board Options Exchange Volatility Index (VIX) (a measure of market risk aversion) and 3-, 12-, and 35-month federal funds rate futures shows that fund flows decline when markets become more risk averse (that is, the VIX is higher) and when market expectations of federal funds rates almost three years in the future increase.[3] Yet the regression shows no statistically significant relationship between the 3- or 12-month future rate and emerging market fund flows. To the extent that EPFR data track approximately actual fluctuations in total portfolio flows to emerging markets as measured by balance of payments data (Figure 2.2.1), these results suggest that longer-term market expectations could be more important than shorter-term rates in transmitting the effects of U.S. monetary policy to emerging market capital flows. Movements in shorter-term interest rates, which tend to be foreseen

The author of this box is Frantisek Ricka.

[1]EPFR data track net flows (investor contributions and redemptions) for individual funds and fund groups. They exclude portfolio performance and currency effects. The data are collected by EPFR Global from managers and administrators of a universe of funds covering more than $23.5 trillion in globally domiciled funds. The emerging-market-specific sample covers country-specific, regional, and general emerging market bond and equity funds.

[2]According to the same EPFR data, bond outflows in the week leading up to the Federal Reserve's decision were above average, suggesting capital moved in anticipation of the rate increase.

[3]The estimated coefficient indicates that every percentage point increase in the expected 35-month federal funds futures rate reduces emerging market fund flows by more than $5 billion, suggesting a loss of at least $1 billion in fund flows during the week after the taper talk, when the 35-month future rate rose by 20 basis points.

Box 2.2 *(continued)*

Table 2.2.1. Short-Term Determinants of Emerging Market Fund Flows

Variables	Weekly Emerging Market Fund Flows
Lagged Emerging Market Fund Flows	0.580***
	(0.0912)
Chicago Board Options Exchange Volatility Index (VIX) (change)	−350.6**
	(145.9)
Three-Month Federal Funds Futures (change)	−22,918
	(16,368)
Twelve-Month Federal Funds Futures (change)	7,517
	(6,760)
Thirty-Five-Month Federal Funds Futures	−5,625**
	(2,233)
Constant	−328.6
	(238.1)
Number of Observations	147

Source: IMF staff estimates.
Note: Newey-West standard errors are in parentheses. The reported regression results are based on weekly data from January 1, 2013, to December 31, 2015.
$**p < .05; ***p < .01.$

by markets and are thus subject to fewer surprises, are not statistically significant at a 5 percent confidence level—though the large absolute value of the estimated coefficient on the 3-month interest rate suggests that the respective effect on capital flows should not be dismissed altogether.

There are important caveats to bear in mind. First, the EPFR data used in the regressions shown in Table 2.2.1 cover only a subset of portfolio flows to emerging markets; while such data may be useful for picking up high-frequency movements in portfolio flows in the absence of comprehensive balance of payments data for intervals shorter than a quarter, a comprehensive picture of overall capital flows to emerging markets can come only from quarterly balance of payments data. Second, at quarterly or annual frequencies, shifts in policy rate expectations can be tightly correlated with growth expectations. If so, part of the effect picked up by the coefficient on the 35-month federal funds futures rate could reflect the impact of expected economic growth in the United States. The latter, by affecting the growth differential between advanced economies and emerging markets, can be an important driver of capital inflows to emerging markets, consistent with the econometric results presented in this chapter.

Figure 2.2.1. Correlation between Emerging Market Fund Flows and Total Emerging Market Portfolio Inflows
(Billions of dollars)

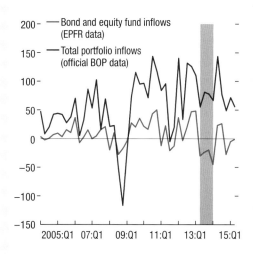

Sources: CEIC Asia database; CEIC China database; Emerging Portfolio Fund Research (EPFR) Global; Haver Analytics; IMF, *Balance of Payments Statistics*; IMF, *International Financial Statistics*; and World Bank, World Development Indicators database.
Note: BOP = balance of payments.

References

Accominotti, Olivier, and Barry Eichengreen. Forthcoming. "The Mother of All Sudden Stops: Capital Flows and Reversals in Europe, 1919–32." *Economic History Review.*

Ahmed, Shaghil, and Andrei Zlate. 2013. "Capital Flows to Emerging Market Economies: A Brave New World?" International Finance Discussion Paper 1081, Board of Governors of the Federal Reserve System, Washington.

Aizenman, Joshua, Menzie D. Chinn, and Hiro Ito. 2015. "Monetary Policy Spillovers and the Trilemma in the New Normal: Periphery Country Sensitivity to Core Country Conditions." NBER Working Paper 21128, National Bureau of Economic Research, Cambridge, Massachusetts.

Araujo, Juliana D., Antonio C. David, Carlos van Hombeeck, and Chris Papageorgiou. 2015. "Capital Flows in Low-Income Developing Countries: Catching the Wave?" IMF Working Paper 15/86, International Monetary Fund, Washington.

Arslanalp, Serkan, and Takahiro Tsuda. 2014. "Tracking Global Demand for Advanced Economy Sovereign Debt." *IMF Economic Review* 62 (3): 430–64.

Avdjiev, Stefan, Michael Chui, and Hyun Song Shin. 2014. "Non-financial Corporations from Emerging Market Economies and Capital Flows." *BIS Quarterly Review* (December): 67–77.

Avdjiev, Stefan, Robert N. McCauley, and Hyun Song Shin. 2015. "Breaking Free of the Triple Coincidence in International Finance." BIS Working Paper 524, Bank for International Settlements, Basel.

Benetrix, Agustin S., Jay C. Shambaugh, and Philip R. Lane. 2015. "International Currency Exposures, Valuation Effects and the Global Financial Crisis." *Journal of International Economics* 96 (1): 98–109.

Blanchard, Olivier, Jonathan D. Ostry, Atish R. Ghosh, and Marcos Chamon. Forthcoming. "Capital Flows: Expansionary or Contractionary?" *American Economic Review.*

Bordo, Michael D., and Joseph G. Haubrich. 2010. "Credit Crises, Money and Contractions: An Historical View." *Journal of Monetary Economics* 57 (1): 1–18.

Broner, Fernando, Tatiana Didier, Aitor Erce, and Sergio L. Schmukler. 2013. "Gross Capital Flows: Dynamics and Crises." *Journal of Monetary Economics* 60 (1): 113–33.

Calvo, Guillermo A. 1998. "Capital Flows and Capital-Market Crises: The Simple Economics of Sudden Stops." *Journal of Applied Economics* 1 (1): 35–54.

———, Leonardo Leiderman, and Carmen M. Reinhart. 1996. "Inflows of Capital to Developing Countries in the 1990s." *Journal of Economic Perspectives* 10 (2): 123–39.

Catão, Luis A. V. 2007. "Sudden Stops and Currency Drops: A Historical Look." In *The Decline of Latin American Economies: Growth, Institutions, and Crises,* edited by Sebastian Edwards, Gerardo Esquivel, and Graciela Márquez. Chicago: University of Chicago Press.

———, and Rui C. Mano. 2015. "Default Premium." IMF Working Paper 15/167, International Monetary Fund, Washington.

Catão, Luis A. V., and Gian Maria Milesi-Ferretti. 2014. "External Liabilities and Crises." *Journal of International Economics* 94 (1): 18–32.

Cerutti, Eugenio, Stijn Claessens, and Damien Puy. 2015. "Push Factors and Capital Flows to Emerging Markets: Why Knowing Your Lender Matters More Than Fundamentals." IMF Working Paper 15/124, International Monetary Fund, Washington.

Choi, Woon G., Sunil Sharma, and Maria Strömqvist. 2009. "Net Capital Flows, Financial Integration, and International Reserve Holdings: The Recent Experience of Emerging Markets and Advanced Economies." *IMF Staff Papers* 56 (3): 516–40.

Claessens, Stijn, and David Naude. 1993. "Recent Estimates of Capital Flight." Policy Research Working Paper 1186, World Bank, Washington.

Dornbusch, Rudiger, Alejandro Werner, Guillermo Calvo, and Stanley Fischer. 1994. "Mexico: Stabilization, Reform, and No Growth." *Brookings Papers on Economic Activity* (1): 253–315.

Eichengreen, Barry, and Ricardo Hausmann. 1998. "Exchange Rates and Financial Fragility." NBER Working Paper 7418, National Bureau of Economic Research, Cambridge, Massachusetts.

———, and Ugo Panizza. 2002. "Original Sin: The Pain, the Mystery, and the Road to Redemption." Paper presented at "Currency and Maturity Matchmaking: Redeeming Debt from Original Sin," Inter-American Development Bank, Washington, November 21–22.

Fernández, Andrés, Michael W. Klein, Alessandro Rebucci, Martin Schindler, and Martin Uribe. 2015. "Capital Control Measures: A New Dataset." NBER Working Paper 20970, National Bureau of Economic Research, Cambridge, Massachusetts.

International Monetary Fund (IMF). 2015a. "Macroeconomic Developments and Prospects in Low-Income Developing Countries: 2015." IMF Policy Paper, Washington.

———. 2015b. *2015 Spillover Report.* Washington.

Kaminsky, Graciela L., and Carmen M. Reinhart. 1999. "The Twin Crises: The Causes of Banking and Balance-of-Payments Problems." *American Economic Review* 89 (3): 473–500.

Karolyi, Andrew G., David T. Ng, and Eswar S. Prasad. 2013. "The Coming Wave." Working Paper 08/2013, Hong Kong Institute for Monetary Research, Hong Kong Special Administrative Region.

Koepke, Robin. 2015. "What Drives Capital Flows to Emerging Markets? A Survey of the Empirical Literature." Working Paper, Institute of International Finance, Washington.

Laeven, Luc, and Fabián Valencia. 2013. "Systemic Banking Crises Database," *IMF Economic Review* 61, 225–70.

Lane, Philip R., and Gian Maria Milesi-Ferretti. 2007. "The External Wealth of Nations Mark II: Revised and Extended Estimates of Foreign Assets and Liabilities, 1970–2004." *Journal of International Economics* 73 (2): 223–50.

Lane, Philip R., and Jay C. Shambaugh. 2010. "Financial Exchange Rates and International Currency Exposures." *American Economic Review* 100 (1): 518–40.

Magud, Nicolas E., Carmen M. Reinhart, and Esteban Vesperoni. 2014. "Capital Inflows, Exchange Rate Flexibility, and Credit Booms." *Review of Development Economics* 18 (3): 415–30.

Mundell, Robert A. 1963. "Capital Mobility and Stabilization Policy under Fixed and Flexible Exchange Rates." *Canadian Journal of Economics and Political Science* 29 (November): 475–85.

Nier, Erlend, Tahsin Saadi Sedik, and Tomas Mondino. 2014. "Gross Private Capital Flows to Emerging Markets: Can the Global Financial Cycle Be Tamed?" IMF Working Paper 14/196, International Monetary Fund, Washington.

Obstfeld, Maurice. 2015. "Trilemmas and Trade-Offs: Living with Financial Globalization." BIS Working Paper 480, Bank for International Settlements, Basel.

Reinhart, Carmen M., and Kenneth S. Rogoff. 2004. "The Modern History of Exchange Rate Arrangements: A Reinterpretation." *Quarterly Journal of Economics* 119 (1): 1–48.

———. 2011. "The Forgotten History of Domestic Debt." *Economic Journal* 121 (552): 319–50.

Rey, Hélène. Forthcoming. "International Channels of Transmission of Monetary Policy and the Mundellian Trilemma." *IMF Economic Review.*

Sahay, Ratna, Vivek Arora, Thanos Arvanitis, Hamid Faruqee, Papa N'Diaye, Tommaso Mancini-Griffoli, and an IMF team. 2014. "Emerging Market Volatility: Lessons from the Taper Tantrum." IMF Staff Discussion Note 14/09, International Monetary Fund, Washington.

CHAPTER 3

TIME FOR A SUPPLY-SIDE BOOST? MACROECONOMIC EFFECTS OF LABOR AND PRODUCT MARKET REFORMS IN ADVANCED ECONOMIES

This chapter finds that product and labor market reforms raise output and employment in the medium term, but complementary macroeconomic policies are needed to maximize their short-term payoff given the current economic slack in most advanced economies. Product market reforms deliver gains in the short term, while the impact of labor market reforms varies across types of reforms and depends on overall economic conditions. Reductions in labor tax wedges and increases in public spending on active labor market policies have larger effects during periods of slack, in part because they usually entail some degree of fiscal stimulus. In contrast, reforms to employment protection arrangements and unemployment benefit systems have positive effects in good times, but can become contractionary in periods of slack. These results suggest the need for carefully prioritizing and sequencing reforms.

Worries have deepened over the persistent sluggishness of growth in advanced economies since the 2008–09 global financial crisis. The growth rate of potential output—defined as the level of output consistent with stable inflation—has declined in major advanced economies, and it is likely to remain below precrisis levels through the medium term (see Chapter 3 in the April 2015 *World Economic Outlook*). Although the global financial crisis was a factor in this slowdown, not least through its effect on investment, the decline in potential growth started in the early 2000s, which suggests that deeper structural factors have been at play (Figure 3.1).

As a result, the continued weakness of growth and shrinking macroeconomic policy space, especially in several euro area countries and in Japan, have led policymakers to emphasize structural reforms. The hope is that such reforms will lift potential output over the medium term while also strengthening aggregate demand in the near term by raising consumer and business confidence.

High on the agenda are several reforms designed to strengthen the functioning of product and labor markets (IMF 2015; OECD 2015). Although the specifics vary widely for individual countries, these reforms broadly involve the following:

- Deregulating retail trade, professional services, and certain segments of network industries (air, rail, and road transportation; electricity and gas distribution; telecommunications and postal services), primarily by reducing barriers to entry
- Increasing the ability of and incentives for the non-employed to find jobs, by boosting resources for and efficiency of active labor market policies, reducing the level or duration of unemployment benefits where these are particularly high, or both
- Lowering the costs of and simplifying the procedures for hiring and dismissing regular (that is, permanent) workers and harmonizing employment protection legislation for both regular and temporary workers
- Improving collective-bargaining frameworks in instances in which they have struggled to deliver high and stable employment
- Cutting the labor tax wedge—that is, the difference between the labor cost to the employer and the worker's net take-home pay
- Implementing targeted policies to boost participation of underrepresented groups in the labor market, including youth, women, and older workers

The reforms on this menu, though highly diverse, all aim either at reducing policy distortions or at improving the way existing institutions address imperfections in markets. For example, governments can improve the way they provide income insurance to workers by more effectively combining unemployment benefits, employment protection legislation, and active labor market policies.

The long-term gains that labor and product market reforms generate for advanced economies and the channels through which they operate (increased productivity,

The authors of this chapter are Romain Duval and Davide Furceri (lead authors), Alexander Hijzen, João Jalles, and Sinem Kılıç Çelik, with contributions from Jaebin Ahn, Romain Bouis, Matteo Cacciatore, Johannes Eugster, Giuseppe Fiori, Peter Gal, Fabio Ghironi, Prakash Loungani and Jakob Miethe, and support from Bingjie Hu, Olivia Ma, Huy Nguyen, and Rachel Szymanski. Alexander Hijzen and Peter Gal contributed as visiting scholars from the Organisation for Economic Co-operation and Development (OECD), whose support is gratefully acknowledged.

Figure 3.1. Evolution of Potential Output Growth and Its Components in Advanced Economies
(Percent)

Potential growth has declined in major advanced economies, and it is likely to remain below precrisis levels through the medium term.

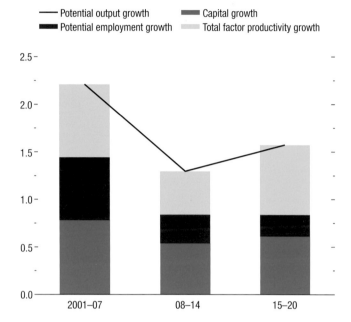

Source: IMF staff estimates.
Note: This figure draws on Figure 3.11 in the April 2015 *World Economic Outlook*.

lower unemployment, higher labor force participation) are fairly well documented (see, for example, Bouis and Duval 2011 and the studies cited therein). Much less is known, however, about the short- to medium-term effects of such reforms on aggregate output, employment, and inflation. On one hand, credible structural reforms may strengthen confidence and enhance expectations and thereby boost aggregate demand (Draghi 2015). On the other, they may further weaken demand through wage and price deflation, which can increase real interest rates in countries where monetary policy is already constrained (Eggertsson, Ferrero, and Raffo 2014; Krugman 2014). Both scenarios presume that reforms have a fairly quick and sizable impact on supply (potential output). A broader concern is that even the most effective reforms might have merely a small short-term supply benefit because of the length of time the economy needs to converge to a (higher) long-term output level (Rodrik 2015).

This chapter employs new data and modeling techniques to assess whether product and labor

market reforms can improve the economic outlook in advanced economies. Specifically, the chapter

- Summarizes the evolution of a wide range of product market regulations and labor market structures across advanced economies over the past four decades and assesses the scope for further reform
- Examines the channels through which reforms affect economic activity under strong versus weak economic conditions, drawing on a new model that differentiates between specific regulations (for example, the costs of layoff procedures and barriers to entry), unlike other model-based studies
- Applies novel empirical strategies to a new database of reforms to create a fresh quantitative assessment of their short- to medium-term macroeconomic effects, including their sensitivity to the state of the business cycle and the stance of macroeconomic policies
- Considers how—in light of the findings—reforms might be sequenced and supported by other policies to maximize their potential quantitative economic benefits in the near and medium term
These are the chapter's main findings:
- A number of advanced economies still have significant room for further deregulation in retail trade and professional services and in a few network industries. Labor market institutions are more varied across countries and are also more stable over time than are product market regulations. In some cases this stability reflects the success of several different institutional models in delivering good labor market outcomes, but in many others it highlights obstacles to reforming poorly functioning institutions and the scope for further efforts.
- The product and labor market reforms considered in this chapter can make important contributions to potential output and employment levels in many advanced economies over the medium term (Table 3.1). They therefore warrant further effort, particularly in most euro area countries and in Japan. Their contributions are likely to be modest in the short term, however, because it takes time for the benefits to materialize, particularly where economic conditions remain weak.
- Product market reforms also have some expansionary effect in the short term. This effect does not depend markedly on overall economic conditions, but the impact on investment tends to be weaker for credit-constrained firms.

Table 3.1. Effect of Product and Labor Market Reforms on Macroeconomic Outcomes

The effects of structural reforms depend on the type of reform, overall economic conditions, and the horizon considered.

Area of Reforms	Normal Economic Conditions		Weak Economic Conditions		Strong Economic Conditions	
	Short Term	Medium Term	Short Term	Medium Term	Short Term	Medium Term
Product Market	+	++		+	+	++
Employment Protection Legislation			−	− −	+	++
Unemployment Benefits	+	++	−		+	++
Labor Tax Wedge	++	++	++	++		
Active Labor Market Policies	++	++	++	++		

Source: IMF staff estimates.
Note: The macroeconomic outcomes are output and/or employment; + (−) indicates positive (negative) effect; the number of + (−) signs denotes the strength of the effect. The effect of labor tax wedge decreases and spending increases on active labor market policies is smaller but remains positive when these measures are implemented in a budget-neutral way.

- The effects of labor market reforms depend on over-all economic conditions:
  - Fiscal structural reforms in the labor market area, such as reduced labor tax wedges and increased public spending on active labor market policies, have larger effects during periods of economic slack, in part because they usually entail some degree of fiscal stimulus.
  - In contrast, reforms to employment protection arrangements and unemployment benefit systems have positive effects in good times, but can become contractionary in periods of slack because they can weaken aggregate demand.
- However, there is no compelling evidence that reform impacts in advanced economies have been weakened in the short term by interest rates that have been at or near zero since the global financial crisis. It is unclear in theory and based on past episodes whether reforms have substantial deflationary (or inflationary) effects.
- Complementary policies can offset the short-term costs of some structural reforms. These include supportive macroeconomic policies and intensified efforts to address weaknesses in bank and corporate balance sheets—for example, through stronger corporate insolvency frameworks and the development of distressed debt markets by improving market infrastructure and using asset management companies to jump-start the market in some cases (Aiyar and others 2015).

These results suggest that prioritizing and sequencing reforms can be particularly important for optimizing their impact in the current environment of persistent slack in most advanced economies. Reforms that entail fiscal stimulus will be the most valuable, including reducing labor tax wedges and increasing public spending on active labor market policies. Such measures will also remain effective when implemented in a budget-neutral way, for example, as part of broad tax and spending reforms. Product market reforms should also be prioritized, because they boost output regardless of overall economic conditions and because they do not weigh on public finances.

Other labor market reforms could be costly in the short term under current conditions, including reductions in unemployment benefits and—especially—reform of job protection rules. One strategy could be to enact such measures with a credible proviso that they will come into force only when the recovery is more robust. Such an approach could induce firms to invest and hire prospectively, in advance of the actual implementation of the reforms. Grandfathering reforms—that is, applying new rules only to new beneficiaries (of permanent job contracts or unemployment benefits) and exempting current beneficiaries—is an alternative, possibly easier-to-implement way to achieve the same goal. Another common concern with these labor market reforms is that they may increase income inequality. Preliminary analysis does not point to significant distributional consequences of the reforms studied in this chapter, with the exception of reductions in unemployment benefits, which appear to raise inequality over the medium term. This possibility provides a case for strengthening job search support and incentives without cutting benefits, or at least for complementing benefit reforms with offsetting fiscal measures targeted at lower-income households.

There is also a case for fiscal rules that accommodate structural reforms, especially in periods of weak economic conditions. Expansionary fiscal policy can offset the short-term costs of certain reforms (for example, to employment protection legislation) and amplify the gains from others (for example, from tax wedge reductions or increased spending on active labor market policies) (see also Chapter 2 in the October 2014 *Fiscal Monitor*). Thus, in countries that have a credible medium-term fiscal framework and available fiscal space, it could be beneficial to use fiscal policy to advance the implementation of reforms while committing to tightening later, when fiscal consolidation becomes less costly. This strategy could facilitate the adoption of reforms while amplifying their payoff over the medium term.

Given the uncertain effects of product and labor market reforms on prices, and amid persistent low inflation in many countries, strong and credible monetary policy frameworks that keep medium-term inflation expectations anchored and ease the zero-lower-bound constraint on policy rates—including quantitative easing or negative deposit rates, where relevant—can preempt the risk that reforms will lead to deflation, increase the real interest rate, and lower aggregate demand.

The policy prescriptions in this chapter represent a first-best strategy to maximize the impact of reforms in the current environment of persistent slack, but it may not always be feasible to implement them. For example, binding macroeconomic policy constraints may sometimes rule out demand support for labor market reforms even under weak macroeconomic conditions. Likewise, in some cases political economy constraints may call for pursuing difficult reforms when there is a window of opportunity—such as during periods of protracted slow growth. In such cases, reforms are pursued for their long-term benefits, but expectations regarding their short-term impact should be realistic.

Finally, despite the clear benefits, reforms in product and labor markets alone cannot counteract the persistent decline in potential growth that started in the early 2000s and was amplified by the global financial crisis. Past reforms have reduced the scope for further progress in some areas, and the empirical evidence in this chapter suggests that the impact of reforms eventually levels off. Product and labor market reforms should therefore be combined with complementary actions in other areas, including education, innovation, and tax and spending policies (April 2016 *Fiscal Monitor*, Chapter 2).

The Economics of Product and Labor Market Reforms: A Primer

Product and labor market reforms are motivated by multiple public policy objectives. They can raise long-term output by boosting productivity, investment, and employment. They may affect income inequality by changing the distribution of jobs, market wages, and nonwage income (social benefits and taxes). Public finances and debt sustainability may also depend on reforms, including through effects on long-term output. Reforms that increase the responsiveness of wages and prices to business conditions can promote microeconomic efficiency while enhancing economic resilience by smoothing adjustment to macroeconomic shocks.

This chapter focuses on how various product and labor market reforms affect macroeconomic outcomes, particularly output and employment. Reforms can be classified according to the nature of their impact:

- *Reforms that enhance productivity*—In theory, pro-competitive product market reforms boost growth by lowering the prices that firms charge consumers, by improving the use and allocation of labor and capital across firms, and by enhancing firms' incentives to invest, absorb cutting-edge technologies, and innovate. Such reforms include, in particular, measures aimed at facilitating new firms' access to markets, lowering the administrative burden on corporations, and easing barriers to foreign direct investment and trade. Advanced economies have made major progress in all of these areas over the past two decades—for instance, in deregulating network industries (Figure 3.2). Nonetheless, there remains scope for further progress in many European countries as well as in Japan and Korea (Koske and others 2015). Although the specifics vary from country to country, there are opportunities to further strengthen competition in nontradables industries, including in some network industry segments, as well as in retail trade and professional services, where significant and rather stable barriers to entry remain in some countries (for example, Canada, France, Germany, Italy, Japan, and Spain). Reform of employment protection systems may also boost productivity by enhancing resource (re)allocation across firms and industries (Bassanini, Nunziata, and Venn 2009). Other important productivity-enhancing reforms that are beyond the scope of this chapter involve strengthening innovation policies and education systems, as well as altering tax and spending policies (see Chapter 2 in the April 2016 *Fiscal Monitor*).

- *Reforms that lower structural unemployment*—Economic theory suggests that easing barriers to entry into product markets, reducing the level or duration of unemployment benefits where particularly high, strengthening active labor market policies, and lowering labor tax wedges can all reduce unemployment over the long term by increasing the demand for labor, unemployed workers' ability and incentives to find jobs, or both (Blanchard and Giavazzi 2003; Nickell and Layard 1999; Pissarides 2000). Easing employment protection legislation enhances the relative job prospects of underrepresented groups, such as low-skilled youth and migrants, in the labor market, but it can have an unpredictable impact on *aggregate* unemployment, since it increases incentives both to hire and to dismiss workers. Reforms in this area may also have different effects depending on their design, such as whether they apply to regular or temporary jobs (for example, Blanchard and Landier 2002). Labor market regulations are much more stable over time than are product market regulations—with the exception of some widespread relaxation of employment protection for temporary workers; to a lesser extent, they also vary more across countries (Figure 3.3). The stability of labor market institutions within countries and their variability across countries partly reflect political economy factors that so far have impeded the reform of poorly functioning institutions (Box 3.1). However, they also illustrate that societal preferences vary (for example, over economic risk) and that different institutional models can be effective in accommodating those preferences (for example, Blanchard, Jaumotte, and Loungani 2014). For instance, despite some cuts in benefits since the early 1990s, Nordic countries have maintained comparatively generous unemployment insurance systems while relying extensively on active labor market policies to reduce unemployment (OECD 2006). Likewise, different collective wage-bargaining systems may deliver high and stable employment, provided they ensure that wages adequately reflect business conditions (Box 3.2). More broadly, experience suggests that both "Anglo-Saxon" and "Nordic" models can deliver high employment rates (OECD 2006; Sapir 2006).

- *Reforms that raise the participation of underrepresented groups in the labor market*—Despite some convergence, the fact that women, youth, low-skilled migrants, and older workers continue to display widely different participation rates across countries contributes to cross-country differences

Figure 3.2. Evolution of Product Market Regulations
(Scale, 0–6; higher score indicates stricter regulations)

Major progress has been achieved in deregulating network industries, but there remains scope for further reform efforts, particularly in the areas of retail trade and professional services.

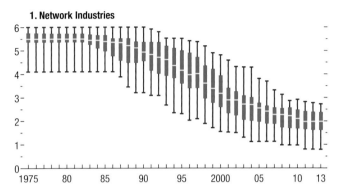

1. Network Industries

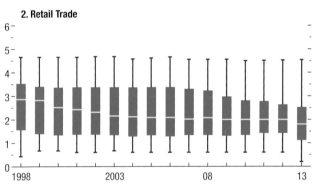

2. Retail Trade

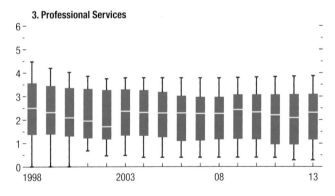

3. Professional Services

Sources: Koske and others 2015; and IMF staff calculations.
Note: The horizontal line inside each box represents the median; the upper and lower edges of each box show the top and bottom quartiles; and the red markers denote the maximum and the minimum. Network industries are air, rail, and road transportation; electricity and gas distribution; and telecommunications and postal services.

Figure 3.3. Evolution of Labor Market Institutions

Labor market regulations are generally more stable over time and also vary more across countries than product market regulations.

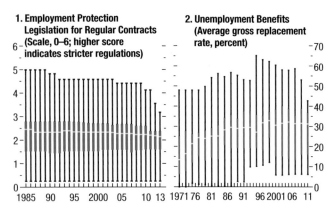

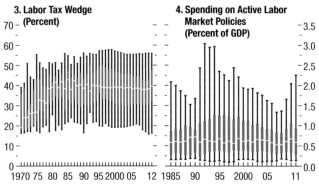

Sources: Organisation for Economic Co-operation and Development, Indicators of Employment Protection, Benefits and Wages, Tax Statistics, and Social Expenditure databases; and IMF staff calculations.
Note: The horizontal line inside each box represents the median; the upper and lower edges of each box show the top and bottom quartiles; and the red markers denote the maximum and the minimum.

in overall employment rates and suggests that there is scope for improving current policies. Options for encouraging more women to enter the labor force include reducing the (marginal) income taxation of second earners, enhancing the availability and reducing the cost of child care, and promoting policies that improve work-life balance—for instance, expanded scope and incentives for part-time work and parental leave (for example, Jaumotte 2003). Among the policies that can strengthen the labor participation of youth and low-skilled migrants are targeted active labor market policies (such as training programs), combined with demand-side policies that create job opportunities, such as lower tax wedges and youth-specific minimum wages. For older workers, it is important to reduce incentives

for early retirement, not least by lowering the implicit taxation on continued work often embedded in old-age pension systems—for example, when bonuses (penalties) for deferred (anticipated) retirement are too weak (Stock and Wise 1990)—but also by limiting the extent to which other social welfare programs can be used as pathways into early retirement (Duval 2003).

The short- to medium-term effects of these product and labor market reforms are more uncertain and are likely to vary widely depending on how they affect current aggregate demand and supply. If demand increases (declines) more than supply, overall use of domestic resources may increase (decrease), and inflation may rise (decline) as a result. This depends, in turn, on how reforms influence expectations (through their credibility and communication), wages and income distribution, the strength of the external competitiveness channel, and income and job security (actual or perceived). Transitory costs also matter. Employment protection reform may trigger immediate layoffs—especially in bad economic times—whereas hiring can take more time. Product market deregulation may lead to rapid downsizing or exit of incumbent firms but only gradual new firm entry, for example, in some network industries in which it can take time to build a network and a customer base. Finally, the short- to medium-term impact of reform can be shaped by macroeconomic policies.

The Macroeconomic Effects of Reforms: A Model-Based Analysis

This section looks at the macroeconomic effects of reforms using a new dynamic general equilibrium model that incorporates key features of product and labor market regulation (see Annex 3.1 for details and Cacciatore and others, forthcoming-b). This model offers some key benefits: it helps shed light on the transmission channels through which reforms affect economic activity, and it addresses relevant policy issues that cannot be fully explored in the empirical analysis—such as how the zero lower bound on nominal interest rates affects the short-term impact of reforms and the immediate impact of credible announcements of future reforms.

Model Description

The model addresses two key limitations of past studies: (1) it explicitly includes, and differentiates among, a broad range of specific product and labor market policies, and (2) it features some real-world imperfections in product and labor markets, such as irreversible (regulatory and other) investment costs that new firms have to pay when entering the market and job-search-and-matching frictions in the labor market that make job creation a gradual and costly process.

The analysis uses the model to explore the impact of four types of product and labor market reforms: lowering anticompetitive barriers to entry in nontradables sectors, reducing administrative costs of firing procedures, cutting the levels or duration of unemployment benefits, and strengthening active labor market policies that more efficiently match prospective workers to job openings. Reforms can be carried out in three distinct macroeconomic environments:

1. *Normal times*—that is, normal business conditions
2. *Bad times with unconstrained monetary policy*—that is, assuming that the policy rate could go below zero, or equivalently, that quantitative easing could in practice fully relax the zero-lower-bound constraint
3. *Bad times with constrained monetary policy*—that is, a combination of major slack in the economy, driven by a large adverse demand shock, and a binding zero lower bound on the monetary policy rate.[1]

The analysis highlights what difference the macroeconomic environment makes for the effect of different reforms.

Short- and Long-Term Effects of Reforms

All four types of reforms studied here increase the level of output in the long term by raising productivity, employment levels, or both. For instance, in an illustrative reform scenario for the euro area as a whole, joint implementation of the four types of reforms would increase the level of output by about 4 percent and reduce the unemployment rate by about 2½ percentage points in the long term. Product market reforms would account for approximately half of the overall output gain, with increased producer entry boosting job creation and the economy also benefiting from decreased

spending on wasteful regulatory costs. These beneficial effects do not factor in any additional productivity gains that may stem from reduced inefficiency among incumbent firms (the so-called X-inefficiency) or from stronger incentives for them to innovate.

Although the types of reforms considered here unambiguously raise output over the long term, they pay off only gradually, and some can entail short-term costs. Gains materialize as new firms start producing and new workers are hired, both of which occur only gradually. By contrast, some reforms can trigger quick downsizing of incumbent firms and dismissal of workers. In particular, in the model-based analysis, easing employment protections induces firms to dismiss relatively less productive workers immediately, whereas its positive impact on hiring incentives creates jobs only gradually. As a result, unemployment increases, aggregate demand declines, and output contracts for a time (Figure 3.4, panels 1 and 2). Lowering entry barriers in nontradables sectors initially boosts demand by triggering entry of new firms, which demand intermediate goods and ultimately labor and capital, but subsequent downsizing of incumbents more than offsets these new firms' (expansionary) contributions to aggregate output, leading to net job and output losses overall in the short term (Figure 3.4, panels 3 and 4).[2]

Unemployment benefit reforms have ambiguous short-term effects. The model-based analysis finds positive short-term effects because reduced unemployment benefits boost hiring by lowering wages, while firing is basically unaffected. However, the model abstracts from a potential counteracting force: a cut in unemployment benefits often disproportionately affects lower-income workers who face credit constraints, inducing them to curtail consumption. Even if the government fully redistributes the fiscal gain from benefit reductions through broad-based tax cuts, aggregate consumption may still decline and output fall (see, for instance, Kollmann and others 2015).

Likewise, the short-term impact of active labor market policy reforms depends on two conflicting effects. By increasing workers' incentives to look for and accept job offers, such reforms boost job creation. But by making it easier for firms to find new workers, they also provide an incentive to lay off relatively less productive workers.

---

[1]Although this chapter focuses on a model calibrated for the euro area, the key insights of the analysis apply to advanced economies more broadly. Alternative versions of the model, such as for a small open economy operating either a flexible or a fixed exchange rate regime, yield qualitatively similar implications—although the quantitative effects of reforms can differ. See related work by Cacciatore and others (2015).

[2]The analysis here focuses on barriers to entry, which offer the greatest scope for reform in most countries. However, other types of product market reforms, such as reductions in administrative burdens on existing corporations, may yield more immediate gains by reducing fixed costs of production.

Figure 3.4. Selected Model Results

Employment protection legislation and product market reforms raise output over the long term, but they pay off only gradually and can entail short-term costs, particularly in bad times. Constraints on monetary policy do not weaken the simulated effects.

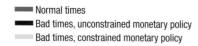

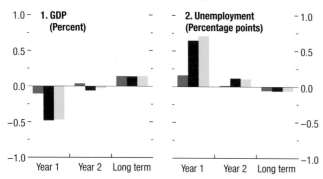

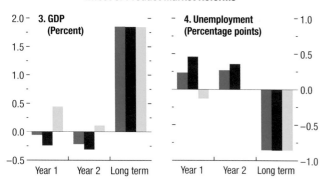

Source: IMF staff estimates.
Note: "Long term" refers to the steady state.

The Role of Macroeconomic Conditions

Not only can the types of reforms considered here entail short-term costs, but their short-term effects can also be very different if the reforms are implemented in bad times rather than in normal times. In particular, employment protection legislation reforms are more contractionary in the short term when there is substantial economic slack—even when the monetary policy response is unconstrained (Figure 3.4, panels 1 and 2). Firms seek to dismiss more workers in bad times than in normal times, but stringent job protections partly discourage them from doing so.

Relaxing the constraint imposed by such protections benefits individual firms taken in isolation. But by triggering a wave of layoffs, reforming employment protections further weakens aggregate demand and delays economic recovery. To a lesser extent, product market reforms also have a weaker short-term impact in bad times compared with normal times (Figure 3.4, panels 3 and 4), although the difference is small, as higher profit margins per firm due to fewer competing firms under adverse macroeconomic conditions offset lower expected profits among prospective entrants. In addition, binding external financial constraints—not considered in the analysis here—that prevent new firms from financing investment can make product market reforms substantially more contractionary in the short term (Cacciatore and others, forthcoming-a). This suggests that easing external borrowing constraints—on firms and the economy as a whole—may enhance the short-term effect of product market deregulation.

Unemployment benefit reforms can have either stronger or weaker short-term effects in bad economic times, depending on various factors. On one hand, the model-based analysis highlights that a sizable pool of unemployed workers makes it easier for firms to recruit, and job creation responds more strongly to the reduction in wages brought about by a cut in benefits. This larger employment *gain* from unemployment benefit reforms in bad times contrasts with the larger job *losses* observed following a relaxation of employment protections and illustrates the broader point that wage flexibility may be more desirable than employment flexibility in bad times (see, for example, Boeri and Jimeno 2015).[3] On the other hand, in periods of economic slack, a reduction in benefits may have a larger adverse effect than in normal times through fiscal multipliers, which tend to be larger in general during recessions (Auerbach and Gorodnichenko 2012; Blanchard and Leigh 2013; Jordà and Taylor 2013; Abiad, Furceri, and Topalova 2015), and this may hold true particularly for changes in unemployment benefits, because households also become more credit constrained during downturns (Mian and Sufi 2010).[4] In addition, a cut in benefits tends to have

[3]Boeri and Jimeno (2015) also argue that high minimum wages for underrepresented groups in the labor market may have higher employment costs in recessions.
[4]The argument could still hold even if reform were implemented in a budget-neutral way, insofar as changes in unemployment benefits entail a higher fiscal multiplier than do offsetting tax cuts (spending increases). On the other hand, liquidity constraints can

a larger effect in recessions on (non-credit-constrained) households' incentives to reduce consumption in favor of precautionary saving, as their ability to insure themselves declines and their risk of idiosyncratic income loss increases.[5]

One way to alleviate the short-term cost of some labor market reforms—especially in bad times—is to announce credibly that they will be implemented only when the economic recovery is more solid, for instance, by passing a law that sets a future date for entry into force.[6] In particular, announcing future employment protection legislation reforms immediately boosts firms' hiring incentives in anticipation of lower future costs of layoff procedures, without inducing them to dismiss more workers in the short term, while the existing rules still apply. By contrast, such a strategy may not be so helpful when applied to product market reforms in bad times. For example, announcing a future reduction of entry barriers encourages new firms to postpone entry and investment until entry costs are effectively lowered, while encouraging incumbent firms to start downsizing immediately in anticipation of stronger future competition.

The Role of Constraints on Monetary Policy

Whether constraints on monetary policy, including the zero lower bound, influence the short-term effects of reforms depends on the relative short-term effect of these reforms on demand and supply and therefore their net effect on inflation and the real interest rate. The results of the model suggest that constraints on monetary policy may have limited effects in shaping the short-term impact of reforms, as these reforms have little or no deflationary effect (Figure 3.4). For example, although relaxing employment protections puts

downward pressure on inflation by weakening aggregate demand in the short term, the immediate positive impact of the reform on productivity, and thereby on bargained wages, offsets this effect.[7] As for product market deregulation, reducing entry barriers may be more beneficial at the zero lower bound because, unlike in normal times, monetary tightening does not offset the short-term increase in demand—and therefore in marginal costs and inflation—created by the additional investment and job creation undertaken by new firms that enter the market (Figure 3.4, panels 3 and 4).[8] As noted earlier, product market reform can also lead to immediate productivity gains by inducing incumbent firms to eliminate existing inefficiencies. Such a reform-driven productivity increase—not considered in the analysis here—would be expansionary even in the short term under all three alternative macroeconomic conditions studied here, but this particular channel of reform would have a milder impact when the economy is at the zero lower bound. The reason is that higher productivity, other things being equal, immediately boosts supply, lowering inflation and thus raising real interest rates.

The Macroeconomic Effects of Reforms: An Empirical Analysis

This section quantifies empirically the macroeconomic effects of reforms and examines whether the data align with the theoretical considerations discussed in the previous sections. In contrast to a large body of literature that focuses on estimating the long-term impact of policies and institutions on economic activity, this chapter adopts a novel empirical strategy that allows estimation of both the short- and medium-term effects of product and labor market reforms on a range of macroeconomic outcomes. Specifically, it identifies major policy changes in the areas of product market regulation, employment protection legislation, unemployment benefits, active labor market policies, and labor taxation, and then traces the evolution of output, (un)employment, and inflation in the aftermath of these reforms.[9]

---

strengthen the response of individual job search, and therefore of job matching, to changes in benefits (Chetty 2008).

[5]The analysis of the impact of benefit reforms in bad versus normal times also bears some connection to the unsettled debate regarding whether unemployment insurance should be made more or less generous in recessions (see, for example, Landais, Michaillat, and Saez 2015 and Mitman and Rabinovich 2015). The answer depends not only on the short-term impact of changes in benefits, but also on the value of income insurance for workers, which is likely to be greater in recessions—an issue that is not taken into account in the analysis here.

[6]Grandfathering reforms may also help on this front. In particular, grandfathering employment protection legislation increases incentives for firms to create jobs—since all new contracts are subject to the new, less stringent rules—without changing their incentives to lay off existing workers. Examples include the 2015 employment protection legislation reform in Italy and some provisions of the 2012 reform in Spain.

[7]For an alternative theoretical analysis applied to Japan's labor market, see Porcellacchia 2016.

[8]Using a similar setup but without focusing on the zero-lower-bound issue, Cacciatore, Fiori, and Ghironi (forthcoming) show that an expansionary monetary policy stance can smooth transition costs and contribute to front-loading the long-term benefits of reforms.

[9]Complementary analysis was carried out to assess the effects of these reforms on income inequality, as measured by Gini coefficients. No statistically significant effects were found, with the exception of

Major reforms are identified primarily by examining documented legislative and regulatory actions reported in all available issues of the Organisation for Economic Co-operation and Development (OECD) *Economic Survey* for advanced economies since 1970, as well as additional country-specific sources. In this respect, the methodology is closely related to the "narrative approach" used to identify monetary and fiscal shocks and periods of high financial distress by Romer and Romer (1989, 2004, 2010, 2015) and Devries and others (2011). The approach considers both reforms and "counterreforms"— that is, policy changes in the opposite direction. These major policy shifts are identified as those legislative or regulatory changes for which at least one of the following three conditions is satisfied: (1) the OECD survey uses strong normative language, suggestive of an important measure (for example, "major reform"), to describe the change; (2) the policy action is mentioned repeatedly across various issues of the OECD survey or in retrospective summaries of key past reforms for the country considered; or (3) the OECD indicator of the regulatory stance in the area considered—if available—displays a very large change. When only the last of these conditions is met, an extensive search through other sources is performed to identify the precise policy action underpinning the change in the indicator.[10]

The main advantage of this approach is that it identifies the precise nature and timing of significant legislative and regulatory actions taken by advanced economies since the early 1970s in all key labor and product market policy areas, including some for which no time-varying indicators exist (for example, regarding conditions for receipt of unemployment benefits or the design of active labor market policies, such as integration of job placement and benefit payment services). These four major gains (nature and timing of policy actions, coverage length and breadth) allow for a richer and more granular analysis of the short- to medium-term effects of reforms than in past studies. This approach, along with others used in the literature on this topic, has three main shortcomings, however. First, the identified events may themselves be driven by macroeconomic outcomes and may coincide with reforms in other areas—issues that are addressed in the empirical analysis. Second, two

large reforms in a given area (for example, employment protection legislation) can involve different specific actions (for example, a major simplification of the procedures for individual and collective dismissals, respectively). As a result, only the average historical impact of reforms can be estimated. Third, the database provides no information regarding the stance of current (or past) product and labor market regulations and as such is not a substitute for existing policy indicators, such as, for instance, those the OECD produces.

Finally, the approach does not rely on a common single metric to identify reforms, unlike some earlier studies that relied on changes in OECD product and labor market indicators to identify reform episodes (Bouis and others 2012; Bordon, Ebeke, and Shirono, 2016). The results presented in the chapter are robust to using this methodology, even though the effects of reforms are weaker and less precisely estimated compared with the narrative approach—suggesting that the latter better identifies major reform events and thereby reduces measurement error.

Once major policy actions are identified, their short- and medium-term impact on economic activity is quantified using two econometric specifications. The first establishes whether reforms have statistically significant effects on macroeconomic variables such as output, (un)employment, and inflation. The second assesses whether these effects vary with overall business conditions prevailing at the time of the reform (weak versus strong economic conditions) or with the stance of accompanying macroeconomic policies—that is, whether the effects of reforms differ between periods of fiscal expansion and fiscal contraction (see Annex 3.3 for details).[11] To provide additional insights into the

---

reductions in unemployment benefits, which are associated with an increase in inequality over the medium term.

[10]See Annex 3.2 for details on the criteria and procedure employed to identify major reform episodes using the accounts in the OECD *Economic Survey*, as well as for examples of reforms.

[11]The baseline specifications control for past economic growth, past reforms, and recessions dummies as well as country and time fixed effects. A possible concern regarding the analysis is that the probability of structural reform is influenced not only by past economic growth and the occurrence of recessions (Box 3.1), but also by contemporaneous economic developments as well as expectations of future growth. However, this is unlikely to be a major issue, given the long lags associated with the implementation of structural reforms and the likelihood that information about future growth is largely embedded in past economic activity. Most important, controlling for expectations of current and future growth delivers results that are very similar to, and not different with statistical significance from, those reported in this chapter. Another possible concern regarding the analysis is that the results may suffer from omitted-variables bias, as reforms may occur across different markets at the same time. However, including all the reforms simultaneously in the estimated equation does not substantially alter the magnitude and the statistical significance of the results. Furthermore, sector-level analyses address omitted-variables concerns by

channels through which product market and employment protection legislation reforms are transmitted, and to address some of the limitations of the macroeconometric analysis (by fully controlling for countrywide economic shocks that coincide with reforms), sector- and firm-level approaches complement the macroeconomic analysis.

Product Market Reforms

This subsection focuses on the effects of product market reforms aimed at reducing domestic barriers to competition. Although this issue is high on policymakers' current structural reform agenda, other related policies, including those directed at easing barriers to international trade and foreign direct investment, also have the potential to boost productivity and output levels (Box 3.3).

Macro Analysis

The analysis here shows that product market reforms have statistically significant medium-term output effects.[12] A major liberalization event, such as, for example, the deregulation of several network industries in Germany in 1998, leads to a statistically significant increase in the output level of about 1½ percent four years after the reform (Figure 3.5, panel 1). The effect eventually levels off, after seven years, at about 2¼ percent. In addition, the point estimates suggest that product market reforms increase employment levels and decrease price levels, though the wide confidence intervals associated with the estimates imply that these effects are not statistically distinguishable from zero (Figure 3.5, panels 2 and 3).

The macroeconomic effects of product market reforms are not statistically significantly weaker under adverse business conditions—though the point estimates suggest smaller effects—but employment (and output) effects are significantly larger where employment protection regulations are more stringent.[13] This

finding is consistent with previous theory and empirical evidence (Blanchard and Giavazzi 2003; Fiori and others 2012). The intuition is that in countries with more stringent employment protection legislation, real wages are more likely to exceed levels that clear the labor market and to leave employment below the full-employment level. In such countries, product market reform has greater potential to deliver job gains.[14]

Sector-Level Analysis

The macroeconomic effects of product market reforms identified in the macro analysis reflect not only the direct impact of deregulation in the industries considered, but also its indirect impact through two kinds of spillovers to other sectors. First, product market reforms in upstream industries (for instance, network industries, banking, professional services) can reduce the price and improve the quality and variety of the intermediate inputs used by downstream sectors (for instance, manufacturing), thereby boosting productivity and competitiveness in these sectors (*backward linkages*). Moreover, lower prices for intermediate inputs may increase profits, and therefore incentives to innovate, in downstream sectors.[15] Second, product market reforms raise output in the affected sectors, increasing their demand for intermediate inputs from upstream sectors (*forward linkages*). For example, deregulation in the electricity sector may positively affect other sectors by both reducing their costs of production (backward linkage) and requiring more inputs from these sectors (forward linkage).

Sector-level analysis shows that product market reforms in network sectors have statistically significant direct and indirect medium-term effects on output. On average, output in the sector affected by a particular reform increases by more than 10 percent four years after the reform, although this impact takes

---

controlling for countrywide economic conditions and, in some cases, using instrumental variables. Such analyses yield results that are qualitatively similar to those from the macroeconomic analysis. See the discussion later in the chapter as well as Annex 3.3 for details.

[12]The macroeconomic analysis focuses on major past reforms across network industries. Qualitatively similar results are obtained for broader reforms identified as major legislative changes aimed at improving overall product market competition.

[13]These results may be driven by the fact that in the sample used here, major product market reforms occur in countries with strong employment protection regulation. However, no statistically significant correlation is found between the probability of major product

market reforms and the degree of employment protection regulation. In addition, the analysis controls for the degree of current and past employment protection regulation.

[14]This result should not necessarily be interpreted as lack of complementarity among structural reforms in general. Indeed, the case studies presented in Box 3.4 point to potential benefits from broad packages of reforms.

[15]For discussion and empirical evidence regarding the impact of reform through backward linkages, see Bourlès and others 2013 and Cette, Lopez, and Mairesse, forthcoming. Theoretically, competition has an ambiguous effect on innovation. Although some models of endogenous technological change would predict that competition curbs innovation (Aghion and Howitt 1992), more recent models predict positive or hump-shaped effects of competition on innovation (Aghion and others 2001; Aghion and Schankerman 2004).

Figure 3.5. Macroeconomic Effects of Product Market Reforms
(Percent; years on x-axis)

Product market reforms have a statistically significant medium-term impact on output, but not on employment and price level.

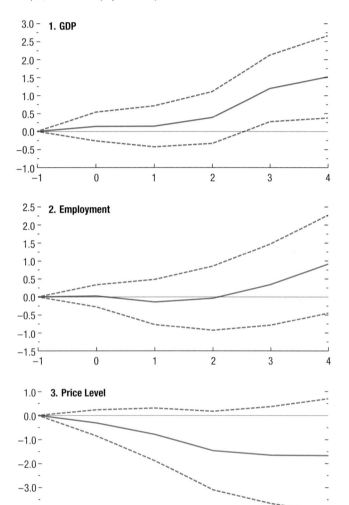

Source: IMF staff estimates.
Note: $t = 0$ is the year of the shock. Solid lines denote the response to a major reform in product market regulation, and dashed lines denote 90 percent confidence bands.

time to materialize, being, for example, zero in the first year.[16] Taken at face value, these estimates imply

[16]To minimize endogeneity concerns due to omitted-variables bias, the specification controls for country-year and country-sector fixed effects (as well as industry-specific trends), and reforms are instrumented by (1) the initial stringency of regulation, as measured by the corresponding OECD indicator; (2) the number of countries that implemented a reform in the same area over the preceding three

that simultaneous major reforms across all network sectors—a major event that has never actually happened—would increase economy-wide output by more than 1 percent (10 percent times the share of these sectors in the whole economy, which is approximately 0.1 on average) in the medium term (Figure 3.6, panel 1). Furthermore, productivity increases, and the (relative) price level falls. In addition to these direct effects, product market reforms in network sectors have statistically significant indirect medium-term effects on output in other sectors. A major reform in one of the network sectors increases output in downstream and upstream sectors by, on average, about 0.3 percent four years after the reform (Figure 3.6, panels 2 and 3).

Firm-Level Analysis

To provide additional insights into the effects of product market reforms and the channels through which they operate, the analysis examines how their effects vary across different types of firms in different sectors, depending on firm characteristics such as their size and financial health and needs. The results of the analysis suggest that product market reforms have statistically significant positive effects on incumbent firms, whose output (sales) increases by about 2 percent in the first year and by about 3 percent three years after the reform (Figure 3.7, panel 1).[17] Furthermore, reforms have statistically significant medium-term effects on employment and capital, which increase by about 1½ and 3 percent, respectively (Figure 3.7, panels 2 and 3). The output effects of reforms in retail trade and professional services are comparable to those in network industries (Figure 3.7, panels 4–6). This finding suggests that the output effects estimated in the macro- and sector-level analyses for network industries may to a large extent be generalized to reforms in other key areas. Moreover, the comparable magnitudes of the (direct) medium-term effects on output estimated in the firm- and sector-level analyses tentatively suggest

years; and (3) the issuance of a new European Union directive since the last reform was implemented.
Dabla-Norris and others (2015) also find that product market reforms have a positive impact on output—via higher productivity—that increases over time. In contrast, no statistically significant employment effects are found in the deregulated sectors, in line with the results from the macroeconomic analysis. Bassanini (2015) finds a negative short-term impact of deregulation in network industries.
[17]Given the shorter time sample of firm-level data compared with macro- and sector-level data, the analysis examines the effect of reforms on firms' economic activity up to three years after the reform (see Annex 3.3 for a detailed description of the data and sources).

that the positive effect on incumbent firms' output contributes more to the response of sectoral output to reforms than do firms' entry and exit—although the response of incumbent firms is itself triggered largely by increased competition from potential new entrants.[18]

Whereas output effects are similar across sectors and firms, employment effects vary with firm size (Figure 3.8). In particular, the employment effect of reforms tends to be larger for smaller firms in network sectors, and to a lesser extent in professional services, and larger for larger firms in retail trade.[19] This reflects differences in production technology and the nature of regulation between these sectors. Network industries tend to be dominated by a rather small number of large firms that scale back employment and investment plans when reforms improve potential entrants' access to the network. By contrast, firms in retail trade tend to be relatively small and labor intensive; when reforms remove restrictions specific to large firms, these large firms benefit.[20]

Product market reforms also have a varied effect across firms depending on the firms' financial health and needs. The medium-term impact of reforms on investment among firms with low debt is about four times larger (about 20 percent) than it is among highly indebted firms (about 5 percent) (Figure 3.9, panels 1 and 2).[21] In addition, when credit conditions are tight across the economy, firms that depend heavily on external financing invest considerably less following a major product market reform than firms that do not (Figure 3.9, panels 3 and 4).[22] These results further strengthen

[18]Comparisons between firm- and sector-level and macro analyses should be treated with caution. First, the firm-level analysis here is restricted to incumbent firms that remain in business. While product market reforms have potentially important effects on the entry and exit of firms, the current data set does not allow those dynamics to be analyzed with confidence. Second, firm-level results are unweighted. This means that they capture the average firms' response rather than the population-weighted aggregate response. Finally, the sample does not cover all firms and industries equally well.

[19]Note that these results are unweighted and that weighting should reduce the estimated effect of product market reforms in network industries, given the predominance of large firms in these sectors.

[20]Another key regulation in retail trade addresses the flexibility of shop opening hours and prices. Regulation in professional services relates to barriers to entry and the way services are delivered and includes, among other things, rules governing the recognition of qualifications and the determination of fees and prices.

[21]In an effort to isolate the role of credit constraints that may be associated with high levels of indebtedness from the confounding role of credit demand, the debt ratios are held constant over time.

[22]The analysis makes use of a triple-differences approach, building on previous work by Rajan and Zingales (1998), which focuses on the differential effects of product market reforms among firms in

Figure 3.6. Direct and Indirect Sectoral Output Effects of Product Market Reforms
(Percent; years on x-axis)

Product market reforms in network sectors have statistically significant direct and indirect medium-term effects on output.

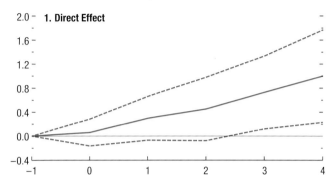

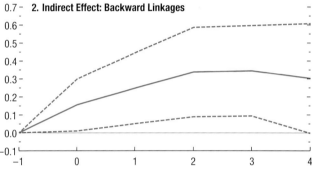

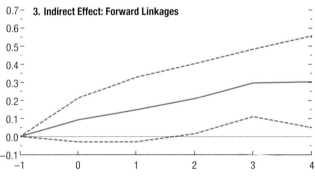

Sources: Timmer and others 2015; and IMF staff estimates.
Note: *t* = 0 is the year of the shock. Solid lines denote the response to a major reform in product market regulation, and dashed lines denote 90 percent confidence bands. The direct effect measures the impact on GDP of deregulating all network industries only through the response of real value added in the deregulated industries themselves. It is computed assuming that all network industries together account for about 10 percent of GDP on average across sample countries. The indirect effect measures the average impact on GDP across sample countries of deregulating one network industry only through the response of real value added in downstream industries (backward linkages) and upstream industries (forward linkages). See the chapter text for details. Network industries are air, rail, and road transportation; electricity and gas distribution; and telecommunications and postal services.

Figure 3.7. Direct Effects of Product Market Reforms on Incumbent Firms' Output
(Percent; years on x-axis)

Product market reforms have statistically significant positive effects on the output, employment, and capital of incumbent firms. The output effects of reforms in retail trade and professional services are comparable to those in network industries.

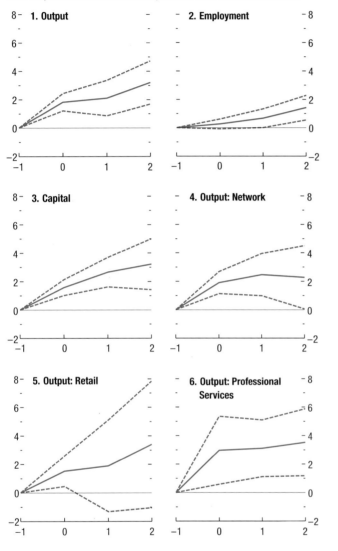

Figure 3.8. Direct Effects of Product Market Reforms on Incumbent Firms' Employment: The Role of Firm Size
(Percent; years on x-axis)

Employment effects of product market reforms vary with firm size. They tend to be larger for smaller firms in network sectors, and to a lesser extent in professional services, and larger for larger firms in retail trade.

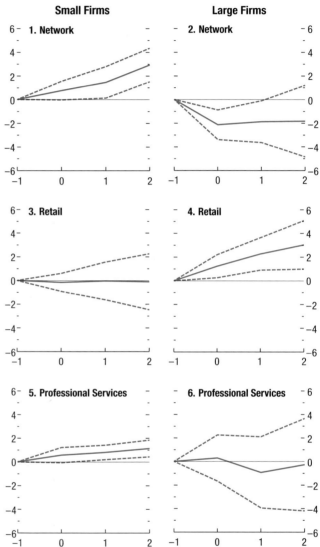

Source: IMF staff estimates.
Note: *t* = 0 is the year of the shock. Solid lines denote the response to a major reform in product market regulation, and dashed lines denote 90 percent confidence bands. Network industries are air, rail, and road transportation; electricity and gas distribution; and telecommunications and postal services.

Source: IMF staff estimates.
Note: *t* = 0 is the year of the shock. Solid lines denote the response to a major reform in product market regulation, and dashed lines denote 90 percent confidence bands. Network industries are air, rail, and road transportation; electricity and gas distribution; and telecommunications and postal services.

the case for policies aimed at addressing weak bank and corporate balance sheets, as these may enhance the investment impact of product market reforms.

Labor Market Reforms

This subsection focuses on the effects of reforms of employment protection legislation for regular (permanent) workers, unemployment benefits, active labor market policies, and labor taxation. In addition to these policies, collective-bargaining systems also matter for high and stable employment (see Box 3.2).

Employment Protection Legislation

The analysis shows that reforms that ease dismissal regulations with respect to regular workers (such as, for instance, those in Spain in the mid-1990s or Austria in 2003) do not have, on average, statistically significant effects on employment and other macroeconomic variables. A look behind the average effects shows, however, that the impacts vary markedly according to overall business conditions. When economic conditions are strong, reforms have a sizable positive impact on output and employment, whereas the impact becomes contractionary if the reforms are undertaken during periods of slack (Figure 3.10, panels 1–4). In addition, the estimates suggest that in bad times, reform of employment protection legislation may reduce inflation in the short and medium term, though the wide confidence intervals associated with the results imply that these estimates are not statistically significantly different from zero (Figure 3.10, panels 5 and 6). As discussed in the chapter's theoretical section, a potential reason for this asymmetric effect across different economic regimes is that whereas in periods of strong economic activity, these reforms may stimulate hiring by reducing the cost of future dismissals, in periods of slack they may trigger immediate layoffs.

Another potential mechanism behind the limited average macroeconomic impact of employment protection legislation reforms could be that the effect varies

industries that are heavily dependent on external financing in periods in which credit supply is constrained and those in which credit is readily available. External dependence is measured by the ratio to capital expenditure of the difference between capital expenditure and cash flows. Firms' intrinsic dependence on external credit is measured by the average level of external dependence in the firms' industry across the United Kingdom and the United States. Credit conditions are measured using the regime-switching method—described in Annex 3.3—applied to credit growth in each country. The analysis is limited to network industries.

Figure 3.9. Direct Effects of Product Market Reforms on Incumbent Firms' Investment: The Role of Financial Conditions

(Percent; years on x-axis)

The effect of product market reforms on investment tends to be weaker for firms with high debt and for firms that depend heavily on external financing during periods of tight credit conditions.

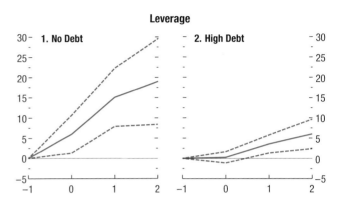

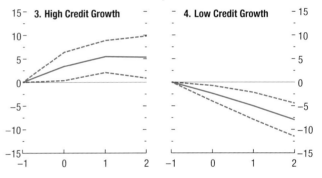

Source: IMF staff estimates.
Note: *t* = 0 is the year of the shock. Solid lines denote the response to a major reform in product market regulation, and dashed lines denote 90 percent confidence bands. External dependence is defined as the difference between capital expenditure and cash flows as a share of capital expenditure. This measure is then averaged across firms over time and across countries within each industry. Only data from the United Kingdom and United States are used for the calculation of this measure. This definition is based on Rajan and Zingales 1998. Under high and low credit growth, respectively, panels 3 and 4 show the difference in the investment response to reform between firms in sectors that depend strongly on external financing and firms in sectors that depend weakly on external financing.

across economic sectors, depending on how binding the regulations are in each sector. Specifically, stringent regulations governing dismissal are likely to be more binding in sectors that are characterized by a higher "natural" propensity to adjust their workforce to idiosyncratic shocks.[23] Reforms to employment protection legislation

[23]An example of a sector among those with highest natural layoff rates is construction; one of those with the lowest layoff rates is electricity and gas.

Figure 3.10. Macro and Sectoral Effects of Employment Protection Legislation Reforms
(Percent; years on x-axis)

Employment protection legislation reforms have a sizable positive impact on output and employment when economic conditions are strong, whereas the impact becomes contractionary if the reforms are undertaken during periods of slack.

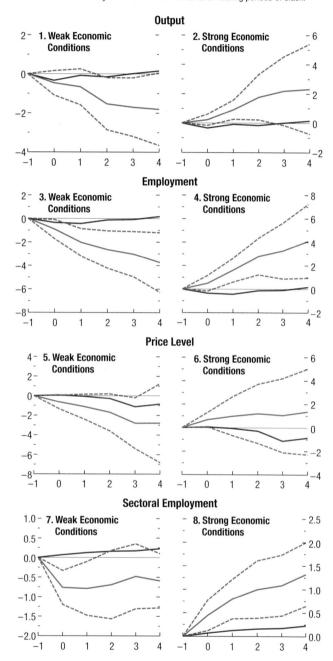

Source: IMF staff estimates.
Note: *t* = 0 is year of the shock. Solid blue lines denote the response to a major reform in employment protection legislation; dashed lines denote 90 percent confidence bands; and solid red lines represent the unconditional result. The differential effect of employment legislation reforms for a sector with relatively high layoff constraints compared with a sector with relatively low layoff constraints is about 1¾ percent.

could then lead to reallocation of workers away from sectors in which regulations are less binding toward those in which regulations are more binding and could thus result in small aggregate employment effects. To test this hypothesis, and also as a robustness check for the economy-wide results presented earlier, the analysis looks at how reforms affect within-country differences in the response of output and employment between sectors with high and low natural layoff rates.[24] The empirical approach follows the methodology proposed by Bassanini, Nunziata, and Venn (2009), who assess the long-term effect of regulations governing dismissal on sectoral total factor productivity growth. The results of this analysis suggest that the effects of employment protection legislation reforms vary positively with the degree of natural layoff, increasing employment more in sectors in which regulations are more binding.[25] The magnitude of the estimated coefficient suggests that the differential effect of employment legislation reforms for a sector that has relatively high constraints on layoffs (at the 75th percentile of the distribution of layoff rates) compared with a sector that has relatively low constraints on layoffs (at the 25th percentile) is about 1¾ percent. In addition, for a given natural layoff rate, the effect is positive under strong economic conditions and negative during periods of slack, confirming the results of the macro analysis (Figure 3.10, panels 7 and 8).

Unemployment Benefits

Reforms that reduce the income replacement rates of unemployment benefits are found to have statistically significant and long-lasting effects on the unemployment rate (Figure 3.11, panel 1). In particular, reforms—which in the sample are associated with reductions in the OECD indicator of average gross income replacement rate that range between 2 and 12 percentage points—reduce the rate of unemployment by about ½ percentage point in the short term (one year after the reform) and by about 1½ percentage points on average in the medium term (four years after). This result is consistent with the evidence provided by Bouis and others (2012), who find that

[24]The main advantage of this approach, compared with the macroeconomic analysis, is that it can control for country-year fixed effects and therefore for all the macroeconomic variables as well as unobserved factors that can affect economic activity and be correlated with employment protection legislation reforms. Data for sectoral layoff rates have been kindly provided by Andrea Bassanini. See Annex 3.3 for details.

[25]Similar results are obtained for sectoral real value added.

large reductions in the initial income replacement rate increase employment rates by, on average, about 1 percentage point over the medium term.

The results also suggest that undertaking unemployment benefit reductions jointly with major reforms aimed at increasing the efficiency of active labor market policies, including through enhanced public employment services—for example, integration between job placement and benefit payment services to create so-called one-stop shops for the unemployed—amplifies their effects. Similarly, although major reductions in the duration of unemployment benefits do not have, on average, statistically significant effects on unemployment, they are associated with a statistically significant medium-term reduction in unemployment (more than 2 percentage points) when implemented together with reforms that enhance the design of active labor market policies.[26]

However, unemployment benefit reforms have weaker—indeed, statistically nonsignificant—effects during periods of slack (Figure 3.11, panels 2 and 3). This asymmetric impact may reflect the larger adverse fiscal multiplier effect from benefit cuts, as well as their bigger impact on workers' incentives to reduce consumption in favor of precautionary saving, in bad times compared with good times (Whang 2015).[27] Furthermore, insofar as the number of jobs is limited in recessions, enhancing search incentives by cutting benefits is likely to be less effective (Landais, Michaillat, and Saez 2015).

Labor Tax Wedges

The analysis shows that shocks to labor tax wedges have statistically significant short- and medium-term effects on output and employment (Figure 3.12, panels 1 and 2).[28] A reduction of 1 percent in labor

[26]Reforms that enhance the design of active labor market policies are not found here to have statistically significant effects on unemployment when implemented alone.

[27]Using a heterogeneous-agents model that combines matching frictions in the labor market with incomplete asset markets and nominal rigidities, Ravn and Sterk (2013) show that a reduction in consumption in favor of precautionary saving (brought about by an increase in job uncertainty) decreases aggregate demand and firms' hiring, thereby further weakening demand. They find that the effect is quantitatively important, being potentially large enough to explain the increase in U.S. unemployment during the Great Recession.

[28]The analysis uses a measure, derived from OECD tax models, that defines a tax wedge as the difference between the labor cost to the employer and the corresponding net take-home pay of the employee for a single-earner couple with two children earning 100 percent of the average productive wage. The measure expresses the sum of personal income tax and all social security contributions as a percentage of total labor cost.

Figure 3.11. Unemployment Effects of Unemployment Benefit Reforms
(Percentage points; years on x-axis)

Reforms that reduce the income replacement rates of unemployment benefits are found to have statistically significant and long-lasting effects on the unemployment rate. However, such reforms have weaker, statistically nonsignificant effects during periods of slack.

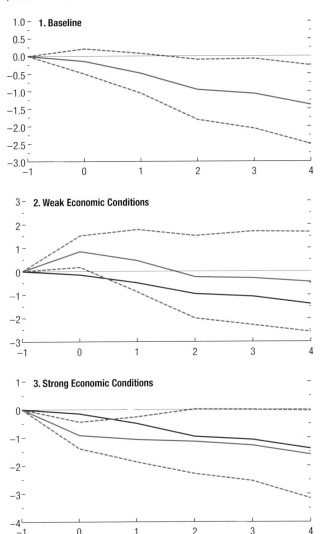

Source: IMF staff estimates.
Note: *t* = 0 is the year of the shock. Solid blue lines denote the response to a major unemployment benefit reform; dashed lines denote 90 percent confidence bands; and solid red lines represent the unconditional result.

tax wedges increases the level of output (employment) by about 0.15 (0.2) percent in the year of the shock and by about 0.6 (0.7) percent after four years. These effects eventually level off. Estimates are consistent with others reported in the literature (for instance, Bassanini and Duval 2006 and references cited therein). The results are also robust, even though the effects

Figure 3.12. Macroeconomic Effects of Labor Tax Wedge Cuts
(Percent; years on x-axis)

Reductions in labor tax wedges have statistically significant short- and medium-term effects on output and employment. These effects are larger under weak economic conditions.

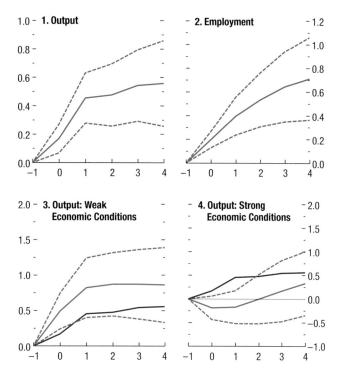

Source: IMF staff estimates.
Note: *t* = 0 is the year of the shock. Solid blue lines denote the response to a 1 percentage point reduction in labor tax wedges; dashed lines denote 90 percent confidence bands; and solid red lines represent the unconditional result.

Figure 3.13. Macroeconomic Effects of Spending Shocks on Active Labor Market Policies
(Percent; years on x-axis)

Discretionary increases in public spending on active labor market policies have statistically significant short- and medium-term effects on output and employment. These effects are larger under weak economic conditions.

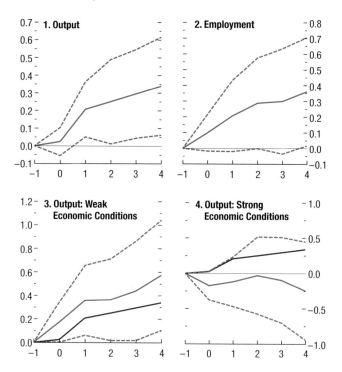

Source: IMF staff estimates.
Note: *t* = 0 is the year of the shock. Solid blue lines denote the response to a 10 percent increase in spending on active labor market policies; dashed lines denote 90 percent confidence bands; and solid red lines represent the unconditional result.

are smaller, when tax wedge cuts are budget neutral. This finding suggests that making tax structures more employment friendly by shifting the tax burden away from labor has positive effects on output and employment (Bouis and others 2012).

Cutting labor tax wedges is found to be more effective in periods of slack (Figure 3.12, panels 3 and 4). In such periods, a 1 percent reduction in labor tax wedges increases output by 0.5 percent in the year of the reform and by 0.8 percent after four years, whereas in expansions, the impact is not statistically distinguishable from zero. This finding is consistent with a growing literature that explores the effect of fiscal policy during recessions and expansions and points to larger fiscal multiplier effects during recessions (see Auerbach and Gorodnichenko 2012; Blanchard and Leigh 2013; Jordà and Taylor 2013; and Abiad, Furceri, and Topalova 2015).

Spending on Active Labor Market Policies

Discretionary increases in public spending on active labor market policies are found to have statistically significant medium-term output and employment effects (Figure 3.13, panels 1 and 2). A 10 percent increase in spending raises output and employment levels by about 0.35 percent four years after the shock, and the levels stabilize afterward. In addition, the effect on output materializes quickly, reaching 0.2 percent one year after the shock.[29] Given that average spending on active labor market policies across the sample is

[29]To isolate changes in discretionary spending from fluctuations in spending driven by the business cycle, the analysis follows the approach inspired by Perotti (1999) and Corsetti, Meier, and Müller (2012), wherein spending shocks are identified as innovations to past spending and economic activity as well as to expectations about current economic activity.

about 1 percent of GDP, this implies a one-year-ahead multiplier of about 1.2, consistent with other estimates reported in the literature (see Coenen and others 2012 and literature cited therein).

Shocks to spending on active labor market policies are found to have bigger effects in bad times. During periods of slack, a 10 percent increase in spending increases output by about 0.2 percent in the year of the shock and by about 0.6 percent after four years, whereas these effects are not statistically significantly different from zero in expansions (Figure 3.13, panels 3 and 4). As is also true in the case of shocks to labor tax wedges, this finding is consistent with the presence of larger fiscal multipliers in recessions. Spending on active labor market policies remains effective—even though the effects are smaller—if implemented in a budget-neutral way, and the effects are amplified when higher spending is combined with major reforms aimed at increasing the efficiency of active labor market policies.[30]

The Role of Macroeconomic Policy

As discussed earlier, the effects of some labor market reforms—in particular, reforms of employment protection legislation and unemployment benefit systems—can become contractionary if the reforms are undertaken under weak economic conditions. A key question, then, is whether accompanying macroeconomic policy stimulus can offset these short-term costs and maximize the benefits from reforms, either directly, through its direct effect on aggregate demand, or indirectly, because higher aggregate demand may make firms more willing to hire and less willing to dismiss workers in the aftermath of the reforms—as suggested by the model-based analysis of employment protection legislation reforms discussed earlier. Exploring this issue requires considering policy actions—both expansionary and contractionary—that are uncorrelated with reforms and can plausibly be deemed exogenous to macroeconomic conditions. For this purpose, the analysis focuses on fiscal policy shocks, which are identified as the forecast error of government consumption expenditure relative to GDP (for a similar approach, see Auerbach and Gorodnichenko 2012, 2013; and Abiad, Furceri, and Topalova 2015).[31]

The analysis indeed confirms that expansionary fiscal policy, in addition to stimulating aggregate demand, maximizes the benefits from labor market reforms (Figure 3.14).[32] During periods of relatively large fiscal expansion, reforms to employment protection legislation (unemployment benefits) are found to reduce the unemployment rate by about 2½ (3) percentage points in the medium term.[33] In contrast, during periods of relatively large fiscal contraction, they have zero or adverse effects on unemployment.[34]

Reforms That Increase Participation of Women and Older Workers

This subsection examines the effects of policies that can raise the labor force participation rates of women and older workers. Other labor market reforms have the potential to boost the participation rates of additional underrepresented population groups, such as youth and low-skilled migrants. Those reforms include well-designed training programs, as well as reductions in tax wedges and youth-specific minimum wages (April 2016 *Fiscal Monitor*, Chapter 2; OECD 2015). The analysis shows that reducing the (marginal) income taxation of second earners has statistically significant effects on women's labor force participation rates (Figure 3.15, panel 1).[35] There is also evidence that increasing incentives for part-time work and public spending on child care tends to increase women's labor force participation rates (see also Christiansen and others, forthcoming). For older workers, reducing early retirement incen-

---

information sets. The correlation between the measure of fiscal shocks and reforms of employment protection legislation or unemployment benefit systems is found to be close to zero. Likewise, the correlation between fiscal shocks and economic regime (or change in economic regime) is only –0.11 (0.01) and is not statistically significant.

[32]Consistent with this finding, Bordon, Ebeke, and Shirono (2016) find that supportive macroeconomic policies enhance the effect of product market reforms on employment.

[33]See Annex 3.3 for details on the empirical specification used, as well as for the definition of expansionary and contractionary fiscal regimes.

[34]Qualitatively similar results are found for employment and output. A potential concern regarding the analysis is that fiscal shocks may respond to output growth surprises. Analysis of the data shows that these shocks are weakly correlated with growth surprises. Moreover, purifying fiscal shocks by removing the portion explained by growth surprises delivers results that are similar to, and not different with statistical significance from, those reported in Figure 3.12.

[35]Given the limited time sample over which a measure of tax wedges on second earners is available (2000–12), the analysis examines the effect on participation rates up to three years after the shock.

---

[30]The effect of budget-neutral spending on active labor market policies does not vary substantially with the business cycle.

[31]This procedure also overcomes the problem of fiscal foresight (Forni and Gambetti 2010; Leeper, Richter, and Walker 2012; Leeper, Walker, and Yang 2013; Ben Zeev and Pappa 2014), because it aligns the economic agents' and the econometrician's

Figure 3.14. Role of Fiscal Policy in Shaping the Effects of Employment Protection Legislation and Unemployment Benefit Reforms on Unemployment
(Percentage points; years on x-axis)

Expansionary fiscal policy enhances the benefits from labor market reforms. During periods of relatively large fiscal expansions, reforms to employment protection legislation and unemployment benefits reduce the unemployment rate. In contrast, during periods of relatively large fiscal contractions, they have zero or adverse effects on unemployment.

Effect of Employment Protection Legislation Reforms

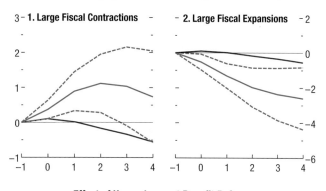

Effect of Unemployment Benefit Reforms

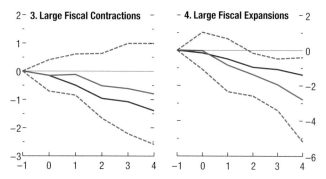

Source: IMF staff estimates.
Note: $t = 0$ is the year of the shock. In panels 1 and 2, solid blue lines denote the response to a major reform in employment protection legislation. In panels 3 and 4, they denote the response to a major reform in unemployment benefits. Dashed lines denote 90 percent confidence bands; and solid red lines represent the unconditional result.

tives by lowering the implicit tax on continued work embedded in old-age pension systems—for example, by increasing bonuses for deferred retirement or minimum statutory retirement ages—is found to boost these workers' labor market participation (Figure 3.15, panel 2), as well as employment rates overall. The magnitude of the effect is consistent with other estimates reported in the literature (see, for example, Duval 2003).

Summary and Policy Implications

Is now a good time to make a big push for additional structural reform in advanced economies? The

Figure 3.15. Effects of Reforms on Participation Rates of Women and Older Workers
(Percentage points; years on x-axis)

Reductions in marginal taxation of second earners and continued work at older ages boost the labor market participation of women and older workers, respectively.

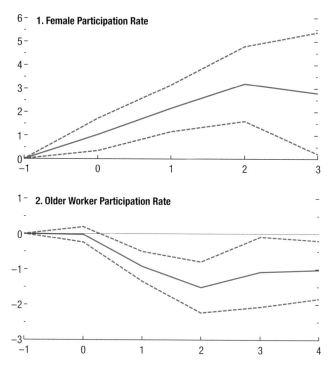

Source: IMF staff estimates.
Note: $t = 0$ is the year of the shock. In panel 1, the solid line denotes the response to a 1 percent reduction in the (marginal) labor tax wedge for second earners. In panel 2, the solid line denotes the response to a 10 percentage point reduction in implicit tax on continued work. Dashed lines denote 90 percent confidence bands.

three basic findings of this chapter support a qualified "yes," for several reasons:

- There is a strong need and scope for substantial further reforms of product market regulations—especially those governing retail trade and professional services—and labor market institutions.
- The political environment is currently conducive to such reforms, at least for product markets, given the worries about weak growth (see Box 3.1).
- Product and labor market reforms can raise potential output and employment levels over the medium term (Table 3.1). These findings justify further reform efforts in many advanced economies, particularly in those with the greatest scope for reform—such as, to various extents, some euro area countries, Japan, and Korea.

But the "yes" must be qualified by three other considerations:

- Most reforms are likely to make only a small near-term contribution to the ongoing economic recovery, as it takes time for the gains to materialize, particularly in countries where economic conditions are weak.
- Wherever possible, labor market reforms need to be accompanied by supportive macroeconomic policies—including fiscal stimulus where space is available and a strong medium-term fiscal framework is in place—to enhance their short-term benefits at the current juncture.
- Structural reforms can raise the long-term level of output, as the chapter shows, but their growth effects appear to be transitory.

The qualifications highlight the need for careful prioritization and sequencing of reforms as well as for complementary macroeconomic policies, especially for labor market reforms. Product market reforms should be implemented forcefully, as they boost output even under weak macroeconomic conditions and would not worsen public finances. In contrast, narrowing unemployment benefits and easing job protections should be accompanied by other policies to offset their short-term cost; alternatively, they might even be grandfathered or be enacted with their implementation deferred until a (suitably defined) better time arrives.

Finally, because product and labor market reforms are no silver bullet, policymakers should undertake them in combination with other growth-oriented reforms.

Annex 3.1. Modeling the Effects of Product and Labor Market Reforms

This annex presents the dynamic stochastic general equilibrium model used to assess the effects of reforms. The model considers a currency union that consists of two countries and two sectors (tradables and nontradables) in each country—although key insights are qualitatively robust to considering a small open economy under a flexible exchange rate regime instead.[36] Full details are provided by Cacciatore and others (forthcoming-b), who in turn build on earlier work by Cacciatore and Fiori (2016) and Cacciatore, Fiori, and Ghironi (forthcoming) that develops a novel theoretical framework for studying the consequences of product and labor market reforms and their interactions with macroeconomic policy. The main features of the model are the following:

- *Households*—These consist of a continuum of members and maximize the present value of their utility, which

depends on consumption of a basket of nontradable and (domestic and foreign) tradable goods. Because of labor and product market imperfections described later, a fraction of the household members will be unemployed and receive unemployment benefits from the government, financed through lump-sum taxes. The representative household owns the capital stock and also invests in a noncontingent bond, as well as in a mutual fund of nontradables sector firms through which new entrants can finance their entry costs.

- *Firms*—In each country, there are two vertically integrated production stages. Upstream, perfectly competitive firms use capital and labor to produce a nontradable intermediate input. Downstream, monopolistically competitive firms purchase intermediate inputs and produce differentiated nontradable goods. These goods are consumed, but also used by competitive firms in the tradables sector to produce a tradable good that is sold to consumers in both countries.

- *Job destruction*—While the rental market for capital is fully competitive, the labor market is imperfect and characterized by job-search-and-matching frictions with endogenous job creation and destruction as in Mortensen and Pissarides 1994 and den Haan, Ramey, and Watson 2000. Jobs are located in the intermediate goods sector. They can be destroyed for exogenous and endogenous motives. One endogenous motive is that jobs are subject to both common and job-specific productivity shocks in each period. If productivity is less than an endogenously determined threshold below which the value of keeping a particular job is less than the cost of discontinuing it, the firm dismisses the worker and pays the firing costs. The higher the firing costs, the lower the productivity threshold below which jobs are destroyed. Firing costs take the form of administrative costs of layoff procedures, and hence, are not transferred to workers and therefore should not be misconstrued as severance payments. Laid-off workers become unemployed and immediately begin searching for a new job.

- *Job creation*—Job creation is subject to matching frictions. To hire a worker, firms post job vacancies, incurring a cost. The probability of finding a worker depends on the degree of tightness of the labor market and the efficiency of the matching process. In turn, matching efficiency may be thought of as being partly affected by active labor market policies, although these are not specifically modeled. The representative intermediate goods producer chooses the number of vacancies, the job destruction threshold, and its capital stock so as

[36]See related work by Cacciatore and others (2015).

to maximize the present value of profits. Profits, and therefore job creation, also depend on wages, which are set through a negotiation process between firms and workers—so-called Nash bargaining. Stronger bargaining power of workers in this process, more generous unemployment benefits, or both raise wage claims and thereby reduce profits and job creation incentives, all else being equal. At the same time, higher wages raise consumption, aggregate demand, and—through this effect—job creation incentives, also all else being equal. The hiring-firing process creates dynamics (turnover) in the labor market, and employment varies depending on endogenous variations in job creation and destruction.

- *Product market dynamics and regulation*—The number of firms serving the nontradable goods market is endogenous.[37] Prior to entry, firms pay a sunk entry cost that reflects both a technological component (for example, sunk technological costs required to start producing electricity) and administrative costs of regulation. New entrants start producing after one period, increasing competition among firms and reducing profit margins and prices for all. Entry occurs until a new entrant's discounted value of future profits equals the sunk entry costs. Firm exit is exogenous and occurs when a firm is hit by a "death shock." This entry-exit process creates firm dynamics in the goods market. Finally, producers face (quadratic) price adjustment costs, resulting in sticky prices.

- *Monetary policy*—Since model parameters are chosen to match features of euro area macroeconomic data, monetary policy is assumed to respond to inflation and the output gap as estimated historically in the euro area. The policy rate cannot fall below a certain threshold—in practice, here, the zero lower bound—but the argument is more general.

Implementation of Reforms under Alternative Macroeconomic Conditions

The analysis simulates permanent unanticipated reforms across the whole currency union. It considers four possible reforms to product market regulation, employment protection legislation, unemployment benefit systems, and active labor market policies. More precisely, the analysis focuses on (1) a reduction in entry barriers to the level estimated for the United

States (for details, see Cacciatore and others, forthcoming-b); (2) the elimination of administrative costs of layoff procedures;[38] (3) a reduction to U.S. levels in workers' average unemployment benefit replacement rate over a five-year unemployment spell; and (4) a 50 percent increase in the efficiency of the job-matching process, which, according to estimates by Murtin and Robin (2014), would bring average matching efficiency across the euro area roughly to the (higher) average level across Sweden and the United Kingdom.

Reforms are carried out under three alternative macroeconomic conditions: (1) in "normal times," corresponding to the economy's initial steady state; (2) in "bad times with constrained monetary policy," which means in the immediate aftermath of a recession driven by a risk-premium shock that increased the required return on financial assets, depressing output and generating deflation (see, for instance, Eggertsson and Woodford 2003);[39] and (3) in "bad times with unconstrained monetary policy," which is situation (2) but now assuming as a thought experiment that the policy rate can freely fall below zero.

Annex 3.2. Identification of Reforms and Policy Shocks

Product Market, Employment Protection Legislation, and Unemployment Benefit Reforms

Identification Approach

Major reforms of product market regulation, employment protection legislation, and unemployment benefit systems are identified by examining documented legislative and regulatory actions reported in all available Organisation for Economic Co-operation and Development (OECD) *Economic Surveys* for 26 individual advanced economies since 1970, as well as additional country-specific sources (see Annex 3.4 for the list of countries covered). In this respect, the methodology is closely related to the "narrative approach" used by Romer and Romer (1989, 2004, 2010, and 2015) and Devries and others (2011) to identify monetary and fiscal shocks and periods of high financial distress. The approach also considers both reforms and "counterreforms"—namely, policy changes in the opposite direction.

---

[37]The model focuses on entry in the nontradables sector to capture the focus of current policy discussions on this sector. Cacciatore, Fiori, and Ghironi (forthcoming) focus on entry in the tradables sector.

[38]Relaxing employment protection legislation may also lower workers' bargaining power (Blanchard and Giavazzi 2003). This effect is not considered here.

[39]The size of the risk premium shock is chosen so as to deliver a 4 percent peak-to-trough decline in output, while its persistence is such that, in the absence of reform, the zero lower bound binds for approximately two years.

In a first step, more than 1,000 legislative and regulatory actions are identified in the areas of product market regulation, employment protection legislation, unemployment benefits, and the design of active labor market policies over the entire sample. In a second step, for any of these actions to qualify as a major reform, one of the following three alternative criteria must be met: (1) the OECD survey uses strong normative language to define the action, suggestive of an important measure (for example, "major reform"); (2) the policy action is mentioned repeatedly across different issues of the OECD survey or in the retrospective summaries of key past reforms that are featured in some issues, for the country considered; or (3) the OECD indicator of the regulatory stance in the area considered—if available—displays a very large change (in the 5th percentile of the distribution of the change in the indicator). When only the last of these conditions is met, an extensive search through other sources is performed to identify the precise policy action underpinning the change in the indicator. Annex Table 3.2.1 provides an example of how these criteria have guided the identification of major reforms and counterreforms in the area of product market regulation, employment protection legislation, and unemployment benefits (for details, see Duval and others, forthcoming).

One important advantage of this approach is that it identifies the precise nature and timing of *major* legislative and regulatory actions taken by advanced economies since the early 1970s in key labor and product market policy areas. Specifically, compared with existing databases on policy actions in the area of labor market institutions (such as the European Commission Labref, Fondazione Rodolfo de Benedetti–IZA, and International Labour Organization EPLex databases), the approach allows identification of major legislative and regulatory reforms as opposed to just actions. This is particularly useful for empirical analysis that seeks to identify, and then estimate, the effects or the drivers of reform shocks.

The approach also improves along several dimensions on indirect methods that rely exclusively on changes in OECD policy indicators to identify policy shocks. Specifically, the approach is able to do the following:

- Identify the exact timing of major legislative and regulatory actions
- Identify the precise reforms that underpin a gradual decline in OECD policy indicators without any obvious break (for example, for some countries in some network industries—air, rail, and road transportation; electricity and gas distribution; telecommunications and postal services)

- Cover reform areas for which no time-varying policy indicators exist, such as conditionality in the provision of unemployment benefits or major reforms regarding the design of activation policies, such as the integration of job placement and benefit payment services
- Identify reforms in areas for which OECD indicators exist but do not cover all relevant policy dimensions (for example, a major reform that lowers the duration of unemployment benefits from an indefinite period to five years is not captured by the corresponding OECD indicator, which covers the first five years of an unemployment spell)
- Cover a longer time period in some policy areas, such as employment protection legislation, for which OECD indicators are available only starting from the mid-1980s
- Document and describe the precise legislative and regulatory actions that underpin observed large changes in the OECD indicator
- Differentiate between announcement and implementation dates of reforms, in some cases[40]

In contrast, the approach does not allow any information to be provided regarding the stance of current or past product and labor market regulations and as such is clearly no substitute for existing policy indicators, for instance, those produced by the OECD.

Number of Identified Reforms

Annex Figure 3.2.1 shows the number of reforms identified in the sample and illustrates the heterogeneity of reform efforts across regulatory areas. Product market reforms have been most frequently implemented, in particular as regards the regulation of network industries (Annex Figure 3.2.1, panel 1).[41] In general, fewer reforms have been implemented in the areas of employment protection legislation and unemployment benefit systems. One exception has been the rather widespread relaxation of employment protection legislation for temporary contracts. In part, this may reflect political

[40]While the limited number of cases for which the announcement and the implementation date of reforms is available prevents systematic use of this information in the cross-country analysis, this information could be useful in microstudies aimed at assessing the impact of reforms, including through anticipation effects.

[41]Economy-wide product market reform episodes are then defined as events during which reform occurs in at least two out of the seven network industries, which corresponds to the 90th percentile of the distribution of the sum of all seven reform dummy variables. Similar results are obtained when the distribution of the weighted sum of the reform dummies is used instead, with weights equal to the (country-sector-specific time-varying) share of value added of each sector in GDP.

Annex Table 3.2.1. Examples of Reforms Identified

Reform (+) or Counter-reform (−)	Announcement Year	Implementation/ Scored Year	Area	Country	Content	Normative Language	Mention in Reports	Large Change in OECD Indicator
+	1982	1984	Product market (telecommun-ications)	United States	Antitrust suit against AT&T	The most important deregulatory move in telecommunications came with the antitrust suit against AT&T by the United States. Competition for long-distance voice services entered a new phase in 1984.	1986, 1989, 2004	No
+	1993	Mid-1994/1995	Employment protection legislation	Spain	Draft law modifying the existing law regulating employment. It introduced dismissals of permanent workers.	... far-reaching labor market reforms aimed at lifting barriers to job creation. A decree was passed at the end of December 1993, and a draft has been presented to Parliament and is expected to become law by the middle of 1994.	No	Yes for 1995
−	...	1970	Employment protection legislation	Italy	Act of 1970, referred to as the "workers' statute"	The Act of 1970 referred to as the "workers' statute" laid the basis for employer-employee relations and regulations concerning hiring. The two main sources of rigidity seem to be the regulations governing hiring and firing. The conditions and procedures for hiring workers are extremely stringent, particularly for large firms.	1986	...
+	...	1994	Unemployment benefits	Denmark	Labor market reforms of 1994: activation of the unemployed, limiting the duration of unemployment benefits, enforcing job availability criteria, compulsory full-time activation, stricter eligibility criteria	The measures taken ... are steps in the right direction. Training and education offers are fully operational, a foundation has been established for reducing the duration of unemployment benefits on a sustainable basis.	2000	Yes for 1994 (replacement rate); other aspects (duration, eligibility, active policies) not captured

Source: Organisation for Economic Co-operation and Development (OECD).

economy obstacles that in some cases have made it diffi-cult to reform poorly functioning institutions (Box 3.1), but also that societal preferences (for insurance against economic risk) vary across countries and that different labor market institutional models can be successful.

Labor Tax Wedge Shocks

Labor tax wedge shocks are identified as the annual change in the main tax wedge measure derived from OECD tax models. This measure is defined as the wedge between the labor cost to the employer and the corresponding net take-home pay of the employee for an average single-earner couple with two children, and it expresses the sum of personal income tax and all social security contributions as a percentage of total labor cost.

Discretionary Shocks to Public Spending on Active Labor Market Policies

The methodology used to identify shocks to dis-cretionary spending on active labor market policies follows the approach inspired by Perotti (1999) and Corsetti, Meier, and Müller (2012). In this approach, spending shocks are identified as innovations to past spending and economic activity as well as to expec-tations about current economic activity.[42] Data for

[42]Specifically, spending shocks are identified as the residuals of the following regression:

$$\Delta s_{it} = \alpha_i + \gamma_t + \beta_t \Delta y_{it-1} + \delta_t \Delta y^E_{it-1} + \vartheta_t \Delta s_{it-1} + \varepsilon_{it},$$

in which Δs denotes the growth rate of public spending on active labor market policies; Δy is GDP growth; Δy^E denotes the forecast for GDP growth at time t, made at $t - 1$; and α_i and γ_t are country and time fixed effects, respectively.

spending on active labor market policies are taken from the OECD Social Expenditure Database.

The Wedge between the Tax Rates of Second Earners and Single Individuals

The wedge between the tax rates of second earners and single individuals is computed as the ratio of *Tax second earner* to *Tax single individual*. The *Tax second earner* variable is calculated as

$$Tax\ second\ earner = 1 -$$
$$\frac{(Household\ Net\ Income)_B - (Household\ Net\ Income)_A}{(Household\ Gross\ Income)_B - (Household\ Gross\ Income)_A},$$

in which A represents the case in which the second earner does not earn any income and B the case in which the second earner's gross earnings are 67 percent of average earnings. The *Tax single individual* variable is computed using the same formula for a single person. Data on tax rates of second earners and single individuals are taken from the OECD Family Database.

Implicit Tax on Continued Work

Data for implicit tax on continued work embedded in old-age pension systems are taken from and updated using the methodology described by Duval (2003). This variable measures the change in pension wealth—calculated as the change in present value of the stream of future pension payments net of contributions to the system—from working five more years, for "typical" workers at ages 55, 60, and 65. It varies depending, for instance, on the minimum age of eligibility for benefits or the existence and magnitude of pension adjustments for early or deferred retirement.

Annex 3.3. The Macroeconomic Effects of Reforms: Empirical Analysis

Cross-Country Analysis

Empirical Strategy

The analysis in this section assesses the macroeconomic impact of reforms. Two econometric specifications are used. The first establishes whether reforms have statistically significant effects on macroeconomic variables such as output, (un)employment, and inflation. The second assesses whether these effects vary with overall business conditions prevailing at the time of a particular reform (weak versus strong economic conditions) or with the stance of accompanying macroeconomic policies (fiscal expansions versus fiscal con-

Annex Figure 3.2.1. Number of Reforms Identified

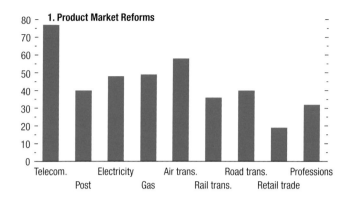

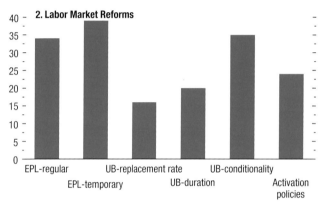

Source: IMF staff calculations.
Note: EPL = employment protection legislation; gas = gas distribution; post = postal services; professions = professional services; telecom. = telecommunications; trans. = transportation; UB = unemployment benefit.

tractions). The statistical method follows the approach proposed by Jordà (2005) to estimate impulse-response functions. This approach has been advocated by Stock and Watson (2007) and Auerbach and Gorodnichenko (2012), among others, as a flexible alternative to vector autoregression (autoregressive distributed-lag) specifications since it does not impose dynamic restrictions. It is also particularly suited to estimating nonlinearities (including interactions between shocks and other variables of interest) in the dynamic response. The first regression specification is estimated as follows:

$$y_{t+k,i} - y_{t-1,i} = \alpha_i + \gamma_t + \beta_k R_{i,t} + \theta X_{i,t} + \varepsilon_{i,t}, \quad (A3.3.1)$$

in which y is the log of output (log of employment, unemployment rate, log of productivity, log of price level); α_i are country fixed effects, included to take account of differences in countries' average growth rates; γ_t are time fixed effects, included to take account of global shocks such as shifts in oil prices or the global business cycle; R denotes the reform; and X is a set of control variables, including past economic growth, past reforms, and recession dummies.

In the second specification, the response is allowed to vary with the state of the economy and the stance of fiscal policy:

$$y_{i,t+k} - y_{i,t-1} = \alpha_i + \gamma_t + \beta_k^L F(z_{i,t}) R_{i,t} + \beta_k^H (1 - F(z_{i,t})) R_{i,t} + \theta Z_{i,t} + \varepsilon_{i,t},$$

(A3.3.2)

with

$$F(z_{it}) = \frac{\exp(-\delta z_{it})}{1 + \exp(-\delta z_{it})}, \delta > 0,$$

in which z is an indicator of the state of the economy (or the stance of fiscal policy) normalized to have zero mean and unit variance and Z is a set of control variables, including past economic growth, past reforms, recession dummies, and the state of the economy or the stance of fiscal policy.[43] The indicator of the state of the economy considered in the analysis is GDP growth.[44] The indicator of the stance of fiscal policy is a government consumption shock, identified as the forecast error of government consumption expenditure relative to GDP (for a similar approach see, for example, Auerbach and Gorodnichenko 2012, 2013; and Abiad, Furceri, and Topalova 2015).[45]

Equations (A3.3.1) and (A3.3.2) are estimated for each $k = 0, \ldots, 4$. Impulse-response functions are computed using the estimated coefficients β_k, and the confidence bands associated with the estimated impulse-response functions are obtained using the

estimated standard errors of the coefficients β_k, based on clustered robust standard errors.

The macroeconomic series used in the analysis come from the Organisation for Economic Co-operation and Development (OECD) *Economic Outlook: Statistics and Projections* database, which covers an unbalanced sample of 26 OECD economies over the period 1970–2014 (see Annex 3.4 for details). The forecasts of government consumption used in the analysis are those reported in the fall issue of the OECD's *Economic Outlook* for the same year. As a robustness check, the forecasts of the spring issue of the same year and the fall issue of the previous year are used.

Robustness Checks

A possible concern regarding the analysis is that the probability of structural reform is influenced not only by past economic growth and the occurrence of recessions (Box 3.1), but also by contemporaneous economic developments as well as expectations of future growth. However, this is unlikely to be a major issue, given the long lags associated with the implementation of structural reforms and that information about future growth is likely to be largely embedded in past economic activity. Most important, controlling for expectations of current and future growth delivers results that are very similar to, and not statistically significantly different from, those reported in the chapter text (Annex Figure 3.3.1).

Another possible concern regarding the analysis is that the results may suffer from omitted-variables bias, as reforms may occur across different areas at the same time. However, including all reforms across all areas simultaneously in the estimated equation does not substantially alter the magnitude and the statistical significance of the results (Annex Figure 3.3.1).

Finally, estimates could be biased in the event of reform reversals. In practice, however, this bias is negligible, as there are only a very few such cases. Furthermore, the results are robust to controlling for future reforms and counterreforms, as well as to focusing exclusively on reform episodes.

Sector- and Firm-Level Analysis

To provide additional insights into the transmission channels of product and labor market reforms and to address some of the limitations of the macroeconometric analysis (by fully controlling for countrywide economic shocks that coincide with reforms), the macroeconomic analysis is complemented by sector- or firm-level approaches or both.

---

[43]This approach is equivalent to the smooth-transition autoregressive model developed by Granger and Teräsvirta (1993). The advantage of this approach is twofold. First, compared with a model in which each reform variable is interacted with the unemployment rate or business cycle measures, this approach tests directly whether the effect of reforms varies across different regimes such as recessions (for example, output growth below a given threshold) and expansions. Second, compared with estimating structural vector autoregressions for each regime, it allows the effect of reforms to change smoothly between recessions and expansions by considering a continuum of states to compute the impulse-response functions, thus making the response more stable and precise.

[44]Following Auerbach and Gorodnichenko (2012), $\delta = 1.5$ is used here for the analysis of recessions and expansions. Periods of very low (high) growth identified in this analysis also correspond to periods of large negative (positive) output gaps. Similar results are indeed found when the output gap rather than GDP growth is used.

[45]This procedure also overcomes the problem of fiscal foresight (Forni and Gambetti 2010; Leeper, Richter, and Walker 2012; Leeper, Walker, and Yang 2013; Ben Zeev and Pappa 2014), because it aligns the economic agents' and the econometrician's information sets. Here, $\delta = 1$ is used to assess the role of the fiscal policy stance. The results do not qualitatively change for different values of $\delta > 0$.

Product Market Reforms: Direct Effects

The direct effects of product market reforms on sectoral (or firm) output are estimated using a specification similar to (A3.3.1) but augmented by country-year (α_{ij}) and country-sector (γ_{ij}) fixed effects as well as by sector time trends (*trend*$_j$):

$$y_{j,i,t+k} - y_{j,i,t-1} = \alpha_{it} + \gamma_{ij} + trend_j + \beta_k R_{j,i,t} + \varepsilon_{j,i,t},$$

$$(A3.3.3)$$

in which i denotes country, j sector (or firm), and t year.

The inclusion of these two types of fixed effects provides two important advantages compared with the cross-country analysis: (1) country-year fixed effects make it possible to control for any variation that is common to all sectors of a country's economy, including aggregate output growth as well as reforms in other areas; and (2) country-industry fixed effects allow industry-specific factors, including, for instance, cross-country differences in the growth of certain sectors that could arise from differences in comparative advantage, to be controlled for. The firm-level analysis in addition controls for past and future reforms, industry-year fixed effects, and key firm characteristics such as age, size, debt, and labor productivity.

The sectoral series used in the analysis of direct effects of product market reforms come from the OECD Structural Analysis (STAN) database, which provides annual information on sectoral input, output, and prices over the period 1970–2011.[46] The firm-level series are taken from the Orbis database, which covers an unbalanced sample of 20 advanced economies over the period 1998–2013.[47]

Product Market Reforms: Indirect Effects

The indirect effects of product market reforms on sectoral output through their spillovers to other sectors are estimated using a specification similar to (A3.3.3) but focusing instead on a term for the interaction between product market reforms in each network industry and the total input requirement of downstream (upstream) industries from upstream (downstream) industries:

$$y_{j,i,t+k} - y_{j,i,t-1} = \alpha_{ij} + \gamma_{it} + trend_j +$$

$$\beta_k \sum_{s \neq j} \omega_{js,i,t}^{I/O} R_{s,i,t} + \varepsilon_{j,i,t},\qquad (A3.3.4)$$

in which $\omega_{js,i,t}^{I}$ is the share of intermediate inputs provided by each network industry s in country i

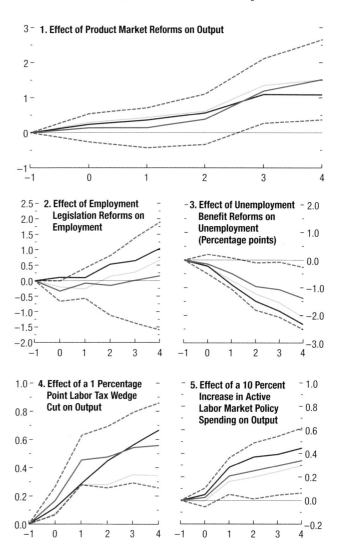

Annex Figure 3.3.1. Effects of Reforms on Economic Activity: Robustness Check
(Percent, unless noted otherwise; years on x-axis)

— Baseline — Controlling for other reforms — Controlling for expectations about future growth

1. Effect of Product Market Reforms on Output

2. Effect of Employment Legislation Reforms on Employment

3. Effect of Unemployment Benefit Reforms on Unemployment (Percentage points)

4. Effect of a 1 Percentage Point Labor Tax Wedge Cut on Output

5. Effect of a 10 Percent Increase in Active Labor Market Policy Spending on Output

Source: IMF staff estimates.
Note: $t = 0$ is the year of the shock. Dashed lines denote 90 percent confidence bands.

to downstream industry j, and $\omega_{js,i,t}^{O}$ is the share of intermediate inputs provided by each industry j in country i to downstream network industry s. To minimize endogeneity issues and measurement errors, the weights $\omega_{js,i,t}^{I/O}$ are based on 2000 input-output data. Similar results are obtained using 1996 input-output data instead.

---

[46]See Bouis, Duval, and Eugster, forthcoming, for further details on the construction of the data set and the analysis.

[47]See Gal and Hijzen, forthcoming, for further details on the construction of the data set and the analysis.

The sectoral series used in this analysis come from the EU KLEMS and World KLEMS databases, which provide annual information on sectoral input, output, and prices over the period 1970–2007.

Employment Protection Legislation Reforms

The empirical approach used to assess the effect of employment protection legislation reforms on sectoral employment builds on the methodology proposed by Bassanini, Nunziata, and Venn (2009). The analysis relies on the identification assumption that stringent dismissal regulations are likely to be more binding in sectors that are characterized by a higher natural propensity to regularly adjust their workforce (L_j):

$$y_{j,i,t+k} - y_{j,i,t-1} = \alpha_{it} + \gamma_{ij} + trend_j + \beta_k L_j R_{i,t} + \varepsilon_{j,i,t}.$$
(A3.3.5)

The sectoral series used in this analysis come from the EU KLEMS and World KLEMS databases (Timmer and others 2015). Data on layoff rates are taken from Bassanini, Nunziata, and Venn 2009 and are computed based on industry-level U.S. layoff rates reported in the 2004 Current Population Survey *Displaced Workers Supplement*. While relying on U.S. layoff rates can be considered a good proxy for underlying layoff propensity in the absence of dismissal regulations, one potential problem with this approach is that they may not be representative for the whole sample—that is, U.S. layoff rates may be affected by U.S.-specific regulations or sectoral patterns. To check for the sensitivity of the results to this assumption, the analysis is replicated using U.K. layoff rates computed from the U.K. *Labour Force Survey*. The results based on U.K. layoff rates are very similar to, and not statistically significantly different from, those based on U.S. layoff rates.

Annex 3.4. Country Coverage and Data Sources

Annex Table 3.4.1. Country Coverage

Australia	Finland	Italy	Norway	United Kingdom
Austria	France	Japan	Portugal	United States
Belgium	Germany	Korea	Slovak Republic	
Canada	Greece	Luxembourg	Spain	
Czech Republic	Iceland	Netherlands	Sweden	
Denmark	Ireland	New Zealand	Switzerland	

Annex Table 3.4.2. Macroeconomic Data Sources

Variable	Source
Potential Output Growth and Components	April 2015 *World Economic Outlook*, Chapter 3
Product Market Regulations	Koske and others 2015 (Organisation for Economic Co-operation and Development, Indicators of Product Market Regulation)
Employment Protection Legislation	Organisation for Economic Co-operation and Development, Indicators of Employment Protection database
Unemployment Benefits	Organisation for Economic Co-operation and Development, Benefits and Wages database
Labor Tax Wedge	Organisation for Economic Co-operation and Development, Tax Statistics database
Spending on Active Labor Market Policies	Organisation for Economic Co-operation and Development, Social Expenditure database
Real GDP	Organisation for Economic Co-operation and Development, *Economic Outlook*
Employment	Organisation for Economic Co-operation and Development, *Economic Outlook*
Consumer Price Index	Organisation for Economic Co-operation and Development, *Economic Outlook*
Unemployment Rate	Organisation for Economic Co-operation and Development, *Economic Outlook*
Female Participation Rate	Organisation for Economic Co-operation and Development, *Labor Force Survey*
Older Worker Participation Rate	Organisation for Economic Co-operation and Development, *Labor Force Survey*

Box 3.1. Breaking the Deadlock: Identifying the Political Economy Drivers of Structural Reforms

Despite broad recognition that many advanced economies are in need of product and labor market reforms, progress in these areas over the past two decades has not always met expectations. This deadlock over major reforms has inspired a significant number of studies in political economy research (see, for instance, Saint-Paul 2000 and Galasso 2014 and references cited therein). This literature has emphasized the role of macroeconomic conditions and policies and the vested interests of incumbents (firms and workers), as well as political factors—such as the degree of fractionalization in the parliament, ideology, political systems, and electoral cycles—as potential determinants of reforms. However, the empirical evidence on each of these reform drivers remains inconclusive, and different studies have often reached contrasting conclusions due to different samples, uncertainty regarding the exact timing of reforms, and the choice of control variables used in the analysis.[1]

This box tries to address the limitations of previous studies by (1) focusing on a more homogenous group of 26 advanced economies (see Annex 3.4 for the list of countries covered in the sample); (2) using this chapter's new database on reforms, which focuses on documented changes in regulation or legislation reported in Organisation for Economic Co-operation and Development (OECD) *Economic Surveys* and additional country-specific sources to identify the exact nature and timing of reforms (see Annex 3.2); and (3) using model averaging techniques to identify the most robust determinants of reforms.[2] The analysis focuses on six reform areas for which major legislative changes are identified in the database: product market, employment protection legislation for regular and temporary contracts, generosity of and conditionality embedded in unemployment protection benefit systems, and efficiency of activation policies—more specifically,

The authors of this box are Jakob Miethe and Davide Furceri. The analysis presented here draws on Duval, Furceri, and Miethe, forthcoming.

[1]For example, for conflicting results on the role of fractionalization, see Wiese 2014; Bortolotti and Pinotti 2008; and Alesina, Ardagna, and Trebbi 2006.

[2]The analysis builds on the approach proposed by Sala-i-Martin (1997) and further extended by Doppelhofer, Miller, and Sala-i-Martin (2000). It applies extreme bounds and model averaging techniques to logit models. For each reform variable, the analysis considers up to 30 possible determinants of reforms suggested in the literature and 100,000 randomly chosen models from 1.3 million different combinations. In this approach, a variable is assessed to be a robust determinant of reforms if more than 90 percent of its effects are either positive or negative. See Duval, Furceri, and Miethe, forthcoming, for details.

major overhauls of public employment services (which, for instance, enhance their effectiveness by merging job placement and benefit payment services).

The analysis points to several common drivers across reforms (Table 3.1.1). First, and most strikingly, product and labor market reforms typically occur during periods of weak economic growth, high unemployment, or both. This highlights that crises can break the political deadlock over reforms. Second, there is also clear evidence across the board that reform pressure is stronger if little action has been taken in the past. For example, if product market regulation is high in the preceding period, the likelihood of reform increases. Third, parliamentary systems are generally more likely to implement reforms, with the exception of major reforms to activation policies. Fourth, peer pressure matters: a given country is more likely to undertake reform in a particular area when neighboring countries and trade partners do so.

In addition to these common drivers, the analysis also points to some important area-specific determinants. The timing of elections seems to be particularly relevant for reforms of employment protection legislation in regard to regular contracts; these reforms tend to occur far away from elections, possibly reflecting their unpopularity. Aging countries tend to implement more product market and employment protection legislation reforms than do younger societies, possibly because such reforms may benefit older nonworking people more than prime-age workers. Furthermore, many product market reforms in European Union countries tend to have occurred during their accession process, reflecting greater pressure for reform during that period. In contrast, other variables that feature prominently in the political economy literature—such as union density, the political orientation of governments, and fiscal positions—are found to be only weakly correlated with the occurrence of product and labor market reforms.

In sum, this box points to weak economic conditions and the size of structural reform gaps as the most robust drivers of product and labor market reforms. This implies that the current economic environment and the remaining scope for reforms in many countries provide political conditions that ought to be conducive to a push for structural reforms.

Box 3.1 *(continued)*

Table 3.1.1. Drivers of Reforms

Category	Area of Reforms					
	PMR	EPR reg.	EPR temp.	UB	UB cond.	ALMP
Initial Stance	+	+	+		+	−
Domestic Spillovers from Reforms in Other Areas						
International Spillovers	+		+		+	−
Weak Economic Conditions	+	+	+	+	+	+
Closeness to Elections		−				
Ideology			−			
Political System	+	+	+	+		+
European Union–Related Variables	+					
Demographic Variables	+		+			

Source: IMF staff estimates.

Note: + = positive effect on reforms (more than 90 percent of cumulative distribution function of coefficient positive); − = negative effect on reforms (more than 90 percent negative). ALMP = active labor market policies; Demographic Variables = population older than 65, population 50–65; Closeness to Elections = the inverse of the number of months to the next elections, the inverse of the number of years of the executive in office, years left in term, dummy variable that takes value 1 if elections occur within the next 18 months, 0 otherwise; EPR reg. = employment protection reforms, regular workers; EPR temp. = employment protection reforms, temporary workers; European Union–Related Variables = Economic and Monetary Union, European Union accession, transition; Ideology = takes value 1 for right-leaning governments, 2 for center-leaning, and 3 for left-leaning; Initial Stance = lagged and initial indicator; PMR = product market regulations; Political System = democracy, union density, regional autonomy, system, centralization, parliamentary stability; Spillovers = domestic and international (raw as well as weighted by trade shares and distance); UB = unemployment benefits; UB cond. = unemployment benefits with conditionality; Weak Economic Conditions = unemployment, low growth, recessions, crises.

Box 3.2. Reforming Collective-Bargaining Systems to Achieve High and Stable Employment

Since the global financial crisis, there has been a renewed focus on the macroeconomic performance of collective-bargaining systems as a key tool to strengthen the responsiveness of wages and working hours to macroeconomic shocks and, ultimately, to help achieve high and stable employment—so-called macro flexibility (Blanchard, Jaumotte, and Loungani 2014). Collective bargaining tends to be particularly important in continental western Europe, where it covers about 80 percent of the workforce and mostly takes the form of sector-level bargaining. Against this backdrop, this box sheds light on some of the key features that can help collective-bargaining systems achieve these goals.

Much of the early policy debate focused on the degree of centralization of wage bargaining. The prevailing view was that highly centralized systems (which provide macro flexibility by inducing unions and firms to internalize the effects of wage claims on economy-wide employment) and decentralized systems (by providing wage flexibility at the firm level) would be preferable to sector-level bargaining (Calmfors and Driffill 1988). However, as flagged, for instance, by Blanchard, Jaumotte, and Loungani (2014), the implications of alternative bargaining structures remain insufficiently understood. Indeed, experiences have diverged noticeably among countries where sector-level bargaining is widespread. This suggests that the ability of collective-bargaining systems to sustain high and stable employment rates depends not only on the degree of centralization, but also on the systems' specific features in terms of institutional design and national practices. This includes the scope for flexibility at the firm level, the reach of sector-level collective-bargaining agreements, and the effectiveness of coordination among bargaining units. These issues are particularly relevant for countries predominantly characterized by sector-level bargaining.

One important feature of a sector-level bargaining system is whether it provides for any flexibility at the firm level to accommodate temporary shocks that affect different firms in different ways—such as the global financial and euro area crises, whose impact on sales and access to credit varied widely

across firms within a number of countries. For example, the widespread use of hardship and opening clauses, which allow firms to set less favorable wages and working conditions than those in the applicable sector-level agreement if certain conditions are met, is often seen as one of the factors behind the resilience of the German labor market during the global financial crisis (Dustmann and others 2014). By contrast, countries such as Portugal and Spain entered the crisis with bargaining systems that continued to rely on strict application of the "favorability principle," which says that working conditions can be no less favorable to workers than those specified in the sector-level agreement. Since the crisis, both countries have introduced reforms to provide more flexibility to firms. Opening clauses come with drawbacks, however, suggesting they need to be carefully calibrated. In the absence of any constraints on timing and scope, depending on the relative importance of their effects on employment levels and the shape of the wage distribution, they might raise inequality—directly, and possibly also indirectly by weakening the position of trade unions.

The presence and design of extensions of collective-bargaining agreements also matter for the ability of a sector-level bargaining system to withstand shocks. Despite the decline in union membership, collective-bargaining coverage has remained largely stable in countries relying on sector-level bargaining. This is due to the role of extensions that expand the coverage of collective-bargaining agreements beyond the membership of employer associations and trade unions to all workers in a sector. Extensions limit the scope of competition on the basis of poor working conditions and also reduce the transaction costs of engaging in negotiations, which may be particularly important for small firms that lack the resources to engage in firm-level bargaining. However, depending on the way they are administered, extensions have the potential to hurt employment and increase its sensitivity to changes in macroeconomic conditions. As an illustrative example, Figure 3.2.1 provides tentative new evidence based on a policy reform in

The author of this box is Alexander Hijzen, with contributions from Eric Gould (Hebrew University) and Pedro Martins (Queen Mary College, University of London).

Box 3.2 *(continued)*

Figure 3.2.1. Portugal: Employment Growth during the Global Financial Crisis among Firms Not Affiliated with an Employer Association
(Percent)

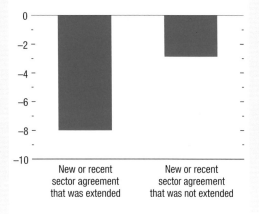

Source: IMF staff estimates.

Portugal that resulted from the unanticipated June 2011 decision by the government to suspend with immediate effect the extension of collective agreements. Because of the usual administrative delay associated with extensions, this effectively implied that any agreements signed in March 2011 or later were not extended. Figure 3.2.1 compares employment growth in firms that were not affiliated with an employer association in sectors in which a collective agreement was introduced or revised just before this date (and hence, the agreement was extended) with firms in sectors in which a collective agreement was introduced or revised just after this date (and hence, the agreement was not extended). It suggests that employment growth between 2010 and 2011 declined considerably more in nonaffiliated firms that were subject to an extension compared with those that were not.[1]

Good policy design can help mitigate the adverse effects of extensions. For instance, subjecting extensions to representativeness criteria (as, for example, in the Netherlands) or a meaningful test of public interest (as, for example, in Germany) can

[1]Similar findings are reported by Martins (2014).

help ensure that the interests of all firms, including small ones, are taken into account. The availability of clear and transparent procedures for exemptions from extensions, as they evolved in the Netherlands, for example, can provide some flexibility at the firm level when needed. By contrast, if in downturns extensions are applied retroactively starting from the date of the collective-bargaining agreement, the implied wage increases may harm liquidity-constrained firms.

When collective bargaining takes place predominantly at the sector level, coordination among bargaining units also matters for macro flexibility. Coordination can arise when smaller players follow the lead of a major one ("pattern bargaining") or through confederations of trade unions and employer associations. Indeed, many countries with some form of coordinated sector-level bargaining, such as Scandinavian countries, Germany, and Japan, have enjoyed comparatively high and stable employment over the years.

However, the effectiveness of coordination is likely to depend on the quality of industrial relations and the degree of trust among the social partners (Blanchard, Jaumotte, and Loungani 2014). Indeed, there is evidence to suggest that the importance of trust for macro flexibility is greatest in countries whose bargaining systems place more emphasis on coordination—in practice, countries with some form of sector-level or national-level bargaining.[2] In these countries, the unemployment response to the global financial crisis was much smaller where trust was high than where it was low (Figure 3.2.2).[3] While determining which fac-

[2]Under a decentralized bargaining system, trust may not matter as much, since the required macro flexibility is readily achieved through flexibility at the firm level.
[3]In Figure 3.2.2, a country is said to have no coordination when collective bargaining is completely decentralized and coordination is absent. The measure of trust is constructed using a question in the *World Values Survey* that asks, "Generally speaking, would you say that most people can be trusted or that you need to be very careful in dealing with people?" The response "most people can be trusted" is coded 1; "you need to be very careful in dealing with people" is coded 0. The responses are averaged across individuals aged 25 to 55 within each country and, subsequently, across years to obtain a time-invariant measure of trust. A country is said to have high trust when trust is above that of the median across the countries considered. Based on the information on trust and coordination, the following

Box 3.2 *(continued)*

tors can enhance trust is beyond the scope of this box, it seems plausible that trust depends to some extent on the way collective-bargaining systems operate in practice, including such factors as the inclusiveness of the system (in particular, whether social partners are broadly representative), the transparency of procedures (for example, for extensions or opt-outs), the effectiveness of agreement implementation, and built-in incentives for regular renegotiation.

three groups of countries are defined: (1) no centralization/coordination (Canada, Czech Republic, Estonia, Israel, New Zealand, Slovak Republic, United Kingdom, United States); (2) some centralization/coordination and low trust (France, Italy, Korea, Slovenia, Spain); and (3) some centralization/coordination and high trust (Finland, Germany, Netherlands, Norway, Sweden). The effects shown here are qualitatively robust to a regression analysis that would control for the role of other institutions, such as the stance of employment protection legislation.

Figure 3.2.2. Change in Unemployment Rate
(Percentage points; mean change before versus after 2008)

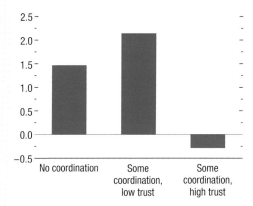

Sources: Organisation for Economic Co-operation and Development; World Values Survey; and IMF staff calculations.
Note: Low and high are defined as below and above the median.

Box 3.3. The Potential Productivity Gains from Further Trade and Foreign Direct Investment Liberalization

While this chapter's analysis of product market reforms focuses primarily on "behind-the-border" barriers to competition, easing barriers to international trade and foreign direct investment (FDI) also has the potential to boost long-term productivity and output levels. This issue features high on policymakers' agendas, as exemplified by the recent Trans-Pacific Partnership agreement. Despite past major liberalization, efforts have stalled more recently, and there remains some scope for further progress in advanced economies, particularly regarding nontariff barriers to trade and barriers to FDI (Figure 3.3.1, panel 1).[1]

Broadly speaking, even though the specifics vary across different types of measures, trade and FDI liberalization may boost productivity and thereby output through three channels:

- *Increased competition*—Lower trade and FDI barriers strengthen competition in the liberalized sector(s), putting pressure on domestic producers to lower price margins, exploit economies of scale (Helpman and Krugman 1985), improve efficiency, absorb foreign technology, or innovate (Aghion and others 2005).
- *Enhanced variety and quality of available inputs*— Trade liberalization can boost productivity by increasing the quality and variety of intermediate inputs available to domestic producers (Grossman and Helpman 1991; Kasahara and Rodrigue 2008; Halpern, Koren, and Szeidl 2015).
- *Resource reallocation across firms and sectors*—Liberalization enables larger and more productive firms to gain market share at the expense of smaller and less productive firms, thereby yielding an aggregate productivity gain within the liberalized sector (Melitz 2003; Pavcnik 2002). Liberalization may further involve productivity-enhancing reallocation of resources across sectors.

This box provides new quantitative evidence on the potential gains from further trade liberalization through these mechanisms and finds a sizable and dominant impact of the input channel. This is consistent with, but generalizes and quantifies the macroeconomic implications of, the recent empirical literature at the firm level.[2] Because of data constraints, the

The authors of this box are JaeBin Ahn and Romain Duval. It draws on Ahn and others 2016.

[1]Figure 3.3.1 presents the Organisation for Economic Co-operation and Development (OECD) indicator of barriers to trade and investment in four subcategories: barriers to FDI, tariff barriers, differential treatment of foreign suppliers, and barriers to trade facilitation. They are expressed as averages across OECD countries in 1998, 2003, 2008, and 2013. More details on the indicator can be found in Koske and others 2015.

[2]See, in particular, Amiti and Konings 2007 and Topalova and Khandelwal 2011.

Figure 3.3.1. Trade Liberalization

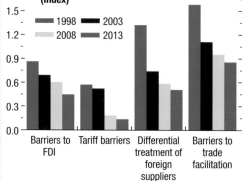

1. Barriers to Trade and Investment (Index)

1998 2003 2008 2013

Barriers to FDI / Tariff barriers / Differential treatment of foreign suppliers / Barriers to trade facilitation

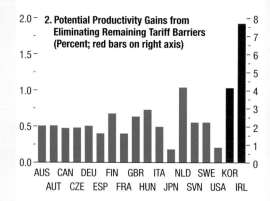

2. Potential Productivity Gains from Eliminating Remaining Tariff Barriers (Percent; red bars on right axis)

AUS CAN DEU FIN GBR ITA NLD SWE KOR
AUT CZE ESP FRA HUN JPN SVN USA IRL

Sources: EU KLEMS; Koske and others 2015; World Bank, Trade Analysis Information System (TRAINS); and IMF staff calculations.
Note: Panel 1 is an average of 28 OECD country indexes, each on a scale of 0 to 6, from least to most restrictive. Panel 2 is based on tariff rate data in latest available years. FDI = foreign direct investment; OECD = Organisation for Economic Co-operation and Development. Data labels in the figure use International Organization for Standardization (ISO) country codes.

analysis focuses exclusively on tariff liberalization and its complementarities with reductions in barriers to FDI. As such, it captures only a fraction of productivity gains to be reaped from comprehensive trade liberalization in advanced economies.[3]

A unique database of effective tariffs is constructed for 18 manufacturing and nonmanufacturing sectors across 18 advanced economies spanning more than two

[3]Indeed, recent trade liberalization efforts have increasingly centered on reducing nontariff barriers, particularly in services sectors, from expediting customs procedures to intellectual-property provisions. Ongoing efforts to enhance data availability on nontariff barrier measures will gradually help complement existing studies of the impact of tariff liberalization (for example, Bacchetta and Beverelli 2012; Staiger 2015).

Box 3.3 *(continued)*

decades. For each country and year observation, the effective "output tariff" in each sector j is computed as a weighted average of most-favored-nation (MFN) preferential tariff and non-MFN rates, in which weights reflect the relative importance of the individual products and trade partners to which each type of rate applies.[4] For each country and year, the effective "input tariff" in each sector j is then computed as a weighted average of output tariff rates in all sectors, with weights reflecting the share of imported inputs from each of these sectors used in the production of sector j's output. Specifically,

$$\tau_j^{input} = \sum_k \omega_{jk}\tau_k^{output},$$

in which the share ω_{jk} of inputs from sector k in total inputs used in sector j is calculated using input-output matrices for each individual country, taking into account all input linkages—that is, factoring in that tariff changes affect not only imported inputs, but also domestic ones, insofar as these in turn can be produced using other imported inputs (for details, see Ahn and others 2016).

To quantify the respective effects of output and input tariffs on productivity at the country-sector level, the following empirical specification is then estimated:

$$\ln TFP_{ist} = \alpha_{is} + \gamma_{it} + \beta_1\tau_{is,t-1}^{output} + \beta_2\tau_{is,t-1}^{input} + \varepsilon_{ist},$$

in which $\ln TFP_{ist}$ denotes log total factor productivity (TFP) in country i and sector s in year t, while $\tau_{is,t-l}^{output}$ and $\tau_{is,t-l}^{input}$ are the corresponding country-sector-level output and input tariff rates lagged by l years. The analysis tests for different lag structures (l = 1 to 5). The specification also includes country-sector (α_{is}) as well as country-year (γ_{it}) fixed effects. This baseline specification is then extended to include interactions between tariffs and barriers to FDI.

This empirical analysis yields the following main findings:[5]
- There is a statistically significant and robust impact of input tariff liberalization on sector-level TFP,

which is much stronger than the effect of output tariff liberalization. In other words, the input variety and quality channels that underpin the input tariff effect appear to matter more for TFP than the procompetition impact of lower output tariffs: a 1 percentage point reduction in the input tariff raises productivity by about 2 percent, whereas the output tariff effect is not statistically significant.
- The productivity gains from liberalization appear to materialize rather quickly within one to five years, with the estimated impact dissipating over time—in line with the findings of the chapter regarding product market deregulation in nontradables industries.
- Although tariff barriers in advanced economies have been reduced substantially over the past decades, there is still much scope for further reductions, and therefore for further productivity gains, in some sectors in some countries.
- A back-of-the-envelope calculation of the potential productivity gains from full elimination of remaining tariffs suggests that aggregate productivity could rise by about 1 percent on average across advanced economies, varying from a 0.2 percent gain in Japan to a 7.7 percent gain in Ireland, depending on current sector-level tariff rates as well as each sector's importance in a particular country (Figure 3.3.1, panel 2). For instance, potential gains for Ireland and Korea are estimated to be larger than those for other advanced economies because Korea has higher remaining tariffs on average than other advanced economies in the sample—partly reflecting that its trade partners differ from those of the European Union countries that dominate the sample, while strong reliance on imported inputs, especially in specific sectors—the chemical and pharmaceutical industries—is estimated to dominate the potential gains for Ireland.
- The effects of both input and output tariff liberalization are greater when barriers to FDI are lower, highlighting the importance of complementarities between trade and FDI liberalization.

These findings provide a clear case for further liberalization efforts to raise productivity and output in advanced economies—all the more so as the estimates vastly understate the potential gains since they ignore the (presumably much larger) benefits to be reaped from easing nontariff trade barriers, as well as gains from reallocation of resources across sectors. Given their comparatively higher barriers to trade, emerging market economies and low-income countries would benefit even more.

[4]On this front, the analysis significantly improves on existing studies that typically consider MFN rates only, which have become increasingly misleading as preferential bilateral or regional agreements have gained prominence around the world.

[5]The main findings are robust to alternative lags of the output and input tariff variables as well as to alternative clustering strategies—at the country-sector or country-year level—for standard errors. Considering the effective rate of protection à la Corden (1966)—which essentially takes into account potential anticompetitive forces from cheaper imported inputs—instead of the output tariff rate yields virtually identical results.

Box 3.4. Can Reform Waves Turn the Tide? Some Case Studies Using the Synthetic Control Method

A number of advanced economies carried out a sequence of extensive reforms of their labor and product markets in the 1990s. Using the Synthetic Control Method, this box studies four cases of well-known waves of reforms—those of Australia, the Netherlands, and New Zealand in the early 1990s, and Germany in the early 2000s.[1] The results suggest that output in three of the cases was higher as a result of the reforms than it was in the control group; the exception was the case of New Zealand, which may partly reflect the fact that reforms were implemented under particularly weak macroeconomic conditions.

The Synthetic Control Method

A vexing problem in assessing the impact of structural reforms is defining the counterfactual, namely, how output would have evolved in the absence of reforms. The Synthetic Control Method is a data-driven way of finding the counterfactual when carrying out a case study. It identifies a control group—in practice, a weighted average of a set of "similar" countries—whose prereform macroeconomic outcomes were similar to those of the reformer country.[2] The performance of the reformer country is then compared with that of the control group in the postreform period. To assess whether the control group is indeed a good counterfactual, a measure of fit developed by Adhikari and Alm (2015) is used in this analysis. The Synthetic Control Method is thus an alternative to a difference-in-difference method, as the difference in outcomes before and after reforms for the reformer country is being compared to the difference in outcomes before and after the reforms for the control group.

Like any method, the Synthetic Control Method has its pros and cons. One advantage is that it avoids

The authors of this box are Prakash Loungani and Bingjie Hu. A companion working paper (Adhikari and others, forthcoming) contains technical details and an extended discussion of the reform episodes.

[1]The Synthetic Control Method was developed by Abadie and Gardeazabal (2003) and has been applied, for instance, to study the effect on growth of trade liberalization (Billmeier and Nannicini 2013) and natural disasters (Cavallo and others 2013). For recent IMF analysis of case studies of major reform events, see IMF 2015.

[2]The macroeconomic outcomes considered here are some of the conventional determinants of GDP per capita used by Billmeier and Nannicini (2013), namely, physical and human capital per capita, trade openness, population growth, and a democracy dummy variable.

subjective biases involved in picking a control group through a statistical procedure for creating a synthetic control group. The method can also reduce any omitted-variables bias. The intuitive explanation is that only countries that are alike in both observed and unobserved predictors of output should produce similar trajectories of the outcome variable over extended periods of time. The method obtains the impact estimates one (country) case at a time, which allows an exploration of the cross-country heterogeneity in the effects of reform in a very flexible way. Among the limitations, the method does not fully address potential reverse causality; if structural reforms are motivated, say, by an expectation of weaker future growth prospects, this would bias the estimates obtained from the method, as long as growth expectations are not captured by the unobservable heterogeneity included in the estimation. Furthermore, the method will tend to ascribe to the treatment—here, a reform episode—the impact of any *idiosyncratic* shock (for instance, a natural disaster or a domestic banking crisis) that may occur around the treatment date—a source of omitted-variables bias that the method cannot address.

The Reform Waves

The cases of big labor and product market reform episodes are well known and have been extensively discussed in policy and academic circles. Nevertheless, to avoid any selection bias in picking cases, the analysis uses the reforms data set assembled for this chapter to cross-check that the selected episodes were indeed associated with major reform initiatives across a broad array of areas. Among the identified episodes, some then had to be discarded because a suitable synthetic control unit could not be found (for example, New Zealand in the early 1980s). The four reform packages this box focuses on are described briefly; while the reforms spanned many years, the initial year is chosen as the treatment date in applying the method:

- *New Zealand (1991)*—In 1991, the Employment Contract Act replaced the country's long-standing centralized bargaining system with decentralized enterprise bargaining. This permitted firms and workers either to negotiate an individual employment contract with one another or to be bound by a collective contract at the firm level. Product market reforms included a massive reduction in direct government assistance to industries as well as an avoidance of policies to boost specific industries.

Box 3.4 *(continued)*

- *Australia (1994)*—Legislation adopted in 1993, which took effect in 1994, strengthened decentralized wage bargaining by increasing the scope for employers to negotiate agreements directly with employees. Product market reforms consisted of privatizing major industries and reducing regulatory protection of incumbent firms. This increased competition in a wide range of industries, such as infrastructure industries, agriculture, network industries (air, rail, and road transportation; electricity and gas distribution; telecommunications and postal services), and professional services. The mid-1990s wave of reforms followed an earlier wave in the second half of the 1980s.

- *Netherlands (1994)*—Starting in 1994, labor reform aimed to make wage agreements more flexible and more conducive to job creation. For instance, an agreement was reached to reduce the gap between the legal minimum wage and minimum wages set in collective labor agreements, and "opening clauses" allowed firms to negotiate with their workers to pay below the minimum set in collective contracts. Various measures were taken to increase competition in a wide range of industries, new legislation resulted in a major liberalization of shopping hours, and the labor tax wedge was significantly reduced.

- *Germany (2003)*—The so-called Hartz reforms created new types of temporary employment contracts, introduced additional wage subsidies, significantly cut unemployment benefits for the long-term unemployed, restructured the public employment agency, and strengthened activation policies more broadly.

Output Effects of Reforms

To analyze the impact of reforms, the path of output in the reformer country before and after reform is compared and how it differs from that of the control group examined (Figure 3.4.1). With the exception of the New Zealand case, structural reforms appear to have had positive output effects. The results also show the advantage of having a counterfactual in assessing the success of reforms: for instance, while growth in New Zealand started to increase substantially a few years after the reforms, this improvement was not noticeably larger than in the ("nonreforming") control group, and a recession had struck in the meantime.

Figure 3.4.1. Log of Real GDP per Capita in Purchasing-Power-Parity Terms
(2005 international dollars)

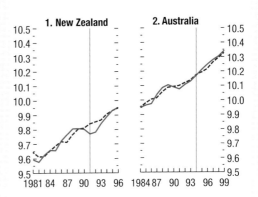

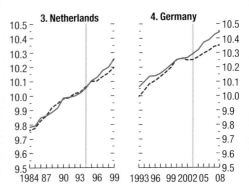

Source: IMF staff calculations.
Note: The two countries with the largest weights in the synthetic control groups are the United States and Greece (for New Zealand and Australia); Belgium and the United States (for the Netherlands); and Italy and Sweden (for Germany). The number and estimated weights of other countries in the synthetic control groups vary across the four case studies. Vertical lines indicate the starting year of the reform episode.

As this chapter shows, the success of some structural reforms depends in part on prevailing macroeconomic conditions at the time the reforms are introduced. In the case of New Zealand, the reforms were carried out at the same time that the government was also trying to tame chronic budget deficits and inflation. Hence, of the four cases considered here, New Zealand's reforms were arguably the ones introduced with the least amount of support from macroeconomic

Box 3.4 *(continued)*

policies.[3] The recession that ensued has been attributed by observers to the macroeconomic stance rather than to short-term adverse effects of the structural reforms themselves (Reddell and Sleeman 2008).

In the other three cases, when compared with that in the synthetic country, per capita output after five years was about 5 percent higher on average in the reformer country, though the range is fairly wide, being weaker for Australia than for Germany and the Netherlands. Earlier studies generally corroborate the view that reforms had positive output effects in these countries. There is general acceptance that reforms

[3]While the Dutch case also has some similarities with respect to the macroeconomic stance, the more effective social dialogue in the country, which led to a shared agreement on wage moderation combined with expanded employment and investment by firms, may have played a role in preventing adverse output effects (see Blanchard 2000).

made a major contribution to the growth surge of the 1990s in Australia (for instance, Parham 2004 and the studies cited therein), although some have provided a more skeptical view (Quiggin 2004). The Netherlands' experience has typically been described as a "miracle" for its positive employment and output effects—see Watson and others 1999 for an early view along these lines, which has been corroborated in later work. The source of the "miracle" has sometimes been traced back as far as the 1982 Wassenaar Arrangement among social partners (for example, Blanchard 2000). Krebs and Scheffel (2013) show an increase in output following the Hartz reforms in Germany, though the magnitude of the effect is considerably larger here than in their calibrated model. Some have suggested that decentralization of wage bargaining may also have played a role (Dustmann and others 2014).

References

Abadie, Alberto, and Javier Gardeazabal. 2003. "The Economic Costs of Conflict: A Case Study of the Basque Country." *American Economic Review* 93 (1): 113–32.

Abiad, Abdul, Davide Furceri, and Petia Topalova. 2015. "The Macroeconomic Effects of Public Investment: Evidence from Advanced Economies." IMF Working Paper 15/95, International Monetary Fund, Washington.

Adhikari, Bibek, and James Alm. 2015. "Evaluating the Economic Effects of Flat Tax Reforms Using Synthetic Control Methods." Tulane University Working Paper, Tulane University, New Orleans, Louisiana.

Adhikari, Bibek, Romain Duval, Bingjie Hu, and Prakash Loungani. Forthcoming. "Can Reform Waves Turn the Tide? Synthetic Control Method." IMF Working Paper, International Monetary Fund, Washington.

Aghion, Philippe, Nick Bloom, Richard Blundell, Rachel Griffith, and Peter Howitt. 2005. "Competition and Innovation: An Inverted-U Relationship." *Quarterly Journal of Economics* 120 (2): 701–28.

Aghion Philippe, Christopher Harris, Peter Howitt, and John Vickers. 2001. "Competition, Imitation and Growth with Step-by-Step Innovation." *Review of Economic Studies* 68 (3): 467–92.

Aghion, Philippe, and Peter Howitt. 1992. "A Model of Growth through Creative Destruction." *Econometrica* 60 (2): 323–51.

Aghion, Philippe, and Mark Schankerman. 2004. "On The Welfare Effects and Political Economy of Competition-Enhancing Policies." *Economic Journal* 114: 800–24.

Ahn, JaeBin, Era Dabla-Norris, Romain Duval, Bingjie Hu, and Lamin Njie. 2016. "Reassessing the Productivity Gains from Trade Liberalization: A Sector-Level Approach." IMF Working Paper 16/77, International Monetary Fund, Washington.

Aiyar, Shekhar, Wolfgang Bergthaler, Jose M. Garrido, Anna Ilyina, Andreas Jobst, Kenneth Kang, Dmitry Kovtun, Yan Liu, Dermot Monaghan, and Marina Moretti. 2015. "A Strategy for Resolving Europe's Problem Loans." IMF Staff Discussion Note 15/19, International Monetary Fund, Washington.

Alesina, Alberto, Silvia Ardagna, and Francesco Trebbi. 2006. "Who Adjusts and When? On The Political Economy of Reforms." NBER Working Paper 12049, National Bureau of Economic Research, Cambridge, Massachusetts.

Amiti, Mary, and Jozef Konings. 2007. "Trade Liberalization, Intermediate Inputs, and Productivity: Evidence from Indonesia." *American Economic Review* 97 (5): 1611–38.

Auerbach, Alan, and Youri Gorodnichenko. 2012. "Measuring the Output Responses to Fiscal Policy." *American Economic Journal: Economic Policy* 4 (2): 1–27.

———. 2013. "Measuring the Output Responses to Fiscal Policy." *American Economic Journal: Economic Policy* 4 (2): 1–27.

Bacchetta, Marc, and Cosimo Beverelli. 2012. "Non-Tariff Measures and the WTO." *VOXEU*, July 13.

Bassanini, Andrea. 2015. "A Bitter Medicine? Short-Term Employment Impact of Deregulation in Network Industries." IZA Discussion Paper 9187, Institute for the Study of Labor (IZA), Bonn, Germany.

———, and Romain Duval. 2006. "Employment Patterns in OECD Countries: Reassessing the Role of Policies and Institutions." OECD Economics Department Working Paper 486, Organisation for Economic Co-operation and Development, Paris.

Bassanini, Andrea, Luca Nunziata, and Danielle Venn. 2009. "Job Protection Legislation and Productivity Growth in OECD Countries." *Economic Policy* 24 (58): 349–402.

Ben Zeev, Nadav, and Evi Pappa. 2014. "Chronicle of a War Foretold: The Macroeconomic Effects of Anticipated Defense Spending Shocks." CEPR Discussion Paper 9948, Centre for Economic Policy Research, London.

Billmeier, Andreas, and Tommaso Nannicini. 2013. "Assessing Economic Liberalization Episodes: A Synthetic Control Approach." *Review of Economics and Statistics* 95 (3): 983–1001.

Blanchard, Olivier. 2000. "The Dutch Jobs Miracle." *Project Syndicate*, July 6.

———, and Francesco Giavazzi. 2003. "Macroeconomic Effects of Regulation and Deregulation in Goods and Labour Markets." *Quarterly Journal of Economics* 118 (3): 879–907.

Blanchard, Olivier, Florence Jaumotte, and Prakash Loungani. 2014. "Labor Market Policies and IMF Advice in Advanced Economies during the Great Recession." *IZA Journal of Labor Policy* 3 (1): 1–23.

Blanchard, Olivier, and Augustin Landier. 2002. "The Perverse Effects of Partial Labor Market Reform: Fixed-Term Contrast in France." *Economic Journal* 112 (480): 214–44.

Blanchard, Olivier, and Daniel Leigh. 2013. "Growth Forecast Errors and Fiscal Multipliers." *American Economic Review: Papers and Proceedings* 103 (3): 117–20.

Boeri, Tito, and Juan Jimeno. 2015. "The Unbearable Divergence of Unemployment in Europe." CEP Discussion Paper 1384, Centre for Economic Performance, London.

Bordon, Anna Rose, Christian Ebeke, and Kazuko Shirono. 2016. "When Do Structural Reforms Work? On the Role of the Business Cycle and Macroeconomic Policies." IMF Working Paper 16/62, International Monetary Fund, Washington.

Bortolotti, Bernardo, and Paolo Pinotti. 2008. "Delayed Privatization." *Public Choice* 136: 331–51.

Bouis, Romain, Orsetta Causa, Lilas Demmou, Romain Duval, and Aleksandra Zdzienicka. 2012. "The Short-Term Effects of Structural Reforms: An Empirical Analysis." OECD Economics Department Working Paper 950, Organisation for Economic Co-operation and Development, Paris.

Bouis, Romain, and Romain Duval. 2011. "Raising Potential Growth after the Crisis: A Quantitative Assessment of the Potential Gains from Various Structural Reforms in the OECD Area and Beyond." OECD Economics Department Working Paper 835, Organisation for Economic Co-operation and Development, Paris.

————, and Johannes Eugster. Forthcoming. "Product Market Deregulation and Growth: New Industry-Level Evidence." IMF Working Paper, International Monetary Fund, Washington.

Bourlès, Renaud, Gilbert Cette, Jimmy Lopez, Jacques Mairesse, and Giuseppe Nicoletti. 2013. "Do Product Market Regulations in Upstream Sectors Curb Productivity Growth? Panel Data Evidence for OECD Countries." *Review of Economics and Statistics* 95 (5): 1750–68.

Cacciatore, Matteo, Romain Duval, Giuseppe Fiori, and Fabio Ghironi. 2015. "Short-Term Pain for Long-Term Gain: Market Deregulation and Monetary Policy in Small Open Economies." *Journal of International Money and Finance* 57 (October): 86–114.

————. Forthcoming-a. "Market Reforms in the Time of Imbalance." *Journal of Economic Dynamics and Control.*

————. Forthcoming-b. "Product and Labor Market Reforms at the Zero Lower Bound." IMF Working Paper, International Monetary Fund, Washington.

Cacciatore, Matteo, and Giuseppe Fiori. 2016. "The Macroeconomic Effects of Goods and Labor Market Deregulation." *Review of Economic Dynamics* 20 (1): 1–24.

————, and Fabio Ghironi. Forthcoming. "Market Deregulation and Optimal Monetary Policy in a Monetary Union." *Journal of International Economics.*

Calmfors, Lars, and John Driffill. 1988. "Bargaining Structure, Corporatism, and Macroeconomic Performance." *Economic Policy* 3 (6): 13–62.

Cavallo, Eduardo, Sebastian Galiani, Ilan Noy, and Juan Pantano. 2013. "Catastrophic Natural Disasters and Economic Growth." *Review of Economics and Statistics* 95 (5): 1549–61.

Cette, Gilbert, Jimmy Lopez, and Jacques Mairesse. Forthcoming. "Market Regulations, Prices and Productivity." *American Economic Review: Papers and Proceedings* 106 (5): 1–6.

Chetty, Raj. 2008. "Moral Hazard versus Liquidity and Optimal Unemployment Insurance." *Journal of Political Economy* 116 (2): 173–234.

Christiansen, Lone, Huidan Lin, Joana Pereira, Petia Topalova, and Rima Turk. Forthcoming. "Unlocking Female Employment Potential in Europe: Drivers and Benefits." IMF Staff Discussion Note, International Monetary Fund, Washington.

Coenen, Günter, Christopher J. Erceg, Charles Freedman, Davide Furceri, Michael Kumhof, René Lalonde, Douglas Laxton, and others. 2012. "Effects of Fiscal Stimulus in Structural Models." *American Economic Journal: Macroeconomics* 4 (1): 22–68.

Corden, Max. 1966. "The Structure of a Tariff System and the Effective Protective Rate." *Journal of Political Economy* 74 (3): 221–37.

Corsetti, Giancarlo, Andre Meier, and Gernot J. Müller. 2012. "What Determines Government Spending Multipliers?" IMF Working Paper 12/150, International Monetary Fund, Washington.

Dabla-Norris, Era, Si Guo, Vikram Haksar, Minsuk Kim, Kalpana Kochhar, Kevin Wiseman, and Aleksandra Zdzienicka. 2015. "The New Normal: A Sector-Level Perspective on Productivity Trends in Advanced Economies." IMF Staff Discussion Note 15/03, International Monetary Fund, Washington.

den Haan, Wouter, Garey Ramey, and Joel Watson. 2000. "Job Destruction and Propagation of Shocks." *American Economic Review* 90 (3): 482–98.

Devries, Pete, Daniel Leigh, Jaime Guajardo, and Andrea Pescatori. 2011. "A New Action-Based Dataset of Fiscal Consolidation." IMF Working Paper 11/128, International Monetary Fund, Washington.

Doppelhofer, Gernot, Ronald I. Miller, and Xavier Sala-i-Martin. 2000. "Determinants of Long-Term Growth: A Bayesian Averaging of Classical Estimates (BACE) Approach." NBER Working Paper 7750, National Bureau of Economic Research, Cambridge, Massachusetts.

Draghi, Mario. 2015. "Monetary Policy and Structural Reforms in the Euro Area." Presented at Prometeia40, Bologna, Italy, December 14.

Dustmann, Christian, Bernd Fitzenberger, Uta Schönberg, and Alexandra Spitz-Oener. 2014. "From Sick Man of Europe to Superstar: Germany's Resurgent Economy." *Journal of Economic Perspectives* 28 (1): 167–88.

Duval, Romain. 2003. "Retirement Behaviour in OECD Countries: Impact of Old-Age Pension Schemes and Other Social Transfer Programmes." *OECD Economic Studies* 2003 (2): 7–50.

————, Davide Furceri, Joao Jalles, and Huy Nguyen. Forthcoming. "A New Narrative Database of Product and Labor Market Reforms in Advanced Economies." IMF Working Paper, International Monetary Fund, Washington.

Duval, Romain, Davide Furceri, and Jakob Miethe. Forthcoming. "Breaking the Deadlock: Identifying the Political Economy Drivers of Structural Reforms." IMF Working Paper, International Monetary Fund, Washington.

Eggertsson, Gauti, Andrea Ferrero, and Andrea Raffo. 2014. "Can Structural Reforms Help Europe?" *Journal of Monetary Economics* 61 (C): 2–22.

Eggertsson, Gauti, and Michael Woodford. 2003. "The Zero Bound on Interest Rates and Optimal Monetary Policy." *Brookings Papers on Economic Activity* 34 (1): 139–235.

Fiori, Giuseppe, Giuseppe Nicoletti, Stefano Scarpetta, and Fabio Schiantarelli. 2012. "Employment Effects of Product and Labour Market Reforms: Are There Synergies?" *Economic Journal, Royal Economic Society* 122 (558): 79–104.

Forni, Mario, and Luca Gambetti. 2010. "Fiscal Foresight and the Effects of Government Spending." CEPR Discussion Paper 7840, Centre for Economic Policy Research, London.

Gal, Peter, and Alexander Hijzen. Forthcoming. "The Short-Term Effects of Product Market Reforms: A Cross-Country Firm-Level Analysis." IMF Working Paper, International Monetary Fund, Washington.

Galasso, Vincenzo. 2014. "The Role of Political Partisanship during Economic Crises." *Public Choice* 158: 143–65.

Granger, Clive W. J., and Timo Teräsvirta. 1993. *Modelling Nonlinear Economic Relationships*. New York: Oxford University Press.

Grossman, Gene, and Elhanan Helpman. 1991. "Quality Ladders in the Theory of Growth." *Review of Economic Studies* 58 (1): 43–61.

Halpern, László, Miklós Koren, and Adam Szeidl. 2015. "Imported Inputs and Productivity." *American Economic Review* 105 (12): 3660–703.

Helpman, Elhanan, and Paul Krugman. 1985. *Market Structure and Foreign Trade*. Cambridge, Massachusetts: MIT Press.

International Monetary Fund (IMF). 2015. "Structural Reforms and Macroeconomic Performance: Initial Considerations for the Fund." IMF Staff Report, Washington.

Jaumotte, Florence. 2003. "Labour Force Participation of Women: Empirical Evidence on the Role of Policy and Other Determinants in OECD Countries." OECD Economic Studies 2003 (2): 51–108.

Jordà, Òscar. 2005. "Estimation and Inference of Impulse Responses by Local Projections." *American Economic Review* 95 (1): 161–82.

———, and Alan Taylor. 2013. "The Time for Austerity: Estimating the Average Treatment Effect of Fiscal Policy." NBER Working Paper, National Bureau of Economic Research, Cambridge, Massachusetts.

Kasahara, Hiroyuki, and Joel Rodrigue. 2008. "Does the Use of Imported Intermediates Increase Productivity? Plant-Level Evidence." *Journal of Development Economics* 87 (1): 106–18.

Kollmann, Robert, Marco Ratto, Werner Roeger, Jan in't Veld, and Lukas Vogel. 2015. "What Drives the German Current Account? And How Does It Affect Other EU Member States?" *Economic Policy* 30 (81): 47–93.

Koske, Isabell, Isabelle Wanner, Rosamaria Bitetti, and Omar Barbiero. 2015. "The 2013 Update of the OECD's Database on Product Market Regulation: Policy Insights for OECD and non-OECD Countries." OECD Economics Department Working Paper 1200, Organisation for Economic Co-operation and Development, Paris.

Krebs, Tom, and Martin Scheffel, 2013. "Macroeconomic Evaluation of Labor Market Reform in Germany." *IMF Economic Review* 61 (4): 664–701.

Krugman, Paul. 2014. "Structural Deformity." *New York Times*, November 20.

Landais, Camille, Pascal Michaillat, and Emmanuel Saez. 2015. "A Theory of Optimal Unemployment Benefit Insurance over the Business Cycle." NBER Working Paper 16526, National Bureau of Economic Research, Cambridge, Massachusetts.

Leeper, Eric M., Alexander W. Richter, and Todd B. Walker. 2012. "Quantitative Effects of Fiscal Foresight." *American Economic Journal: Economic Policy* 4 (2): 115–44.

Leeper, Eric M., Todd B. Walker, and Shu-Chun S. Yang. 2013. "Fiscal Foresight and Information Flows." *Econometrica* 81 (3): 1115–45.

Martins, Pedro S. 2014. "30,000 Minimum Wages: The Economic Effects of Collective Bargaining Extensions." IZA Discussion Paper 8540, Institute for the Study of Labor (IZA), Bonn, Germany.

Melitz, Marc. 2003. "The Impact of Trade on Intra-Industry Reallocations and Aggregate Industry Productivity." *Econometrica* 71 (6): 1696–725.

Mian, Atif R., and Amir Sufi. 2010. "Household Leverage and the Recession of 2007 to 2009." NBER Working Paper 15896, National Bureau of Economic Research, Cambridge, Massachusetts.

Mitman, Kurt, and Stanislav Rabinovich. 2015. "Optimal Unemployment Insurance in an Equilibrium Business-Cycle Model." *Journal of Monetary Economics* 71 (C): 99–118.

Mortensen, Dale, and Christopher Pissarides. 1994. "Job Creation and Job Destruction in the Theory of Unemployment." *Review of Economic Studies* 61: 397–415.

Murtin, Fabrice, and Jean-Marc Robin. 2014. "Labor Market Reforms and Unemployment Dynamics." CeMMAP Working Paper CWP13/14, Centre for Microdata Methods and Practice, Institute for Fiscal Studies, London.

Nickell, Stephen, and Richard Layard. 1999. "Labor Market Institutions and Economic Performance." In *Handbook of Labor Economics*, edited by Orley Ashenfelter and David Card, 3029–084. Philadelphia: Elsevier.

Organisation for Economic Co-operation and Development (OECD). 2006. "Boosting Jobs and Incomes: The OECD Jobs Strategy," Paris.

———. 2015. "Economic Policy Reforms: Going for Growth," Paris.

Parham, Dean. 2004. "Australia's 1990s Productivity Surge and Its Determinants." In *Growth and Productivity in East Asia*, edited by Takatoshi Ito and Andrew Rose. Chicago: University of Chicago Press.

Pavcnik, Nina. 2002. "Trade Liberalization, Exit, and Productivity Improvements: Evidence from Chilean Plants." *Review of Economic Studies* 69 (1): 245–76.

Perotti, Roberto. 1999. "Fiscal Policy in Good Times and Bad." *Quarterly Journal of Economics* 114 (4): 1399–436.

Pissarides, Christopher. 2000. *Equilibrium Unemployment Theory*. Cambridge, Massachusetts: MIT Press.

Porcellacchia, Davide. 2016. "Wage-Price Dynamics and Structural Reforms in Japan." IMF Working Paper 16/20, International Monetary Fund, Washington.

Quiggin, John. 2004. "Looking Back on Microeconomic Reform: A Skeptical Viewpoint." Australian Public Policy Program Working Paper 1/P03, University of Queensland, Brisbane, Australia.

Rajan, Raghuram G., and Luigi Zingales. 1998. "Financial Dependence and Growth." *American Economic Review* 88 (3): 559–86.

Ravn, Morten O., and Vincent Sterk. 2013. "Job Uncertainty and Deep Recessions." Meeting Paper 921, Society for Economic Dynamics, Stonybrook, New York.

Reddell, Michael, and Cath Sleeman. 2008. "Some Perspectives on Past Recessions." *Reserve Bank of New Zealand: Bulletin* 71 (2): 5–21.

Rodrik, Dani. 2015. "The Mirage of Structural Reform." *Project Syndicate*, October 8.

Romer, Christina D., and David H. Romer. 1989. "Does Monetary Policy Matter? A New Test in the Spirit of Friedman and Schwartz." In *NBER Macroeconomics Annual 1989*, edited by Olivier J. Blanchard and Stanley Fischer, 121–70. Cambridge, Massachusetts: MIT Press.

———. 2004. "A New Measure of Monetary Shocks: Derivation and Implications." *American Economic Review* 94 (4): 1055–84.

———. 2010. "The Macroeconomic Effects of Tax Changes: Estimates Based on a New Measure of Fiscal Shocks." *American Economic Review* 100 (3): 763–801.

———. 2015. "New Evidence on the Impact of Financial Crises in Advanced Countries." NBER Working Paper 21021, National Bureau of Economic Research, Cambridge, Massachusetts.

Saint-Paul, Gilles. 2000. *The Political Economy of Labor Market Institutions.* New York: Oxford University Press.

Sala-i-Martin, Xavier. 1997. "I Just Ran Two Million Regressions." *American Economic Review* 87 (2): 178–83.

Sapir, Andre. 2006. "Globalization and the Reform of European Social Models." *Journal of Common Market Studies* 44 (2): 369–90.

Staiger, Robert. 2015. "Non-Tariff Measures and the WTO." Unpublished Working Paper. Dartmouth College, Hanover, New Hampshire.

Stock, James H., and Mark W. Watson. 2007. "Why Has U.S. Inflation Become Harder to Forecast?" *Journal of Money, Credit and Banking* 39 (S1): 3–33.

Stock, James H., and David Wise. 1990. "Pensions, the Option Value of Work, and Retirement." *Econometrica* 58 (5): 1151–180.

Timmer, Marcel P., Erik Dietzenbacher, Bart Los, Robert Stehrer, and Gaaitzen J. de Vries. 2015. "An Illustrated User Guide to the World Input-Output Database: The Case of Global Automotive Production." *Review of International Economics* 23 (3): 575–605.

Topalova, Petia, and Amit Khandelwal. 2011. "Trade Liberalization and Firm Productivity: The Case of India." *Review of Economics and Statistics* 93 (3): 995–1009.

Watson, Maxwell C., Bas Bakker, Jan Kees Martijn, and Ioannis Halikias. 1999. "The Netherlands: Transforming a Market Economy." IMF Occasional Paper 181, International Monetary Fund, Washington.

Whang, Eunah. 2015. "The Effects of Hartz IV Reform on Precautionary Savings." Netspar Discussion Paper 07/2015-015, Tilburg, Netherlands.

Wiese, Rasmus, 2014. "What Triggers Reforms in OECD Countries? Improved Reform Measurement and Evidence from the Healthcare Sector." *European Journal of Political Economy* 34: 332–52.

STATISTICAL APPENDIX

The Statistical Appendix presents historical data as well as projections. It comprises seven sections: Assumptions, What's New, Data and Conventions, Country Notes, Classification of Countries, Key Data Documentation, and Statistical Tables.

The assumptions underlying the estimates and projections for 2016–17 and the medium-term scenario for 2018–21 are summarized in the first section. The second section presents a brief description of the changes to the database and statistical tables since the October 2015 *World Economic Outlook* (WEO). The third section provides a general description of the data and the conventions used for calculating country group composites. The fourth section summarizes selected key information for each country. The classification of countries in the various groups presented in the WEO is summarized in the fifth section. The sixth section provides information on methods and reporting standards for the member countries' national account and government finance indicators included in the report.

The last, and main, section comprises the statistical tables. (Statistical Appendix A is included here; Statistical Appendix B is available online.) Data in these tables have been compiled on the basis of information available through March 25, 2016. The figures for 2016 and beyond are shown with the same degree of precision as the historical figures solely for convenience; because they are projections, the same degree of accuracy is not to be inferred.

Assumptions

Real effective *exchange rates* for the advanced economies are assumed to remain constant at their average levels measured during the period February 2 to March 1, 2016. For 2016 and 2017, these assumptions imply average U.S. dollar/special drawing right (SDR) conversion rates of 1.395 and 1.400, U.S. dollar/euro conversion rates of 1.111 and 1.119, and yen/U.S. dollar conversion rates of 114.8 and 113.3, respectively.

It is assumed that the *price of oil* will average $34.75 a barrel in 2016 and $40.99 a barrel in 2017.

Established *policies* of national authorities are assumed to be maintained. The more specific policy

assumptions underlying the projections for selected economies are described in Box A1.

With regard to *interest rates*, it is assumed that the London interbank offered rate (LIBOR) on six-month U.S. dollar deposits will average 0.9 percent in 2016 and 1.5 percent in 2017, that three-month euro deposits will average –0.3 percent in 2016 and –0.4 percent in 2017, and that six-month yen deposits will average –0.1 percent in 2016 and –0.3 percent in 2017.

As a reminder, with respect to *introduction of the euro*, on December 31, 1998, the Council of the European Union decided that, effective January 1, 1999, the irrevocably fixed conversion rates between the euro and currencies of the member countries adopting the euro are as follows:

1 euro	=	13.7603	Austrian schillings
	=	40.3399	Belgian francs
	=	0.585274	Cyprus pound[1]
	=	1.95583	Deutsche marks
	=	15.6466	Estonian krooni[2]
	=	5.94573	Finnish markkaa
	=	6.55957	French francs
	=	340.750	Greek drachmas[3]
	=	0.787564	Irish pound
	=	1,936.27	Italian lire
	=	0.702804	Latvian lat[4]
	=	3.45280	Lithuanian litas[5]
	=	40.3399	Luxembourg francs
	=	0.42930	Maltese lira[1]
	=	2.20371	Netherlands guilders
	=	200.482	Portuguese escudos
	=	30.1260	Slovak koruna[6]
	=	239.640	Slovenian tolars[7]
	=	166.386	Spanish pesetas

[1]Established on January 1, 2008.
[2]Established on January 1, 2011.
[3]Established on January 1, 2001.
[4]Established on January 1, 2014.
[5]Established on January 1, 2015.
[6]Established on January 1, 2009.
[7]Established on January 1, 2007.

See Box 5.4 of the October 1998 WEO for details on how the conversion rates were established.

What's New

- Data for Macao Special Administrative Region and the Commonwealth of Puerto Rico are included in data aggregated for the advanced economies. Macao is a Special Administrative Region of China, and Puerto Rico is a territory of the United States, but the WEO maintains statistical data for both economies on a separate and independent basis.
- Argentina's and Venezuela's consumer prices are excluded from all the WEO groups' aggregates.

Data and Conventions

Data and projections for 191 economies form the statistical basis of the WEO database. The data are maintained jointly by the IMF's Research Department and regional departments, with the latter regularly updating country projections based on consistent global assumptions.

Although national statistical agencies are the ultimate providers of historical data and definitions, international organizations are also involved in statistical issues, with the objective of harmonizing methodologies for the compilation of national statistics, including analytical frameworks, concepts, definitions, classifications, and valuation procedures used in the production of economic statistics. The WEO database reflects information from both national source agencies and international organizations.

Most countries' macroeconomic data presented in the WEO conform broadly to the 1993 version of the *System of National Accounts* (SNA). The IMF's sector statistical standards—the sixth edition of the *Balance of Payments and International Investment Position Manual* (BPM6), the *Monetary and Financial Statistics Manual* (MFSM 2000), and the *Government Finance Statistics Manual 2001* (GFSM 2001)—have been or are being aligned with the SNA 2008.[1] These standards reflect the IMF's special interest in countries' external positions, financial sector stability, and public sector fiscal positions. The process of adapting country data to the new standards begins in earnest when the manuals are released. However, full concordance with the manuals is ultimately dependent on the provision by national

statistical compilers of revised country data; hence, the WEO estimates are only partially adapted to these manuals. Nonetheless, for many countries the impact, on major balances and aggregates, of conversion to the updated standards will be small. Many other countries have partially adopted the latest standards and will continue implementation over a period of years.

Composite data for country groups in the WEO are either sums or weighted averages of data for individual countries. Unless noted otherwise, multiyear averages of growth rates are expressed as compound annual rates of change.[2] Arithmetically weighted averages are used for all data for the emerging market and developing economies group except data on inflation and money growth, for which geometric averages are used. The following conventions apply:

- Country group composites for exchange rates, interest rates, and growth rates of monetary aggregates are weighted by GDP converted to U.S. dollars at market exchange rates (averaged over the preceding three years) as a share of group GDP.
- Composites for other data relating to the domestic economy, whether growth rates or ratios, are weighted by GDP valued at purchasing power parity as a share of total world or group GDP.[3]
- Unless noted otherwise, composites for all sectors for the euro area are corrected for reporting discrepancies in intra-area transactions. Annual data are not adjusted for calendar-day effects. For data prior to 1999, data aggregations apply 1995 European currency unit exchange rates.
- Composites for fiscal data are sums of individual country data after conversion to U.S. dollars at the average market exchange rates in the years indicated.
- Composite unemployment rates and employment growth are weighted by labor force as a share of group labor force.
- Composites relating to external sector statistics are sums of individual country data after conversion to

---

[1]Many countries are implementing the SNA 2008 or European System of National and Regional Accounts (ESA) 2010, and a few countries use versions of the SNA older than 1993. A similar adoption pattern is expected for the BPM6. Please refer to Table G, which lists the statistical standards adhered to by each country.

[2]Averages for real GDP and its components, employment, GDP per capita, inflation, factor productivity, trade, and commodity prices are calculated based on the compound annual rate of change, except in the case of the unemployment rate, which is based on the simple arithmetic average.

[3]See "Revised Purchasing Power Parity Weights" in the July 2014 *WEO Update* for a summary of the revised purchasing-power-parity-based weights, as well as Box A2 of the April 2004 WEO and Annex IV of the May 1993 WEO. See also Anne-Marie Gulde and Mari-anne Schulze-Ghattas, "Purchasing Power Parity Based Weights for the *World Economic Outlook*," in *Staff Studies for the World Economic Outlook* (Washington: International Monetary Fund, December 1993), pp. 106–23.

U.S. dollars at the average market exchange rates in the years indicated for balance of payments data and at end-of-year market exchange rates for debt denominated in currencies other than U.S. dollars.

- Composites of changes in foreign trade volumes and prices, however, are arithmetic averages of percent changes for individual countries weighted by the U.S. dollar value of exports or imports as a share of total world or group exports or imports (in the preceding year).

- Unless noted otherwise, group composites are computed if 90 percent or more of the share of group weights is represented.

- Data refer to calendar years, except in the case of a few countries that use fiscal years. Please refer to Table F, which lists the economies with exceptional reporting periods for national accounts and government finance data for each country.

For some countries, the figures for 2015 and earlier are based on estimates rather than actual outturns. Please refer to Table G, which lists the latest actual outturns for the indicators in the national accounts, prices, government finance, and balance of payments indicators for each country.

Country Notes

- The GDP data for *Argentina* before 2015 reflect official data, while for 2015 the data reflect IMF staff estimates. On February 1, 2013, the IMF issued a declaration of censure, and in June 2015 called on Argentina to implement additional specified actions to address the quality of its official GDP data according to a specified timetable. The new government that took office in December 2015 has announced its determination to improve the quality of GDP statistics. The Managing Director will report to the Executive Board on this issue again by July 15, 2016. At that time, the Executive Board will review the issue in line with IMF procedures.

- The consumer price data for *Argentina* before December 2013 reflect the CPI for the Greater Buenos Aires Area (CPI-GBA), while from December 2013 to October 2015 the data reflect the national CPI (IPCNu). Given the differences in geographical coverage, weights, sampling, and methodology of the two series and the authorities' decision in December 2015 to discontinue the IPCNu, the average CPI inflation for 2014, 2015, and 2016 and

end-period inflation for 2015 are not reported in the April 2016 *World Economic Outlook*. On February 1, 2013, the IMF issued a declaration of censure and in June 2015 called on Argentina to implement additional specified actions to address the quality of its official CPI data according to a specified timetable. The new government that took office in December 2015 has stated that it considers that the IPCNu is flawed and announced its determination to discontinue it and to improve the quality of CPI statistics. It has temporarily suspended the publication of CPI data to review sources and methodology. The Managing Director will report to the Executive Board on this issue again by July 15, 2016. At that time, the Executive Board will review the issue in line with IMF procedures.

- The series from which the nominal exchange rate assumptions are calculated are not made public for *Egypt* because the nominal exchange rate is a market-sensitive issue in Egypt.

- The 2015 data for *Greece* are preliminary. Fiscal projections for 2016–21 are not available at this time, given ongoing negotiations with the authorities and European partners on the fiscal targets in a potential new adjustment program.

- Because of the ongoing IMF program with *Pakistan*, the series from which nominal exchange rate assumptions are calculated are not made public—the nominal exchange rate is a market-sensitive issue in Pakistan.

- Data for *Syria* are excluded from 2011 onward because of the uncertain political situation.

- Projecting the economic outlook in *Venezuela* is complicated by the lack of any Article IV consultation since 2004 and delays in the publication of key economic data.

Classification of Countries

Summary of the Country Classification

The country classification in the WEO divides the world into two major groups: advanced economies and emerging market and developing economies.[4] This classification is not based on strict criteria, economic

[4]As used here, the terms "country" and "economy" do not always refer to a territorial entity that is a state as understood by international law and practice. Some territorial entities included here are not states, although their statistical data are maintained on a separate and independent basis.

or otherwise, and it has evolved over time. The objective is to facilitate analysis by providing a reasonably meaningful method of organizing data. Table A provides an overview of the country classification, showing the number of countries in each group by region and summarizing some key indicators of their relative size (GDP valued by purchasing power parity, total exports of goods and services, and population).

Some countries remain outside the country classification and therefore are not included in the analysis. Anguilla, Cuba, the Democratic People's Republic of Korea, and Montserrat are examples of countries that are not IMF members, and their economies therefore are not monitored by the IMF. Somalia is omitted from the emerging market and developing economies group composites because of data limitations.

General Features and Composition of Groups in the *World Economic Outlook* Classification

Advanced Economies

The 39 advanced economies are listed in Table B. The seven largest in terms of GDP based on market exchange rates—the United States, Japan, Germany, France, Italy, the United Kingdom, and Canada—constitute the subgroup of *major advanced economies* often referred to as the Group of Seven (G7). The members of the *euro area* are also distinguished as a subgroup. Composite data shown in the tables for the euro area cover the current members for all years, even though the membership has increased over time.

Table C lists the member countries of the European Union, not all of which are classified as advanced economies in the WEO.

Emerging Market and Developing Economies

The group of emerging market and developing economies (152) includes all those that are not classified as advanced economies.

The *regional breakdowns* of emerging market and developing economies are *Commonwealth of Independent States (CIS), emerging and developing Asia, emerging and developing Europe* (sometimes also referred to as "central and eastern Europe"), *Latin America and the Caribbean (LAC), Middle East, North Africa, Afghanistan, and Pakistan (MENAP)*, and *sub-Saharan Africa (SSA)*.

Emerging market and developing economies are also classified according to *analytical criteria*. The analytical criteria reflect the composition of export earnings and a distinction between net creditor and net debtor economies. The detailed composition of emerging market and developing economies in the regional and analytical groups is shown in Tables D and E.

The analytical criterion *source of export earnings* distinguishes between categories *fuel* (Standard International Trade Classification [SITC] 3) and *nonfuel* and then focuses on *nonfuel primary products* (SITCs 0, 1, 2, 4, and 68). Economies are categorized into one of these groups when their main source of export earnings exceeded 50 percent of total exports on average between 2010 and 2014.

The financial criteria focus on *net creditor economies, net debtor economies, heavily indebted poor countries* (HIPCs), and *low-income developing countries* (LIDCs). Economies are categorized as net debtors when their latest net international investment position, where available, was less than zero or their current account balance accumulations from 1972 (or earliest available data) to 2014 were negative. Net debtor economies are further differentiated on the basis of *experience with debt servicing.*[5]

The HIPC group comprises the countries that are or have been considered by the IMF and the World Bank for participation in their debt initiative known as the HIPC Initiative, which aims to reduce the external debt burdens of all the eligible HIPCs to a "sustainable" level in a reasonably short period of time.[6] Many of these countries have already benefited from debt relief and have graduated from the initiative.

The LIDCs are countries that were designated as eligible to use the IMF's concessional financing resources under the Poverty Reduction and Growth Trust (PRGT) in the 2013 PRGT eligibility review and had a level of per capita gross national income less than the PRGT income graduation threshold for non–small states (that is, twice the World Bank International Development Association operational threshold, or US$2,390 in 2011 as measured by the World Bank's Atlas method) and Zimbabwe.

[5] During 2010–14, 17 economies incurred external payments arrears or entered into official or commercial bank debt-rescheduling agreements. This group is referred to as *economies with arrears and/or rescheduling during 2010–14.*

[6] See David Andrews, Anthony R. Boote, Syed S. Rizavi, and Sukwinder Singh, *Debt Relief for Low-Income Countries: The Enhanced HIPC Initiative*, IMF Pamphlet Series 51 (Washington: International Monetary Fund, November 1999).

Table A. Classification by *World Economic Outlook* Groups and Their Shares in Aggregate GDP, Exports of Goods and Services, and Population, 2015[1]
(Percent of total for group or world)

	Number of Economies	GDP — Advanced Economies	GDP — World	Exports of Goods and Services — Advanced Economies	Exports of Goods and Services — World	Population — Advanced Economies	Population — World
Advanced Economies	39	100.0	42.4	100.0	63.3	100.0	14.6
United States		37.2	15.8	16.8	10.6	30.5	4.5
Euro Area	19	28.1	11.9	40.3	25.5	32.0	4.7
Germany		8.0	3.4	11.9	7.5	7.8	1.1
France		5.5	2.3	5.7	3.6	6.1	0.9
Italy		4.5	1.9	4.2	2.6	5.8	0.8
Spain		3.4	1.4	3.0	1.9	4.4	0.6
Japan		10.0	4.3	5.9	3.8	12.0	1.8
United Kingdom		5.6	2.4	5.9	3.7	6.2	0.9
Canada		3.4	1.4	3.7	2.3	3.4	0.5
Other Advanced Economies	16	15.6	6.6	27.4	17.3	15.9	2.3
Memorandum							
Major Advanced Economies	7	74.2	31.5	54.1	34.2	71.7	10.5

	Number of Economies	GDP — Emerging Market and Developing Economies	GDP — World	Exports of Goods and Services — Emerging Market and Developing Economies	Exports of Goods and Services — World	Population — Emerging Market and Developing Economies	Population — World
Emerging Market and Developing Economies	152	100.0	57.6	100.0	36.7	100.0	85.4
Regional Groups							
Commonwealth of Independent States[2]	12	8.0	4.6	7.6	2.8	4.7	4.0
Russia		5.7	3.3	5.1	1.9	2.4	2.0
Emerging and Developing Asia	29	53.2	30.6	50.0	18.4	57.1	48.7
China		29.7	17.1	31.0	11.4	22.3	19.0
India		12.2	7.0	5.8	2.1	21.0	17.9
Excluding China and India	27	11.4	6.5	13.3	4.9	13.8	11.8
Emerging and Developing Europe	12	5.7	3.3	9.5	3.5	2.8	2.4
Latin America and the Caribbean	32	14.5	8.3	13.8	5.1	10.0	8.5
Brazil		4.9	2.8	2.9	1.1	3.3	2.8
Mexico		3.4	2.0	5.3	1.9	2.1	1.8
Middle East, North Africa, Afghanistan, and Pakistan	22	13.2	7.6	14.5	5.3	10.5	9.0
Middle East and North Africa	20	11.7	6.7	14.1	5.2	7.0	5.9
Sub-Saharan Africa	45	5.4	3.1	4.6	1.7	14.9	12.8
Excluding Nigeria and South Africa	43	2.6	1.5	2.6	1.0	11.1	9.5
Analytical Groups[3]							
By Source of Export Earnings							
Fuel	29	20.2	11.6	21.8	8.0	12.4	10.6
Nonfuel	122	79.8	45.9	78.2	28.7	87.6	74.8
Of Which, Primary Products	29	4.8	2.7	4.5	1.7	7.6	6.5
By External Financing Source							
Net Debtor Economies	118	51.8	29.8	48.2	17.7	67.6	57.7
Net Debtor Economies by Debt-Servicing Experience							
Economies with Arrears and/or Rescheduling during 2010–14	17	2.9	1.7	1.9	0.7	4.0	3.4
Other Groups							
Heavily Indebted Poor Countries	38	2.4	1.4	1.9	0.7	11.2	9.6
Low-Income Developing Countries	59	7.4	4.2	6.5	2.4	22.5	19.2

[1]The GDP shares are based on the purchasing-power-parity valuation of economies' GDP. The number of economies comprising each group reflects those for which data are included in the group aggregates.

[2]Georgia, Turkmenistan, and Ukraine, which are not members of the Commonwealth of Independent States, are included in this group for reasons of geography and similarity in economic structure.

[3]Syria is omitted from the source of export earnings and South Sudan is omitted from the net external position group composites because of insufficient data.

Table B. Advanced Economies by Subgroup

Major Currency Areas

United States
Euro Area
Japan

Euro Area

Austria	Greece	Netherlands
Belgium	Ireland	Portugal
Cyprus	Italy	Slovak Republic
Estonia	Latvia	Slovenia
Finland	Lithuania	Spain
France	Luxembourg	
Germany	Malta	

Major Advanced Economies

Canada	Italy	United States
France	Japan	
Germany	United Kingdom	

Other Advanced Economies

Australia	Korea	Singapore
Czech Republic	Macao SAR[2]	Sweden
Denmark	New Zealand	Switzerland
Hong Kong SAR[1]	Norway	Taiwan Province of China
Iceland	Puerto Rico	
Israel	San Marino	

[1]On July 1, 1997, Hong Kong was returned to the People's Republic of China and became a Special Administrative Region of China.

[2]On December 20, 1999, Macao was returned to the People's Republic of China and became a Special Administrative Region of China.

Table C. European Union

Austria	Germany	Poland
Belgium	Greece	Portugal
Bulgaria	Hungary	Romania
Croatia	Ireland	Slovak Republic
Cyprus	Italy	Slovenia
Czech Republic	Latvia	Spain
Denmark	Lithuania	Sweden
Estonia	Luxembourg	United Kingdom
Finland	Malta	
France	Netherlands	

Table D. Emerging Market and Developing Economies by Region and Main Source of Export Earnings

	Fuel	Nonfuel Primary Products
Commonwealth of Independent States		
	Azerbaijan	Uzbekistan
	Kazakhstan	
	Russia	
	Turkmenistan[1]	
Emerging and Developing Asia		
	Brunei Darussalam	Marshall Islands
	Timor-Leste	Mongolia
		Papua New Guinea
		Solomon Islands
		Tuvalu
Latin America and the Caribbean		
	Bolivia	Argentina
	Colombia	Chile
	Ecuador	Guyana
	Trinidad and Tobago	Paraguay
	Venezuela	Suriname
		Uruguay
Middle East, North Africa, Afghanistan, and Pakistan		
	Algeria	Afghanistan
	Bahrain	Mauritania
	Iran	Sudan
	Iraq	
	Kuwait	
	Libya	
	Oman	
	Qatar	
	Saudi Arabia	
	United Arab Emirates	
	Yemen	
Sub-Saharan Africa		
	Angola	Burkina Faso
	Chad	Burundi
	Republic of Congo	Central African Republic
	Equatorial Guinea	Democratic Republic of the Congo
	Gabon	Côte d'Ivoire
	Nigeria	Eritrea
	South Sudan	Guinea-Bissau
		Liberia
		Malawi
		Mali
		Niger
		Sierra Leone
		South Africa
		Zambia

[1]Turkmenistan, which is not a member of the Commonwealth of Independent States, is included in this group for reasons of geography and similarity in economic structure.

Table E. Emerging Market and Developing Economies by Region, Net External Position, and Status as Heavily Indebted Poor Countries and Low-Income Developing Countries

	Net External Position[1]	Heavily Indebted Poor Countries[2]	Low-Income Developing Countries		Net External Position[1]	Heavily Indebted Poor Countries[2]	Low-Income Developing Countries
Commonwealth of Independent States				Bulgaria	*		
Armenia	*			Croatia	*		
Azerbaijan	●			Hungary	*		
Belarus	*			Kosovo	*		
Georgia[3]	*			FYR Macedonia	*		
Kazakhstan	*			Montenegro	*		
Kyrgyz Republic	*		*	Poland	*		
Moldova	*		*	Romania	*		
Russia	●			Serbia	*		
Tajikistan	*		*	Turkey	*		
Turkmenistan[3]	●			**Latin America and the Caribbean**			
Ukraine[3]	*			Antigua and Barbuda	*		
Uzbekistan	●		*	Argentina	●		
Emerging and Developing Asia				The Bahamas	*		
Bangladesh	*		*	Barbados	*		
Bhutan	*		*	Belize	*		
Brunei Darussalam	●			Bolivia	●	●	*
Cambodia	*		*	Brazil	*		
China	●			Chile	*		
Fiji	*			Colombia	*		
India	*			Costa Rica	*		
Indonesia	*			Dominica	*		
Kiribati	●		*	Dominican Republic	*		
Lao P.D.R.	*		*	Ecuador	*		
Malaysia	*			El Salvador	*		
Maldives	*			Grenada	*		
Marshall Islands	*			Guatemala	*		
Micronesia	●			Guyana	*	●	
Mongolia	*		*	Haiti	*	●	*
Myanmar	*		*	Honduras	*	●	*
Nepal	●		*	Jamaica	*		
Palau	●			Mexico	*		
Papua New Guinea	*		*	Nicaragua	*	●	*
Philippines	*			Panama	*		
Samoa	*			Paraguay	*		
Solomon Islands	*		*	Peru	*		
Sri Lanka	*			St. Kitts and Nevis	*		
Thailand	*			St. Lucia	*		
Timor-Leste	●			St. Vincent and the Grenadines	*		
Tonga	*			Suriname	*		
Tuvalu	*			Trinidad and Tobago	●		
Vanuatu	*			Uruguay	*		
Vietnam	*		*	Venezuela	●		
Emerging and Developing Europe							
Albania	*						
Bosnia and Herzegovina	*						

Table E. Emerging Market and Developing Economies by Region, Net External Position, and Status as Heavily Indebted Poor Countries and Low-Income Developing Countries (continued)

	Net External Position[1]	Heavily Indebted Poor Countries[2]	Low-Income Developing Countries		Net External Position[1]	Heavily Indebted Poor Countries[2]	Low-Income Developing Countries
Middle East, North Africa, Afghanistan, and Pakistan				Republic of Congo	*	•	*
Afghanistan	•	•	*	Côte d'Ivoire	•	•	*
Algeria	•			Equatorial Guinea	*		
Bahrain	•			Eritrea	*	*	*
Djibouti	*		*	Ethiopia	*	•	*
Egypt	*			Gabon	•		
Iran	•			The Gambia	*	•	*
Iraq	•			Ghana	*	•	*
Jordan	*			Guinea	*	•	*
Kuwait	•			Guinea-Bissau	*	•	*
Lebanon	*			Kenya	*		*
Libya	•			Lesotho	*		*
Mauritania	*	•	*	Liberia	*	•	*
Morocco	*			Madagascar	*	•	*
Oman	•			Malawi	*	•	*
Pakistan	*			Mali	*	•	*
Qatar	•			Mauritius	•		
Saudi Arabia	•			Mozambique	*	•	*
Sudan	*	*	*	Namibia	•		
Syria	*			Niger	*	•	*
Tunisia	*			Nigeria	*		*
United Arab Emirates	•			Rwanda	*	•	*
Yemen	*		*	São Tomé and Príncipe	*	•	*
Sub-Saharan Africa				Senegal	*	•	*
Angola	•			Seychelles	*		
Benin	*	•	*	Sierra Leone	*	•	*
Botswana	•			South Africa	*		
Burkina Faso	*	•	*	South Sudan[4]	...		*
Burundi	*	•	*	Swaziland	*		
Cabo Verde	*			Tanzania	*	•	*
Cameroon	*	•	*	Togo	*	•	*
Central African Republic	*	•	*	Uganda	*	•	*
Chad	*	•	*	Zambia	*	•	*
Comoros	*	•	*	Zimbabwe	*		*
Democratic Republic of the Congo	*	•	*				

[1]Dot (star) indicates that the country is a net creditor (net debtor).
[2]Dot instead of star indicates that the country has reached the completion point.
[3]Georgia, Turkmenistan, and Ukraine, which are not members of the Commonwealth of Independent States, are included in this group for reasons of geography and similarity in economic structure.
[4]South Sudan is omitted from the net external position group composite for lack of a fully developed database.

Table F. Economies with Exceptional Reporting Periods[1]

	National Accounts	Government Finance
The Bahamas		Jul/Jun
Bangladesh		Jul/Jun
Barbados		Apr/Mar
Belize		Apr/Mar
Bhutan	Jul/Jun	Jul/Jun
Botswana		Apr/Mar
Dominica		Jul/Jun
Egypt	Jul/Jun	Jul/Jun
Ethiopia	Jul/Jun	Jul/Jun
Haiti	Oct/Sep	Oct/Sep
Hong Kong SAR		Apr/Mar
India	Apr/Mar	Apr/Mar
Iran	Apr/Mar	Apr/Mar
Jamaica		Apr/Mar
Lao P.D.R.		Oct/Sep
Lesotho		Apr/Mar
Malawi		Jul/Jun
Marshall Islands	Oct/Sep	Oct/Sep
Micronesia	Oct/Sep	Oct/Sep
Myanmar	Apr/Mar	Apr/Mar
Namibia		Apr/Mar
Nepal	Aug/Jul	Aug/Jul
Pakistan	Jul/Jun	Jul/Jun
Palau	Oct/Sep	Oct/Sep
Puerto Rico	Jul/Jun	Jul/Jun
Samoa	Jul/Jun	Jul/Jun
Singapore		Apr/Mar
St. Lucia		Apr/Mar
Swaziland		Apr/Mar
Thailand		Oct/Sep
Trinidad and Tobago		Oct/Sep

[1]Unless noted otherwise, all data refer to calendar years.

Table G. Key Data Documentation

Country	Currency	National Accounts Historical Data Source[1]	Latest Actual Annual Data	Base Year[2]	System of National Accounts	Use of Chain-Weighted Methodology[3]	Prices (CPI) Historical Data Source[1]	Latest Actual Annual Data
Afghanistan	Afghan Afghani	NSO	2014	2002	SNA 1993		NSO	2015
Albania	Albanian lek	IMF staff	2012	1996	SNA 1993	From 1996	NSO	2014
Algeria	Algerian dinar	NSO	2014	2001	SNA 1993	From 2005	NSO	2014
Angola	Angolan kwanza	MEP	2014	2002	ESA 1995		NSO	2015
Antigua and Barbuda	Eastern Caribbean dollar	CB	2014	2006[6]	SNA 1993		NSO	2014
Argentina	Argentine peso	MEP	2014	2004	SNA 2008		NSO	2015
Armenia	Armenian dram	NSO	2014	2005	SNA 1993		NSO	2015
Australia	Australian dollar	NSO	2015	2013/14	SNA 2008	From 1980	NSO	2015
Austria	Euro	NSO	2015	2010	ESA 2010	From 1995	NSO	2015
Azerbaijan	Azerbaijan manat	NSO	2014	2003	SNA 1993	From 1994	NSO	2014
The Bahamas	Bahamian dollar	NSO	2014	2006	SNA 1993		NSO	2015
Bahrain	Bahrain dinar	MoF	2014	2010	SNA 2008		NSO	2015
Bangladesh	Bangladesh taka	NSO	2013	2005	SNA 1993		NSO	2014
Barbados	Barbados dollar	NSO and CB	2013	1974[6]	SNA 1993		CB	2014
Belarus	Belarusian rubel	NSO	2013	2009	ESA 1995	From 2005	NSO	2014
Belgium	Euro	CB	2014	2013	ESA 2010	From 1995	CB	2015
Belize	Belize dollar	NSO	2013	2000	SNA 1993		NSO	2013
Benin	CFA franc	NSO	2012	2007	SNA 1993		NSO	2013
Bhutan	Bhutanese ngultrum	NSO	2011/12	2000[6]	SNA 1993		CB	2014/15
Bolivia	Bolivian boliviano	NSO	2014	1990	Other		NSO	2015
Bosnia and Herzegovina	Bosnia convertible marka	NSO	2015	2010	ESA 2010	From 2000	NSO	2015
Botswana	Botswana pula	NSO	2012	2006	SNA 1993		NSO	2013
Brazil	Brazilian real	NSO	2014	1995	SNA 2008		NSO	2014
Brunei Darussalam	Brunei dollar	NSO and PMO	2014	2010	SNA 1993		NSO and PMO	2015
Bulgaria	Bulgarian lev	NSO	2014	2010	ESA 2010	From 1996	NSO	2015
Burkina Faso	CFA franc	NSO and MEP	2012	1999	SNA 1993		NSO	2015
Burundi	Burundi franc	NSO	2012	2005	SNA 1993		NSO	2015
Cabo Verde	Cabo Verdean escudo	NSO	2014	2007	SNA 2008	From 2011	NSO	2014
Cambodia	Cambodian riel	NSO	2013	2000	SNA 1993		NSO	2014
Cameroon	CFA franc	NSO	2014	2000	SNA 1993		NSO	2014
Canada	Canadian dollar	NSO	2014	2007	SNA 2008	From 1980	NSO	2015
Central African Republic	CFA franc	NSO	2012	2005	SNA 1993		NSO	2014
Chad	CFA franc	CB	2013	2005	Other		NSO	2014
Chile	Chilean peso	CB	2014	2008	SNA 2008	From 2003	NSO	2015
China	Chinese yuan	NSO	2015	2010	SNA 2008		NSO	2015
Colombia	Colombian peso	NSO	2014	2005	Other	From 2000	NSO	2014
Comoros	Comorian franc	NSO	2013	2000	Other		NSO	2014
Democratic Republic of the Congo	Congolese franc	NSO	2013	2005	SNA 1993		CB	2015
Republic of Congo	CFA franc	NSO	2014	1990	SNA 1993		NSO	2014
Costa Rica	Costa Rican colón	CB	2015	2012	SNA 1993		CB	2015

Table G. Key Data Documentation *(continued)*

Country	Government Finance					Balance of Payments		
	Historical Data Source[1]	Latest Actual Annual Data	Statistics Manual in Use at Source	Subsectors Coverage[4]	Accounting Practice[5]	Historical Data Source[1]	Latest Actual Annual Data	Statistics Manual in Use at Source
Afghanistan	MoF	2014	2001	CG	C	NSO	2014	BPM 5
Albania	IMF staff	2014	1986	CG,LG,SS,MPC, NFPC	Other	CB	2014	BPM 6
Algeria	CB	2014	1986	CG	C	CB	2015	BPM 5
Angola	MoF	2014	2001	CG,LG	Other	CB	2014	BPM 5
Antigua and Barbuda	MoF	2014	2001	CG	C	CB	2014	BPM 5
Argentina	MEP	2015	1986	CG,SG,LG,SS	C	CB	2014	BPM 5
Armenia	MoF	2014	2001	CG	C	CB	2014	BPM 5
Australia	MoF	2014/15	2001	CG,SG,LG,TG	A	NSO	2015	BPM 6
Austria	NSO	2015	2001	CG,SG,LG,SS	A	CB	2015	BPM 6
Azerbaijan	MoF	2014	Other	CG	C	CB	2014	BPM 5
The Bahamas	MoF	2014/15	2001	CG	C	CB	2014	BPM 5
Bahrain	MoF	2014	2001	CG	C	CB	2014	BPM 6
Bangladesh	MoF	2013/14	Other	CG	C	CB	2013	BPM 4
Barbados	MoF	2014/15	1986	CG,SS,NFPC	C	CB	2014	BPM 5
Belarus	MoF	2013	2001	CG,LG,SS	C	CB	2013	BPM 6
Belgium	CB	2014	ESA 2010	CG,SG,LG,SS	A	CB	2014	BPM 6
Belize	MoF	2013/14	1986	CG,MPC	C/A	CB	2013	BPM 5
Benin	MoF	2013	2001	CG	C	CB	2012	BPM 5
Bhutan	MoF	2012/13	1986	CG	C	CB	2011/12	BPM 6
Bolivia	MoF	2014	2001	CG,LG,SS,MPC, NMPC, NFPC	C	CB	2014	BPM 5
Bosnia and Herzegovina	MoF	2014	2001	CG,SG,LG,SS	A	CB	2014	BPM 6
Botswana	MoF	2011/12	1986	CG	C	CB	2012	BPM 5
Brazil	MoF	2014	2001	CG,SG,LG,SS, MPC,NFPC	C	CB	2014	BPM 6
Brunei Darussalam	MoF	2014	Other	CG, BCG	C	MEP	2014	BPM 6
Bulgaria	MoF	2014	2001	CG,LG,SS	C	CB	2014	BPM 6
Burkina Faso	MoF	2014	2001	CG	Other	CB	2013	BPM 5
Burundi	MoF	2013	2001	CG	A	CB	2012	BPM 6
Cabo Verde	MoF	2014	2001	CG,SS	A	NSO	2014	BPM 5
Cambodia	MoF	2014	1986	CG,LG	A	CB	2014	BPM 5
Cameroon	MoF	2014	2001	CG,NFPC	C	MoF	2013	BPM 5
Canada	MoF	2015	2001	CG,SG,LG,SS	A	NSO	2015	BPM 6
Central African Republic	MoF	2014	2001	CG	C	CB	2012	BPM 5
Chad	MoF	2014	1986	CG,NFPC	C	CB	2012	BPM 5
Chile	MoF	2015	2001	CG,LG	A	CB	2015	BPM 6
China	MoF	2015	2001	CG,LG	C	SAFE	2015	BPM 6
Colombia	MoF	2014	2001	CG,SG,LG,SS	C/A	CB and NSO	2014	BPM 5
Comoros	MoF	2014	1986	CG	C/A	CB and IMF staff	2014	BPM 5
Democratic Republic of the Congo	MoF	2015	2001	CG,LG	A	CB	2015	BPM 5
Republic of Congo	MoF	2014	2001	CG	A	CB	2007	BPM 5
Costa Rica	MoF and CB	2015	1986	CG	C	CB	2015	BPM 5

Table G. Key Data Documentation *(continued)*

Country	Currency	National Accounts Historical Data Source[1]	Latest Actual Annual Data	Base Year[2]	System of National Accounts	Use of Chain-Weighted Methodology[3]	Prices (CPI) Historical Data Source[1]	Latest Actual Annual Data
Côte d'Ivoire	CFA franc	NSO	2014	2009	SNA 1993		NSO	2015
Croatia	Croatian kuna	NSO	2014	2010	ESA 2010		NSO	2014
Cyprus	Euro	NSO	2015	2005	ESA 2010	From 1995	NSO	2015
Czech Republic	Czech koruna	NSO	2015	2010	ESA 2010	From 1995	NSO	2015
Denmark	Danish krone	NSO	2015	2010	ESA 2010	From 1980	NSO	2015
Djibouti	Djibouti franc	NSO	2014	1990	Other		NSO	2015
Dominica	Eastern Caribbean dollar	NSO	2014	2006	SNA 1993		NSO	2014
Dominican Republic	Dominican peso	CB	2014	2007	SNA 2008	From 2007	CB	2015
Ecuador	U.S. dollar	CB	2014	2007	SNA 1993		NSO and CB	2015
Egypt	Egyptian pound	MEP	2014/15	2011/12	SNA 1993		NSO	2014/15
El Salvador	U.S. dollar	CB	2014	1990	Other		NSO	2015
Equatorial Guinea	CFA franc	MEP and CB	2013	2006	SNA 1993		MEP	2014
Eritrea	Eritrean nakfa	IMF staff	2006	2005	SNA 1993		NSO	2009
Estonia	Euro	NSO	2015	2010	ESA 2010	From 2010	NSO	2015
Ethiopia	Ethiopian birr	NSO	2013/14	2010/11	SNA 1993		NSO	2015
Fiji	Fijian dollar	NSO	2013	2008[6]	SNA 1993/ 2008		NSO	2015
Finland	Euro	NSO	2015	2010	ESA 2010	From 1980	NSO	2015
France	Euro	NSO	2015	2010	ESA 2010	From 1980	NSO	2015
Gabon	CFA franc	MoF	2013	2001	SNA 1993		MoF	2014
The Gambia	Gambian dalasi	NSO	2012	2004	SNA 1993		NSO	2013
Georgia	Georgian lari	NSO	2014	2000	SNA 1993	From 1996	NSO	2015
Germany	Euro	NSO	2015	2010	ESA 2010	From 1991	NSO	2015
Ghana	Ghanaian cedi	NSO	2014	2006	SNA 1993		NSO	2014
Greece	Euro	NSO	2015	2010	ESA 2010	From 1995	NSO	2015
Grenada	Eastern Caribbean dollar	NSO	2014	2006	SNA 1993		NSO	2013
Guatemala	Guatemalan quetzal	CB	2014	2001	SNA 1993	From 2001	NSO	2014
Guinea	Guinean franc	NSO	2009	2003	SNA 1993		NSO	2015
Guinea-Bissau	CFA franc	NSO	2013	2005	SNA 1993		NSO	2015
Guyana	Guyanese dollar	NSO	2012	2006[6]	SNA 1993		NSO	2012
Haiti	Haitian gourde	NSO	2014/15	1986/87	SNA 2008		NSO	2014/15
Honduras	Honduran lempira	CB	2015	2000	SNA 1993		CB	2015
Hong Kong SAR	Hong Kong dollar	NSO	2015	2013	SNA 2008	From 1980	NSO	2015
Hungary	Hungarian forint	NSO	2015	2005	ESA 2010	From 2005	IEO	2015
Iceland	Icelandic króna	NSO	2015	2005	ESA 2010	From 1990	NSO	2015
India	Indian rupee	NSO	2014/15	2011/12	SNA 2008		NSO	2014/15
Indonesia	Indonesian rupiah	NSO	2014	2010	SNA 2008		NSO	2015
Iran	Iranian rial	CB	2014/15	2004/05	SNA 1993		CB	2014/15
Iraq	Iraqi dinar	NSO	2014	2007	SNA 1968		NSO	2014
Ireland	Euro	NSO	2015	2013	ESA 2010	From 2012	NSO	2015

Table G. Key Data Documentation (continued)

Country	Government Finance					Balance of Payments		
	Historical Data Source[1]	Latest Actual Annual Data	Statistics Manual in Use at Source	Subsectors Coverage[4]	Accounting Practice[5]	Historical Data Source[1]	Latest Actual Annual Data	Statistics Manual in Use at Source
Côte d'Ivoire	MoF	2015	1986	CG	A	CB	2014	BPM 6
Croatia	MoF	2014	2001	CG,LG	A	CB	2013	BPM 6
Cyprus	NSO	2015	ESA 2010	CG,LG,SS	C/A	NSO	2015	BPM 5
Czech Republic	MoF	2015	2001	CG,LG,SS	A	NSO	2015	BPM 6
Denmark	NSO	2014	2001	CG,LG,SS	A	NSO	2015	BPM 6
Djibouti	MoF	2015	2001	CG	A	CB	2015	BPM 5
Dominica	MoF	2013/14	1986	CG	C	CB	2014	BPM 5
Dominican Republic	MoF	2014	2001	CG,SG,LG,SS	A	CB	2014	BPM 6
Ecuador	CB and MoF	2015	1986	CG,SG,LG,SS,NFPC	C	CB	2014	BPM 5
Egypt	MoF	2014/15	2001	CG,LG,SS,MPC	C	CB	2014/15	BPM 5
El Salvador	MoF	2015	1986	CG,LG,SS	C	CB	2014	BPM 6
Equatorial Guinea	MoF	2014	1986	CG	C	CB	2013	BPM 5
Eritrea	MoF	2008	2001	CG	C	CB	2008	BPM 5
Estonia	MoF	2015	1986/2001	CG,LG,SS	C	CB	2015	BPM 6
Ethiopia	MoF	2014/15	1986	CG,SG,LG,NFPC	C	CB	2014/15	BPM 5
Fiji	MoF	2014	2001	CG	C	CB	2013	BPM 5
Finland	MoF	2014	2001	CG,LG,SS	A	NSO	2015	BPM 6
France	NSO	2014	2001	CG,LG,SS	A	CB	2015	BPM 6
Gabon	IMF staff	2014	2001	CG	A	CB	2014	BPM 5
The Gambia	MoF	2013	2001	CG	C	CB and IMF staff	2012	BPM 4
Georgia	MoF	2014	2001	CG,LG	C	NSO and CB	2014	BPM 5
Germany	NSO	2015	2001	CG,SG,LG,SS	A	CB	2014	BPM 6
Ghana	MoF	2014	2001	CG	C	CB	2014	BPM 5
Greece	MoF	2014	1986	CG,LG,SS	A	CB	2015	BPM 6
Grenada	MoF	2014	2001	CG	C	CB	2013	BPM 5
Guatemala	MoF	2014	1986	CG	C	CB	2014	BPM 5
Guinea	MoF	2015	2001	CG	Other	CB and MEP	2014	BPM 6
Guinea-Bissau	MoF	2014	2001	CG	A	CB	2014	BPM 6
Guyana	MoF	2012	2001	CG,SS	C	CB	2012	BPM 5
Haiti	MoF	2014/15	2001	CG	C	CB	2014/15	BPM 5
Honduras	MoF	2015	1986	CG,LG,SS,NFPC	A	CB	2014	BPM 5
Hong Kong SAR	NSO	2014/15	2001	CG	C	NSO	2015	BPM 6
Hungary	MEP and NSO	2014	ESA 2010	CG,LG,SS,NMPC	A	CB	2014	BPM 6
Iceland	NSO	2014	2001	CG,LG,SS	A	CB	2015	BPM 6
India	MoF	2013/14	2001	CG,SG	C	CB	2014/15	BPM 6
Indonesia	MoF	2014	2001	CG,LG	C	CB	2014	BPM 6
Iran	MoF	2014/15	2001	CG	C	CB	2014/15	BPM 5
Iraq	MoF	2014	2001	CG	C	CB	2014	BPM 5
Ireland	MoF	2014	2001	CG,LG,SS	A	NSO	2015	BPM 6

Table G. Key Data Documentation *(continued)*

Country	Currency	National Accounts Historical Data Source[1]	Latest Actual Annual Data	Base Year[2]	System of National Accounts	Use of Chain-Weighted Methodology[3]	Prices (CPI) Historical Data Source[1]	Latest Actual Annual Data
Israel	New Israeli shekel	NSO	2015	2010	SNA 2008	From 1995	Haver Analytics	2015
Italy	Euro	NSO	2015	2010	ESA 2010	From 1980	NSO	2015
Jamaica	Jamaican dollar	NSO	2014	2007	SNA 1993		NSO	2014
Japan	Japanese yen	GAD	2015	2005	SNA 1993	From 1980	GAD	2015
Jordan	Jordanian dinar	NSO	2014	1994	Other		NSO	2015
Kazakhstan	Kazakhstani tenge	NSO	2014	2007	SNA 1993	From 1994	CB	2014
Kenya	Kenya shilling	NSO	2014	2009	SNA 2008		NSO	2015
Kiribati	Australian dollar	NSO	2014	2006	SNA 2008		NSO	2014
Korea	South Korean won	CB	2014	2010	SNA 2008	From 1980	MoF	2015
Kosovo	Euro	NSO	2015	2013	ESA 2010		NSO	2015
Kuwait	Kuwaiti dinar	MEP and NSO	2014	2010	SNA 1993		NSO and MEP	2014
Kyrgyz Republic	Kyrgyz som	NSO	2015	1995	SNA 1993		NSO	2015
Lao P.D.R.	Lao kip	NSO	2013	2002	SNA 1993		NSO	2013
Latvia	Euro	NSO	2015	2010	ESA 2010	From 1995	NSO	2015
Lebanon	Lebanese pound	NSO	2013	2010	SNA 2008	From 2010	NSO	2015
Lesotho	Lesotho loti	NSO	2014	2004	Other		NSO	2014
Liberia	U.S. dollar	CB	2014	1992	SNA 1993		CB	2015
Libya	Libyan dinar	MEP	2014	2003	SNA 1993		NSO	2014
Lithuania	Euro	NSO	2015	2010	ESA 2010	From 2005	NSO	2015
Luxembourg	Euro	NSO	2014	2010	ESA 2010	From 1995	NSO	2014
Macao SAR	Macanese pataca	NSO	2015	2013	SNA 2008	From 2001	NSO	2015
FYR Macedonia	Macedonian denar	NSO	2014	2005	ESA 2010		NSO	2014
Madagascar	Malagasy ariary	NSO	2014	2000	SNA 1968		NSO	2015
Malawi	Malawian kwacha	NSO	2011	2010	SNA 2008		NSO	2015
Malaysia	Malaysian ringgit	NSO	2014	2010	SNA 2008		NSO	2015
Maldives	Maldivian rufiyaa	MoF and NSO	2014	2003[6]	SNA 1993		CB	2014
Mali	CFA franc	MoF	2013	1999	SNA 1993		MoF	2015
Malta	Euro	NSO	2015	2010	ESA 2010	From 2000	NSO	2015
Marshall Islands	U.S. dollar	NSO	2012/13	2003/04	Other		NSO	2013
Mauritania	Mauritanian ouguiya	NSO	2014	2004	SNA 1993		NSO	2014
Mauritius	Mauritian rupee	NSO	2014	2006	SNA 1993	From 1999	NSO	2015
Mexico	Mexican peso	NSO	2015	2008	SNA 2008		NSO	2015
Micronesia	U.S. dollar	NSO	2013	2004	Other		NSO	2013
Moldova	Moldovan leu	NSO	2015	1995	SNA 1993		NSO	2015
Mongolia	Mongolian tögrög	NSO	2015	2010	SNA 1993		NSO	2015
Montenegro	Euro	NSO	2014	2006	ESA 1995		NSO	2015
Morocco	Moroccan dirham	NSO	2014	2007	SNA 1993	From 1998	NSO	2014
Mozambique	Mozambican metical	NSO	2014	2009	SNA 1993		NSO	2015
Myanmar	Myanmar kyat	MEP	2014/15	2010/11	Other		NSO	2014/15
Namibia	Namibia dollar	NSO	2014	2000	SNA 1993		NSO	2014
Nepal	Nepalese rupee	NSO	2014/15	2000/01	SNA 1993		CB	2014/15
Netherlands	Euro	NSO	2015	2010	ESA 2010	From 1980	NSO	2015
New Zealand	New Zealand dollar	NSO	2015	2009/10	Other	From 1987	NSO	2015
Nicaragua	Nicaraguan córdoba	IMF staff	2014	2006	SNA 1993	From 1994	CB	2015

Table G. Key Data Documentation *(continued)*

Country	Government Finance					Balance of Payments		
	Historical Data Source[1]	Latest Actual Annual Data	Statistics Manual in Use at Source	Subsectors Coverage[4]	Accounting Practice[5]	Historical Data Source[1]	Latest Actual Annual Data	Statistics Manual in Use at Source
Israel	MoF	2015	2001	CG,LG,SS	Other	Haver Analytics	2015	BPM 6
Italy	NSO	2014	2001	CG,LG,SS	A	NSO	2015	BPM 6
Jamaica	MoF	2014/15	1986	CG	C	CB	2014	BPM 5
Japan	GAD	2014	2001	CG,LG,SS	A	MoF	2015	BPM 6
Jordan	MoF	2014	2001	CG,NFPC	C	CB	2014	BPM 5
Kazakhstan	IMF staff	2015	2001	CG,LG	A	CB	2014	BPM 6
Kenya	MoF	2014	2001	CG	A	CB	2014	BPM 6
Kiribati	MoF	2013	1986	CG,LG	C	NSO	2014	BPM 6
Korea	MoF	2014	2001	CG	C	CB	2014	BPM 6
Kosovo	MoF	2015	Other	CG,LG	C	CB	2015	BPM 5
Kuwait	MoF	2014	1986	CG	C/A	CB	2014	BPM 5
Kyrgyz Republic	MoF	2014	Other	CG,LG,SS	C	MoF	2014	BPM 5
Lao P.D.R.	MoF	2012/13	2001	CG	C	CB	2013	BPM 5
Latvia	MoF	2015	Other	CG,LG,SS,NFPC	C	CB	2014	BPM 6
Lebanon	MoF	2014	2001	CG	C	CB and IMF staff	2014	BPM 5
Lesotho	MoF	2014/15	2001	CG,LG	C	CB	2013	BPM 6
Liberia	MoF	2013	2001	CG	A	CB	2013	BPM 5
Libya	MoF	2014	1986	CG,SG,LG	C	CB	2014	BPM 5
Lithuania	MoF	2014	2014	CG,LG,SS	A	CB	2015	BPM 6
Luxembourg	MoF	2014	2001	CG,LG,SS	A	NSO	2014	BPM 6
Macao SAR	MoF	2015	2001	CG	C	NSO	2014	BPM 6
FYR Macedonia	MoF	2014	1986	CG,SG,SS	C	CB	2014	BPM 6
Madagascar	MoF	2014	1986	CG,LG	C	CB	2014	BPM 5
Malawi	MoF	2014/15	1986	CG	C	NSO	2014	BPM 5
Malaysia	MoF	2013	1986	CG,SG,LG	C	NSO	2014	BPM 6
Maldives	MoF	2014	1986	CG	C	CB	2014	BPM 5
Mali	MoF	2015	2001	CG	C/A	CB	2013	BPM 5
Malta	NSO	2015	2001	CG,SS	A	NSO	2015	BPM 6
Marshall Islands	MoF	2012/13	2001	CG,LG,SS	A	NSO	2013	Other
Mauritania	MoF	2014	1986	CG	C	CB	2013	BPM 5
Mauritius	MoF	2014	2001	CG,LG,NFPC	C	CB	2014	BPM 5
Mexico	MoF	2015	2001	CG,SS,NFPC	C	CB	2015	BPM 5
Micronesia	MoF	2013/14	2001	CG,SG,LG,SS	Other	NSO	2013	Other
Moldova	MoF	2015	1986	CG,LG,SS	C	CB	2014	BPM 5
Mongolia	MoF	2015	2001	CG,SG,LG,SS	C	CB	2015	BPM 5
Montenegro	MoF	2014	1986	CG,LG,SS	C	CB	2014	BPM 5
Morocco	MEP	2014	2001	CG	A	FEO	2014	BPM 5
Mozambique	MoF	2015	2001	CG,SG	C/A	CB	2015	BPM 6
Myanmar	MoF	2014/15	2001	CG,NFPC	C/A	IMF staff	2014/15	Other
Namibia	MoF	2014/15	2001	CG	C	CB	2013	BPM 5
Nepal	MoF	2014/15	2001	CG	C	CB	2014/15	BPM 5
Netherlands	MoF	2015	2001	CG,LG,SS	A	CB	2014	BPM 6
New Zealand	MoF	2014/15	2001	CG	A	NSO	2015	BPM 6
Nicaragua	MoF	2014	1986	CG,LG,SS	C	IMF staff	2014	BPM 6

Table G. Key Data Documentation *(continued)*

Country	Currency	National Accounts					Prices (CPI)	
		Historical Data Source[1]	Latest Actual Annual Data	Base Year[2]	System of National Accounts	Use of Chain-Weighted Methodology[3]	Historical Data Source[1]	Latest Actual Annual Data
Niger	CFA franc	NSO	2014	2000	SNA 1993		NSO	2015
Nigeria	Nigerian naira	NSO	2015	2010	SNA 2008		NSO	2015
Norway	Norwegian krone	NSO	2015	2013	ESA 2010	From 1980	NSO	2015
Oman	Omani rial	NSO	2012	2010	SNA 1993		NSO	2014
Pakistan	Pakistan rupee	NSO	2014/15	2005/06[6]	SNA 1968/ 1993		NSO	2014/15
Palau	U.S. dollar	MoF	2013/14	2005	Other		MoF	2013/14
Panama	U.S. dollar	NSO	2014	2007	SNA 1993	From 2007	NSO	2014
Papua New Guinea	Papua New Guinea kina	NSO and MoF	2013	1998	SNA 1993		NSO	2013
Paraguay	Paraguayan guaraní	CB	2014	1994	SNA 1993		CB	2015
Peru	Peruvian nuevo sol	CB	2015	2007	SNA 1993		CB	2015
Philippines	Philippine peso	NSO	2015	2000	SNA 2008		NSO	2015
Poland	Polish zloty	NSO	2015	2010	ESA 2010	From 1995	NSO	2015
Portugal	Euro	NSO	2015	2011	ESA 2010	From 1980	NSO	2015
Puerto Rico	U.S. dollar	MEP	2013/14	1954	SNA 1968		MEP	2015
Qatar	Qatari riyal	NSO and MEP	2014	2013	SNA 1993		NSO and MEP	2015
Romania	Romanian leu	NSO	2015	2010	ESA 2010	From 2000	NSO	2015
Russia	Russian ruble	NSO	2015	2008	SNA 2008	From 1995	NSO	2015
Rwanda	Rwanda franc	MoF	2014	2011	SNA 1993		MoF	2015
Samoa	Samoa tala	NSO	2014/15	2009/10	SNA 1993		NSO	2014/15
San Marino	Euro	NSO	2014	2007	Other		NSO	2015
São Tomé and Príncipe	São Tomé and Príncipe dobra	NSO	2012	2000	SNA 1993		NSO	2015
Saudi Arabia	Saudi riyal	NSO and MEP	2015	2010	SNA 1993		NSO and MEP	2015
Senegal	CFA franc	NSO	2013	2000	SNA 1993		NSO	2011
Serbia	Serbian dinar	NSO	2015	2010	ESA 2010	From 2010	NSO	2015
Seychelles	Seychellois rupee	NSO	2013	2006	SNA 1993		NSO	2014
Sierra Leone	Sierra Leonean leone	NSO	2014	2006	SNA 1993	From 2010	NSO	2015
Singapore	Singapore dollar	NSO	2014	2010	SNA 1993	From 2010	NSO	2014
Slovak Republic	Euro	NSO	2015	2010	ESA 2010	From 1997	NSO	2015
Slovenia	Euro	NSO	2015	2010	ESA 2010	From 2000	NSO	2015
Solomon Islands	Solomon Islands dollar	CB	2014	2004	SNA 1993		NSO	2014
South Africa	South African rand	CB	2014	2010	SNA 1993		NSO	2015
South Sudan	South Sudanese pound	NSO	2014	2010	SNA 1993		NSO	2014
Spain	Euro	NSO	2015	2010	ESA 2010	From 1995	NSO	2015
Sri Lanka	Sri Lankan rupee	NSO	2015	2002	SNA 1993		NSO	2015
St. Kitts and Nevis	Eastern Caribbean dollar	NSO	2013	2006[6]	SNA 1993		NSO	2013
St. Lucia	Eastern Caribbean dollar	NSO	2014	2006	SNA 1993		NSO	2015

Table G. Key Data Documentation (continued)

Country	Historical Data Source[1]	Latest Actual Annual Data	Statistics Manual in Use at Source	Subsectors Coverage[4]	Accounting Practice[5]	Historical Data Source[1]	Latest Actual Annual Data	Statistics Manual in Use at Source
	Government Finance					Balance of Payments		
Niger	MoF	2015	1986	CG	A	CB	2014	BPM 6
Nigeria	MoF	2015	2001	CG,SG,LG,NFPC	C	CB	2015	BPM 5
Norway	NSO and MoF	2014	2001	CG,LG,SS	A	NSO	2015	BPM 6
Oman	MoF	2014	2001	CG	C	CB	2013	BPM 5
Pakistan	MoF	2014/15	1986	CG,SG,LG	C	CB	2014/15	BPM 5
Palau	MoF	2013/14	2001	CG	Other	MoF	2013/14	BPM 6
Panama	MEP	2014	1986	CG,SG,LG,SS,NFPC	C	NSO	2014	BPM 5
Papua New Guinea	MoF	2013	1986	CG	C	CB	2013	BPM 5
Paraguay	MoF	2015	2001	CG,SG,LG,SS,MPC, NMPC,NFPC	C	CB	2014	BPM 5
Peru	MoF	2015	1986	CG,SG,LG,SS	C	CB	2015	BPM 5
Philippines	MoF	2015	2001	CG,LG,SS	C	CB	2015	BPM 6
Poland	MoF and NSO	2014	ESA 2010	CG,LG,SS	A	CB	2014	BPM 6
Portugal	NSO	2014	2001	CG,LG,SS	A	CB	2015	BPM 6
Puerto Rico	MEP	2014/15	2001	Other	A	...	...	...
Qatar	MoF	2015	1986	CG	C	CB and IMF staff	2014	BPM 5
Romania	MoF	2015	2001	CG,LG,SS	C	CB	2015	BPM 6
Russia	MoF	2014	2001	CG,SG,SS	C/A	CB	2014	BPM 6
Rwanda	MoF	2014	2001	CG,LG	C/A	CB	2014	BPM 5
Samoa	MoF	2014/15	2001	CG	A	CB	2014/15	BPM 6
San Marino	MoF	2014	Other	CG	Other	...	...	...
São Tomé and Príncipe	MoF and Customs	2015	2001	CG	C	CB	2015	BPM 6
Saudi Arabia	MoF	2015	1986	CG	C	CB	2015	BPM 5
Senegal	MoF	2011	1986	CG	C	CB and IMF staff	2011	BPM 5
Serbia	MoF	2015	Other	CG,SG,LG,SS	C	CB	2015	BPM 6
Seychelles	MoF	2015	1986	CG,SS	C	CB	2014	BPM 6
Sierra Leone	MoF	2014	1986	CG	C	CB	2014	BPM 5
Singapore	MoF	2013/14	2001	CG	C	NSO	2014	BPM 6
Slovak Republic	NSO	2015	2001	CG,LG,SS	A	CB	2015	BPM 6
Slovenia	MoF	2015	1986	CG,SG,LG,SS	C	NSO	2015	BPM 6
Solomon Islands	MoF	2014	1986	CG	C	CB	2014	BPM 6
South Africa	MoF	2014/15	2001	CG,SG,SS	C	CB	2014	BPM 6
South Sudan	MoF and MEP	2015	Other	CG	C	MoF, NSO, and MEP	2015	BPM 5
Spain	MoF and NSO	2014	2001	CG,SG,LG,SS	A	CB	2014	BPM 6
Sri Lanka	MoF	2014	2001	CG,SG,LG,SS	C	CB	2012	BPM 5
St. Kitts and Nevis	MoF	2013	2001	CG	C	CB	2013	BPM 5
St. Lucia	MoF	2013/14	1986	CG	C	CB	2014	BPM 5

Table G. Key Data Documentation *(continued)*

Country	Currency	National Accounts					Prices (CPI)	
		Historical Data Source[1]	Latest Actual Annual Data	Base Year[2]	System of National Accounts	Use of Chain-Weighted Methodology[3]	Historical Data Source[1]	Latest Actual Annual Data
St. Vincent and the Grenadines	Eastern Caribbean dollar	NSO	2014	2006[6]	SNA 1993		NSO	2015
Sudan	Sudanese pound	NSO	2010	2007	Other		NSO	2015
Suriname	Surinamese dollar	NSO	2011	2007	SNA 1993		NSO	2014
Swaziland	Swazi lilangeni	NSO	2014	2011	SNA 1993		NSO	2014
Sweden	Swedish krona	NSO	2015	2014	ESA 2010	From 1993	NSO	2015
Switzerland	Swiss franc	NSO	2015	2010	ESA 2010	From 1980	NSO	2015
Syria	Syrian pound	NSO	2010	2000	SNA 1993		NSO	2011
Taiwan Province of China	New Taiwan dollar	NSO	2015	2011	SNA 2008		NSO	2015
Tajikistan	Tajik somoni	NSO	2014	1995	SNA 1993		NSO	2014
Tanzania	Tanzania shilling	NSO	2014	2007	SNA 1993		NSO	2015
Thailand	Thai baht	NESDB	2014	2002	SNA 1993	From 1993	MEP	2015
Timor-Leste	U.S. dollar	MoF	2013	2010[6]	Other		NSO	2014
Togo	CFA franc	MoF and NSO	2010	2000	SNA 1993		NSO	2015
Tonga	Tongan pa'anga	CB	2013	2010	SNA 1993		CB	2013
Trinidad and Tobago	Trinidad and Tobago dollar	NSO	2012	2000	SNA 1993		NSO	2013
Tunisia	Tunisian dinar	NSO	2014	2004	SNA 1993	From 2009	NSO	2014
Turkey	Turkish lira	NSO	2014	1998	ESA 1995		NSO	2015
Turkmenistan	New Turkmen manat	NSO	2014	2005	SNA 1993	From 2000	NSO	2014
Tuvalu	Australian dollar	PFTAC advisors	2012	2005	SNA 1993		NSO	2013
Uganda	Ugandan shilling	NSO	2014	2010	SNA 1993		CB	2014/15
Ukraine	Ukrainian hryvnia	NSO	2015	2010	SNA 2008	From 2005	NSO	2015
United Arab Emirates	U.A.E. dirham	NSO	2014	2007	SNA 1993		NSO	2014
United Kingdom	Pound sterling	NSO	2015	2012	ESA 2010	From 1980	NSO	2015
United States	U.S. dollar	NSO	2015	2009	Other	From 1980	NSO	2015
Uruguay	Uruguayan peso	CB	2014	2005	SNA 1993		NSO	2014
Uzbekistan	Uzbek sum	NSO	2014	1995	SNA 1993		NSO	2012
Vanuatu	Vanuatu vatu	NSO	2014	2006	SNA 1993		NSO	2015
Venezuela	Venezuelan bolívar fuerte	CB	2013	1997	SNA 2008		CB	2013
Vietnam	Vietnamese dong	NSO	2015	2010	SNA 1993		NSO	2015
Yemen	Yemeni rial	IMF staff	2008	1990	SNA 1993		NSO and CB	2009
Zambia	Zambian kwacha	NSO	2013	2010	SNA 1993		NSO	2015
Zimbabwe	U.S. dollar	NSO	2013	2009	Other		NSO	2014

Table G. Key Data Documentation *(continued)*

Country	Government Finance					Balance of Payments		
	Historical Data Source[1]	Latest Actual Annual Data	Statistics Manual in Use at Source	Subsectors Coverage[4]	Accounting Practice[5]	Historical Data Source[1]	Latest Actual Annual Data	Statistics Manual in Use at Source
St. Vincent and the Grenadines	MoF	2014	1986	CG	C	CB	2015	BPM 5
Sudan	MoF	2015	2001	CG	C/A	CB	2015	BPM 5
Suriname	MoF	2014	1986	CG	C	CB	2014	BPM 5
Swaziland	MoF	2014/15	2001	CG	A	CB	2014	BPM 6
Sweden	MoF	2015	2001	CG,LG,SS	A	NSO	2015	BPM 6
Switzerland	MoF	2013	2001	CG,SG,LG,SS	A	CB	2015	BPM 6
Syria	MoF	2009	1986	CG	C	CB	2009	BPM 5
Taiwan Province of China	MoF	2014	1986	CG,LG,SS	C	CB	2015	BPM 6
Tajikistan	MoF	2015	1986	CG,LG,SS	C	CB	2014	BPM 5
Tanzania	MoF	2014	1986	CG,LG	C	CB	2014	BPM 5
Thailand	MoF	2013/14	2001	CG,BCG,LG,SS	A	CB	2014	BPM 6
Timor-Leste	MoF	2013	2001	CG	C	CB	2014	BPM 5
Togo	MoF	2014	2001	CG	C	CB	2013	BPM 5
Tonga	CB and MoF	2012	2001	CG	C	CB and NSO	2015	BPM 6
Trinidad and Tobago	MoF	2012/13	1986	CG,NFPC	C	CB and NSO	2012	BPM 5
Tunisia	MoF	2014	1986	CG	C	CB	2014	BPM 5
Turkey	MoF	2014	2001	CG,LG,SS	A	CB	2014	BPM 6
Turkmenistan	MoF	2014	1986	CG,LG	C	NSO and IMF staff	2013	BPM 5
Tuvalu	IMF staff	2013	Other	CG	C/A	IMF staff	2013	BPM 6
Uganda	MoF	2014	2001	CG	C	CB	2014	BPM 6
Ukraine	MoF	2015	2001	CG,SG,LG,SS	C	CB	2015	BPM 6
United Arab Emirates	MoF	2014	2001	CG,BCG,SG,SS	C	CB	2014	BPM 5
United Kingdom	NSO	2014	2001	CG,LG	A	NSO	2015	BPM 6
United States	MEP	2014	2001	CG,SG,LG	A	NSO	2015	BPM 6
Uruguay	MoF	2014	1986	CG,LG,SS,MPC, NFPC	A	CB	2014	BPM 6
Uzbekistan	MoF	2014	Other	CG,SG,LG,SS	C	MEP	2014	BPM 5
Vanuatu	MoF	2015	2001	CG	C	CB	2014	BPM 5
Venezuela	MoF	2010	2001	CG,LG,SS,NFPC	C	CB	2012	BPM 5
Vietnam	MoF	2014	2001	CG,SG,LG	C	CB	2014	BPM 5
Yemen	MoF	2013	2001	CG,LG	C	IMF staff	2009	BPM 5
Zambia	MoF	2015	1986	CG	C	CB	2015	BPM 6
Zimbabwe	MoF	2014	1986	CG	C	CB and MoF	2013	BPM 4

Note: BPM = *Balance of Payments Manual* (number following abbreviation signifies edition); CPI = consumer price index; ESA = European System of National and Regional Accounts; SNA = System of National Accounts.

[1]CB = Central Bank; FEO = Foreign Exchange Office; GAD = General Administration Department; IEO = International Economic Organization; MEP = Ministry of Economy, Planning, Commerce, and/or Development; MoF = Ministry of Finance and/or Treasury; NESDB = National Economic and Social Development Board; NSO = National Statistics Office; PFTAC = Pacific Financial Technical Assistance Centre; PMO = Prime Minister's Office; SAFE = State Administration of Foreign Exchange.

[2]National accounts base year is the period with which other periods are compared and the period for which prices appear in the denominators of the price relationships used to calculate the index.

[3]Use of chain-weighted methodology allows countries to measure GDP growth more accurately by reducing or eliminating the downward biases in volume series built on index numbers that average volume components using weights from a year in the moderately distant past.

[4]For some countries, the structures of government consist of a broader coverage than specified for the general government. Coverage: BCG = Budgetary Central Government; CG = Central Government; EUA = Extrabudgetary Units/Accounts; LG = Local Government; MPC = Monetary Public Corporation, including Central Bank; NMPC = Nonmonetary Financial Public Corporations; NFPC = Nonfinancial Public Corporations; SG = State Government; SS = Social Security Funds; TG = Territorial Governments.

[5]Accounting Standard: A = Accrual; C = Cash.

[6]Nominal GDP is not measured in the same way as real GDP.

Box A1. Economic Policy Assumptions Underlying the Projections for Selected Economies

Fiscal Policy Assumptions

The short-term fiscal policy assumptions used in the *World Economic Outlook* (WEO) are based on officially announced budgets, adjusted for differences between the national authorities and the IMF staff regarding macroeconomic assumptions and projected fiscal outturns. The medium-term fiscal projections incorporate policy measures that are judged likely to be implemented. For cases in which the IMF staff has insufficient information to assess the authorities' budget intentions and prospects for policy implementation, an unchanged structural primary balance is assumed unless indicated otherwise. Specific assumptions used in regard to some of the advanced economies follow. (See also Tables B5 to B9 in the online section of the Statistical Appendix for data on fiscal net lending/borrowing and structural balances.)[1]

Argentina: Fiscal projections are based on the available information regarding budget outturn for the federal government, fiscal measures announced by the authorities, and budget plans for provinces and on IMF staff macroeconomic projections.

Australia: Fiscal projections are based on Australian Bureau of Statistics data, the Mid-Year Economic and Fiscal Outlook 2015–16, and IMF staff estimates.

Austria: For 2014, the creation of a defeasance structure for Hypo Alpe Adria is assumed to increase the general-government-debt-to-GDP ratio by 4.2 percentage points, and the deficit effect arising from Hypo is assumed to be 1.4 percentage points.

Belgium: Projections reflect the IMF staff's assessment of policies and measures laid out in the 2016 budget and the 2015–18 Stability Programme, incorporated into the IMF staff's macroeconomic framework.

---

[1] The output gap is actual minus potential output, as a percentage of potential output. Structural balances are expressed as a percentage of potential output. The structural balance is the actual net lending/borrowing minus the effects of cyclical output from potential output, corrected for one-time and other factors, such as asset and commodity prices and output composition effects. Changes in the structural balance consequently include effects of temporary fiscal measures, the impact of fluctuations in interest rates and debt-service costs, and other noncyclical fluctuations in net lending/borrowing. The computations of structural balances are based on IMF staff estimates of potential GDP and revenue and expenditure elasticities. (See Annex I of the October 1993 WEO.) Net debt is calculated as gross debt minus financial assets corresponding to debt instruments. Estimates of the output gap and of the structural balance are subject to significant margins of uncertainty.

Brazil: For 2015, outturn estimates are based on the information available as of January 2016. Projections for 2016 take into account budget performance through December 31, 2015, and the 2016 budget law approved by Congress on December 18, 2015. Projections do not include the revised target or the fiscal measures announced by the government on February 19, 2016.

Canada: Projections use the baseline forecasts in the Update of Economic and Fiscal Projections 2015 (November 2015), Backgrounder: Canadian Economic Outlook (February 2016), 2015 provincial budget updates, and 2016 provincial budgets as available. The IMF staff makes adjustments to these forecasts for differences in macroeconomic projections. The IMF staff forecast also incorporates the most recent data releases from Statistics Canada's Canadian System of National Economic Accounts, including federal, provincial, and territorial budgetary outturns through the end of 2015.

Chile: Projections are based on the authorities' budget projections, adjusted to reflect the IMF staff's projections for GDP and copper prices.

China: The pace of fiscal consolidation is likely to be more gradual, reflecting reforms to strengthen social safety nets and the social security system announced as part of the Third Plenum reform agenda.

Denmark: Projections for 2014–15 are aligned with the latest official budget estimates and the underlying economic projections, adjusted where appropriate for the IMF staff's macroeconomic assumptions. For 2016–20, the projections incorporate key features of the medium-term fiscal plan as embodied in the authorities' 2014 Convergence Programme submitted to the European Union (EU).

France: Projections for 2016 reflect the budget law. For 2017–18, they are based on the multiyear budget and the April 2015 Stability Programme, adjusted for differences in assumptions on macro and financial variables, and revenue projections. Historical fiscal data reflect the statistical institute's May 2015 revision and update of the fiscal accounts and national accounts.

Germany: The IMF staff's projections for 2016 and beyond reflect the authorities' adopted core federal government budget plan and the German Stability Programme: 2015 Update, adjusted for the differences in the IMF staff's macroeconomic framework. The estimate of gross debt includes portfolios of impaired assets and noncore business transferred to institutions

Box A1 *(continued)*

that are winding up, as well as other financial sector and EU support operations.

Greece: For 2015, data reflect the IMF staff's preliminary estimates of the fiscal outturn, which are subject to revision, given high uncertainty regarding potentially significant accrual adjustments. Fiscal projections are not available at this time, given ongoing negotiations with the authorities and European partners on the fiscal targets and underlying fiscal measures that could be included in a potential new adjustment program.

Hong Kong SAR: Projections are based on the authorities' medium-term fiscal projections on expenditures.

Hungary: Fiscal projections include IMF staff projections of the macroeconomic framework and of the impact of recent legislative measures, as well as fiscal policy plans announced in the 2016 budget.

India: Historical data are based on budgetary execution data. Projections are based on available information on the authorities' fiscal plans, with adjustments for IMF staff assumptions. Subnational data are incorporated with a lag of up to two years; general government data are thus finalized well after central government data. IMF and Indian presentations differ, particularly regarding divestment and license auction proceeds, net versus gross recording of revenues in certain minor categories, and some public sector lending.

Indonesia: IMF projections are based on moderate tax policy and administration reforms, fuel subsidy pricing reforms introduced in January 2015, and a gradual increase in social and capital spending over the medium term in line with fiscal space.

Ireland: Fiscal projections are based on the 2015 budget, adjusted for differences between the IMF staff's macroeconomic projections and those of the Irish authorities.

Italy: IMF staff estimates and projections are based on the fiscal plans included in the government's 2016 budget. Estimates of the cyclically adjusted balance include the expenditures to clear capital arrears in 2013, which are excluded from the structural balance. After 2016, the IMF staff projects convergence to a structural balance in line with Italy's fiscal rule, which implies corrective measures in some years, as yet unidentified.

Japan: The projections include fiscal measures already announced by the government, including the consumption tax increase with a reduced rate in April 2017, earthquake reconstruction spending, and the stimulus package.

Korea: The medium-term forecast incorporates the government's announced medium-term consolidation path.

Mexico: Fiscal projections for 2015 are broadly in line with the approved budget; projections for 2016 onward assume compliance with rules established in the Fiscal Responsibility Law.

Netherlands: Fiscal projections for the period 2016–21 are based on the authorities' Bureau for Economic Policy Analysis budget projections, after differences in macroeconomic assumptions are adjusted for. Historical data were revised following the June 2014 Central Bureau of Statistics release of revised macro data because of the adoption of the European System of National and Regional Accounts (ESA 2010) and the revisions of data sources.

New Zealand: Fiscal projections are based on the authorities' 2015 Half Year Economic and Fiscal Update and on IMF staff estimates.

Portugal: The estimate for 2015 reflects the cash outturn and January through September data on a national accounts basis; the projection for 2016 reflects the authorities' draft budget and the IMF staff's macroeconomic forecast. Projections thereafter are based on the assumption of unchanged policies.

Russia: Projections for 2016–18 are IMF staff estimates. Projections for 2019–21 are based on the oil-price-based fiscal rule introduced in December 2012, with adjustments by the IMF staff.

Saudi Arabia: IMF staff projections of oil revenues are based on WEO baseline oil prices. On the expenditure side, wage bill estimates incorporate 13th-month pay awards every three years in accordance with the lunar calendar. Expenditure projections take the 2016 budget as a starting point and assume that, to adjust to lower oil prices, capital spending falls as a percentage of GDP over the medium term.

Singapore: For fiscal years 2014/15 and 2015/16, projections are based on budget numbers. For the remainder of the projection period, the IMF staff assumes unchanged policies.

South Africa: Fiscal projections are based on the authorities' 2016 Budget Review.

Spain: For 2015 and beyond, fiscal projections are based on the measures specified in the Stability Programme Update 2015–18, other measures included in the 2016 budget approved in October 2015, and the 2015 budget approved in December 2014.

Box A1 *(continued)*

Sweden: Fiscal projections take into account the authorities' projections based on the Budget Bill for 2016. The impact of cyclical developments on the fiscal accounts is calculated using the Organisation for Economic Co-operation and Development's 2005 elasticity to take into account output and employment gaps.

Switzerland: The projections assume that fiscal policy is adjusted as necessary to keep fiscal balances in line with the requirements of Switzerland's fiscal rules.

Turkey: Fiscal projections assume that both current and capital spending will be in line with the authorities' 2014–16 Medium Term Programme based on current trends and policies.

United Kingdom: Fiscal projections are based on the 2016 budget, published in March 2016. However, on the revenue side, the authorities' projections are adjusted for differences between IMF staff forecasts of macroeconomic variables (such as GDP growth) and the forecasts of these variables assumed in the authorities' fiscal projections. IMF staff data exclude public sector banks and the effect of transferring assets from the Royal Mail Pension Plan to the public sector in April 2012. Real government consumption and investment are part of the real GDP path, which, according to the IMF staff, may or may not be the same as projected by the U.K. Office for Budget Responsibility.

United States: Fiscal projections are based on the January 2016 Congressional Budget Office baseline adjusted for the IMF staff's policy and macroeconomic assumptions. The baseline incorporates the key provisions of the Bipartisan Budget Act of 2015, including a partial rollback of the sequester spending cuts in fiscal year 2016. In fiscal years 2017 through 2021, the IMF staff assumes that the sequester cuts will continue to be partially replaced, in proportions similar to those already implemented in fiscal years 2014 and 2015, with back-loaded measures generating savings in mandatory programs and additional revenues. Projections also incorporate the Protecting Americans from Tax Hikes Act of 2015, which extended some existing tax cuts for the short term and some permanently. Finally, fiscal projections are adjusted to reflect the IMF staff's forecasts for key macroeconomic and financial variables and different accounting treatment of financial sector support and of defined-benefit pension plans

and are converted to a general government basis. Historical data start at 2001 for most series because data compiled according to the 2001 *Government Finance Statistics Manual* (GFSM 2001) may not be available for earlier years.

Monetary Policy Assumptions

Monetary policy assumptions are based on the established policy framework in each country. In most cases, this implies a nonaccommodative stance over the business cycle: official interest rates will increase when economic indicators suggest that inflation will rise above its acceptable rate or range; they will decrease when indicators suggest that inflation will not exceed the acceptable rate or range, that output growth is below its potential rate, and that the margin of slack in the economy is significant. On this basis, the London interbank offered rate (LIBOR) on six-month U.S. dollar deposits is assumed to average 0.9 percent in 2016 and 1.5 percent in 2017 (see Table 1.1). The rate on three-month euro deposits is assumed to average –0.3 percent in 2016 and –0.4 percent in 2017. The interest rate on six-month Japanese yen deposits is assumed to average –0.1 percent in 2016 and –0.3 percent in 2017.

Australia: Monetary policy assumptions are in line with market expectations.

Brazil: Monetary policy assumptions are consistent with gradual convergence of inflation toward the middle of the target range over the relevant horizon.

Canada: Monetary policy assumptions are in line with market expectations.

China: Monetary policy will remain broadly unchanged from its current status, consistent with the authorities' announcement of maintaining stable economic growth.

Denmark: The monetary policy is to maintain the peg to the euro.

Euro area: Monetary policy assumptions for euro area member countries are in line with market expectations.

Hong Kong SAR: The IMF staff assumes that the currency board system remains intact.

India: The policy (interest) rate assumption is consistent with an inflation rate within the Reserve Bank of India's targeted band.

Indonesia: Monetary policy assumptions are in line with a reduction of inflation to within the central bank's targeted band by the end of 2015.

Box A1 *(continued)*

Japan: The current monetary policy conditions are maintained for the projection period, and no further tightening or loosening is assumed.

Korea: Monetary policy assumptions are in line with market expectations.

Mexico: Monetary assumptions are consistent with attaining the inflation target.

Russia: Monetary projections assume increasing exchange rate flexibility as part of the transition to the new full-fledged inflation-targeting regime, as indicated in recent statements by the Central Bank of Russia. Specifically, policy rates are assumed to remain at the current levels, gradually reducing the number of interventions in the foreign exchange markets.

Saudi Arabia: Monetary policy projections are based on the continuation of the exchange rate peg to the U.S. dollar.

Singapore: Broad money is projected to grow in line with the projected growth in nominal GDP.

South Africa: Monetary projections are consistent with South Africa's 3–6 percent inflation target range.

Sweden: Monetary projections are in line with Riksbank projections.

Switzerland: The projections assume no change in the policy rate in 2016–17.

Turkey: Broad money and the long-term bond yield are based on IMF staff projections. The short-term deposit rate is projected to evolve with a constant spread against the interest rate of a similar U.S. instrument.

United Kingdom: Projections assume no change in monetary policy or the level of asset purchases until 2019, consistent with market expectations.

United States: Following the Federal Reserve's 25 basis point rate hike in mid-December, financial conditions have tightened more than expected, and wage growth has yet to exert significant price pressure. The IMF staff expects the federal funds target rate to increase by 50 basis points in 2016 and rise gradually thereafter.

List of Tables

Table A1. Summary of World Output[1]
(Annual percent change)

	Average 1998–2007	2008	2009	2010	2011	2012	2013	2014	2015	Projections 2016	2017	2021
World	**4.2**	**3.0**	**−0.1**	**5.4**	**4.2**	**3.5**	**3.3**	**3.4**	**3.1**	**3.2**	**3.5**	**3.9**
Advanced Economies	**2.8**	**0.2**	**−3.4**	**3.1**	**1.7**	**1.2**	**1.2**	**1.8**	**1.9**	**1.9**	**2.0**	**1.8**
United States	3.0	−0.3	−2.8	2.5	1.6	2.2	1.5	2.4	2.4	2.4	2.5	2.0
Euro Area	2.4	0.5	−4.5	2.1	1.6	−0.9	−0.3	0.9	1.6	1.5	1.6	1.5
Japan	1.0	−1.0	−5.5	4.7	−0.5	1.7	1.4	0.0	0.5	0.5	−0.1	0.7
Other Advanced Economies[2]	3.6	1.1	−2.0	4.5	3.0	1.9	2.3	2.8	1.9	2.0	2.3	2.4
Emerging Market and Developing Economies	**5.8**	**5.8**	**3.0**	**7.4**	**6.3**	**5.3**	**4.9**	**4.6**	**4.0**	**4.1**	**4.6**	**5.1**
Regional Groups												
Commonwealth of Independent States[3]	6.2	5.3	−6.4	4.6	4.8	3.5	2.1	1.1	−2.8	−1.1	1.3	2.4
Emerging and Developing Asia	7.6	7.2	7.5	9.6	7.8	6.9	6.9	6.8	6.6	6.4	6.3	6.4
Emerging and Developing Europe	4.2	3.1	−3.0	4.7	5.4	1.2	2.8	2.8	3.5	3.5	3.3	3.3
Latin America and the Caribbean	3.1	3.9	−1.2	6.1	4.9	3.2	3.0	1.3	−0.1	−0.5	1.5	2.8
Middle East, North Africa, Afghanistan, and Pakistan	5.3	4.8	1.5	4.9	4.5	5.0	2.3	2.8	2.5	3.1	3.5	3.8
Middle East and North Africa	5.3	4.8	1.5	5.2	4.6	5.1	2.1	2.6	2.3	2.9	3.3	3.6
Sub-Saharan Africa	5.3	6.0	4.0	6.6	5.0	4.3	5.2	5.1	3.4	3.0	4.0	5.0
Memorandum												
European Union	2.7	0.7	−4.3	2.0	1.8	−0.4	0.3	1.4	2.0	1.8	1.9	1.8
Low-Income Developing Countries	6.1	5.9	5.9	7.1	5.3	5.2	6.1	6.1	4.5	4.7	5.5	5.8
Analytical Groups												
By Source of Export Earnings												
Fuel	5.6	5.1	−1.4	5.1	5.0	4.8	2.5	2.4	0.1	0.8	2.1	2.8
Nonfuel	5.9	6.0	4.3	8.1	6.6	5.4	5.6	5.2	5.0	4.9	5.2	5.6
Of Which, Primary Products	3.8	3.8	1.0	6.5	5.6	3.1	4.0	2.5	2.4	1.4	2.9	3.6
By External Financing Source												
Net Debtor Economies	4.7	4.4	2.1	6.8	5.1	4.2	4.5	4.1	3.7	3.9	4.6	5.3
Net Debtor Economies by Debt-Servicing Experience												
Economies with Arrears and/or Rescheduling during 2010–14	5.7	5.3	−0.4	3.6	3.1	1.9	2.3	0.9	1.0	2.4	3.2	4.5
Memorandum												
Median Growth Rate												
Advanced Economies	3.5	0.8	−3.8	2.3	2.0	1.1	1.4	2.2	1.6	1.8	2.2	2.1
Emerging Market and Developing Economies	4.6	5.0	1.7	4.5	4.5	4.1	4.0	3.7	3.0	3.2	3.5	4.0
Low-Income Developing Countries	4.7	5.6	3.9	6.2	5.8	5.2	5.4	5.3	4.0	4.4	4.8	5.4
Output per Capita												
Advanced Economies	2.1	−0.6	−4.0	2.5	1.2	0.7	0.6	1.2	1.3	1.2	1.4	1.3
Emerging Market and Developing Economies	4.4	4.2	1.8	6.3	5.1	4.0	3.8	3.3	2.9	3.0	3.6	4.1
Low-Income Developing Countries	3.8	3.8	3.7	4.9	4.1	2.9	4.0	4.0	2.5	2.6	3.5	3.9
World Growth Rate Based on Market Exchange Rates	**3.1**	**1.5**	**−2.0**	**4.1**	**3.0**	**2.5**	**2.4**	**2.7**	**2.4**	**2.5**	**2.9**	**3.1**
Value of World Output (billions of U.S. dollars)												
At Market Exchange Rates	40,305	63,268	59,921	65,571	72,681	74,186	75,905	77,825	73,171	73,994	77,779	96,387
At Purchasing Power Parities	58,506	83,014	83,351	88,830	94,337	99,089	103,919	109,143	113,524	118,170	123,973	155,752

[1]Real GDP.
[2]Excludes the United States, euro area countries, and Japan.
[3]Georgia, Turkmenistan, and Ukraine, which are not members of the Commonwealth of Independent States, are included in this group for reasons of geography and similarity in economic structure.

Table A2. Advanced Economies: Real GDP and Total Domestic Demand[1]

(Annual percent change)

	Average 1998–2007	2008	2009	2010	2011	2012	2013	2014	2015	Projections 2016	Projections 2017	Projections 2021	Fourth Quarter[2] 2015:Q4	Fourth Quarter[2] Projections 2016:Q4	Fourth Quarter[2] Projections 2017:Q4
Real GDP															
Advanced Economies	**2.8**	**0.2**	**−3.4**	**3.1**	**1.7**	**1.2**	**1.2**	**1.8**	**1.9**	**1.9**	**2.0**	**1.8**	**1.8**	**2.1**	**1.9**
United States	3.0	−0.3	−2.8	2.5	1.6	2.2	1.5	2.4	2.4	2.4	2.5	2.0	2.0	2.6	2.4
Euro Area	2.4	0.5	−4.5	2.1	1.6	−0.9	−0.3	0.9	1.6	1.5	1.6	1.5	1.6	1.6	1.5
Germany	1.7	0.8	−5.6	3.9	3.7	0.6	0.4	1.6	1.5	1.5	1.6	1.2	1.3	1.6	1.6
France	2.4	0.2	−2.9	2.0	2.1	0.2	0.7	0.2	1.1	1.1	1.3	1.9	1.4	1.3	1.0
Italy	1.5	−1.1	−5.5	1.7	0.6	−2.8	−1.7	−0.3	0.8	1.0	1.1	0.8	1.0	1.3	1.0
Spain	3.9	1.1	−3.6	0.0	−1.0	−2.6	−1.7	1.4	3.2	2.6	2.3	1.6	3.5	2.1	2.5
Netherlands	2.8	1.7	−3.8	1.4	1.7	−1.1	−0.5	1.0	1.9	1.8	1.9	2.1	1.0	2.6	1.2
Belgium	2.4	0.7	−2.3	2.7	1.8	0.2	0.0	1.3	1.4	1.2	1.4	1.4	1.4	1.2	1.5
Austria	2.6	1.5	−3.8	1.9	2.8	0.8	0.3	0.4	0.9	1.2	1.4	1.1	1.2	1.6	1.3
Greece	3.9	−0.3	−4.3	−5.5	−9.1	−7.3	−3.2	0.7	−0.2	−0.6	2.7	1.5	−0.8	0.5	3.2
Portugal	2.1	0.2	−3.0	1.9	−1.8	−4.0	−1.1	0.9	1.5	1.4	1.3	1.2	1.3	1.6	1.2
Ireland	6.8	−2.2	−5.6	0.4	2.6	0.2	1.4	5.2	7.8	5.0	3.6	2.7	9.3	2.1	5.7
Finland	3.8	0.7	−8.3	3.0	2.6	−1.4	−0.8	−0.7	0.4	0.9	1.1	1.6	0.7	1.3	1.0
Slovak Republic	4.9	5.7	−5.5	5.1	2.8	1.5	1.4	2.5	3.6	3.3	3.4	3.2	4.0	3.4	3.5
Lithuania	6.7	2.6	−14.8	1.6	6.0	3.8	3.5	3.0	1.6	2.7	3.1	3.3	2.7	−0.4	−9.5
Slovenia	4.3	3.3	−7.8	1.2	0.6	−2.7	−1.1	3.0	2.9	1.9	2.0	1.5	2.6	1.6	2.2
Luxembourg	5.1	−0.8	−5.4	5.7	2.6	−0.8	4.3	4.1	4.5	3.5	3.4	3.0	1.1	5.5	2.2
Latvia	7.7	−3.6	−14.3	−3.8	6.2	4.0	3.0	2.4	2.7	3.2	3.6	4.0	2.5	4.5	3.5
Estonia	6.7	−5.4	−14.7	2.5	7.6	5.2	1.6	2.9	1.1	2.2	2.8	3.4	0.8	2.4	3.0
Cyprus	4.3	3.7	−2.0	1.4	0.4	−2.4	−5.9	−2.5	1.6	1.6	2.0	2.0	2.7	1.5	2.3
Malta	2.2	3.3	−2.5	3.6	2.0	2.9	4.0	4.1	5.4	3.5	3.0	2.8	3.5	3.6	2.8
Japan	1.0	−1.0	−5.5	4.7	−0.5	1.7	1.4	0.0	0.5	0.5	−0.1	0.7	0.8	1.1	−0.8
United Kingdom	3.0	−0.5	−4.2	1.5	2.0	1.2	2.2	2.9	2.2	1.9	2.2	2.1	1.9	2.0	2.2
Korea	4.8	2.8	0.7	6.5	3.7	2.3	2.9	3.3	2.6	2.7	2.9	3.0	3.0	2.4	3.0
Canada	3.2	1.0	−2.9	3.1	3.1	1.7	2.2	2.5	1.2	1.5	1.9	2.0	0.5	1.7	2.0
Australia	3.6	2.6	1.8	2.3	2.7	3.5	2.0	2.6	2.5	2.5	3.0	2.8	3.0	2.3	3.2
Taiwan Province of China	5.0	0.7	−1.6	10.6	3.8	2.1	2.2	3.9	0.7	1.5	2.2	2.9	−0.1	1.2	2.3
Switzerland	2.4	2.2	−2.1	2.9	1.9	1.1	1.8	1.9	0.9	1.2	1.5	1.8	0.3	1.5	1.5
Sweden	3.5	−0.6	−5.2	6.0	2.7	−0.3	1.2	2.3	4.1	3.7	2.8	2.1	4.5	2.7	2.9
Singapore	5.5	1.8	−0.6	15.2	6.2	3.7	4.7	3.3	2.0	1.8	2.2	2.8	1.7	1.8	2.2
Hong Kong SAR	3.8	2.1	−2.5	6.8	4.8	1.7	3.1	2.6	2.4	2.2	2.4	3.1	2.0	2.7	2.0
Norway	2.4	0.4	−1.6	0.6	1.0	2.7	1.0	2.2	1.6	1.0	1.5	2.1	0.3	2.0	1.0
Czech Republic	3.7	2.7	−4.8	2.3	2.0	−0.9	−0.5	2.0	4.2	2.5	2.4	2.2	4.0	3.2	2.0
Israel	3.9	3.1	1.3	5.5	5.0	2.9	3.3	2.6	2.6	2.8	3.0	2.9	2.4	2.9	3.2
Denmark	2.0	−0.7	−5.1	1.6	1.2	−0.1	−0.2	1.3	1.2	1.6	1.8	2.1	0.6	2.6	1.8
New Zealand	3.5	−0.4	0.3	2.0	1.8	2.8	1.7	3.0	3.4	2.0	2.5	2.4	3.7	0.8	2.9
Puerto Rico	2.5	−1.8	−2.0	−0.4	−0.4	0.0	0.0	−0.1	−1.3	−1.3	−1.4	−0.5	. . .	. . .	. . .
Macao SAR	5.0	3.4	1.3	25.3	21.7	9.2	11.2	−0.9	−20.3	−7.2	0.7	3.0	. . .	. . .	. . .
Iceland	4.6	1.5	−4.7	−3.6	2.0	1.2	4.4	2.0	4.0	4.2	3.2	2.4	2.7	7.6	2.7
San Marino	. . .	1.7	−12.8	−4.6	−9.5	−7.5	−3.0	−1.0	1.0	1.1	1.2	1.3	. . .	. . .	. . .
Memorandum															
Major Advanced Economies	2.4	−0.3	−3.8	2.8	1.6	1.4	1.2	1.7	1.8	1.8	1.9	1.7	1.6	2.1	1.7
Real Total Domestic Demand															
Advanced Economies	**2.8**	**−0.3**	**−3.7**	**3.0**	**1.4**	**0.8**	**0.9**	**1.8**	**2.1**	**2.0**	**2.1**	**2.0**	**2.1**	**2.3**	**2.0**
United States	3.4	−1.3	−3.8	2.9	1.6	2.1	1.2	2.5	3.0	2.8	2.9	2.2	2.5	3.2	2.7
Euro Area	2.4	0.3	−3.9	1.5	0.7	−2.4	−0.7	0.9	1.8	1.7	1.7	1.5	2.2	1.3	1.7
Germany	1.0	1.0	−3.2	2.9	3.0	−0.9	0.9	1.3	1.4	2.1	1.9	1.6	1.8	2.0	1.9
France	2.7	0.5	−2.5	2.1	2.0	−0.3	0.7	0.6	1.4	1.3	1.4	1.8	2.4	0.5	1.6
Italy	1.8	−1.2	−4.1	2.0	−0.6	−5.6	−2.6	−0.4	1.1	1.1	1.2	0.7	1.9	1.1	1.2
Spain	4.9	−0.4	−6.0	−0.5	−3.1	−4.7	−3.1	1.6	3.8	2.8	2.1	1.2	4.3	2.2	2.2
Japan	0.6	−1.3	−4.0	2.9	0.4	2.6	1.7	0.0	0.0	0.4	0.0	0.6	0.8	1.3	−0.9
United Kingdom	3.5	−1.6	−4.7	2.2	−0.2	2.3	2.6	3.2	2.7	1.9	2.2	2.2	2.7	1.6	2.3
Canada	3.4	2.6	−3.0	5.1	3.4	2.0	1.9	1.3	0.2	0.3	1.8	2.0	−1.2	1.6	1.8
Other Advanced Economies[3]	3.4	1.5	−2.7	6.1	3.1	1.9	1.4	2.4	2.2	2.2	2.5	2.9	2.2	2.2	2.8
Memorandum															
Major Advanced Economies	2.5	−0.8	−3.7	2.8	1.4	1.2	1.1	1.7	2.0	2.0	2.1	1.8	2.0	2.3	1.9

[1]In this and other tables, when countries are not listed alphabetically, they are ordered on the basis of economic size.
[2]From the fourth quarter of the preceding year.
[3]Excludes the G7 (Canada, France, Germany, Italy, Japan, United Kingdom, United States) and euro area countries.

Table A3. Advanced Economies: Components of Real GDP
(Annual percent change)

| | Averages | | 2008 | 2009 | 2010 | 2011 | 2012 | 2013 | 2014 | 2015 | Projections | |
	1998–2007	2008–17									2016	2017
Private Consumer Expenditure												
Advanced Economies	**2.9**	**1.2**	**0.1**	**−1.2**	**1.9**	**1.4**	**0.9**	**1.2**	**1.7**	**2.2**	**2.1**	**2.1**
United States	3.7	1.7	−0.3	−1.6	1.9	2.3	1.5	1.7	2.7	3.1	2.9	2.7
Euro Area	2.1	0.4	0.3	−1.1	0.8	0.0	−1.2	−0.6	0.8	1.7	1.6	1.6
Germany	0.9	1.0	0.5	0.3	0.3	1.3	0.9	0.8	1.0	1.9	1.6	1.7
France	2.7	0.8	0.4	0.2	1.8	0.5	−0.2	0.4	0.6	1.4	1.5	1.5
Italy	1.4	−0.4	−1.1	−1.5	1.2	0.0	−4.0	−2.4	0.6	0.9	1.0	1.1
Spain	3.9	−0.4	−0.7	−3.6	0.3	−2.4	−3.5	−3.1	1.2	3.1	3.0	2.3
Japan	0.9	0.3	−0.9	−0.7	2.8	0.3	2.3	1.7	−0.9	−1.3	0.3	−0.2
United Kingdom	3.7	1.0	−0.7	−3.2	0.0	0.1	1.8	1.9	2.5	2.9	2.4	2.3
Canada	3.5	2.1	2.9	0.0	3.6	2.3	1.9	2.4	2.5	1.9	1.4	1.9
Other Advanced Economies[1]	3.5	2.2	1.1	0.0	3.7	3.0	2.1	2.3	2.3	2.6	2.5	2.7
Memorandum												
Major Advanced Economies	2.7	1.2	−0.2	−1.2	1.7	1.4	1.1	1.3	1.7	2.1	2.1	2.0
Public Consumption												
Advanced Economies	**2.2**	**1.0**	**2.3**	**3.0**	**0.9**	**−0.6**	**0.2**	**−0.3**	**0.6**	**1.2**	**1.4**	**1.0**
United States	2.0	0.3	2.5	3.7	0.1	−2.7	−0.9	−2.5	−0.5	0.4	1.3	1.2
Euro Area	1.9	0.9	2.4	2.4	0.8	−0.1	−0.2	0.2	0.8	1.3	1.1	0.7
Germany	0.9	1.9	3.4	3.0	1.3	0.9	1.3	0.8	1.7	2.4	2.5	1.6
France	1.4	1.4	1.1	2.4	1.3	1.0	1.6	1.7	1.5	1.6	0.9	0.4
Italy	1.4	−0.3	1.0	0.4	0.6	−1.8	−1.4	−0.3	−1.0	−0.7	0.8	−0.1
Spain	4.9	0.7	5.9	4.1	1.5	−0.3	−4.5	−2.8	0.0	2.7	0.6	0.3
Japan	2.1	1.0	−0.1	2.3	1.9	1.2	1.7	1.9	0.1	1.1	1.2	−1.1
United Kingdom	3.0	1.1	2.2	1.2	0.2	0.1	1.8	0.5	2.5	1.7	0.1	0.6
Canada	2.4	1.5	3.8	2.7	2.3	1.3	0.7	0.3	0.3	1.4	1.1	1.4
Other Advanced Economies[1]	2.8	2.4	2.9	3.4	2.8	1.5	2.0	2.2	2.2	2.5	2.3	2.2
Memorandum												
Major Advanced Economies	1.9	0.7	2.1	2.9	0.7	−1.0	0.1	−0.7	0.2	0.9	1.3	0.8
Gross Fixed Capital Formation												
Advanced Economies	**3.1**	**0.4**	**−2.7**	**−11.1**	**1.9**	**2.9**	**2.3**	**0.9**	**2.8**	**2.5**	**2.5**	**3.2**
United States	3.7	1.0	−4.8	−13.1	1.1	3.7	6.3	2.4	4.1	3.7	3.6	4.4
Euro Area	3.3	−0.8	−0.7	−11.2	−0.3	1.6	−3.3	−2.6	1.3	2.7	2.6	2.8
Germany	1.3	1.1	0.8	−9.9	5.0	7.4	0.1	−1.3	3.5	1.7	2.2	2.3
France	3.9	−0.3	0.8	−9.1	2.1	2.1	0.2	−0.6	−1.2	−0.2	1.1	2.1
Italy	3.0	−3.0	−3.1	−9.9	−0.5	−1.9	−9.3	−6.6	−3.4	0.8	1.9	2.6
Spain	6.9	−2.7	−3.9	−16.9	−4.9	−6.9	−7.1	−2.5	3.5	6.4	4.5	2.9
Japan	−1.1	−0.5	−4.1	−10.6	−0.2	1.4	3.4	2.5	1.3	−0.1	0.8	0.9
United Kingdom	3.2	0.7	−5.9	−14.4	5.0	2.0	1.5	2.6	7.3	4.2	2.5	3.9
Canada	5.1	0.6	1.5	−11.8	11.4	4.6	4.9	−0.4	0.7	−3.6	−1.9	1.8
Other Advanced Economies[1]	3.7	1.7	0.0	−5.2	6.0	4.0	2.9	2.3	1.9	1.1	1.6	2.7
Memorandum												
Major Advanced Economies	2.7	0.4	−3.4	−11.9	2.0	3.2	3.3	1.1	2.9	2.2	2.5	3.3

Table A3. Advanced Economies: Components of Real GDP *(continued)*

(Annual percent change)

	Averages		2008	2009	2010	2011	2012	2013	2014	2015	Projections	
	1998–2007	2008–17									2016	2017
Final Domestic Demand												
Advanced Economies	**2.8**	**1.0**	**−0.2**	**−2.6**	**1.7**	**1.3**	**1.0**	**0.9**	**1.7**	**2.1**	**2.1**	**2.1**
United States	3.4	1.3	−0.9	−3.1	1.5	1.7	1.9	1.2	2.5	2.8	2.8	2.8
Euro Area	2.3	0.2	0.5	−2.7	0.5	0.3	−1.5	−0.9	0.9	1.8	1.7	1.6
Germany	1.0	1.2	1.1	−1.4	1.4	2.5	0.8	0.3	1.7	1.9	1.9	1.8
France	2.6	0.7	0.7	−1.5	1.8	0.9	0.3	0.5	0.5	1.1	1.3	1.4
Italy	1.8	−0.9	−1.2	−2.9	0.7	−0.8	−4.5	−2.7	−0.4	0.6	1.1	1.1
Spain	4.9	−0.8	−0.5	−5.9	−0.7	−3.0	−4.5	−2.9	1.4	3.7	2.9	2.0
Japan	0.6	0.3	−1.6	−2.3	2.0	0.7	2.4	1.9	−0.3	−0.5	0.6	−0.2
United Kingdom	3.5	0.9	−1.1	−4.2	0.8	0.4	1.8	1.7	3.2	2.9	2.0	2.2
Canada	3.7	1.6	2.8	−2.2	5.0	2.6	2.4	1.3	1.6	0.5	0.6	1.8
Other Advanced Economies[1]	3.3	2.1	1.1	−0.7	4.3	2.9	2.2	2.2	2.2	2.3	2.3	2.6
Memorandum												
Major Advanced Economies	2.6	1.0	−0.5	−2.7	1.6	1.4	1.3	0.9	1.7	1.9	2.0	2.0
Stock Building[2]												
Advanced Economies	**0.0**	**0.0**	**−0.2**	**−1.1**	**1.3**	**0.1**	**−0.2**	**0.0**	**0.1**	**0.1**	**0.0**	**0.0**
United States	0.0	0.1	−0.5	−0.8	1.5	−0.1	0.1	0.1	0.1	0.2	0.0	0.0
Euro Area	0.0	−0.1	−0.2	−1.2	0.9	0.4	−0.9	0.2	0.0	0.0	0.0	0.0
Germany	0.0	−0.2	−0.1	−1.7	1.4	0.5	−1.6	0.5	−0.3	−0.5	0.2	0.1
France	0.1	0.0	−0.2	−1.1	0.3	1.1	−0.6	0.2	0.2	0.3	0.0	0.0
Italy	0.0	0.0	−0.1	−1.2	1.3	0.2	−1.1	0.2	0.0	0.5	−0.1	0.0
Spain	0.0	0.0	0.1	−0.2	0.2	−0.1	−0.3	−0.3	0.3	0.1	−0.1	0.0
Japan	0.0	0.0	0.2	−1.5	0.9	−0.2	0.2	−0.2	0.2	0.5	−0.1	0.1
United Kingdom	0.0	0.1	−0.5	−0.5	1.5	−0.6	0.4	0.7	0.2	−0.4	0.2	0.0
Canada	0.0	0.0	0.0	−0.7	0.1	0.7	−0.3	0.5	−0.4	−0.2	−0.3	0.1
Other Advanced Economies[1]	0.1	0.0	0.3	−1.9	1.9	0.2	−0.3	−0.8	0.3	0.0	0.0	−0.1
Memorandum												
Major Advanced Economies	0.0	0.0	−0.3	−1.0	1.2	0.0	−0.2	0.2	0.0	0.1	0.0	0.1
Foreign Balance[2]												
Advanced Economies	**−0.1**	**0.1**	**0.5**	**0.3**	**0.1**	**0.3**	**0.4**	**0.3**	**0.0**	**−0.3**	**−0.2**	**−0.2**
United States	−0.5	0.0	1.1	1.2	−0.5	0.0	0.1	0.2	−0.2	−0.6	−0.5	−0.5
Euro Area	0.1	0.3	0.1	−0.6	0.6	0.9	1.5	0.4	0.0	−0.1	−0.2	0.0
Germany	0.6	0.0	−0.1	−2.6	1.1	0.9	1.5	−0.4	0.4	0.1	−0.5	−0.2
France	−0.3	−0.1	−0.3	−0.4	−0.1	−0.1	0.5	0.0	−0.5	−0.2	−0.2	−0.1
Italy	−0.3	0.3	0.2	−1.3	−0.3	1.2	2.8	0.8	0.1	−0.3	−0.1	0.1
Spain	−0.9	1.0	1.6	2.8	0.5	2.1	2.1	1.4	−0.2	−0.5	−0.1	0.2
Japan	0.4	−0.1	0.2	−2.0	2.0	−0.8	−0.8	−0.2	0.3	0.4	0.0	0.0
United Kingdom	−0.5	−0.1	0.9	0.3	−0.9	1.5	−0.7	−0.5	−0.4	−0.5	−0.3	0.0
Canada	−0.3	−0.1	−1.9	0.0	−2.1	−0.3	−0.4	0.4	1.1	0.9	1.1	0.1
Other Advanced Economies[1]	0.6	0.4	0.3	1.5	0.1	0.5	0.5	0.8	0.4	−0.2	0.0	0.1
Memorandum												
Major Advanced Economies	−0.2	0.0	0.5	−0.1	0.0	0.2	0.2	0.0	0.0	−0.3	−0.3	−0.3

[1]Excludes the G7 (Canada, France, Germany, Italy, Japan, United Kingdom, United States) and euro area countries.
[2]Changes expressed as percent of GDP in the preceding period.

Table A4. Emerging Market and Developing Economies: Real GDP

(Annual percent change)

	Average 1998–2007	2008	2009	2010	2011	2012	2013	2014	2015	Projections 2016	2017	2021
Commonwealth of Independent States[1,2]	**6.2**	**5.3**	**−6.4**	**4.6**	**4.8**	**3.5**	**2.1**	**1.1**	**−2.8**	**−1.1**	**1.3**	**2.4**
Russia	5.8	5.2	−7.8	4.5	4.3	3.5	1.3	0.7	−3.7	−1.8	0.8	1.5
Excluding Russia	7.5	5.6	−2.5	5.0	6.2	3.6	4.2	1.9	−0.6	0.9	2.3	4.2
Armenia	10.4	6.9	−14.1	2.2	4.7	7.1	3.3	3.5	3.0	1.9	2.5	4.0
Azerbaijan	14.1	10.8	9.3	5.0	0.1	2.2	5.8	2.8	1.1	−3.0	1.0	1.8
Belarus	7.3	10.3	0.1	7.7	5.5	1.7	1.0	1.6	−3.9	−2.7	0.4	1.2
Georgia	6.6	2.4	−3.7	6.2	7.2	6.4	3.4	4.6	2.8	2.5	4.5	5.0
Kazakhstan	8.1	3.3	1.2	7.3	7.5	5.0	6.0	4.3	1.2	0.1	1.0	4.9
Kyrgyz Republic	4.2	7.6	2.9	−0.5	6.0	−0.9	10.5	3.6	3.5	3.5	2.7	4.5
Moldova	3.4	7.8	−6.0	7.1	6.8	−0.7	9.4	4.8	−1.1	0.5	2.5	3.8
Tajikistan	7.9	7.9	3.9	6.5	7.4	7.5	7.4	6.7	3.0	3.0	3.5	4.5
Turkmenistan	14.4	14.7	6.1	9.2	14.7	11.1	10.2	10.3	6.5	4.3	4.5	6.2
Ukraine[3]	5.8	2.2	−15.1	0.3	5.5	0.2	0.0	−6.6	−9.9	1.5	2.5	4.0
Uzbekistan	5.6	9.0	8.1	8.5	8.3	8.2	8.0	8.1	8.0	5.0	5.5	6.0
Emerging and Developing Asia	**7.6**	**7.2**	**7.5**	**9.6**	**7.8**	**6.9**	**6.9**	**6.8**	**6.6**	**6.4**	**6.3**	**6.4**
Bangladesh	5.7	5.5	5.3	6.0	6.5	6.3	6.0	6.3	6.4	6.6	6.9	6.5
Bhutan	7.7	10.8	5.7	9.3	10.1	6.4	4.9	6.4	7.7	8.4	8.6	7.5
Brunei Darussalam	2.0	−2.0	−1.8	2.7	3.7	0.9	−2.1	−2.3	−0.2	−2.0	3.0	6.8
Cambodia	9.3	6.7	0.1	6.0	7.1	7.3	7.4	7.1	6.9	7.0	7.0	6.7
China	9.9	9.6	9.2	10.6	9.5	7.7	7.7	7.3	6.9	6.5	6.2	6.0
Fiji	2.3	1.0	−1.4	3.0	2.7	1.4	4.7	5.3	4.3	2.5	3.9	3.6
India	7.1	3.9	8.5	10.3	6.6	5.6	6.6	7.2	7.3	7.5	7.5	7.8
Indonesia	2.7	7.4	4.7	6.4	6.2	6.0	5.6	5.0	4.8	4.9	5.3	6.0
Kiribati	1.9	−1.8	0.3	−1.6	0.5	5.2	5.8	2.4	4.2	2.7	2.5	2.0
Lao P.D.R.	6.3	7.8	7.5	8.1	8.0	7.9	8.0	7.4	7.0	7.4	7.4	7.3
Malaysia	4.2	4.8	−1.5	7.5	5.3	5.5	4.7	6.0	5.0	4.4	4.8	5.0
Maldives	8.8	12.7	−5.3	7.2	8.7	2.5	4.7	6.5	1.9	3.5	3.9	4.7
Marshall Islands	1.8	−1.7	6.2	1.3	4.0	1.9	−1.1	1.0	1.6	1.8	1.8	1.3
Micronesia	1.0	−2.2	1.0	3.5	1.8	−0.5	−3.6	−3.4	−0.2	1.1	0.7	0.6
Mongolia	5.7	7.8	−2.1	7.3	17.3	12.3	11.6	7.9	2.3	0.4	2.5	7.2
Myanmar	12.0	3.6	5.1	5.3	5.6	7.3	8.4	8.7	7.0	8.6	7.7	7.7
Nepal	3.8	6.1	4.5	4.8	3.4	4.8	4.1	5.4	3.4	0.5	4.5	3.8
Palau	...	−5.6	−9.1	3.3	5.0	3.2	−2.4	4.2	9.4	2.0	5.0	3.0
Papua New Guinea	2.4	6.6	6.1	7.7	10.7	8.1	5.5	8.5	9.0	3.1	4.4	3.3
Philippines	4.2	4.2	1.1	7.6	3.7	6.7	7.1	6.1	5.8	6.0	6.2	6.5
Samoa	3.7	2.9	−6.4	−1.4	5.4	0.4	−1.9	1.2	1.7	1.2	−0.1	1.9
Solomon Islands	1.1	7.1	−4.7	6.9	12.9	4.7	3.0	2.0	3.3	3.0	3.3	3.2
Sri Lanka	4.3	6.0	3.5	8.0	8.4	9.1	3.4	4.5	5.2	5.0	5.0	5.0
Thailand	3.8	1.7	−0.7	7.5	0.8	7.2	2.7	0.8	2.8	3.0	3.2	3.0
Timor-Leste[4]	...	14.2	13.0	9.4	9.5	6.4	2.8	5.5	4.3	5.0	5.5	5.5
Tonga	1.2	2.7	3.0	3.2	1.8	−1.1	−0.6	2.0	2.6	2.8	2.6	1.8
Tuvalu	...	8.0	−4.4	−2.7	8.5	0.2	1.3	2.2	2.6	3.9	1.9	1.7
Vanuatu	2.5	6.5	3.3	1.6	1.2	1.8	2.0	2.3	−0.8	4.5	4.0	2.5
Vietnam	6.8	5.7	5.4	6.4	6.2	5.2	5.4	6.0	6.7	6.3	6.2	6.2
Emerging and Developing Europe	**4.2**	**3.1**	**−3.0**	**4.7**	**5.4**	**1.2**	**2.8**	**2.8**	**3.5**	**3.5**	**3.3**	**3.3**
Albania	7.0	7.5	3.4	3.7	2.5	1.4	1.1	2.0	2.6	3.4	3.8	4.1
Bosnia and Herzegovina	6.2	5.6	−0.8	0.8	0.9	−0.9	2.4	1.1	2.8	3.0	3.2	4.0
Bulgaria	5.3	5.6	−4.2	0.1	1.6	0.2	1.3	1.5	3.0	2.3	2.3	2.6
Croatia	3.8	2.1	−7.4	−1.7	−0.3	−2.2	−1.1	−0.4	1.6	1.9	2.1	2.0
Hungary	3.7	0.8	−6.6	0.7	1.8	−1.7	1.9	3.7	2.9	2.3	2.5	2.1
Kosovo	...	4.5	3.6	3.3	4.4	2.8	3.4	1.2	3.3	3.4	4.3	4.0
FYR Macedonia	3.4	5.5	−0.4	3.4	2.3	−0.5	2.9	3.5	3.7	3.6	3.6	3.8
Montenegro	...	6.9	−5.7	2.5	3.2	−2.7	3.5	1.8	4.1	4.7	2.5	4.2
Poland	4.2	3.9	2.6	3.7	5.0	1.6	1.3	3.3	3.6	3.6	3.6	3.5
Romania	4.0	8.5	−7.1	−0.8	1.1	0.6	3.5	3.0	3.7	4.2	3.6	3.3
Serbia	3.8	5.4	−3.1	0.6	1.4	−1.0	2.6	−1.8	0.7	1.8	2.3	4.0
Turkey	4.0	0.7	−4.8	9.2	8.8	2.1	4.2	2.9	3.8	3.8	3.4	3.5

Table A4. Emerging Market and Developing Economies: Real GDP *(continued)*
(Annual percent change)

	Average 1998–2007	2008	2009	2010	2011	2012	2013	2014	2015	Projections 2016	2017	2021
Latin America and the Caribbean	**3.1**	**3.9**	**−1.2**	**6.1**	**4.9**	**3.2**	**3.0**	**1.3**	**−0.1**	**−0.5**	**1.5**	**2.8**
Antigua and Barbuda	4.6	1.5	−10.7	−8.5	−1.9	3.6	1.5	4.2	2.2	2.0	2.4	2.7
Argentina[5]	2.5	3.1	0.1	9.5	8.4	0.8	2.9	0.5	1.2	−1.0	2.8	2.9
The Bahamas	2.8	−2.3	−4.2	1.5	0.6	2.2	0.0	1.0	0.5	1.5	1.5	1.5
Barbados	2.2	0.4	−4.0	0.3	0.8	0.3	0.0	0.2	0.5	2.1	2.3	2.0
Belize	5.7	3.2	0.7	3.3	2.1	3.8	1.5	3.6	1.5	2.5	2.7	2.0
Bolivia	3.3	6.1	3.4	4.1	5.2	5.1	6.8	5.5	4.8	3.8	3.5	3.5
Brazil	3.0	5.1	−0.1	7.5	3.9	1.9	3.0	0.1	−3.8	−3.8	0.0	2.0
Chile	4.0	3.2	−1.1	5.7	5.8	5.5	4.0	1.8	2.1	1.5	2.1	3.4
Colombia	3.1	3.5	1.7	4.0	6.6	4.0	4.9	4.4	3.1	2.5	3.0	4.0
Costa Rica	5.5	2.7	−1.0	5.0	4.5	5.2	1.8	3.0	3.7	4.2	4.2	4.0
Dominica	2.4	7.1	−1.2	0.7	−0.1	−1.3	0.6	3.9	−4.3	4.9	3.5	1.7
Dominican Republic	5.6	3.1	0.9	8.3	2.8	2.6	4.8	7.3	7.0	5.4	4.5	4.5
Ecuador	3.0	6.4	0.6	3.5	7.9	5.6	4.6	3.7	0.0	−4.5	−4.3	1.0
El Salvador	2.9	1.3	−3.1	1.4	2.2	1.9	1.8	2.0	2.4	2.5	2.6	2.0
Grenada	4.8	0.9	−6.6	−0.5	0.8	−1.2	2.4	5.7	4.6	3.0	2.5	2.5
Guatemala	3.8	3.3	0.5	2.9	4.2	3.0	3.7	4.2	4.0	4.0	3.9	4.0
Guyana	1.4	2.0	3.3	4.4	5.4	4.8	5.2	3.8	3.0	3.4	3.5	3.3
Haiti	0.9	0.8	3.1	−5.5	5.5	2.9	4.2	2.7	1.0	2.3	3.3	3.5
Honduras	4.4	4.2	−2.4	3.7	3.8	4.1	2.8	3.1	3.6	3.5	3.7	4.0
Jamaica	1.3	−0.8	−3.4	−1.5	1.4	−0.5	0.2	0.5	1.1	2.2	2.5	2.7
Mexico	2.9	1.4	−4.7	5.1	4.0	4.0	1.3	2.3	2.5	2.4	2.6	3.1
Nicaragua	4.0	2.9	−2.8	3.2	6.2	5.1	4.5	4.7	4.5	4.5	4.3	4.0
Panama	5.6	8.6	1.6	5.8	11.8	9.2	6.6	6.1	5.8	6.1	6.4	6.0
Paraguay	1.6	6.4	−4.0	13.1	4.3	−1.2	14.0	4.7	3.0	2.9	3.2	4.0
Peru	4.1	9.1	1.0	8.5	6.5	6.0	5.9	2.4	3.3	3.7	4.1	3.5
St. Kitts and Nevis	3.5	3.4	−3.8	−3.8	−1.9	−0.9	6.2	6.1	6.6	4.7	2.8	2.5
St. Lucia	2.5	2.8	−0.5	−1.7	0.7	−1.1	0.1	0.5	1.6	1.4	1.9	2.1
St. Vincent and the Grenadines	4.0	−0.5	−2.0	−2.3	0.2	1.3	2.3	−0.2	1.6	2.2	3.1	3.1
Suriname	3.9	4.1	3.0	5.1	5.3	3.1	2.8	1.8	0.1	−2.0	2.5	3.0
Trinidad and Tobago	8.2	3.4	−4.4	3.3	−0.3	1.3	2.3	−1.0	−1.8	−1.1	1.8	1.3
Uruguay	1.2	7.2	4.2	7.8	5.2	3.3	5.1	3.5	1.5	1.4	2.6	3.1
Venezuela	2.9	5.3	−3.2	−1.5	4.2	5.6	1.3	−3.9	−5.7	−8.0	−4.5	0.0
Middle East, North Africa, Afghanistan, and Pakistan	**5.3**	**4.8**	**1.5**	**4.9**	**4.5**	**5.0**	**2.3**	**2.8**	**2.5**	**3.1**	**3.5**	**3.8**
Afghanistan	. . .	3.9	20.6	8.4	6.5	14.0	3.9	1.3	1.5	2.0	3.0	4.0
Algeria	4.3	2.4	1.6	3.6	2.8	3.3	2.8	3.8	3.7	3.4	2.9	3.4
Bahrain	5.8	6.2	2.5	4.3	2.1	3.6	5.4	4.5	3.2	2.2	2.0	2.2
Djibouti	2.8	5.8	1.6	4.1	7.3	4.8	5.0	6.0	6.5	6.5	7.0	6.0
Egypt	5.1	7.2	4.7	5.1	1.8	2.2	2.1	2.2	4.2	3.3	4.3	5.0
Iran[6]	5.2	0.9	2.3	6.6	3.7	−6.6	−1.9	4.3	0.0	4.0	3.7	4.1
Iraq	. . .	8.2	3.4	6.4	7.5	13.9	6.6	−2.1	2.4	7.2	3.3	4.8
Jordan	5.9	7.2	5.5	2.3	2.6	2.7	2.8	3.1	2.5	3.2	3.7	4.0
Kuwait	6.0	2.5	−7.1	−2.4	10.6	7.7	1.0	0.0	0.9	2.4	2.6	2.8
Lebanon	3.2	9.1	10.3	8.0	0.9	2.8	2.5	2.0	1.0	1.0	2.0	3.0
Libya	4.2	2.7	−0.8	5.0	−62.1	104.5	−13.6	−24.0	−6.4	−2.0	12.2	4.8
Mauritania	5.4	1.1	−1.0	4.8	4.7	5.8	6.4	6.6	1.9	4.1	3.9	3.2
Morocco	4.6	5.9	4.2	3.8	5.2	3.0	4.7	2.4	4.5	2.3	4.1	4.8
Oman	2.4	8.2	6.1	4.8	4.1	5.8	4.7	2.9	4.1	1.8	1.7	2.1
Pakistan	4.9	5.0	0.4	2.6	3.6	3.8	3.7	4.0	4.2	4.5	4.7	5.5
Qatar	10.7	17.7	12.0	19.6	13.4	4.9	4.6	4.0	3.3	3.4	3.4	1.7
Saudi Arabia	2.9	6.2	−2.1	4.8	10.0	5.4	2.7	3.6	3.4	1.2	1.9	2.1
Sudan[7]	11.2	3.0	4.7	3.0	−1.3	−3.4	3.9	3.3	3.5	3.7	4.0	4.1
Syria[8]	3.6	4.5	5.9	3.4	. . .	. . .	. . .	. . .	. . .	. . .	. . .	. . .
Tunisia	4.9	4.5	3.1	2.6	−1.9	3.9	2.4	2.3	0.8	2.0	3.0	4.5
United Arab Emirates	5.7	3.2	−5.2	1.6	4.9	7.2	4.3	4.6	3.9	2.4	2.6	3.4
Yemen	4.3	3.6	3.9	7.7	−12.7	2.4	4.8	−0.2	−28.1	0.7	11.9	3.5

Table A4. Emerging Market and Developing Economies: Real GDP *(continued)*
(Annual percent change)

	Average 1998–2007	2008	2009	2010	2011	2012	2013	2014	2015	Projections 2016	2017	2021
Sub-Saharan Africa	**5.3**	**6.0**	**4.0**	**6.6**	**5.0**	**4.3**	**5.2**	**5.1**	**3.4**	**3.0**	**4.0**	**5.0**
Angola	10.3	13.8	2.4	3.4	3.9	5.2	6.8	4.8	3.0	2.5	2.7	4.3
Benin	4.4	4.9	2.3	2.1	3.0	4.6	6.9	6.5	5.2	5.0	5.2	5.6
Botswana	4.7	6.2	−7.7	8.6	6.0	4.5	9.9	3.2	−0.3	3.7	4.3	4.0
Burkina Faso	5.9	5.8	3.0	8.4	6.6	6.5	6.6	4.0	4.0	5.0	5.7	6.0
Burundi	3.1	4.9	3.8	5.1	4.0	4.4	4.5	4.7	−4.1	3.4	3.9	5.4
Cabo Verde	7.5	6.7	−1.3	1.5	4.0	1.1	1.0	1.8	1.8	2.9	3.5	4.0
Cameroon	3.8	2.9	1.9	3.3	4.1	4.6	5.6	5.9	5.9	4.9	4.6	4.6
Central African Republic	1.4	2.1	1.7	3.0	3.3	4.1	−36.0	1.0	4.3	5.7	5.9	3.5
Chad	8.2	3.1	4.2	13.6	0.1	8.9	5.7	6.9	1.8	−0.4	1.6	3.5
Comoros	2.0	1.0	1.8	2.1	2.2	3.0	3.5	2.0	1.0	2.2	3.3	4.0
Democratic Republic of the Congo	1.4	6.2	2.9	7.1	6.9	7.1	8.5	9.2	7.7	4.9	5.1	5.7
Republic of Congo	3.3	5.6	7.5	8.7	3.4	3.8	3.3	6.8	2.5	4.4	4.3	2.4
Côte d'Ivoire	0.8	2.5	3.3	2.0	−4.4	10.7	8.7	7.9	8.6	8.5	8.0	6.8
Equatorial Guinea	27.3	9.9	−4.5	−3.8	2.0	5.7	−6.5	−0.3	−12.2	−7.4	−1.9	−1.1
Eritrea	0.7	−9.8	3.9	2.2	8.7	7.0	3.1	5.0	4.8	3.7	3.2	3.9
Ethiopia	6.5	11.2	10.0	10.6	11.4	8.7	9.9	10.3	10.2	4.5	7.0	7.3
Gabon	0.1	1.7	−2.3	6.3	7.1	5.3	5.6	4.3	4.0	3.2	4.5	4.9
The Gambia	3.8	5.7	6.4	6.5	−4.3	5.6	4.8	−0.2	4.4	2.3	3.3	5.5
Ghana	4.9	9.1	4.8	7.9	14.0	9.3	7.3	4.0	3.5	4.5	7.7	4.6
Guinea	3.0	4.9	−0.3	1.9	3.9	3.8	2.3	1.1	0.1	4.1	5.4	6.0
Guinea-Bissau	0.6	3.2	3.3	4.4	9.4	−1.8	0.8	2.5	4.8	4.8	5.0	5.0
Kenya	3.6	0.2	3.3	8.4	6.1	4.6	5.7	5.3	5.6	6.0	6.1	6.5
Lesotho	3.2	5.1	4.5	6.9	4.5	5.3	3.6	3.4	2.5	2.6	4.1	3.8
Liberia	...	6.0	5.1	6.1	7.4	8.2	8.7	0.7	0.0	2.5	4.7	6.4
Madagascar	3.7	7.2	−4.7	0.3	1.5	3.0	2.3	3.3	3.0	4.1	4.5	5.0
Malawi	3.1	7.6	8.3	6.9	4.9	1.9	5.2	5.7	2.9	3.0	4.0	5.5
Mali	5.1	4.8	4.7	5.4	3.2	−0.8	2.3	7.5	6.1	5.0	5.2	4.5
Mauritius	4.4	5.5	3.0	4.1	3.9	3.2	3.2	3.6	3.4	3.8	3.9	4.0
Mozambique	8.4	6.9	6.4	6.7	7.1	7.2	7.1	7.4	6.3	6.0	6.8	38.9
Namibia	4.2	2.6	0.3	6.0	5.1	5.1	5.7	6.4	4.5	4.2	5.8	4.5
Niger	4.7	9.6	−0.7	8.4	2.2	11.8	5.3	7.0	4.0	4.9	6.9	5.4
Nigeria	7.6	8.0	9.0	10.0	4.9	4.3	5.4	6.3	2.7	2.3	3.5	4.0
Rwanda	7.7	11.1	6.3	7.3	7.8	8.8	4.7	7.0	6.9	6.3	6.7	7.5
São Tomé and Príncipe	3.8	8.1	4.0	4.5	4.8	4.5	4.0	4.5	4.0	5.0	5.5	6.0
Senegal	4.6	3.7	2.4	4.3	1.9	4.5	3.6	4.3	6.5	6.6	6.8	7.0
Seychelles	2.6	−2.1	−1.1	5.9	5.4	3.7	5.0	6.2	4.4	3.3	3.5	3.3
Sierra Leone	12.0	5.4	3.2	5.3	6.0	15.2	20.7	4.6	−21.5	5.3	−0.7	5.6
South Africa	3.7	3.2	−1.5	3.0	3.2	2.2	2.2	1.5	1.3	0.6	1.2	2.4
South Sudan	...	...	...	...	...	−52.4	29.3	2.9	−0.2	−7.8	8.2	0.9
Swaziland	3.5	4.3	1.9	1.4	1.2	3.0	2.9	2.5	1.7	0.5	1.1	1.3
Tanzania	5.9	5.6	5.4	6.4	7.9	5.1	7.3	7.0	7.0	6.9	6.8	6.5
Togo	1.1	2.4	3.5	4.1	4.8	5.9	5.4	5.4	5.3	5.2	5.2	5.4
Uganda	7.0	10.4	8.1	7.7	6.8	2.6	4.0	4.9	5.0	5.3	5.7	6.4
Zambia	5.5	7.8	9.2	10.3	5.6	7.6	5.1	5.0	3.6	3.4	4.8	5.5
Zimbabwe[9]	...	−16.6	7.5	11.4	11.9	10.6	4.5	3.8	1.5	2.7	3.5	4.2

[1]Data for some countries refer to real net material product (NMP) or are estimates based on NMP. The figures should be interpreted only as indicative of broad orders of magnitude because reliable, comparable data are not generally available. In particular, the growth of output of new private enterprises of the informal economy is not fully reflected in the recent figures.
[2]Georgia, Turkmenistan, and Ukraine, which are not members of the Commonwealth of Independent States, are included in this group for reasons of geography and similarity in economic structure.
[3]Data are based on the 2008 System of National Accounts. The revised national accounts data are available beginning in 2000 and exclude Crimea and Sevastopol from 2010 onward.
[4]In this table only, the data for Timor-Leste are based on non-oil GDP.
[5]See country-specific notes for Argentina in the "Country Notes" section of the Statistical Appendix.
[6]For Iran, data are based on GDP at market prices. Corresponding data used by the IMF staff for GDP growth at factor prices are −6.8 percent for 2012/13, −1.9 percent for 2013/14, 3.0 percent for 2014/15, 0.0 percent for 2015/16, 4.0 percent for 2016/17, and 3.7 percent for 2017/18.
[7]Data for 2011 exclude South Sudan after July 9. Data for 2012 and onward pertain to the current Sudan.
[8]Data for Syria are excluded for 2011 onward owing to the uncertain political situation.
[9]The Zimbabwe dollar ceased circulating in early 2009. Data are based on IMF staff estimates of price and exchange rate developments in U.S. dollars. IMF staff estimates of U.S. dollar values may differ from authorities' estimates. Real GDP is in constant 2009 prices.

Table A5. Summary of Inflation
(Percent)

	Average 1998–2007	2008	2009	2010	2011	2012	2013	2014	2015	Projections 2016	2017	2021
GDP Deflators												
Advanced Economies	**1.8**	**1.9**	**0.8**	**1.0**	**1.3**	**1.2**	**1.3**	**1.3**	**1.1**	**1.0**	**1.4**	**1.8**
United States	2.2	2.0	0.8	1.2	2.1	1.8	1.6	1.6	1.0	1.0	1.4	2.1
Euro Area	1.9	2.0	1.0	0.7	1.1	1.2	1.3	0.9	1.2	1.1	1.1	1.6
Japan	−1.2	−1.3	−0.5	−2.2	−1.9	−0.9	−0.6	1.7	2.0	1.0	1.0	0.7
Other Advanced Economies[1]	2.0	3.0	1.0	2.4	2.0	1.3	1.5	1.3	0.9	0.8	1.7	2.1
Consumer Prices												
Advanced Economies	**2.0**	**3.4**	**0.2**	**1.5**	**2.7**	**2.0**	**1.4**	**1.4**	**0.3**	**0.7**	**1.5**	**1.9**
United States	2.6	3.8	−0.3	1.6	3.1	2.1	1.5	1.6	0.1	0.8	1.5	2.2
Euro Area[2]	2.0	3.3	0.3	1.6	2.7	2.5	1.3	0.4	0.0	0.4	1.1	1.7
Japan	−0.2	1.4	−1.3	−0.7	−0.3	0.0	0.4	2.7	0.8	−0.2	1.2	1.2
Other Advanced Economies[1]	1.9	3.9	1.4	2.4	3.3	2.1	1.7	1.5	0.6	1.1	1.8	2.1
Emerging Market and Developing Economies[3]	**7.9**	**9.2**	**5.0**	**5.6**	**7.1**	**5.8**	**5.5**	**4.7**	**4.7**	**4.5**	**4.2**	**3.9**
Regional Groups												
Commonwealth of Independent States[4]	19.8	15.4	11.1	7.2	9.7	6.2	6.4	8.1	15.5	9.4	7.4	4.8
Emerging and Developing Asia	4.2	7.6	2.8	5.1	6.5	4.6	4.7	3.5	2.7	2.9	3.2	3.7
Emerging and Developing Europe	18.5	8.0	4.8	5.6	5.4	5.9	4.3	3.8	2.9	4.1	4.8	4.2
Latin America and the Caribbean	7.0	6.4	4.6	4.2	5.2	4.6	4.6	4.9	5.5	5.7	4.3	3.6
Middle East, North Africa, Afghanistan, and Pakistan	5.8	11.8	7.3	6.6	9.2	9.8	9.1	6.8	5.7	5.2	4.8	4.0
Middle East and North Africa	5.7	11.7	6.1	6.2	8.6	9.7	9.3	6.6	5.9	5.5	4.7	3.9
Sub-Saharan Africa	10.1	13.0	9.8	8.2	9.5	9.3	6.6	6.4	7.0	9.0	8.3	6.3
Memorandum												
European Union	2.6	3.7	1.0	2.0	3.1	2.6	1.5	0.5	0.0	0.4	1.3	1.9
Low-Income Developing Countries	9.3	14.6	8.2	9.2	11.8	9.9	8.0	7.3	7.2	8.0	7.7	6.2
Analytical Groups												
By Source of Export Earnings												
Fuel	12.2	12.6	7.6	6.5	8.3	7.8	7.7	6.3	8.6	7.2	5.7	4.1
Nonfuel	6.7	8.2	4.3	5.4	6.8	5.3	4.9	4.3	3.8	3.8	3.8	3.9
Of Which, Primary Products[5]	...	...	...	...	...	...	...	...	...	...	...	...
By External Financing Source												
Net Debtor Economies	8.7	9.3	7.0	6.6	7.5	6.8	6.2	5.7	5.4	5.4	5.3	4.6
Net Debtor Economies by Debt-Servicing Experience												
Economies with Arrears and/or Rescheduling during 2010–14	8.9	15.2	13.6	10.1	10.1	8.2	6.9	11.4	16.0	9.8	8.7	6.1
Memorandum												
Median Inflation Rate												
Advanced Economies	2.1	4.1	0.9	1.9	3.2	2.6	1.3	0.7	0.1	0.7	1.4	2.0
Emerging Market and Developing Economies[3]	4.9	10.3	3.7	4.2	5.4	4.6	4.0	3.3	2.9	3.2	3.4	3.1

[1]Excludes the United States, euro area countries, and Japan.
[2]Based on Eurostat's harmonized index of consumer prices.
[3]Excludes Argentina and Venezuela. See country-specific notes for Argentina in the "Country Notes" section of the Statistical Appendix.
[4]Georgia, Turkmenistan, and Ukraine, which are not members of the Commonwealth of Independent States, are included in this group for reasons of geography and similarity in economic structure.
[5]Data are missing because of Argentina, which accounts for more than 30 percent of the weights of the group. See country-specific notes for Argentina in the "Country Notes" section of the Statistical Appendix.

Table A6. Advanced Economies: Consumer Prices[1]

(Annual percent change)

	Average 1998–2007	2008	2009	2010	2011	2012	2013	2014	2015	Projections 2016	Projections 2017	Projections 2021	End of Period[2] 2015	End of Period[2] Projections 2016	End of Period[2] Projections 2017
Advanced Economies	**2.0**	**3.4**	**0.2**	**1.5**	**2.7**	**2.0**	**1.4**	**1.4**	**0.3**	**0.7**	**1.5**	**1.9**	**0.6**	**0.9**	**1.8**
United States	2.6	3.8	−0.3	1.6	3.1	2.1	1.5	1.6	0.1	0.8	1.5	2.2	0.8	0.8	2.2
Euro Area[3]	2.0	3.3	0.3	1.6	2.7	2.5	1.3	0.4	0.0	0.4	1.1	1.7	0.2	0.9	1.2
Germany	1.5	2.8	0.2	1.1	2.5	2.1	1.6	0.8	0.1	0.5	1.4	2.0	0.3	1.2	1.5
France	1.7	3.2	0.1	1.7	2.3	2.2	1.0	0.6	0.1	0.4	1.1	1.7	0.3	1.1	1.3
Italy	2.3	3.5	0.8	1.6	2.9	3.3	1.2	0.2	0.1	0.2	0.7	1.3	0.1	0.5	0.8
Spain	3.0	4.1	−0.3	1.8	3.2	2.4	1.4	−0.1	−0.5	−0.4	1.0	1.6	0.0	0.7	0.7
Netherlands	2.3	2.2	1.0	0.9	2.5	2.8	2.6	0.3	0.2	0.3	0.7	1.2	0.3	0.5	0.8
Belgium	1.9	4.5	0.0	2.3	3.4	2.6	1.2	0.5	0.6	1.2	1.1	1.5	1.5	0.6	1.6
Austria	1.7	3.2	0.4	1.7	3.6	2.6	2.1	1.5	0.8	1.4	1.8	2.0	1.2	1.8	1.8
Greece	3.3	4.2	1.3	4.7	3.1	1.0	−0.9	−1.4	−1.1	0.0	0.6	1.9	0.4	0.2	0.9
Portugal	2.9	2.7	−0.9	1.4	3.6	2.8	0.4	−0.2	0.5	0.7	1.2	1.8	0.3	0.8	1.5
Ireland	3.3	3.1	−1.7	−1.6	1.2	1.9	0.5	0.3	0.0	0.9	1.4	2.0	0.0	0.5	1.2
Finland	1.5	3.9	1.6	1.7	3.3	3.2	2.2	1.2	−0.2	0.4	1.4	2.0	−0.2	0.8	1.5
Slovak Republic	6.4	3.9	0.9	0.7	4.1	3.7	1.5	−0.1	−0.3	0.2	1.4	2.0	−0.4	0.7	1.8
Lithuania	2.2	11.1	4.2	1.2	4.1	3.2	1.2	0.2	−0.7	0.6	1.9	2.3	−0.3	1.4	2.3
Slovenia	5.6	5.7	0.9	1.8	1.8	2.6	1.8	0.2	−0.5	0.1	1.0	2.0	−0.4	0.7	0.8
Luxembourg	2.5	4.1	0.0	2.8	3.7	2.9	1.7	0.7	0.1	0.5	1.3	2.1	0.9	1.0	1.1
Latvia	4.6	15.2	3.2	−1.2	4.2	2.3	0.0	0.7	0.2	0.5	1.5	1.8	0.4	1.6	2.1
Estonia	4.4	10.6	0.2	2.7	5.1	4.2	3.2	0.5	0.1	2.0	2.9	2.7	−0.2	2.1	2.9
Cyprus[3]	2.5	4.4	0.2	2.6	3.5	3.1	0.4	−0.3	−1.5	0.6	1.3	1.9	−0.4	0.6	1.3
Malta	2.5	4.7	1.8	2.0	2.5	3.2	1.0	0.8	1.2	1.6	1.8	1.8	1.3	1.8	1.8
Japan	−0.2	1.4	−1.3	−0.7	−0.3	0.0	0.4	2.7	0.8	−0.2	1.2	1.2	0.3	−0.2	1.6
United Kingdom[3]	1.6	3.6	2.2	3.3	4.5	2.8	2.6	1.5	0.1	0.8	1.9	2.0	0.1	1.3	1.9
Korea	3.2	4.7	2.8	2.9	4.0	2.2	1.3	1.3	0.7	1.3	2.2	2.0	1.3	1.7	2.4
Canada	2.1	2.4	0.3	1.8	2.9	1.5	0.9	1.9	1.1	1.3	1.9	2.0	1.3	1.4	2.0
Australia	2.8	4.3	1.8	2.9	3.3	1.7	2.5	2.5	1.5	2.1	2.4	2.5	1.7	2.5	2.2
Taiwan Province of China	0.9	3.5	−0.9	1.0	1.4	1.9	0.8	1.2	−0.3	0.7	1.1	2.2	0.1	0.8	1.1
Switzerland	0.8	2.4	−0.5	0.7	0.2	−0.7	−0.2	0.0	−1.1	−0.6	−0.1	1.0	−1.3	−0.3	0.1
Sweden	1.5	3.3	1.9	1.9	1.4	0.9	0.4	0.2	0.7	1.1	1.4	2.1	0.7	1.4	1.7
Singapore	0.7	6.6	0.6	2.8	5.2	4.6	2.4	1.0	−0.5	0.2	1.3	1.9	−0.7	1.3	1.9
Hong Kong SAR	−0.8	4.3	0.6	2.3	5.3	4.1	4.3	4.4	3.0	2.5	2.6	3.0	3.0	2.5	2.6
Norway	1.9	3.8	2.2	2.4	1.3	0.7	2.1	2.0	2.2	2.8	2.5	2.5	2.3	2.5	2.5
Czech Republic	3.3	6.3	1.0	1.5	1.9	3.3	1.4	0.4	0.3	1.0	2.2	2.0	0.1	1.5	2.6
Israel	2.3	4.6	3.3	2.7	3.5	1.7	1.5	0.5	−0.6	−0.1	0.9	2.0	−1.0	0.5	1.2
Denmark	2.1	3.4	1.3	2.3	2.8	2.4	0.8	0.6	0.5	0.8	1.4	2.0	0.5	0.8	1.4
New Zealand	2.2	4.0	2.1	2.3	4.0	1.1	1.1	1.2	0.3	1.5	1.9	2.0	0.1	2.5	1.7
Puerto Rico	2.3	5.2	0.3	2.5	2.9	1.3	1.1	0.6	−0.8	−0.6	1.2	1.8	−0.2	−0.6	1.2
Macao SAR	...	8.5	1.2	2.8	5.8	6.1	5.5	6.0	4.6	3.0	3.0	3.0	3.7	3.0	3.0
Iceland	...	12.7	12.0	5.4	4.0	5.2	3.9	2.0	1.6	2.6	3.9	2.5	1.9	3.2	4.1
San Marino	4.2	4.1	2.4	2.6	2.0	2.8	1.3	1.1	0.4	0.9	1.1	1.5	0.4	0.9	1.1
Memorandum															
Major Advanced Economies	1.9	3.2	−0.1	1.4	2.6	1.9	1.3	1.5	0.2	0.6	1.4	1.9	0.6	0.8	1.9

[1]Movements in consumer prices are shown as annual averages.
[2]Monthly year-over-year changes and, for several countries, on a quarterly basis.
[3]Based on Eurostat's harmonized index of consumer prices.

Table A7. Emerging Market and Developing Economies: Consumer Prices[1]

(Annual percent change)

	Average 1998–2007	2008	2009	2010	2011	2012	2013	2014	2015	Projections 2016	Projections 2017	Projections 2021	End of Period[2] 2015	End of Period[2] Projections 2016	End of Period[2] Projections 2017
Commonwealth of Independent States[3,4]	**19.8**	**15.4**	**11.1**	**7.2**	**9.7**	**6.2**	**6.4**	**8.1**	**15.5**	**9.4**	**7.4**	**4.8**	**13.9**	**8.7**	**6.4**
Russia	21.2	14.1	11.7	6.9	8.4	5.1	6.8	7.8	15.5	8.4	6.5	4.0	12.9	7.9	5.9
Excluding Russia	15.4	19.3	9.6	8.1	13.2	9.1	5.6	8.7	15.4	11.9	9.4	6.6	16.4	10.8	7.7
Armenia	3.2	9.0	3.5	7.3	7.7	2.5	5.8	3.0	3.7	2.6	4.0	4.0	−0.1	3.5	4.0
Azerbaijan	3.8	20.8	1.6	5.7	7.9	1.0	2.4	1.4	4.0	12.8	9.5	4.0	7.6	18.0	1.0
Belarus	55.3	14.8	13.0	7.7	53.2	59.2	18.3	18.1	13.5	13.6	12.1	9.3	12.0	14.5	11.3
Georgia	7.3	10.0	1.7	7.1	8.5	−0.9	−0.5	3.1	4.0	4.3	4.5	3.0	4.9	5.0	4.0
Kazakhstan	8.3	17.1	7.3	7.1	8.3	5.1	5.8	6.7	6.5	13.1	9.3	7.1	12.0	9.0	9.0
Kyrgyz Republic	9.7	24.5	6.8	7.8	16.6	2.8	6.6	7.5	6.5	5.5	6.9	5.1	3.4	7.0	6.5
Moldova	15.0	12.7	0.0	7.4	7.6	4.6	4.6	5.1	9.6	9.8	7.4	5.0	13.5	8.1	6.4
Tajikistan	20.2	20.4	6.4	6.5	12.4	5.8	5.0	6.1	5.8	9.2	8.5	6.0	5.1	11.0	6.4
Turkmenistan	10.4	14.5	−2.7	4.4	5.3	5.3	6.8	6.0	5.5	5.4	4.4	6.1	6.5	4.3	4.5
Ukraine[5]	12.1	25.2	15.9	9.4	8.0	0.6	−0.3	12.1	48.7	15.1	11.0	5.0	43.3	13.0	8.5
Uzbekistan	18.9	13.1	12.3	12.3	12.4	11.9	11.7	9.1	8.5	8.5	9.4	10.0	8.4	8.0	9.8
Emerging and Developing Asia	**4.2**	**7.6**	**2.8**	**5.1**	**6.5**	**4.6**	**4.7**	**3.5**	**2.7**	**2.9**	**3.2**	**3.7**	**2.7**	**3.0**	**3.2**
Bangladesh	5.7	8.9	4.9	9.4	11.5	6.2	7.5	7.0	6.4	6.7	6.9	5.7	6.5	7.0	7.0
Bhutan	5.0	6.3	7.1	4.8	8.6	10.1	8.6	9.6	7.2	6.1	6.0	5.6	7.4	7.6	6.9
Brunei Darussalam	0.2	2.1	1.0	0.2	0.1	0.1	0.4	−0.2	−0.4	0.2	0.1	0.0	−1.0	0.2	0.1
Cambodia	3.8	25.0	−0.7	4.0	5.5	2.9	3.0	3.9	1.2	2.1	2.8	0.2	2.8	2.4	2.9
China	1.1	5.9	−0.7	3.3	5.4	2.6	2.6	2.0	1.4	1.8	2.0	3.0	1.6	1.8	2.0
Fiji	3.0	7.7	3.7	3.7	7.3	3.4	2.9	0.5	2.8	3.3	2.8	2.8	2.8	3.3	2.8
India	5.2	9.2	10.6	9.5	9.5	9.9	9.4	5.9	4.9	5.3	5.3	4.9	5.4	5.1	5.4
Indonesia	14.1	9.8	5.0	5.1	5.3	4.0	6.4	6.4	6.4	4.3	4.5	4.0	3.4	4.5	4.4
Kiribati	1.8	13.7	9.8	−3.9	1.5	−3.0	−1.5	2.1	1.4	0.3	0.7	2.1	1.4	0.3	0.8
Lao P.D.R.	24.0	7.6	0.0	6.0	7.6	4.3	6.4	5.5	5.3	1.5	2.3	3.1	5.5	1.2	2.3
Malaysia	2.4	5.4	0.6	1.7	3.2	1.7	2.1	3.1	2.1	3.1	2.9	3.0	2.7	3.1	2.9
Maldives	1.8	12.0	4.5	6.2	11.3	10.9	4.0	2.5	1.4	2.1	2.6	4.2	1.9	2.0	3.2
Marshall Islands	. . .	14.7	0.5	1.8	5.4	4.3	1.9	1.1	−4.0	−1.3	0.8	2.1	−4.0	−1.3	0.8
Micronesia	2.0	6.6	7.7	3.7	4.3	6.3	2.0	0.6	−1.0	1.9	1.3	3.0	−1.0	1.9	1.3
Mongolia	7.3	26.8	6.3	10.2	7.7	15.0	8.6	12.9	5.9	1.9	4.3	6.4	1.1	3.7	6.5
Myanmar	23.4	11.5	2.2	8.2	2.8	2.8	5.7	5.9	11.5	9.6	8.2	6.4	10.5	8.7	7.7
Nepal	5.5	6.7	12.6	9.6	9.6	8.3	9.9	9.0	7.2	10.2	11.1	5.6	7.6	12.9	9.3
Palau	. . .	9.9	4.7	1.1	2.6	5.4	2.8	4.0	2.2	2.5	2.5	2.0	2.7	2.3	2.6
Papua New Guinea	8.6	10.8	6.9	5.1	4.4	4.5	5.0	5.3	6.0	6.0	5.0	5.0	6.0	6.0	5.0
Philippines	5.2	8.2	4.2	3.8	4.7	3.2	2.9	4.2	1.4	2.0	3.4	3.5	1.5	2.9	3.2
Samoa	4.5	11.6	6.3	0.8	5.2	2.0	0.6	−0.4	0.9	1.2	2.0	3.0	0.4	2.0	2.0
Solomon Islands	8.7	17.3	7.1	0.9	7.4	5.9	5.4	5.2	−0.4	2.1	2.6	3.1	2.2	2.9	2.6
Sri Lanka	9.8	22.4	3.5	6.2	6.7	7.5	6.9	3.3	0.9	3.4	4.5	5.0	2.8	4.1	5.0
Thailand	2.8	5.5	−0.9	3.3	3.8	3.0	2.2	1.9	−0.9	0.2	2.0	2.5	−0.9	1.6	1.8
Timor-Leste	. . .	7.4	−0.2	5.2	13.2	10.9	9.5	0.7	0.6	1.5	3.8	4.0	−0.6	3.6	4.0
Tonga	7.6	7.5	3.5	3.9	4.6	2.0	1.5	1.2	−0.1	−0.3	0.7	2.4	−0.4	−0.4	1.7
Tuvalu	. . .	10.4	−0.3	−1.9	0.5	1.4	2.0	1.1	3.3	3.0	2.9	2.5	3.3	3.0	2.9
Vanuatu	2.5	4.2	5.2	2.7	0.7	1.4	1.3	1.0	3.3	2.5	3.2	3.0	3.5	3.0	3.3
Vietnam	4.9	23.1	6.7	9.2	18.7	9.1	6.6	4.1	0.6	1.3	2.3	4.0	0.6	2.0	2.6
Emerging and Developing Europe	**18.5**	**8.0**	**4.8**	**5.6**	**5.4**	**5.9**	**4.3**	**3.8**	**2.9**	**4.1**	**4.8**	**4.2**	**3.5**	**5.1**	**4.0**
Albania	4.1	3.4	2.3	3.6	3.4	2.0	1.9	1.6	1.9	1.9	2.5	3.0	2.0	2.2	2.7
Bosnia and Herzegovina	2.4	7.4	−0.4	2.1	3.7	2.0	−0.1	−0.9	−1.0	−0.7	1.1	2.1	−1.2	−0.3	1.5
Bulgaria	7.3	12.0	2.5	3.0	3.4	2.4	0.4	−1.6	−1.1	0.2	1.2	2.1	−0.9	1.1	1.3
Croatia	3.4	6.1	2.4	1.0	2.3	3.4	2.2	−0.2	−0.5	0.4	1.3	2.0	−0.2	0.8	1.5
Hungary	7.5	6.1	4.2	4.9	4.0	5.7	1.7	−0.2	−0.1	0.5	2.4	3.0	0.9	1.2	2.6
Kosovo	. . .	9.4	−2.4	3.5	7.3	2.5	1.8	0.4	−0.5	0.2	1.5	2.2	−0.1	1.2	1.7
FYR Macedonia	1.9	7.2	−0.6	1.7	3.9	3.3	2.8	−0.1	−0.2	0.5	1.5	2.0	−0.3	1.4	1.6
Montenegro	. . .	9.0	3.6	0.7	3.1	3.6	2.2	−0.7	1.6	0.9	1.3	1.8	1.4	1.4	1.4
Poland	4.6	4.2	3.4	2.6	4.3	3.7	0.9	0.0	−0.9	−0.2	1.3	2.5	−0.5	0.5	1.7
Romania	24.2	7.8	5.6	6.1	5.8	3.3	4.0	1.1	−0.6	−0.4	3.1	2.5	−0.9	1.5	3.4
Serbia	25.3	12.4	8.1	6.1	11.1	7.3	7.7	2.1	1.4	1.7	3.1	4.0	1.6	2.6	3.3
Turkey	33.9	10.4	6.3	8.6	6.5	8.9	7.5	8.9	7.7	9.8	8.8	6.5	8.8	10.9	6.5

Table A7. Emerging Market and Developing Economies: Consumer Prices[1] (continued)

(Annual percent change)

	Average 1998–2007	2008	2009	2010	2011	2012	2013	2014	2015	Projections 2016	Projections 2017	Projections 2021	End of Period[2] 2015	End of Period[2] Projections 2016	End of Period[2] Projections 2017
Latin America and the Caribbean[6]	**7.0**	**6.4**	**4.6**	**4.2**	**5.2**	**4.6**	**4.6**	**4.9**	**5.5**	**5.7**	**4.3**	**3.6**	**6.2**	**5.0**	**4.2**
Antigua and Barbuda	1.8	5.3	−0.6	3.4	3.5	3.4	1.1	1.1	1.0	1.4	1.8	2.5	0.9	1.4	2.2
Argentina[7]	6.8	8.6	6.3	10.5	9.8	10.0	10.6	. . .	. . .	. . .	19.9	4.8	. . .	25.0	20.0
The Bahamas	1.9	4.4	1.7	1.6	3.1	1.9	0.4	1.2	1.9	0.8	1.1	1.4	2.0	0.8	1.1
Barbados	2.4	8.1	3.7	5.7	9.4	4.5	1.8	1.9	0.5	−0.2	1.2	2.5	−0.7	0.4	1.9
Belize	1.8	6.4	−1.1	0.9	1.7	1.2	0.5	1.2	−0.6	0.0	1.5	2.0	−0.7	0.8	2.3
Bolivia	4.1	14.0	3.3	2.5	9.9	4.5	5.7	5.8	4.1	4.0	5.0	5.0	3.0	5.0	5.0
Brazil	6.6	5.7	4.9	5.0	6.6	5.4	6.2	6.3	9.0	8.7	6.1	4.5	10.7	7.1	6.0
Chile	3.3	8.7	1.5	1.4	3.3	3.0	1.9	4.4	4.3	4.1	3.0	3.0	4.4	3.5	3.0
Colombia	8.0	7.0	4.2	2.3	3.4	3.2	2.0	2.9	5.0	7.3	3.4	3.0	6.8	5.3	3.3
Costa Rica	10.9	13.4	7.8	5.7	4.9	4.5	5.2	4.5	0.8	1.1	3.0	3.0	−0.8	3.0	3.0
Dominica	1.6	6.4	0.0	2.8	1.1	1.4	0.0	0.8	−0.8	−0.2	1.6	2.2	−0.1	−0.1	1.8
Dominican Republic	12.2	10.6	1.4	6.3	8.5	3.7	4.8	3.0	0.8	3.6	4.0	4.0	2.3	3.3	4.0
Ecuador	22.4	8.4	5.2	3.6	4.5	5.1	2.7	3.6	4.0	1.6	0.2	0.4	3.4	0.8	0.0
El Salvador	3.1	7.3	0.5	1.2	5.1	1.7	0.8	1.1	−0.7	2.1	1.9	2.0	1.0	1.9	2.0
Grenada	2.3	8.0	−0.3	3.4	3.0	2.4	0.0	−0.8	−1.3	−0.9	2.2	2.1	−1.2	−0.1	2.8
Guatemala	6.9	11.4	1.9	3.9	6.2	3.8	4.3	3.4	2.4	4.0	3.8	4.0	3.1	4.0	4.0
Guyana	6.2	8.1	3.0	4.3	4.4	2.4	2.2	1.0	−0.3	0.1	2.1	3.0	−1.8	2.1	2.1
Haiti	15.1	14.4	3.4	4.1	7.4	6.8	6.8	3.9	7.5	12.6	8.2	5.0	11.3	10.4	7.0
Honduras	9.1	11.4	5.5	4.7	6.8	5.2	5.2	6.1	3.2	4.2	3.4	5.4	2.4	4.0	5.4
Jamaica	9.3	22.0	9.6	12.6	7.5	6.9	9.4	8.3	4.7	4.2	5.9	5.9	3.0	5.3	6.5
Mexico	7.3	5.1	5.3	4.2	3.4	4.1	3.8	4.0	2.7	2.9	3.0	3.0	2.1	3.3	3.0
Nicaragua	9.0	19.8	3.7	5.5	8.1	7.2	7.1	6.0	4.0	6.1	6.8	7.7	3.1	6.1	6.8
Panama	1.5	8.8	2.4	3.5	5.9	5.7	4.0	2.6	0.1	0.8	2.0	2.0	0.3	0.8	2.0
Paraguay	8.8	10.2	2.6	4.7	8.3	3.7	2.7	5.0	2.9	3.8	4.5	4.5	3.1	4.5	4.5
Peru	2.8	5.8	2.9	1.5	3.4	3.7	2.8	3.2	3.5	3.1	2.5	2.5	4.2	3.4	2.5
St. Kitts and Nevis	3.4	5.3	2.1	0.7	7.1	1.4	1.0	0.7	−2.8	−1.3	0.8	1.8	−2.9	0.2	1.3
St. Lucia	2.8	5.5	−0.2	3.3	2.8	4.2	1.5	3.5	−0.7	−0.8	0.2	2.3	−2.1	−0.7	2.3
St. Vincent and the Grenadines	2.2	10.1	0.4	0.8	3.2	2.6	0.8	0.2	−1.7	0.4	1.1	1.9	−1.7	1.1	1.7
Suriname	20.5	14.6	−0.4	6.7	17.8	5.0	1.9	3.4	6.9	36.8	13.3	4.0	25.0	26.0	8.0
Trinidad and Tobago	5.3	12.1	7.0	10.5	5.1	9.2	5.3	5.7	4.7	4.1	4.7	4.6	1.5	4.6	4.7
Uruguay	8.6	7.9	7.1	6.7	8.1	8.1	8.6	8.9	8.7	9.4	8.4	6.2	9.4	9.1	8.1
Venezuela	21.0	30.4	27.1	28.0	26.8	21.5	39.5	62.2	121.7	481.5	1,642.8	4,505.0	180.9	720.0	2,200.0
Middle East, North Africa, Afghanistan, and Pakistan	**5.8**	**11.8**	**7.3**	**6.6**	**9.2**	**9.8**	**9.1**	**6.8**	**5.7**	**5.2**	**4.8**	**4.0**	**5.2**	**5.6**	**4.8**
Afghanistan	. . .	26.4	−6.8	2.2	11.8	6.4	7.4	4.7	−1.5	3.0	4.5	6.0	0.1	2.9	4.8
Algeria	2.9	4.9	5.7	3.9	4.5	8.9	3.3	2.9	4.8	4.3	4.0	4.0	4.4	4.3	4.0
Bahrain	0.8	3.5	2.8	2.0	−0.4	2.8	3.3	2.7	1.8	3.2	2.3	2.4	0.7	3.1	2.3
Djibouti	2.3	12.0	1.7	4.0	5.1	3.7	2.4	2.9	2.1	3.5	3.5	3.0	1.9	3.0	3.0
Egypt	5.1	11.7	16.2	11.7	11.1	8.6	6.9	10.1	11.0	9.6	9.5	7.2	11.4	10.2	10.4
Iran	14.9	25.3	10.7	12.4	21.2	30.8	34.7	15.6	12.0	8.9	8.2	5.0	9.4	9.0	7.5
Iraq	. . .	2.7	−2.2	2.4	5.6	6.1	1.9	2.2	1.4	2.0	2.0	2.0	2.3	2.0	2.0
Jordan	2.7	14.0	−0.7	4.8	4.2	4.5	4.8	2.9	−0.9	0.2	2.1	2.5	−1.6	1.7	2.5
Kuwait	2.2	6.3	4.6	4.5	4.9	3.2	2.7	2.9	3.4	3.4	3.5	3.6	3.4	3.4	3.5
Lebanon	1.7	10.8	1.2	4.0	5.0	6.6	4.8	1.9	−3.7	−0.7	2.0	2.0	−3.4	2.0	2.0
Libya	−0.7	10.4	2.4	2.5	15.9	6.1	2.6	2.8	8.0	9.2	6.0	0.0	11.7	7.2	5.0
Mauritania	6.5	7.5	2.1	6.3	5.7	4.9	4.1	3.8	0.5	3.8	4.9	5.1	−2.8	3.8	4.9
Morocco	1.8	3.9	1.0	1.0	0.9	1.3	1.9	0.4	1.6	1.5	2.0	2.0	1.6	1.3	2.0
Oman	1.0	12.6	3.5	3.3	4.0	2.9	1.2	1.0	0.2	0.3	2.8	2.7	0.2	0.3	2.8
Pakistan	5.8	12.0	19.6	10.1	13.7	11.0	7.4	8.6	4.5	3.3	5.0	5.0	3.2	4.5	5.0
Qatar	5.1	15.2	−4.9	−2.4	1.9	1.9	3.1	3.3	1.7	2.4	2.7	2.4	. . .	. . .	. . .
Saudi Arabia	0.4	6.1	4.1	3.8	3.7	2.9	3.5	2.7	2.2	3.8	1.0	2.0	2.3	3.8	1.0
Sudan[8]	9.4	14.3	11.3	13.0	18.1	35.5	36.5	36.9	16.9	13.0	12.3	9.0	12.6	13.5	11.0
Syria[9]	2.6	15.2	2.8	4.4	. . .	. . .	. . .	. . .	. . .	. . .	. . .	. . .	. . .	. . .	. . .
Tunisia	2.6	4.3	3.7	3.3	3.5	5.1	5.8	4.9	4.9	4.0	3.9	3.5	4.1	4.0	3.9
United Arab Emirates	4.5	12.3	1.6	0.9	0.9	0.7	1.1	2.3	4.1	3.2	2.7	3.5	3.6	3.2	2.7
Yemen	10.6	19.0	3.7	11.2	19.5	9.9	11.0	8.2	30.0	27.5	24.0	9.5	20.0	32.0	21.0

Table A7. Emerging Market and Developing Economies: Consumer Prices[1] *(continued)*

(Annual percent change)

	Average 1998–2007	2008	2009	2010	2011	2012	2013	2014	2015	Projections 2016	2017	2021	End of Period[2] 2015	Projections 2016	2017
Sub-Saharan Africa	**10.1**	**13.0**	**9.8**	**8.2**	**9.5**	**9.3**	**6.6**	**6.4**	**7.0**	**9.0**	**8.3**	**6.3**	**8.1**	**9.2**	**7.8**
Angola	93.1	12.5	13.7	14.5	13.5	10.3	8.8	7.3	10.3	19.1	15.2	9.0	14.3	19.2	14.0
Benin	2.9	7.4	0.9	2.2	2.7	6.7	1.0	−1.1	0.3	2.0	2.3	2.8	2.3	2.2	2.4
Botswana	8.1	12.6	8.1	6.9	8.5	7.5	5.9	4.4	3.0	3.3	3.6	4.5	3.1	3.6	3.6
Burkina Faso	2.1	10.7	0.9	−0.6	2.8	3.8	0.5	−0.3	0.9	1.6	2.0	2.0	1.3	1.6	2.0
Burundi	8.9	24.4	10.6	6.5	9.6	18.2	7.9	4.4	5.6	7.6	6.2	5.0	7.1	10.7	2.6
Cabo Verde	2.1	6.8	1.0	2.1	4.5	2.5	1.5	−0.2	0.1	0.8	1.3	2.0	−0.5	1.0	1.5
Cameroon	2.2	5.3	3.0	1.3	2.9	2.4	2.1	1.9	2.7	2.2	2.2	2.2	2.8	2.2	2.2
Central African Republic	1.8	9.3	3.5	1.5	1.2	5.9	6.6	11.6	5.4	4.9	4.3	2.4	6.5	2.5	2.5
Chad	1.3	8.3	10.1	−2.1	1.9	7.7	0.2	1.7	3.6	3.2	3.1	3.0	−1.0	3.0	3.0
Comoros	3.6	4.8	4.8	3.9	2.2	5.9	1.6	1.3	2.0	2.2	2.2	2.2	3.4	2.2	2.2
Democratic Republic of the Congo	79.6	18.0	46.2	23.5	15.5	2.1	0.8	1.0	1.0	1.7	2.5	2.7	0.9	2.5	2.5
Republic of Congo	2.5	6.0	4.3	5.0	1.8	5.0	4.6	0.9	2.0	2.3	2.4	2.1	2.2	2.3	2.5
Côte d'Ivoire	2.8	6.3	1.0	1.4	4.9	1.3	2.6	0.4	1.2	2.1	2.0	2.0	1.3	2.1	2.0
Equatorial Guinea	5.4	4.7	5.7	5.3	4.8	3.4	3.2	4.3	3.2	2.0	2.8	2.8	2.0	2.0	2.8
Eritrea	15.3	19.9	33.0	11.2	3.9	6.0	6.5	10.0	9.0	9.0	9.0	9.0	9.0	9.0	9.0
Ethiopia	6.6	44.4	8.5	8.1	33.2	24.1	8.1	7.4	10.1	10.6	11.6	11.6	10.0	14.0	8.5
Gabon	0.3	5.3	1.9	1.4	1.3	2.7	0.5	4.5	0.1	2.5	2.5	2.5	0.1	2.5	2.5
The Gambia	6.1	4.5	4.6	5.0	4.8	4.6	5.2	6.2	6.8	8.3	7.6	5.0	6.7	10.0	5.2
Ghana	17.9	16.5	13.1	6.7	7.7	7.1	11.7	15.5	17.2	15.7	8.9	6.0	17.7	12.4	7.1
Guinea	13.7	18.4	4.7	15.5	21.4	15.2	11.9	9.7	8.2	7.9	8.0	5.0	7.3	8.5	7.5
Guinea-Bissau	2.6	10.4	−1.6	1.1	5.1	2.1	0.8	−1.0	1.5	2.6	2.8	3.0	2.9	2.5	2.5
Kenya	5.9	15.1	10.6	4.3	14.0	9.4	5.7	6.9	6.6	6.3	6.0	5.0	8.0	5.8	5.5
Lesotho	7.2	10.7	5.9	3.4	6.0	5.5	5.0	4.0	4.8	6.5	6.0	5.0	5.5	6.4	6.0
Liberia	. . .	17.5	7.4	7.3	8.5	6.8	7.6	9.9	7.7	8.2	8.0	7.4	8.0	8.3	7.7
Madagascar	10.0	9.3	9.0	9.2	9.5	5.7	5.8	6.1	7.4	7.2	7.0	5.5	7.6	7.1	7.0
Malawi	19.5	8.7	8.4	7.4	7.6	21.3	28.3	23.8	21.9	19.7	13.9	7.6	24.9	16.0	9.6
Mali	1.7	9.1	2.2	1.3	3.1	5.3	−0.6	0.9	1.4	1.0	1.3	2.5	1.0	1.0	1.5
Mauritius	6.1	9.7	2.5	2.9	6.5	3.9	3.5	3.2	1.3	1.5	2.1	2.6	1.3	2.0	2.2
Mozambique	9.6	10.3	3.3	12.7	10.4	2.1	4.2	2.3	2.4	6.0	5.6	5.6	11.1	5.6	5.6
Namibia	7.4	9.1	9.5	4.9	5.0	6.7	5.6	5.3	3.4	5.2	6.0	5.8	3.5	5.0	5.7
Niger	1.8	11.3	4.3	−2.8	2.9	0.5	2.3	−0.9	1.0	1.5	1.5	2.0	2.2	1.2	1.7
Nigeria	11.3	11.6	12.5	13.7	10.8	12.2	8.5	8.0	9.0	10.4	12.4	8.5	9.6	12.0	12.5
Rwanda	5.9	15.4	10.3	2.3	5.7	6.3	4.2	1.8	2.5	4.8	5.0	5.0	4.5	5.0	5.0
São Tomé and Príncipe	16.2	32.0	17.0	13.3	14.3	10.6	8.1	7.0	5.3	3.0	3.5	3.0	4.0	4.0	3.0
Senegal	1.8	6.3	−2.2	1.2	3.4	1.4	0.7	−1.1	0.1	1.2	1.2	1.2	0.4	1.2	−0.1
Seychelles	3.2	37.0	31.8	−2.4	2.6	7.1	4.3	1.4	4.0	2.2	2.6	3.0	3.2	2.8	3.1
Sierra Leone	11.6	14.8	9.2	17.8	18.5	13.8	9.8	8.3	9.0	9.5	9.0	6.5	10.1	9.5	9.0
South Africa	5.4	11.5	7.1	4.3	5.0	5.7	5.8	6.1	4.6	6.5	6.3	5.6	4.9	6.9	5.8
South Sudan	. . .	. . .	. . .	. . .	. . .	45.1	0.0	1.7	52.8	212.4	21.6	7.5	109.9	119.1	7.5
Swaziland	7.0	12.7	7.4	4.5	6.1	8.9	5.6	5.7	5.0	6.6	5.9	5.8	4.9	8.9	3.4
Tanzania	6.3	10.3	12.1	7.2	12.7	16.0	7.9	6.1	5.6	6.1	5.1	5.1	6.8	5.4	5.0
Togo	2.0	8.7	3.7	1.4	3.6	2.6	1.8	0.2	1.8	2.1	2.5	2.0	1.8	2.3	2.5
Uganda	4.5	12.0	13.1	4.0	18.7	14.0	4.8	4.6	5.8	6.7	5.9	5.0	6.6	6.8	5.1
Zambia	19.7	12.4	13.4	8.5	8.7	6.6	7.0	7.8	10.1	22.5	9.9	5.0	21.1	14.3	8.7
Zimbabwe[10]	−18.5	157.0	6.2	3.0	3.5	3.7	1.6	−0.2	−2.4	−1.2	1.2	2.0	−2.4	−1.1	1.2

[1]Movements in consumer prices are shown as annual averages.
[2]Monthly year-over-year changes and, for several countries, on a quarterly basis.
[3]For many countries, inflation for the earlier years is measured on the basis of a retail price index. Consumer price index (CPI) inflation data with broader and more up-to-date coverage are typically used for more recent years.
[4]Georgia, Turkmenistan, and Ukraine, which are not members of the Commonwealth of Independent States, are included in this group for reasons of geography and similarity in economic structure.
[5]Starting in 2014 data exclude Crimea and Sevastopol.
[6]Excludes Argentina and Venezuela.
[7]See country-specific notes for Argentina in the "Country Notes" section of the Statistical Appendix.
[8]Data for 2011 exclude South Sudan after July 9. Data for 2012 and onward pertain to the current Sudan.
[9]Data for Syria are excluded for 2011 onward owing to the uncertain political situation.
[10]The Zimbabwe dollar ceased circulating in early 2009. Data are based on IMF staff estimates of price and exchange rate developments in U.S. dollars. IMF staff estimates of U.S. dollar values may differ from authorities' estimates.

Table A8. Major Advanced Economies: General Government Fiscal Balances and Debt[1]

(Percent of GDP unless noted otherwise)

	Average 1998–2007	2010	2011	2012	2013	2014	2015	Projections 2016	Projections 2017	Projections 2021
Major Advanced Economies										
Net Lending/Borrowing	–3.2	–8.8	–7.4	–6.4	–4.3	–3.8	–3.4	–3.4	–3.0	–2.4
Output Gap[2]	0.9	–2.9	–2.3	–2.1	–2.2	–1.9	–1.5	–1.1	–0.8	–0.1
Structural Balance[2]	–3.6	–7.3	–6.4	–5.1	–3.7	–3.1	–2.7	–2.9	–2.7	–2.4
United States										
Net Lending/Borrowing[3]	–3.1	–10.9	–9.6	–7.9	–4.4	–4.1	–3.7	–3.8	–3.7	–3.9
Output Gap[2]	1.8	–3.7	–3.4	–2.7	–2.9	–2.2	–1.6	–1.1	–0.6	0.0
Structural Balance[2]	–3.6	–9.4	–8.1	–6.1	–4.0	–3.5	–3.0	–3.4	–3.4	–3.9
Net Debt	41.7	69.5	75.9	79.4	80.9	80.6	80.6	82.2	82.2	81.6
Gross Debt	60.7	94.7	99.0	102.5	104.8	105.0	105.8	107.5	107.5	106.0
Euro Area										
Net Lending/Borrowing	–2.0	–6.2	–4.2	–3.7	–3.0	–2.6	–2.0	–1.9	–1.5	–0.3
Output Gap[2]	0.4	–1.6	–0.7	–2.0	–2.8	–2.6	–2.0	–1.5	–1.0	0.1
Structural Balance[2]	–2.3	–4.5	–3.7	–2.0	–1.2	–1.0	–0.9	–1.1	–0.9	–0.3
Net Debt	48.3	56.6	58.8	66.9	69.2	70.3	69.4	69.3	68.6	62.6
Gross Debt	67.9	84.0	86.6	91.3	93.4	94.5	93.2	92.5	91.3	83.2
Germany										
Net Lending/Borrowing	–2.2	–4.1	–0.9	0.1	0.1	0.3	0.6	0.1	0.1	0.7
Output Gap[2]	–0.2	–1.3	1.0	0.4	–0.4	–0.2	–0.1	0.0	0.3	0.2
Structural Balance[2]	–2.2	–2.2	–1.3	0.0	0.4	0.7	0.7	0.1	–0.2	0.7
Net Debt	45.1	56.7	55.0	54.4	53.4	51.9	48.8	46.7	44.9	37.3
Gross Debt	61.9	81.0	78.4	79.7	77.4	74.9	71.0	68.2	65.9	56.0
France										
Net Lending/Borrowing	–2.5	–6.8	–5.1	–4.8	–4.1	–3.9	–3.6	–3.4	–2.9	–0.4
Output Gap[2]	0.3	–1.8	–0.8	–1.5	–1.8	–2.5	–2.2	–2.0	–1.7	0.2
Structural Balance[2]	–2.8	–5.7	–4.6	–3.7	–2.8	–2.4	–2.1	–2.1	–1.8	–0.5
Net Debt	53.8	73.7	76.4	81.7	84.6	87.9	89.1	90.5	91.1	84.9
Gross Debt	62.2	81.5	85.0	89.4	92.3	95.6	96.8	98.2	98.8	92.6
Italy										
Net Lending/Borrowing	–2.9	–4.2	–3.5	–2.9	–2.9	–3.0	–2.6	–2.7	–1.6	0.0
Output Gap[2]	–0.2	–1.3	–0.5	–2.8	–4.1	–4.1	–3.3	–2.5	–1.6	0.0
Structural Balance[2,4]	–3.5	–3.7	–3.9	–1.6	–0.6	–1.0	–0.8	–1.3	–0.8	0.0
Net Debt	88.5	98.3	100.4	104.9	109.7	112.6	111.4	111.8	110.7	102.2
Gross Debt	103.7	115.4	116.5	123.3	128.9	132.5	132.6	133.0	131.7	121.6
Japan										
Net Lending/Borrowing	–5.8	–9.3	–9.8	–8.8	–8.5	–6.2	–5.2	–4.9	–3.9	–3.3
Output Gap[2]	–0.7	–2.6	–3.3	–2.0	–1.1	–1.6	–1.6	–1.6	–2.0	–1.2
Structural Balance[2]	–5.6	–7.9	–8.5	–7.9	–8.2	–5.8	–4.9	–4.5	–3.5	–3.0
Net Debt	70.0	113.1	127.2	129.0	124.2	126.2	128.1	129.6	131.2	132.0
Gross Debt[5]	162.4	215.8	231.6	238.0	244.5	249.1	248.1	249.3	250.9	251.7
United Kingdom										
Net Lending/Borrowing	–1.6	–9.6	–7.7	–7.7	–5.6	–5.6	–4.4	–3.2	–2.2	0.6
Output Gap[2]	1.0	–2.5	–2.0	–2.3	–1.7	–0.7	–0.3	–0.2	0.0	0.0
Structural Balance[2]	–2.3	–7.6	–6.0	–6.0	–4.2	–4.9	–4.1	–3.1	–2.2	0.6
Net Debt	35.6	69.2	73.3	76.6	77.8	79.7	80.7	80.6	79.3	67.2
Gross Debt	40.1	76.6	81.8	85.3	86.2	88.2	89.3	89.1	87.9	75.8
Canada										
Net Lending/Borrowing	1.1	–4.7	–3.3	–2.5	–1.9	–0.5	–1.7	–2.4	–1.8	–0.1
Output Gap[2]	1.3	–2.4	–1.1	–1.2	–0.9	–0.4	–0.7	–0.8	–0.5	0.0
Structural Balance[2]	0.4	–3.4	–2.7	–1.9	–1.4	–0.5	–1.3	–2.0	–1.5	–0.1
Net Debt	38.2	26.8	27.1	28.2	29.4	28.1	26.7	27.5	25.8	15.8
Gross Debt	78.1	81.1	81.5	84.8	86.1	86.2	91.5	92.3	90.6	80.6

Note: The methodology and specific assumptions for each country are discussed in Box A1. The country group composites for fiscal data are calculated as the sum of the U.S. dollar values for the relevant individual countries.

[1]Debt data refer to the end of the year and are not always comparable across countries. Gross and net debt levels reported by national statistical agencies for countries that have adopted the System of National Accounts (SNA) 2008 (Australia, Canada, Hong Kong SAR, United States) are adjusted to exclude unfunded pension liabilities of government employees' defined-benefit pension plans. Fiscal data for the aggregated Major Advanced Economies and the United States start in 2001, and the average for the aggregate and the United States is therefore for the period 2001–07.

[2]Percent of potential GDP.

[3]Figures reported by the national statistical agency are adjusted to exclude items related to the accrual-basis accounting of government employees' defined-benefit pension plans.

[4]Excludes one-time measures based on the authorities' data and, in the absence of the latter, receipts from the sale of assets.

[5]Includes equity shares; nonconsolidated basis.

Table A9. Summary of World Trade Volumes and Prices
(Annual percent change)

	Averages		2008	2009	2010	2011	2012	2013	2014	2015	Projections	
	1998–2007	2008–17									2016	2017
Trade in Goods and Services												
World Trade[1]												
Volume	6.7	3.0	3.0	−10.5	12.4	7.1	2.8	3.4	3.5	2.8	3.1	3.8
Price Deflator												
In U.S. Dollars	2.7	−0.5	11.4	−10.3	5.6	11.1	−1.7	−0.6	−1.8	−12.9	−4.7	1.9
In SDRs	1.7	0.4	8.0	−8.1	6.7	7.4	1.3	0.2	−1.7	−5.4	−4.3	1.5
Volume of Trade												
Exports												
Advanced Economies	5.8	2.5	2.0	−11.2	12.0	5.9	2.3	3.0	3.5	3.4	2.5	3.5
Emerging Market and Developing Economies	8.8	3.9	4.9	−8.2	13.3	9.0	4.0	4.4	3.1	1.7	3.8	3.9
Imports												
Advanced Economies	6.2	2.2	0.4	−11.7	11.4	5.0	1.1	2.2	3.5	4.3	3.4	4.1
Emerging Market and Developing Economies	8.8	4.6	9.5	−8.5	14.0	11.4	5.6	5.2	3.7	0.5	3.0	3.7
Terms of Trade												
Advanced Economies	−0.2	0.1	−2.3	2.6	−0.9	−1.5	−0.7	0.8	0.3	1.9	1.1	−0.3
Emerging Market and Developing Economies	1.8	−0.2	3.5	−4.7	2.1	3.6	0.5	0.0	−0.4	−3.9	−2.3	−0.3
Trade in Goods												
World Trade[1]												
Volume	6.9	2.8	2.5	−11.6	14.3	6.9	2.5	3.1	3.2	2.4	2.8	3.6
Price Deflator												
In U.S. Dollars	2.6	−0.7	12.3	−11.7	6.6	12.5	−1.8	−1.1	−2.5	−13.9	−5.7	1.9
In SDRs	1.5	0.2	8.9	−9.6	7.7	8.7	1.2	−0.3	−2.4	−6.6	−5.4	1.5
World Trade Prices in U.S. Dollars[2]												
Manufactures	1.5	0.1	6.2	−5.6	2.4	6.4	0.5	−1.0	−0.7	−4.0	−2.7	0.7
Oil	14.0	−5.4	36.4	−36.3	27.9	31.6	1.0	−0.9	−7.5	−47.2	−31.6	17.9
Nonfuel Primary Commodities	3.9	−1.5	7.9	−16.0	26.6	18.0	−10.0	−1.4	−4.0	−17.5	−9.4	−0.7
Food	2.1	0.4	24.3	−15.2	12.1	20.2	−2.4	0.7	−4.1	−17.1	−5.6	−0.9
Beverages	−0.6	1.7	23.3	1.6	14.1	16.6	−18.6	−11.9	20.7	−3.1	−15.2	0.2
Agricultural Raw Materials	0.2	−0.5	−0.7	−17.1	33.2	22.7	−12.7	1.6	1.9	−13.5	−10.3	0.4
Metal	10.4	−5.3	−7.8	−19.2	48.2	13.5	−16.8	−4.3	−10.3	−23.1	−14.1	−1.5
World Trade Prices in SDRs[2]												
Manufactures	0.4	1.0	2.9	−3.3	3.5	2.8	3.6	−0.2	−0.6	4.2	−2.4	0.3
Oil	12.7	−4.5	32.2	−34.8	29.3	27.2	4.1	−0.1	−7.5	−42.7	−31.4	17.5
Nonfuel Primary Commodities	2.8	−0.6	4.6	−13.9	28.0	14.0	−7.3	−0.6	−3.9	−10.4	−9.1	−1.1
Food	1.0	1.3	20.5	−13.1	13.3	16.1	0.6	1.5	−4.1	−10.0	−5.3	−1.2
Beverages	−1.6	2.7	19.5	4.1	15.3	12.7	−16.1	−11.2	20.8	5.2	−14.9	−0.2
Agricultural Raw Materials	−0.8	0.3	−3.8	−15.1	34.6	18.6	−10.0	2.4	2.0	−6.1	−10.0	0.0
Metal	9.3	−4.4	−10.7	−17.2	49.8	9.7	−14.3	−3.5	−10.2	−16.6	−13.8	−1.9
World Trade Prices in Euros[2]												
Manufactures	−0.4	2.2	−1.1	−0.3	7.5	1.5	8.8	−4.2	−0.7	14.9	−2.8	−0.1
Oil	11.8	−3.4	27.1	−32.7	34.3	25.5	9.3	−4.1	−7.6	−36.8	−31.6	17.1
Nonfuel Primary Commodities	1.9	0.5	0.5	−11.2	32.9	12.5	−2.6	−4.5	−4.0	−1.2	−9.5	−1.5
Food	0.2	2.4	15.8	−10.4	17.7	14.6	5.6	−2.5	−4.2	−0.7	−5.7	−1.6
Beverages	−2.4	3.8	14.8	7.3	19.8	11.2	−11.9	−14.7	20.7	16.1	−15.2	−0.6
Agricultural Raw Materials	−1.6	1.5	−7.5	−12.5	39.8	17.0	−5.5	−1.6	1.8	3.6	−10.4	−0.4
Metal	8.4	−3.3	−14.1	−14.6	55.5	8.3	−10.0	−7.3	−10.3	−7.9	−14.2	−2.2

Table A9. Summary of World Trade Volumes and Prices *(continued)*
(Annual percent change)

	Averages										Projections	
	1998–2007	2008–17	2008	2009	2010	2011	2012	2013	2014	2015	2016	2017
Trade in Goods												
Volume of Trade												
Exports												
Advanced Economies	5.9	2.3	1.7	−13.1	14.7	6.0	1.9	2.6	3.3	2.9	2.1	3.2
Emerging Market and Developing Economies	9.0	3.7	4.1	−8.7	14.8	8.1	4.2	4.3	3.1	1.5	3.6	3.7
Fuel Exporters	5.2	2.4	4.2	−7.9	5.1	7.7	3.9	1.2	1.0	2.5	5.5	1.8
Nonfuel Exporters	10.6	4.2	4.0	−9.1	18.8	8.3	4.3	5.7	4.0	1.1	3.1	4.1
Imports												
Advanced Economies	6.3	2.0	−0.3	−12.8	13.1	5.3	0.3	1.8	3.4	3.8	3.1	4.1
Emerging Market and Developing Economies	8.9	4.3	9.0	−9.6	15.3	10.5	5.4	4.8	3.0	0.4	2.9	3.6
Fuel Exporters	9.6	2.6	14.6	−13.1	7.2	9.8	9.9	4.5	2.6	−7.2	−1.7	2.1
Nonfuel Exporters	8.8	4.7	7.5	−8.8	17.4	10.7	4.3	4.9	3.0	2.2	3.9	3.9
Price Deflators in SDRs												
Exports												
Advanced Economies	0.8	−0.2	5.6	−7.2	4.4	6.4	−0.3	0.5	−1.9	−5.5	−3.4	0.8
Emerging Market and Developing Economies	4.1	0.7	14.6	−12.9	13.2	12.6	2.8	−0.7	−3.3	−8.8	−8.4	2.2
Fuel Exporters	9.1	−1.9	24.8	−24.7	22.7	23.5	3.4	−1.6	−7.1	−28.6	−21.0	8.7
Nonfuel Exporters	2.1	1.5	10.1	−7.0	9.2	8.1	2.4	−0.3	−1.6	−0.7	−4.7	0.6
Imports												
Advanced Economies	1.1	−0.1	8.6	−10.5	6.3	8.7	1.0	−0.4	−2.1	−7.2	−4.6	1.2
Emerging Market and Developing Economies	2.4	0.9	10.0	−8.4	11.2	8.8	2.2	−0.8	−2.9	−4.9	−6.6	2.2
Fuel Exporters	2.0	1.0	8.5	−5.7	9.2	8.2	1.7	−0.9	−3.5	−2.6	−4.7	0.8
Nonfuel Exporters	2.5	0.8	10.4	−9.1	11.7	9.0	2.3	−0.8	−2.8	−5.4	−7.1	2.5
Terms of Trade												
Advanced Economies	−0.3	−0.1	−2.7	3.7	−1.8	−2.1	−1.3	0.8	0.1	1.8	1.2	−0.4
Emerging Market and Developing Economies	1.6	−0.2	4.2	−4.9	1.8	3.5	0.5	0.1	−0.4	−4.1	−1.9	0.0
Regional Groups												
Commonwealth of Independent States[3]	5.3	−1.4	15.5	−16.8	11.7	10.7	2.0	−1.6	0.7	−19.9	−14.6	5.8
Emerging and Developing Asia	−1.8	0.8	−1.3	3.3	−6.4	−2.4	1.2	1.1	2.4	9.2	4.1	−2.2
Emerging and Developing Europe	0.0	0.1	−0.4	3.3	−3.9	−1.8	−1.0	1.8	1.0	2.6	1.2	−2.1
Latin America and the Caribbean	2.8	−0.6	4.7	−4.8	8.4	5.6	−1.4	−0.9	−3.1	−9.8	−2.8	−0.5
Middle East, North Africa, Afghanistan, and												
Pakistan	6.1	−3.1	11.5	−17.6	9.7	12.8	−0.2	−0.2	−5.0	−25.3	−14.7	6.7
Middle East and North Africa	6.4	−3.2	12.1	−17.9	9.6	12.9	0.4	−0.2	−5.0	−26.0	−15.5	7.0
Sub-Saharan Africa	3.0	−0.9	9.0	−11.2	12.4	10.7	−0.4	−2.1	−3.5	−15.4	−7.1	2.5
Analytical Groups												
By Source of Export Earnings												
Fuel	7.0	−2.8	15.1	−20.2	12.4	14.1	1.7	−0.7	−3.7	−26.7	−17.2	7.8
Nonfuel	−0.4	0.6	−0.3	2.3	−2.2	−0.7	0.1	0.5	1.2	5.0	2.6	−1.9
Memorandum												
World Exports in Billions of U.S. Dollars												
Goods and Services	10,172	20,839	19,580	15,725	18,662	22,208	22,443	23,144	23,494	20,942	20,532	21,663
Goods	8,084	16,440	15,666	12,226	14,901	17,913	18,049	18,486	18,591	16,266	15,739	16,564
Average Oil Price[4]	14.0	−5.4	36.4	−36.3	27.9	31.6	1.0	−0.9	−7.5	−47.2	−31.6	17.9
In U.S. Dollars a Barrel	36.40	77.37	97.04	61.78	79.03	104.01	105.01	104.07	96.25	50.79	34.75	40.99
Export Unit Value of Manufactures[5]	1.5	0.1	6.2	−5.6	2.4	6.4	0.5	−1.0	−0.7	−4.0	−2.7	0.7

[1]Average of annual percent change for world exports and imports.
[2]As represented, respectively, by the export unit value index for manufactures of the advanced economies and accounting for 83 percent of the advanced economies' trade (export of goods) weights; the average of U.K. Brent, Dubai Fateh, and West Texas Intermediate crude oil prices; and the average of world market prices for nonfuel primary commodities weighted by their 2002–04 shares in world commodity exports.
[3]Georgia, Turkmenistan, and Ukraine, which are not members of the Commonwealth of Independent States, are included in this group for reasons of geography and similarity in economic structure.
[4]Percent change of average of U.K. Brent, Dubai Fateh, and West Texas Intermediate crude oil prices.
[5]Percent change for manufactures exported by the advanced economies.

Table A10. Summary of Current Account Balances
(Billions of U.S. dollars)

	2008	2009	2010	2011	2012	2013	2014	2015	2016	2017	2021
									Projections		
Advanced Economies	**−577.5**	**−85.1**	**3.7**	**−40.4**	**18.8**	**222.1**	**232.9**	**302.7**	**305.1**	**189.1**	**−53.1**
United States	−690.8	−384.0	−442.0	−460.4	−449.7	−376.8	−389.5	−484.1	−540.6	−639.1	−877.6
Euro Area	−192.8	7.9	36.6	33.2	159.8	257.6	320.1	344.7	419.6	397.6	356.6
Germany	210.9	196.7	192.3	229.0	248.9	252.9	282.9	285.2	292.0	287.0	281.9
France	−27.6	−22.5	−22.2	−28.3	−32.0	−22.6	−26.2	−3.0	15.2	6.5	0.6
Italy	−68.8	−42.5	−74.0	−70.1	−8.9	19.0	40.9	38.7	41.9	37.2	19.4
Spain	−152.0	−64.3	−56.2	−47.4	−3.1	20.7	13.6	16.5	23.7	25.8	27.3
Japan	142.6	145.3	221.0	129.8	59.7	40.7	24.4	137.5	167.5	165.5	179.1
United Kingdom	−101.2	−70.4	−67.2	−43.9	−86.7	−121.8	−152.2	−123.5	−119.5	−114.0	−117.0
Canada	1.5	−40.4	−58.2	−49.6	−65.7	−57.9	−40.6	−51.4	−51.7	−45.6	−41.2
Other Advanced Economies[1]	169.6	209.5	285.7	269.2	280.7	357.2	369.3	374.6	364.6	357.3	370.3
Emerging Market and Developing Economies	**679.6**	**243.9**	**280.3**	**380.3**	**360.6**	**189.6**	**145.5**	**−71.7**	**−163.7**	**−176.8**	**−298.7**
Regional Groups											
Commonwealth of Independent States[2]	108.3	42.9	69.2	107.9	67.2	18.1	57.7	51.4	30.5	51.0	103.4
Russia	103.9	50.4	67.5	97.3	71.3	34.1	59.5	65.8	48.0	64.3	103.8
Excluding Russia	4.4	−7.5	1.7	10.7	−4.1	−16.0	−1.8	−14.4	−17.5	−13.3	−0.4
Emerging and Developing Asia	424.5	273.4	233.5	98.1	120.9	100.9	208.4	290.3	270.5	192.1	−43.2
China	420.6	243.3	237.8	136.1	215.4	148.2	219.7	293.2	296.4	252.6	93.5
India	−27.9	−38.2	−48.1	−78.2	−88.2	−32.4	−26.7	−26.2	−34.5	−51.8	−94.7
ASEAN-5[3]	29.9	64.6	43.9	48.9	6.5	−3.9	22.4	36.9	24.8	11.0	−16.8
Emerging and Developing Europe	−148.9	−53.9	−86.5	−119.3	−81.7	−72.0	−58.6	−32.4	−35.7	−45.8	−78.4
Latin America and the Caribbean	−42.3	−30.7	−96.6	−113.6	−136.8	−157.3	−185.1	−181.1	−127.4	−112.6	−102.3
Brazil	−30.6	−26.3	−75.8	−77.0	−74.2	−74.8	−104.2	−58.9	−31.1	−23.6	2.3
Mexico	−20.7	−8.7	−5.2	−13.4	−16.6	−30.3	−24.8	−32.4	−27.7	−29.8	−35.2
Middle East, North Africa, Afghanistan, and Pakistan	334.3	41.7	171.2	416.6	419.3	339.4	192.6	−111.7	−210.5	−173.1	−76.6
Sub-Saharan Africa	3.7	−29.4	−10.4	−9.4	−28.4	−39.5	−69.6	−88.2	−91.1	−88.4	−101.6
South Africa	−15.9	−8.1	−5.6	−9.0	−19.7	−21.1	−19.1	−13.7	−11.6	−13.3	−13.1
Analytical Groups											
By Source of Export Earnings											
Fuel	583.4	132.5	306.1	616.9	591.7	454.8	288.4	−78.6	−191.3	−108.9	55.3
Nonfuel	96.9	113.0	−24.1	−236.6	−231.0	−265.2	−143.0	6.8	27.6	−68.0	−354.0
Of Which, Primary Products	−20.1	−1.3	−10.2	−23.2	−55.3	−60.3	−48.6	−55.8	−45.7	−51.6	−62.4
By External Financing Source											
Net Debtor Economies	−298.7	−145.7	−262.2	−362.0	−438.7	−408.4	−376.2	−314.7	−304.7	−338.8	−451.8
Net Debtor Economies by Debt-Servicing Experience											
Economies with Arrears and/or Rescheduling during 2010–14	−15.7	−15.5	−14.0	−24.2	−38.4	−38.1	−22.9	−29.7	−34.9	−35.0	−35.3
Memorandum											
World	**102.2**	**158.9**	**284.0**	**339.9**	**379.4**	**411.7**	**378.4**	**231.0**	**141.4**	**12.3**	**−351.8**
European Union	−241.5	−18.7	2.1	84.3	216.2	314.9	319.1	382.4	413.1	395.2	340.1
Low-Income Developing Countries	−10.3	−24.7	−18.4	−27.9	−39.4	−43.8	−58.8	−89.9	−95.0	−96.7	−121.0
Middle East and North Africa	347.9	49.4	174.0	415.3	422.8	340.3	194.1	−109.9	−207.8	−168.4	−68.8

Table A10. Summary of Current Account Balances *(continued)*
(Percent of GDP)

	2008	2009	2010	2011	2012	2013	2014	2015	Projections 2016	2017	2021
Advanced Economies	**−1.3**	**−0.2**	**0.0**	**−0.1**	**0.0**	**0.5**	**0.5**	**0.7**	**0.7**	**0.4**	**−0.1**
United States	−4.7	−2.7	−3.0	−3.0	−2.8	−2.3	−2.2	−2.7	−2.9	−3.3	−3.9
Euro Area	−1.4	0.1	0.3	0.2	1.3	2.0	2.4	3.0	3.5	3.2	2.6
Germany	5.6	5.7	5.6	6.1	7.0	6.8	7.3	8.5	8.4	8.0	6.9
France	−0.9	−0.8	−0.8	−1.0	−1.2	−0.8	−0.9	−0.1	0.6	0.3	0.0
Italy	−2.9	−1.9	−3.5	−3.1	−0.4	0.9	1.9	2.1	2.3	2.0	0.9
Spain	−9.3	−4.3	−3.9	−3.2	−0.2	1.5	1.0	1.4	1.9	2.0	1.9
Japan	2.9	2.9	4.0	2.2	1.0	0.8	0.5	3.3	3.8	3.7	3.7
United Kingdom	−3.6	−3.0	−2.8	−1.7	−3.3	−4.5	−5.1	−4.3	−4.3	−4.0	−3.5
Canada	0.1	−2.9	−3.6	−2.8	−3.6	−3.2	−2.3	−3.3	−3.5	−3.0	−2.3
Other Advanced Economies[1]	3.2	4.3	5.0	4.1	4.3	5.3	5.4	6.0	5.9	5.5	4.9
Emerging Market and Developing											
Economies	**3.4**	**1.3**	**1.2**	**1.4**	**1.3**	**0.6**	**0.5**	**−0.2**	**−0.6**	**−0.6**	**−0.7**
Regional Groups											
Commonwealth of Independent States[2]	4.7	2.5	3.3	4.1	2.4	0.6	2.1	2.8	2.0	3.0	4.6
Russia	5.9	3.9	4.1	4.8	3.3	1.5	2.9	5.0	4.2	5.1	6.5
Excluding Russia	0.8	−1.8	0.4	1.8	−0.6	−2.3	−0.3	−2.8	−4.2	−2.9	−0.1
Emerging and Developing Asia	5.7	3.4	2.4	0.9	1.0	0.7	1.4	1.9	1.7	1.1	−0.2
China	9.2	4.8	4.0	1.8	2.5	1.6	2.1	2.7	2.6	2.1	0.5
India	−2.3	−2.8	−2.8	−4.3	−4.8	−1.7	−1.3	−1.3	−1.5	−2.1	−2.6
ASEAN-5[3]	2.2	4.8	2.6	2.5	0.3	−0.2	1.1	1.8	1.1	0.5	−0.5
Emerging and Developing Europe	−8.0	−3.5	−5.1	−6.5	−4.6	−3.8	−3.1	−1.9	−2.1	−2.6	−3.5
Latin America and the Caribbean	−1.0	−0.8	−1.9	−1.9	−2.3	−2.6	−3.1	−3.6	−2.8	−2.4	−1.8
Brazil	−1.8	−1.6	−3.4	−2.9	−3.0	−3.0	−4.3	−3.3	−2.0	−1.5	0.1
Mexico	−1.9	−1.0	−0.5	−1.1	−1.4	−2.4	−1.9	−2.8	−2.6	−2.6	−2.4
Middle East, North Africa, Afghanistan, and Pakistan	12.6	1.8	6.2	12.9	11.9	10.0	5.5	−3.6	−6.9	−5.2	−1.8
Sub-Saharan Africa	0.3	−2.8	−0.8	−0.6	−1.8	−2.4	−4.1	−5.9	−6.2	−5.5	−4.9
South Africa	−5.5	−2.7	−1.5	−2.2	−5.0	−5.8	−5.4	−4.4	−4.4	−4.9	−4.0
Analytical Groups											
By Source of Export Earnings											
Fuel	11.5	3.2	6.0	10.0	8.8	6.8	4.4	−1.5	−4.1	−2.1	0.9
Nonfuel	0.7	0.8	−0.1	−1.2	−1.1	−1.1	−0.6	0.0	0.1	−0.3	−1.0
Of Which, Primary Products	−1.8	−0.1	−0.7	−1.5	−3.3	−3.6	−3.0	−3.5	−3.3	−3.6	−3.5
By External Financing Source											
Net Debtor Economies	−2.9	−1.5	−2.2	−2.7	−3.2	−2.9	−2.6	−2.4	−2.3	−2.4	−2.4
Net Debtor Economies by Debt-Servicing Experience											
Economies with Arrears and/or Rescheduling during 2010–14	−3.0	−3.2	−2.5	−3.9	−5.8	−5.5	−3.4	−4.4	−5.1	−4.8	−3.7
Memorandum											
World	**0.2**	**0.3**	**0.4**	**0.5**	**0.5**	**0.5**	**0.5**	**0.3**	**0.2**	**0.0**	**−0.4**
European Union	−1.3	−0.1	0.0	0.5	1.3	1.8	1.7	2.4	2.5	2.3	1.7
Low-Income Developing Countries	−0.9	−2.2	−1.4	−1.9	−2.4	−2.4	−3.0	−4.8	−4.8	−4.5	−4.2
Middle East and North Africa	14.1	2.2	6.8	13.9	12.9	10.8	6.0	−3.9	−7.5	−5.6	−1.8

Table A10. Summary of Current Account Balances *(continued)*
(Percent of exports of goods and services)

	2008	2009	2010	2011	2012	2013	2014	2015	Projections 2016	Projections 2017	Projections 2021
Advanced Economies	**−4.5**	**−0.8**	**0.0**	**−0.3**	**0.1**	**1.5**	**1.6**	**2.3**	**2.3**	**1.4**	**−0.3**
United States	−37.5	−24.3	−23.8	−21.6	−20.3	−16.5	−16.6	−21.8	−25.4	−29.7	−35.1
Euro Area	−6.2	0.3	1.3	1.0	5.0	7.6	9.0	11.0	. . .	. . .	. . .
Germany	12.9	15.2	13.3	13.6	15.3	14.8	16.0	18.1	18.1	16.9	13.6
France	−3.3	−3.4	−3.1	−3.4	−4.0	−2.7	−3.0	−0.4	2.0	0.8	0.1
Italy	−10.6	−8.6	−13.8	−11.4	−1.5	3.1	6.5	7.1	7.3	6.2	2.6
Spain	−36.5	−18.9	−15.3	−11.0	−0.8	4.7	3.0	4.1	5.7	5.9	4.9
Japan	16.0	21.7	25.4	13.9	6.5	4.9	2.8	17.5	21.6	20.5	19.1
United Kingdom	−13.1	−11.3	−9.8	−5.5	−10.9	−15.0	−18.0	−15.8	−16.1	−14.3	−12.1
Canada	0.3	−10.4	−12.4	−9.1	−11.9	−10.4	−7.2	−10.6	−11.6	−9.6	−7.0
Other Advanced Economies[1]	5.3	7.9	8.7	6.9	7.2	8.8	9.1	10.4	10.3	9.6	8.4
Emerging Market and Developing											
Economies	**9.6**	**4.4**	**4.0**	**4.6**	**3.9**	**2.0**	**1.8**	**−0.7**	**−2.0**	**−2.0**	**−2.9**
Regional Groups											
Commonwealth of Independent States[2]	13.7	8.2	10.3	12.2	7.4	2.0	6.8	8.8	6.4	9.7	15.1
Russia	19.9	14.7	15.3	17.0	12.1	5.8	10.6	16.9	15.1	18.2	23.2
Excluding Russia	1.6	−4.1	0.8	3.4	−1.3	−5.2	−0.6	−7.3	−10.8	−7.6	−0.2
Emerging and Developing Asia	16.5	12.5	8.3	2.8	3.3	2.6	5.2	7.6	7.1	4.8	−0.9
China	28.1	19.5	14.8	6.8	9.9	6.3	8.9	12.3	12.7	10.6	3.3
India	−9.5	−13.7	−12.6	−17.3	−19.5	−6.9	−5.6	−5.9	−7.8	−10.8	−13.8
ASEAN-5[3]	4.2	10.7	5.9	5.5	0.7	−0.4	2.3	4.1	2.7	1.1	−1.3
Emerging and Developing Europe	−22.8	−10.3	−14.7	−17.2	−11.8	−9.7	−7.4	−4.5	−4.9	−5.9	−7.9
Latin America and the Caribbean	−4.2	−3.8	−9.7	−9.3	−11.0	−12.6	−15.1	−17.1	−12.4	−10.2	−7.2
Brazil	−13.5	−14.6	−32.7	−26.3	−26.4	−26.8	−39.5	−26.3	−14.4	−10.3	0.8
Mexico	−6.7	−3.5	−1.7	−3.7	−4.3	−7.6	−5.9	−8.0	−6.7	−6.7	−6.0
Middle East, North Africa, Afghanistan, and											
Pakistan	23.4	3.5	13.8	27.2	24.8	20.7	13.5	−8.5	−19.3	−14.2	−4.8
Sub-Saharan Africa	1.0	−9.8	−2.7	−1.9	−5.9	−8.3	−15.3	−25.3	−28.1	−24.8	−21.8
South Africa	−15.5	−9.8	−5.2	−7.1	−16.7	−18.6	−17.4	−14.1	−12.3	−13.9	−11.5
Analytical Groups											
By Source of Export Earnings											
Fuel	26.0	8.5	16.0	24.6	21.8	17.2	12.3	−3.7	−12.2	−5.7	3.4
Nonfuel	2.1	3.0	−0.5	−4.1	−3.9	−4.2	−2.2	0.1	0.5	−1.1	−4.4
Of Which, Primary Products	−5.7	−0.4	−2.7	−5.2	−13.2	−14.4	−12.1	−16.1	−13.5	−14.5	−14.0
By External Financing Source											
Net Debtor Economies	−9.3	−5.5	−8.0	−9.2	−11.0	−10.0	−9.2	−8.5	−8.4	−8.7	−8.6
Net Debtor Economies by											
Debt-Servicing Experience											
Economies with Arrears and/or											
Rescheduling during 2010–14	−8.3	−10.9	−8.3	−12.3	−19.8	−19.8	−13.3	−20.7	−26.4	−24.7	−18.7
Memorandum											
World	**0.3**	**1.0**	**1.4**	**1.5**	**1.6**	**1.7**	**1.7**	**1.2**	**0.8**	**0.1**	**−1.3**
European Union	−3.2	−0.3	0.0	1.1	2.9	4.1	4.0	5.4	5.7	5.1	3.6
Low-Income Developing Countries	−2.9	−8.2	−4.8	−5.7	−7.9	−8.2	−10.7	−18.0	−18.7	−16.8	−13.9
Middle East and North Africa	25.0	4.4	14.4	27.8	25.5	21.3	13.9	−8.6	−19.6	−14.1	−4.4

[1]Excludes the G7 (Canada, France, Germany, Italy, Japan, United Kingdom, United States) and euro area countries.
[2]Georgia, Turkmenistan, and Ukraine, which are not members of the Commonwealth of Independent States, are included in this group for reasons of geography and similarity in economic structure.
[3]Indonesia, Malaysia, Philippines, Thailand, Vietnam.

Table A11. Advanced Economies: Balance on Current Account
(Percent of GDP)

	2008	2009	2010	2011	2012	2013	2014	2015	Projections 2016	Projections 2017	Projections 2021
Advanced Economies	**−1.3**	**−0.2**	**0.0**	**−0.1**	**0.0**	**0.5**	**0.5**	**0.7**	**0.7**	**0.4**	**−0.1**
United States	−4.7	−2.7	−3.0	−3.0	−2.8	−2.3	−2.2	−2.7	−2.9	−3.3	−3.9
Euro Area[1]	−1.4	0.1	0.3	0.2	1.3	2.0	2.4	3.0	3.5	3.2	2.6
Germany	5.6	5.7	5.6	6.1	7.0	6.8	7.3	8.5	8.4	8.0	6.9
France	−0.9	−0.8	−0.8	−1.0	−1.2	−0.8	−0.9	−0.1	0.6	0.3	0.0
Italy	−2.9	−1.9	−3.5	−3.1	−0.4	0.9	1.9	2.1	2.3	2.0	0.9
Spain	−9.3	−4.3	−3.9	−3.2	−0.2	1.5	1.0	1.4	1.9	2.0	1.9
Netherlands	4.1	5.8	7.4	9.1	10.8	11.0	10.6	11.0	10.6	10.2	8.8
Belgium	−1.0	−1.1	1.8	−1.1	−0.1	−0.2	−0.2	0.5	0.5	0.1	−0.8
Austria	4.5	2.6	2.9	1.6	1.5	2.0	1.9	3.6	3.6	3.5	3.1
Greece	−14.4	−12.4	−11.4	−10.0	−3.8	−2.0	−2.1	0.0	−0.2	−0.3	0.3
Portugal	−12.1	−10.4	−10.1	−6.0	−1.9	1.5	0.1	0.5	0.9	0.4	−0.6
Ireland	−5.7	−3.0	0.6	0.8	−1.5	3.1	3.6	4.5	4.0	3.5	3.1
Finland	2.2	1.9	1.2	−1.8	−1.9	−1.7	−0.9	0.1	0.0	−0.1	0.3
Slovak Republic	−6.4	−3.5	−4.7	−5.0	0.9	2.0	0.1	−1.1	−1.0	−1.0	0.6
Lithuania	−13.3	2.1	−0.3	−3.9	−1.2	1.5	3.6	−2.3	−3.0	−2.9	−2.7
Slovenia	−5.3	−0.6	−0.1	0.2	2.6	5.6	7.0	7.3	7.6	7.1	3.9
Luxembourg	7.7	7.4	6.8	6.2	6.1	5.7	5.5	5.2	5.1	5.0	5.0
Latvia	−12.4	8.1	2.3	−2.8	−3.3	−2.4	−2.0	−1.6	−2.0	−2.2	−1.9
Estonia	−8.7	2.5	1.8	1.3	−2.4	−0.1	1.0	1.9	1.2	0.5	−2.4
Cyprus	−15.6	−7.7	−10.7	−4.0	−5.6	−4.5	−4.6	−5.1	−4.8	−4.7	−4.9
Malta	−1.1	−6.6	−4.7	−2.5	1.3	3.6	3.9	4.1	5.3	5.3	6.7
Japan	2.9	2.9	4.0	2.2	1.0	0.8	0.5	3.3	3.8	3.7	3.7
United Kingdom	−3.6	−3.0	−2.8	−1.7	−3.3	−4.5	−5.1	−4.3	−4.3	−4.0	−3.5
Korea	0.3	3.7	2.6	1.6	4.2	6.2	6.0	7.7	8.2	7.4	5.6
Canada	0.1	−2.9	−3.6	−2.8	−3.6	−3.2	−2.3	−3.3	−3.5	−3.0	−2.3
Australia	−5.0	−4.7	−3.6	−3.0	−4.3	−3.4	−3.0	−4.6	−3.6	−3.5	−3.2
Taiwan Province of China	6.6	10.9	8.9	8.2	9.9	10.8	12.3	14.5	15.0	14.4	14.0
Switzerland	3.0	8.0	14.9	7.7	10.3	11.1	8.8	11.4	9.3	8.8	8.8
Sweden	8.5	5.9	6.0	6.1	5.9	6.0	5.4	5.9	5.8	5.7	5.0
Singapore	14.4	16.8	23.7	22.0	17.2	17.9	17.4	19.7	21.2	20.5	18.0
Hong Kong SAR	15.0	9.9	7.0	5.6	1.6	1.5	1.3	3.0	3.1	3.2	3.6
Norway	15.7	10.6	10.9	12.4	12.4	10.2	11.9	9.0	6.5	7.3	8.3
Czech Republic	−1.9	−2.4	−3.7	−2.1	−1.6	−0.5	0.2	0.9	0.6	0.6	−1.0
Israel	1.1	3.4	3.6	2.3	1.4	3.1	3.8	4.1	4.0	3.5	2.4
Denmark	2.7	3.3	5.7	5.7	5.7	7.1	7.7	6.9	6.6	6.5	6.1
New Zealand	−7.7	−2.3	−2.2	−2.8	−3.9	−3.1	−3.1	−3.0	−3.7	−3.7	−2.9
Puerto Rico	. . .	. . .	. . .	. . .	. . .	. . .	. . .	. . .	. . .	. . .	. . .
Macao SAR	19.1	31.0	43.0	43.1	41.7	42.6	38.0	26.2	20.0	17.2	24.5
Iceland	−22.8	−9.7	−6.6	−5.3	−4.2	5.7	3.7	4.2	4.1	2.4	0.9
San Marino	. . .	. . .	. . .	. . .	. . .	. . .	. . .	. . .	. . .	. . .	. . .
Memorandum											
Major Advanced Economies	−1.6	−0.7	−0.8	−0.8	−1.0	−0.8	−0.7	−0.6	−0.6	−0.8	−1.3
Euro Area[2]	−0.7	0.4	0.5	0.8	2.2	2.9	3.1	3.9	4.1	3.8	3.1

[1]Data corrected for reporting discrepancies in intra-area transactions.
[2]Data calculated as the sum of the balances of individual euro area countries.

Table A12. Emerging Market and Developing Economies: Balance on Current Account
(Percent of GDP)

	2008	2009	2010	2011	2012	2013	2014	2015	Projections 2016	2017	2021
Commonwealth of Independent States[1]	**4.7**	**2.5**	**3.3**	**4.1**	**2.4**	**0.6**	**2.1**	**2.8**	**2.0**	**3.0**	**4.6**
Russia	5.9	3.9	4.1	4.8	3.3	1.5	2.9	5.0	4.2	5.1	6.5
Excluding Russia	0.8	−1.8	0.4	1.8	−0.6	−2.3	−0.3	−2.8	−4.2	−2.9	−0.1
Armenia	−14.2	−16.5	−13.6	−10.4	−10.0	−7.6	−7.3	−3.2	−4.3	−5.1	−5.7
Azerbaijan	35.5	23.0	28.0	26.5	21.5	16.4	13.9	0.2	−0.2	0.2	5.9
Belarus	−8.2	−12.6	−15.0	−8.5	−2.9	−10.4	−6.8	−1.9	−3.5	−3.1	−2.9
Georgia	−22.0	−10.5	−10.2	−12.8	−11.7	−5.8	−10.6	−11.6	−10.3	−9.1	−5.6
Kazakhstan	4.7	−3.6	0.9	5.4	0.5	0.4	2.8	−2.6	−4.0	−1.5	2.6
Kyrgyz Republic	−15.3	−2.2	−6.1	−9.6	−15.6	−15.0	−16.7	−14.7	−18.4	−15.4	−9.8
Moldova	−16.1	−8.2	−7.5	−11.0	−7.4	−5.0	−3.7	−6.6	−4.0	−4.4	−4.8
Tajikistan	−7.6	−5.9	−1.1	−4.8	−2.5	−2.9	−9.7	−10.2	−8.4	−7.3	−2.9
Turkmenistan	16.5	−14.7	−10.6	2.0	0.0	−7.2	−6.7	−12.7	−15.4	−11.6	−1.9
Ukraine[2]	−6.8	−1.4	−2.2	−6.3	−8.1	−9.2	−4.0	−0.3	−2.6	−2.3	−2.5
Uzbekistan	8.7	2.2	6.2	5.8	1.8	2.9	0.7	0.0	0.2	0.5	2.0
Emerging and Developing Asia	**5.7**	**3.4**	**2.4**	**0.9**	**1.0**	**0.7**	**1.4**	**1.9**	**1.7**	**1.1**	**−0.2**
Bangladesh	1.2	2.4	0.4	−1.0	0.7	1.2	−0.1	−1.1	−1.3	−1.5	−2.1
Bhutan	−2.2	−2.2	−9.9	−23.5	−19.0	−22.7	−23.1	−26.7	−24.9	−26.1	−4.5
Brunei Darussalam	44.1	36.3	41.0	32.8	29.8	20.9	27.8	7.8	−6.9	0.7	19.0
Cambodia	−6.6	−6.9	−6.8	−10.2	−11.0	−12.3	−12.1	−11.2	−8.3	−8.0	−5.9
China	9.2	4.8	4.0	1.8	2.5	1.6	2.1	2.7	2.6	2.1	0.5
Fiji	−15.9	−4.2	−4.1	−4.9	−1.3	−9.8	−7.2	−5.4	−7.9	−6.5	−4.9
India	−2.3	−2.8	−2.8	−4.3	−4.8	−1.7	−1.3	−1.3	−1.5	−2.1	−2.6
Indonesia	0.0	1.8	0.7	0.2	−2.7	−3.2	−3.1	−2.1	−2.6	−2.8	−3.0
Kiribati	−6.5	−13.5	−2.2	−13.4	−4.5	8.3	24.0	45.7	18.7	−2.9	0.5
Lao P.D.R.	−19.3	−22.0	−18.8	−18.4	−29.3	−28.9	−23.2	−23.2	−21.0	−19.8	−14.4
Malaysia	16.5	15.0	10.1	10.9	5.2	3.5	4.3	2.9	2.3	1.9	1.6
Maldives	−28.9	−10.5	−8.2	−16.9	−7.4	−4.3	−4.1	−8.0	−7.8	−14.7	−10.6
Marshall Islands	0.5	−14.2	−26.5	−5.6	−9.3	−14.7	−7.3	−0.8	2.7	3.3	−4.7
Micronesia	−16.5	−18.8	−15.0	−17.8	−12.6	−10.0	6.8	1.0	−0.1	−0.7	−2.9
Mongolia	−8.9	−6.9	−13.0	−26.5	−27.4	−25.4	−11.5	−4.8	−10.7	−17.7	−8.5
Myanmar	−4.2	−1.2	−1.1	−1.8	−4.0	−4.9	−5.6	−8.9	−8.4	−8.0	−7.3
Nepal	2.7	4.2	−2.4	−1.0	4.8	3.3	4.6	5.0	6.2	0.5	−3.1
Palau	−20.0	−7.7	−6.7	−9.2	−8.7	−9.3	−11.8	−0.5	0.2	−10.4	−4.7
Papua New Guinea	8.5	−15.2	−21.5	−23.6	−53.6	−31.8	−4.2	2.8	0.8	3.6	−0.5
Philippines	0.1	5.0	3.6	2.5	2.8	4.2	3.8	2.9	2.6	2.4	1.6
Samoa	−5.6	−4.9	−7.8	−5.3	−8.6	−0.2	−7.6	−4.0	−4.1	−3.8	−3.9
Solomon Islands	−18.2	−21.9	−33.4	−8.7	1.8	−3.5	−4.3	−2.6	−4.5	−7.8	−3.4
Sri Lanka	−9.5	−0.5	−2.2	−7.8	−6.7	−3.8	−2.7	−2.0	−0.8	−1.4	−2.9
Thailand	0.3	7.3	2.9	2.4	−0.4	−1.2	3.8	8.8	8.0	5.7	1.4
Timor-Leste	46.1	38.7	41.2	40.6	40.2	42.7	25.1	16.5	2.0	−11.9	−7.8
Tonga	−11.5	−20.9	−19.1	−15.1	−8.6	−6.2	−8.5	−7.7	−6.6	−6.6	−3.2
Tuvalu	7.1	−1.0	−42.0	−61.3	−25.2	−24.1	−26.3	−26.7	−57.7	−8.9	−11.6
Vanuatu	−10.8	−7.9	−6.5	−8.4	−9.4	−1.4	0.5	−10.1	−15.6	−15.1	−6.2
Vietnam	−11.0	−6.5	−3.8	0.2	6.0	4.6	5.0	1.4	0.6	0.2	0.9
Emerging and Developing Europe	**−8.0**	**−3.5**	**−5.1**	**−6.5**	**−4.6**	**−3.8**	**−3.1**	**−1.9**	**−2.1**	**−2.6**	**−3.5**
Albania	−15.8	−15.9	−11.3	−13.2	−10.1	−10.8	−12.9	−11.4	−12.7	−12.6	−10.9
Bosnia and Herzegovina	−14.1	−6.4	−6.1	−9.5	−8.9	−5.5	−7.8	−6.8	−5.8	−5.5	−5.5
Bulgaria	−22.0	−8.4	−0.9	0.9	−0.3	1.8	1.2	2.1	1.7	0.8	−1.7
Croatia	−8.8	−5.1	−1.1	−0.8	−0.1	0.8	0.7	4.4	2.7	2.1	−0.6
Hungary	−7.1	−0.8	0.3	0.7	1.8	4.0	2.3	5.1	5.4	5.2	1.9
Kosovo	−16.2	−9.2	−11.7	−13.7	−7.5	−6.4	−7.9	−8.0	−8.3	−8.9	−7.8
FYR Macedonia	−12.8	−6.8	−2.0	−2.5	−3.2	−1.6	−0.8	−1.4	−1.7	−2.6	−3.4
Montenegro	−49.8	−27.9	−22.7	−17.6	−18.5	−14.5	−15.2	−13.2	−16.5	−17.0	−11.0
Poland	−6.8	−4.1	−5.4	−5.2	−3.7	−1.3	−2.0	−0.5	−1.8	−2.1	−3.0
Romania	−11.8	−4.8	−5.1	−4.9	−4.8	−1.1	−0.5	−1.1	−1.7	−2.5	−3.5
Serbia	−21.0	−6.2	−6.4	−8.6	−11.5	−6.1	−6.0	−4.8	−4.4	−4.3	−4.0
Turkey	−5.4	−1.8	−6.1	−9.6	−6.1	−7.7	−5.5	−4.4	−3.6	−4.1	−4.6

Table A12. Emerging Market and Developing Economies: Balance on Current Account *(continued)*

(Percent of GDP)

	2008	2009	2010	2011	2012	2013	2014	2015	Projections 2016	Projections 2017	Projections 2021
Latin America and the Caribbean	**−1.0**	**−0.8**	**−1.9**	**−1.9**	**−2.3**	**−2.6**	**−3.1**	**−3.6**	**−2.8**	**−2.4**	**−1.8**
Antigua and Barbuda	−26.7	−14.0	−14.7	−10.4	−14.6	−14.8	−14.5	−10.0	−6.2	−7.0	−9.5
Argentina[3]	1.6	2.9	−0.3	−0.7	−0.2	−0.7	−1.4	−2.8	−1.7	−2.2	−3.0
The Bahamas	−10.6	−10.3	−10.1	−15.1	−18.3	−17.7	−22.3	−11.7	−9.8	−8.9	−4.8
Barbados	−10.6	−6.7	−5.8	−12.8	−9.3	−9.1	−8.9	−5.2	−4.6	−5.1	−6.7
Belize	−10.6	−4.9	−2.4	−1.1	−1.2	−4.4	−7.6	−10.2	−6.8	−6.7	−5.9
Bolivia	11.9	4.3	3.9	0.3	7.2	3.4	0.2	−6.9	−8.3	−7.1	−3.7
Brazil	−1.8	−1.6	−3.4	−2.9	−3.0	−3.0	−4.3	−3.3	−2.0	−1.5	0.1
Chile	−3.2	2.0	1.7	−1.2	−3.5	−3.7	−1.3	−2.0	−2.1	−2.7	−3.2
Colombia	−2.6	−2.0	−3.0	−2.9	−3.1	−3.3	−5.2	−6.5	−6.0	−4.3	−3.6
Costa Rica	−9.1	−1.9	−3.4	−5.3	−5.2	−5.0	−4.7	−4.0	−4.2	−4.3	−4.4
Dominica	−28.3	−22.7	−16.2	−13.5	−18.8	−13.3	−13.1	−14.1	−16.6	−19.2	−7.1
Dominican Republic	−9.4	−4.8	−7.4	−7.5	−6.6	−4.1	−3.2	−1.9	−1.7	−2.2	−3.2
Ecuador	2.9	0.5	−2.3	−0.5	−0.2	−1.0	−0.6	−2.9	−2.3	−0.2	−0.2
El Salvador	−7.1	−1.5	−2.5	−4.8	−5.4	−6.5	−4.7	−3.2	−3.0	−4.1	−5.0
Grenada	−29.0	−24.3	−23.7	−23.6	−21.1	−23.2	−15.5	−15.1	−12.2	−13.8	−14.8
Guatemala	−3.6	0.7	−1.4	−3.4	−2.6	−2.5	−2.1	−0.5	−0.7	−1.0	−2.1
Guyana	−13.7	−9.1	−9.6	−13.0	−11.6	−14.3	−12.6	−4.8	−5.2	−7.6	−7.6
Haiti	−3.1	−1.9	−1.5	−4.3	−5.7	−6.3	−6.3	−2.4	−1.9	−2.3	−2.5
Honduras	−15.4	−3.8	−4.3	−8.0	−8.5	−9.5	−7.4	−6.4	−5.9	−5.9	−5.7
Jamaica	−17.7	−11.0	−8.0	−12.1	−10.7	−8.8	−7.1	−4.3	−2.9	−2.6	−1.1
Mexico	−1.9	−1.0	−0.5	−1.1	−1.4	−2.4	−1.9	−2.8	−2.6	−2.6	−2.4
Nicaragua	−17.8	−8.6	−8.9	−11.8	−10.6	−11.1	−7.1	−8.8	−8.8	−10.0	−9.5
Panama	−10.8	−0.8	−10.8	−13.2	−10.5	−9.8	−9.8	−6.5	−6.1	−5.0	−2.5
Paraguay	1.0	3.0	−0.3	0.4	−2.0	1.7	−0.4	−1.8	−1.2	−1.1	−0.5
Peru	−4.3	−0.5	−2.4	−1.9	−2.7	−4.3	−4.0	−4.4	−3.9	−3.3	−2.1
St. Kitts and Nevis	−26.8	−25.7	−20.8	−15.9	−9.8	−6.6	−7.6	−13.0	−18.4	−19.1	−17.6
St. Lucia	−28.5	−11.5	−16.2	−18.8	−13.5	−11.2	−6.7	−7.5	−7.9	−8.6	−10.4
St. Vincent and the Grenadines	−33.1	−29.2	−30.6	−29.4	−27.6	−30.9	−29.6	−24.8	−21.3	−20.0	−14.3
Suriname	9.2	2.9	13.0	5.7	3.3	−3.8	−8.0	−15.6	−8.0	0.8	−1.3
Trinidad and Tobago	30.5	8.5	18.9	11.4	3.2	7.3	4.6	−5.4	−4.4	−3.7	−2.6
Uruguay	−5.7	−1.2	−1.8	−2.7	−5.0	−4.9	−4.3	−3.9	−3.9	−3.7	−3.5
Venezuela	10.8	0.2	1.9	4.9	0.8	2.0	1.4	−7.6	−6.6	−2.5	1.3
Middle East, North Africa, Afghanistan, and Pakistan	**12.6**	**1.8**	**6.2**	**12.9**	**11.9**	**10.0**	**5.5**	**−3.6**	**−6.9**	**−5.2**	**−1.8**
Afghanistan	2.7	13.1	7.5	6.0	5.9	7.9	7.8	4.5	3.3	0.2	−3.0
Algeria	20.1	0.3	7.5	9.9	5.9	0.4	−4.4	−15.7	−17.1	−16.2	−8.0
Bahrain	8.8	2.4	3.0	8.7	8.4	7.3	4.5	−3.2	−6.7	−5.8	−1.1
Djibouti	−24.3	−9.7	0.7	−13.7	−20.3	−23.3	−25.6	−29.2	−23.4	−14.1	−14.5
Egypt	0.5	−2.2	−1.9	−2.5	−3.7	−2.2	−0.8	−3.7	−5.3	−5.3	−3.1
Iran	5.8	2.4	5.9	10.5	4.0	7.0	3.8	0.4	−0.8	0.0	1.2
Iraq	15.9	−6.8	3.0	12.0	6.7	1.4	−0.8	−6.4	−14.4	−11.0	1.9
Jordan	−9.4	−5.2	−7.1	−10.3	−15.2	−10.3	−6.6	−8.8	−6.4	−5.6	−6.4
Kuwait	40.9	26.7	31.8	42.7	45.2	39.5	31.3	11.5	−1.0	3.3	5.5
Lebanon	−10.5	−11.9	−20.7	−15.1	−24.3	−26.7	−26.9	−25.0	−21.3	−21.2	−19.6
Libya	42.5	14.9	19.5	9.1	29.1	13.5	−27.8	−43.6	−48.7	−39.2	−15.1
Mauritania	−13.2	−13.4	−7.6	−6.0	−24.6	−22.6	−27.7	−19.3	−13.6	−15.8	−10.5
Morocco	−7.1	−5.3	−4.4	−7.9	−9.5	−7.9	−5.7	−1.4	0.4	0.1	−0.3
Oman	8.5	−1.1	8.9	13.2	10.3	6.6	6.0	−12.6	−25.1	−19.6	−8.5
Pakistan	−8.1	−5.5	−2.2	0.1	−2.1	−1.1	−1.3	−1.0	−1.1	−1.6	−1.8
Qatar	23.1	6.5	19.1	30.7	32.6	29.9	23.6	4.9	−5.0	−4.9	−1.5
Saudi Arabia	25.5	4.9	12.7	23.7	22.4	18.2	9.8	−6.3	−10.2	−6.1	−1.3
Sudan[4]	−1.6	−9.6	−2.1	−0.4	−9.3	−8.5	−6.7	−7.7	−6.3	−5.5	−4.9
Syria[5]	−1.3	−2.9	−2.8	. . .	. . .	. . .	. . .	. . .	. . .	. . .	. . .
Tunisia	−3.8	−2.8	−4.8	−7.4	−8.3	−8.4	−9.1	−8.9	−7.7	−7.0	−4.5
United Arab Emirates	7.1	3.1	2.5	14.7	21.3	18.4	13.7	3.9	−1.0	0.1	0.7
Yemen	−4.6	−10.1	−3.4	−3.0	−1.7	−3.1	−1.7	−5.6	−7.0	−4.8	−5.2

Table A12. Emerging Market and Developing Economies: Balance on Current Account *(continued)*
(Percent of GDP)

	2008	2009	2010	2011	2012	2013	2014	2015	Projections 2016	2017	2021
Sub-Saharan Africa	**0.3**	**−2.8**	**−0.8**	**−0.6**	**−1.8**	**−2.4**	**−4.1**	**−5.9**	**−6.2**	**−5.5**	**−4.9**
Angola	8.5	−10.0	9.1	12.6	12.0	6.7	−2.9	−8.5	−11.6	−8.8	−3.7
Benin	−7.5	−8.3	−8.2	−7.3	−9.5	−9.5	−9.3	−11.1	−11.1	−10.6	−9.2
Botswana	−1.1	−6.3	−2.6	3.1	0.3	8.9	15.7	9.3	2.2	2.9	10.3
Burkina Faso	−11.5	−4.7	−2.2	−1.5	−7.2	−11.0	−8.0	−5.6	−5.3	−4.6	−6.6
Burundi	−1.0	1.7	−12.2	−14.4	−18.6	−19.5	−18.8	−15.4	−8.9	−6.4	−7.4
Cabo Verde	−13.7	−14.6	−12.4	−16.3	−12.6	−4.9	−8.0	−9.2	−9.9	−9.6	−5.6
Cameroon	−1.2	−3.5	−2.8	−3.0	−3.6	−3.9	−4.4	−5.8	−5.7	−5.5	−4.3
Central African Republic	−9.9	−9.1	−10.2	−7.6	−4.6	−3.0	−5.5	−12.8	−10.9	−10.2	−6.1
Chad	3.7	−9.2	−9.0	−5.6	−8.7	−9.2	−8.9	−12.8	−13.0	−8.8	−6.3
Comoros	−18.7	−15.4	−5.8	−14.0	−17.6	−15.9	−10.7	−10.2	−15.2	−15.7	−12.4
Democratic Republic of the Congo	−0.8	−6.1	−10.5	−5.2	−4.6	−10.6	−9.6	−12.2	−14.2	−12.3	−9.6
Republic of Congo	−0.5	−14.1	7.5	4.9	−2.4	−4.5	−9.4	−14.2	−23.1	−10.8	−6.2
Côte d'Ivoire	1.9	6.6	1.9	10.5	−1.2	−1.4	−0.7	−1.7	−1.8	−2.7	−2.7
Equatorial Guinea	26.7	−23.1	−34.4	−0.1	−2.2	−4.0	−9.6	−6.6	−8.3	−6.0	3.6
Eritrea	−5.5	−7.6	−5.6	0.6	2.3	−0.1	0.6	−2.2	0.2	0.9	−1.4
Ethiopia	−6.7	−6.7	−1.4	−2.5	−6.9	−5.9	−7.9	−12.8	−10.7	−9.7	−6.2
Gabon	21.6	4.4	14.9	15.2	15.9	11.6	8.1	−2.8	−7.2	−5.8	−2.3
The Gambia	−12.2	−12.5	−16.3	−12.3	−7.9	−10.2	−10.9	−15.2	−10.5	−10.3	−8.3
Ghana	−11.9	−5.4	−8.6	−9.0	−11.7	−11.9	−9.6	−8.3	−7.2	−5.4	−6.4
Guinea	−10.2	−8.2	−9.3	−25.1	−26.0	−26.8	−25.7	−22.4	−13.5	−25.5	−45.0
Guinea-Bissau	−2.5	−5.4	−8.7	−4.2	−11.8	−7.4	−3.4	−0.9	1.8	−1.0	−4.6
Kenya	−5.5	−4.6	−5.9	−9.1	−8.4	−8.9	−10.4	−8.2	−8.3	−6.9	−6.9
Lesotho	21.1	3.9	−10.0	−14.7	−9.8	−10.3	−7.9	−2.6	−13.9	−9.7	−14.7
Liberia	−46.6	−23.2	−32.0	−27.5	−21.5	−28.4	−31.6	−39.3	−39.8	−39.4	−36.1
Madagascar	−20.6	−21.1	−9.7	−6.9	−6.9	−5.9	−0.3	−2.2	−3.0	−4.4	−4.8
Malawi	−15.1	−10.2	−8.6	−8.6	−9.3	−8.7	−8.2	−8.9	−11.1	−9.3	−9.0
Mali	−10.9	−6.4	−11.1	−5.1	−2.2	−2.8	−4.6	−2.8	−4.0	−4.4	−6.4
Mauritius	−10.1	−7.4	−10.3	−13.8	−7.3	−6.3	−5.6	−5.1	−4.5	−4.6	−4.9
Mozambique	−9.9	−10.9	−16.1	−25.3	−44.7	−39.1	−34.4	−41.3	−43.0	−70.3	−89.2
Namibia	−0.1	−1.5	−3.5	−3.0	−5.7	−4.0	−8.5	−9.8	−14.5	−7.9	−2.7
Niger	−12.0	−24.4	−19.8	−22.3	−14.7	−15.0	−16.0	−18.0	−17.3	−18.2	−13.7
Nigeria	9.0	5.1	3.9	3.0	4.4	3.9	0.2	−2.4	−2.8	−1.8	−0.9
Rwanda	−5.1	−7.1	−7.3	−7.5	−11.4	−7.4	−11.5	−13.8	−14.2	−12.5	−8.9
São Tomé and Príncipe	−33.1	−23.2	−21.7	−25.5	−21.3	−23.4	−27.5	−11.3	−9.4	−9.8	−9.5
Senegal	−14.2	−6.7	−4.4	−8.1	−10.8	−10.4	−8.9	−7.6	−6.0	−5.8	−4.8
Seychelles	−19.1	−14.8	−19.1	−22.6	−21.3	−12.3	−22.2	−14.2	−13.3	−12.9	−10.9
Sierra Leone	−9.0	−13.3	−22.7	−65.3	−31.9	−17.6	−19.2	−13.8	−9.7	−12.8	−12.3
South Africa	−5.5	−2.7	−1.5	−2.2	−5.0	−5.8	−5.4	−4.4	−4.4	−4.9	−4.0
South Sudan	. . .	. . .	. . .	18.4	−15.9	−1.2	2.1	−12.6	−6.1	−6.5	−8.9
Swaziland	−7.1	−11.6	−8.6	−6.8	3.1	5.1	3.3	0.5	−1.8	−0.8	−0.2
Tanzania	−7.8	−7.6	−7.7	−10.8	−11.6	−10.6	−9.5	−8.7	−7.7	−7.4	−6.8
Togo	−7.0	−5.6	−6.3	−8.0	−7.5	−13.0	−12.8	−12.6	−10.1	−10.1	−10.1
Uganda	−6.8	−5.7	−8.0	−10.0	−6.8	−7.0	−9.5	−8.9	−8.4	−8.5	−11.2
Zambia	−3.3	6.0	7.5	4.7	5.4	−0.6	2.1	−3.5	−3.8	−1.7	3.8
Zimbabwe[6]	−16.6	−47.1	−16.0	−30.8	−24.5	−23.9	−18.6	−17.3	−16.3	−16.4	−16.7

[1]Georgia, Turkmenistan, and Ukraine, which are not members of the Commonwealth of Independent States, are included in this group for reasons of geography and similarity in economic structure.
[2]Starting in 2014 data exclude Crimea and Sevastopol.
[3]See country-specific notes for Argentina in the "Country Notes" section of the Statistical Appendix.
[4]Data for 2011 exclude South Sudan after July 9. Data for 2012 and onward pertain to the current Sudan.
[5]Data for Syria are excluded for 2011 onward owing to the uncertain political situation.
[6]The Zimbabwe dollar ceased circulating in early 2009. Data are based on IMF staff estimates of price and exchange rate developments in U.S. dollars. IMF staff estimates of U.S. dollar values may differ from authorities' estimates.

Table A13. Summary of Financial Account Balances
(Billions of U.S. dollars)

	2008	2009	2010	2011	2012	2013	2014	2015	Projections 2016	Projections 2017
Advanced Economies										
Financial Account Balance	−689.9	20.4	−82.8	−185.6	−77.5	237.3	456.8	643.2	691.9	574.7
Direct Investment, Net	655.9	306.4	344.8	370.9	149.4	−15.6	362.9	118.5	192.3	203.5
Portfolio Investment, Net	−1,204.2	−375.1	−737.8	−898.5	−209.9	−309.9	−153.9	353.0	95.3	21.3
Financial Derivatives, Net	320.7	−91.8	−118.2	0.7	−78.5	22.5	−52.8	−13.2	41.8	37.5
Other Investment, Net	−559.5	−283.8	66.7	−35.5	−213.9	388.7	165.4	0.7	297.6	258.3
Change in Reserves	76.5	469.5	352.9	350.7	274.1	152.7	135.3	182.8	64.9	54.6
United States										
Financial Account Balance	−730.6	−231.0	−437.0	−515.8	−441.2	−395.8	−239.6	−209.2	−156.9	−255.4
Direct Investment, Net	19.0	159.9	95.2	183.0	145.9	112.0	225.4	−64.8	92.8	88.0
Portfolio Investment, Net	−808.0	18.5	−620.8	−226.3	−508.2	−25.7	−167.0	−77.0	−295.4	−353.4
Financial Derivatives, Net	32.9	−44.8	−14.1	−35.0	7.1	2.2	−54.4	−25.4	−22.0	−28.8
Other Investment, Net	20.6	−416.9	100.9	−453.4	−90.4	−481.2	−240.1	−35.7	67.7	38.8
Change in Reserves	4.8	52.3	1.8	15.9	4.5	−3.1	−3.6	−6.3	0.0	0.0
Euro Area										
Financial Account Balance	−503.5	43.8	−101.9	−206.6	167.5	425.7	403.3	239.6	. . .	. . .
Direct Investment, Net	326.0	72.2	90.7	147.5	27.4	−92.5	61.9	36.4	. . .	. . .
Portfolio Investment, Net	−379.0	−356.0	−119.5	−487.2	−190.3	−12.8	96.8	299.0	. . .	. . .
Financial Derivatives, Net	−56.4	29.6	−4.3	6.2	41.1	19.1	55.5	42.9	. . .	. . .
Other Investment, Net	−398.9	240.1	−82.9	112.2	270.4	505.7	183.3	−150.5	. . .	. . .
Change in Reserves	4.7	57.9	14.1	14.7	19.0	6.3	5.8	11.9	. . .	. . .
Germany										
Financial Account Balance	182.0	184.4	123.7	167.7	202.3	276.5	323.3	285.2	292.0	287.0
Direct Investment, Net	67.1	43.0	60.6	10.3	45.6	11.1	110.3	20.8	21.5	22.3
Portfolio Investment, Net	−44.5	119.2	154.1	−51.4	70.6	218.1	168.3	148.4	152.0	149.4
Financial Derivatives, Net	44.0	−7.5	17.6	39.8	31.2	32.3	42.3	37.3	38.2	37.5
Other Investment, Net	112.8	17.4	−110.7	165.1	53.1	13.9	5.8	78.7	80.4	77.8
Change in Reserves	2.7	12.4	2.1	3.9	1.7	1.2	−3.3	0.0	0.0	0.0
France										
Financial Account Balance	−26.9	−30.7	−34.2	−74.6	−52.7	−23.7	−14.4	−10.3	17.3	8.7
Direct Investment, Net	66.0	70.3	34.3	19.8	14.7	−17.9	27.7	10.5	15.3	20.2
Portfolio Investment, Net	−37.8	−328.7	−155.0	−333.7	−50.6	−80.5	−9.8	29.6	55.0	37.9
Financial Derivatives, Net	24.1	23.6	−34.8	−19.4	−18.4	−22.3	−31.8	12.0	15.1	19.1
Other Investment, Net	−86.5	212.0	105.1	240.3	−3.6	98.9	−1.6	−70.3	−70.3	−70.8
Change in Reserves	−12.5	−5.5	7.7	−7.7	5.2	−1.9	1.0	8.0	2.2	2.3
Italy										
Financial Account Balance	−45.7	−54.5	−113.7	−92.6	−15.5	14.6	61.4	46.1	43.7	39.1
Direct Investment, Net	76.2	−0.3	21.3	17.1	6.8	0.8	6.6	8.5	8.7	9.2
Portfolio Investment, Net	−110.7	−55.4	56.4	13.5	−33.3	−19.3	−5.9	106.8	30.5	20.4
Financial Derivatives, Net	−0.4	−6.9	6.6	−10.1	7.5	4.0	−4.8	1.7	0.0	0.0
Other Investment, Net	−19.0	−0.7	−199.4	−114.5	1.6	27.1	66.7	−71.5	4.5	9.5
Change in Reserves	8.2	8.8	1.4	1.3	1.9	2.0	−1.3	0.6	0.0	0.0

Table A13. Summary of Financial Account Balances *(continued)*
(Billions of U.S. dollars)

	2008	2009	2010	2011	2012	2013	2014	2015	Projections 2016	2017
Spain										
Financial Account Balance	−147.6	−70.8	−56.9	−41.4	2.4	46.6	28.1	21.6	29.0	31.3
Direct Investment, Net	−2.3	2.7	−1.9	12.8	−27.2	−19.1	12.4	8.8	8.4	8.2
Portfolio Investment, Net	1.9	−69.6	−46.6	43.1	53.7	−59.1	−13.0	−18.8	−20.8	−21.5
Financial Derivatives, Net	10.4	8.4	−11.4	2.9	−10.7	1.4	1.5	0.0	0.0	0.0
Other Investment, Net	−158.6	−18.4	1.9	−114.1	−16.3	122.8	22.0	31.6	41.4	44.6
Change in Reserves	0.9	6.0	1.1	13.9	2.8	0.7	5.2	0.0	0.0	0.0
Japan										
Financial Account Balance	181.6	168.8	247.3	158.4	53.9	−9.6	51.1	174.7	164.4	162.6
Direct Investment, Net	89.1	61.2	72.5	117.8	117.5	139.4	110.9	132.6	107.0	107.2
Portfolio Investment, Net	289.0	211.7	147.9	−162.9	28.8	−280.6	−42.9	131.2	146.1	152.4
Financial Derivatives, Net	−24.9	−10.5	−11.9	−17.1	6.7	58.1	32.9	17.8	62.0	63.5
Other Investment, Net	−202.3	−120.9	−5.5	43.4	−61.1	34.8	−58.2	−111.9	−160.3	−170.6
Change in Reserves	30.8	27.2	44.3	177.3	−37.9	38.7	8.5	5.1	9.5	10.0
United Kingdom										
Financial Account Balance	−72.1	−45.2	−46.8	−29.2	−71.0	−108.1	−166.2	−124.0	−120.0	−114.6
Direct Investment, Net	105.8	−60.8	−10.1	53.4	−34.9	−66.4	−134.3	−76.9	−71.8	−63.5
Portfolio Investment, Net	−450.2	−48.3	21.3	19.7	337.6	−79.3	−188.9	14.2	13.8	14.4
Financial Derivatives, Net	223.2	−45.4	−39.4	4.8	−47.7	21.8	−24.3	−16.3	−11.1	−14.2
Other Investment, Net	51.6	100.3	−28.0	−115.1	−338.2	8.0	169.5	−54.4	−59.8	−60.5
Change in Reserves	−2.5	9.0	9.4	7.9	12.1	7.8	11.7	9.4	8.8	9.2
Canada										
Financial Account Balance	−3.0	−41.6	−58.3	−49.4	−62.7	−54.6	−39.1	−43.2	−51.7	−45.6
Direct Investment, Net	17.7	16.9	6.3	12.5	12.8	−16.9	−2.8	18.5	1.9	0.0
Portfolio Investment, Net	−47.6	−91.0	−109.9	−104.3	−63.8	−21.4	−17.1	−27.5	−27.8	−22.1
Financial Derivatives, Net	. . .	. . .	. . .	. . .	. . .	. . .	. . .	. . .	. . .	. . .
Other Investment, Net	25.3	22.3	41.4	34.3	−13.4	−21.1	−24.4	−42.7	−25.9	−23.5
Change in Reserves	1.6	10.2	3.9	8.1	1.7	4.7	5.3	8.5	0.0	0.0
Other Advanced Economies[1]										
Financial Account Balance	64.0	148.8	290.0	293.3	263.1	366.1	367.8	377.9	355.2	346.5
Direct Investment, Net	16.0	14.9	91.8	−13.7	−27.2	7.7	−22.5	12.5	−2.2	1.6
Portfolio Investment, Net	180.6	−105.4	−48.7	42.7	134.7	123.3	183.4	193.6	205.1	208.4
Financial Derivatives, Net	−12.6	20.0	−17.9	41.0	−28.9	−28.9	−30.9	−24.8	−32.6	−35.5
Other Investment, Net	−165.7	−110.6	−14.5	98.3	−91.6	164.2	131.5	37.2	141.3	140.1
Change in Reserves	44.9	332.5	279.4	125.1	275.3	101.0	106.8	158.3	43.6	32.5
Emerging Market and Developing Economies										
Financial Account Balance	554.7	55.2	134.3	257.6	119.6	58.6	−49.8	−182.1	−98.6	−97.4
Direct Investment, Net	−469.9	−329.1	−453.0	−534.4	−486.5	−470.7	−456.7	−344.6	−366.2	−322.5
Portfolio Investment, Net	120.6	−91.1	−229.8	−129.0	−245.7	−142.6	−138.1	203.5	64.2	−37.0
Financial Derivatives, Net	. . .	. . .	. . .	. . .	. . .	. . .	. . .	. . .	. . .	. . .
Other Investment, Net	211.6	−45.3	−2.5	163.4	431.1	96.0	415.7	514.8	671.1	280.6
Change in Reserves	685.9	519.5	817.8	756.6	423.7	578.5	126.8	−558.9	−468.5	−17.5

Table A13. Summary of Financial Account Balances *(continued)*
(Billions of U.S. dollars)

	2008	2009	2010	2011	2012	2013	2014	2015	Projections 2016	Projections 2017
Regional Groups										
Commonwealth of Independent States[2]										
Financial Account Balance	92.7	23.1	66.0	92.9	49.2	24.5	−6.0	58.5	50.9	70.1
Direct Investment, Net	−49.4	−17.2	−9.4	−16.1	−27.8	2.4	19.8	1.9	−6.7	8.0
Portfolio Investment, Net	35.8	−6.3	−14.4	17.9	3.5	17.4	23.4	6.9	0.0	−6.2
Financial Derivatives, Net	. . .	. . .	. . .	. . .	. . .	. . .	. . .	. . .	. . .	. . .
Other Investment, Net	131.8	36.3	35.9	66.0	44.5	28.1	69.0	82.7	54.9	52.5
Change in Reserves	−26.7	7.2	52.0	23.9	27.5	−23.8	−118.3	−32.6	3.5	16.7
Emerging and Developing Asia										
Financial Account Balance	443.9	211.2	141.3	65.6	11.5	33.5	57.2	147.0	273.8	195.5
Direct Investment, Net	−153.7	−115.3	−224.9	−277.9	−222.9	−274.0	−268.8	−138.7	−138.1	−103.0
Portfolio Investment, Net	5.9	−70.4	−96.1	−58.7	−115.7	−64.7	−125.4	159.2	103.5	9.4
Financial Derivatives, Net	. . .	. . .	0.2	−0.3	−3.2	2.0	−5.4	−0.8	−0.2	−0.3
Other Investment, Net	114.2	−63.9	−104.3	−30.7	215.5	−81.1	254.6	454.5	639.0	259.1
Change in Reserves	476.5	462.1	566.7	434.4	135.2	451.7	196.6	−327.6	−330.4	30.5
Emerging and Developing Europe										
Financial Account Balance	−160.1	−53.0	−89.1	−107.6	−65.3	−64.3	−40.2	−5.5	−24.2	−36.7
Direct Investment, Net	−63.3	−30.7	−27.0	−40.0	−27.2	−25.2	−30.5	−29.6	−31.0	−33.4
Portfolio Investment, Net	14.4	−10.1	−45.4	−53.2	−70.2	−39.9	−19.2	23.2	−1.9	−11.2
Financial Derivatives, Net	2.5	0.9	0.0	1.6	−3.0	−1.4	0.3	0.0	0.1	−1.6
Other Investment, Net	−120.0	−42.4	−52.6	−30.2	7.2	−13.9	8.7	7.2	7.2	5.5
Change in Reserves	5.9	31.0	35.9	14.6	27.9	18.5	−0.1	−5.3	2.4	4.9
Latin America and the Caribbean										
Financial Account Balance	−53.9	−33.1	−104.6	−99.0	−169.5	−201.7	−185.6	−212.0	−147.2	−110.6
Direct Investment, Net	−102.6	−72.7	−111.9	−147.1	−150.4	−142.9	−140.9	−131.9	−129.5	−122.2
Portfolio Investment, Net	−9.9	−27.8	−98.7	−92.4	−96.4	−110.9	−116.9	−68.2	−47.8	−45.6
Financial Derivatives, Net	. . .	. . .	. . .	. . .	. . .	. . .	. . .	. . .	. . .	. . .
Other Investment, Net	16.0	12.4	26.3	15.8	18.5	45.2	30.8	15.6	37.1	47.3
Change in Reserves	41.3	54.5	79.0	122.4	59.5	6.1	37.9	−33.5	−10.5	6.3
Middle East, North Africa, Afghanistan, and Pakistan										
Financial Account Balance	237.9	−43.6	122.9	314.3	314.9	314.8	196.5	−93.3	−170.2	−135.6
Direct Investment, Net	−64.6	−64.0	−46.0	−22.7	−26.6	−9.2	−10.3	−16.1	−28.9	−33.4
Portfolio Investment, Net	51.0	32.0	25.0	73.1	57.2	72.1	112.8	90.1	17.6	24.1
Financial Derivatives, Net	. . .	. . .	. . .	. . .	. . .	. . .	. . .	. . .	. . .	. . .
Other Investment, Net	80.2	15.9	59.1	124.3	130.4	126.3	75.2	−20.4	−37.7	−48.5
Change in Reserves	171.4	−27.6	84.8	139.5	154.0	125.6	18.8	−146.8	−121.2	−77.8
Sub-Saharan Africa										
Financial Account Balance	−5.8	−49.3	−2.2	−8.7	−21.1	−48.2	−71.7	−76.7	−81.7	−80.1
Direct Investment, Net	−36.4	−29.2	−33.8	−30.6	−31.5	−21.8	−26.1	−30.2	−32.0	−38.5
Portfolio Investment, Net	23.5	−8.4	−0.3	−15.8	−24.0	−16.6	−12.8	−7.6	−7.1	−7.4
Financial Derivatives, Net	. . .	. . .	. . .	. . .	. . .	. . .	. . .	. . .	. . .	. . .
Other Investment, Net	−10.5	−3.7	33.0	18.1	14.8	−8.6	−22.6	−24.8	−29.4	−35.4
Change in Reserves	17.5	−7.6	−0.5	21.7	19.6	0.4	−8.0	−13.2	−12.2	1.9

Table A13. Summary of Financial Account Balances *(continued)*
(Billions of U.S. dollars)

	2008	2009	2010	2011	2012	2013	2014	2015	Projections 2016	Projections 2017
Analytical Groups										
By Source of Export Earnings										
Fuel										
Financial Account Balance	421.1	−2.0	221.3	499.7	463.8	367.5	213.0	−69.5	−147.7	−67.9
Direct Investment, Net	−88.7	−60.7	−28.0	−30.7	−46.4	1.8	12.2	−18.9	−38.3	−22.2
Portfolio Investment, Net	87.9	9.4	16.9	81.2	44.2	72.6	132.2	97.8	12.0	12.6
Financial Derivatives, Net	. . .	. . .	. . .	. . .	. . .	. . .	. . .	. . .	. . .	. . .
Other Investment, Net	264.3	102.0	133.8	245.1	228.2	190.1	173.8	73.1	43.4	30.3
Change in Reserves	156.5	−55.4	97.0	202.8	237.0	102.5	−105.6	−222.7	−164.0	−87.6
Nonfuel										
Financial Account Balance	129.2	59.7	−85.3	−242.1	−344.2	−308.8	−262.7	−112.6	49.1	−29.5
Direct Investment, Net	−379.8	−265.8	−422.7	−503.7	−440.2	−472.5	−468.9	−325.7	−327.9	−300.3
Portfolio Investment, Net	32.6	−100.7	−246.7	−210.2	−289.8	−215.2	−270.2	105.7	52.2	−49.6
Financial Derivatives, Net	. . .	. . .	. . .	. . .	. . .	. . .	. . .	. . .	. . .	. . .
Other Investment, Net	−53.5	−147.5	−135.9	−81.8	202.9	−94.0	241.9	441.6	627.7	250.3
Change in Reserves	524.4	575.2	719.7	553.7	186.7	475.9	232.5	−336.2	−304.5	70.1
By External Financing Source										
Net Debtor Economies										
Financial Account Balance	−321.5	−180.0	−260.6	−358.5	−467.4	−413.1	−373.1	−299.5	−272.0	−302.9
Direct Investment, Net	−287.1	−196.0	−221.9	−284.5	−276.6	−265.6	−274.5	−253.5	−275.3	−291.1
Portfolio Investment, Net	71.6	−80.8	−232.8	−183.0	−248.1	−174.8	−197.5	−41.5	−52.0	−90.9
Financial Derivatives, Net	. . .	. . .	. . .	. . .	. . .	. . .	. . .	. . .	. . .	. . .
Other Investment, Net	−159.9	−60.6	−44.2	−62.1	−45.6	−28.4	−11.6	−6.5	−6.4	−9.0
Change in Reserves	48.8	159.5	238.4	171.6	107.2	58.7	108.1	−1.4	60.2	88.1
Net Debtor Economies by Debt-Servicing Experience										
Economies with Arrears and/or Rescheduling during 2010–14										
Financial Account Balance	−15.0	−12.3	−11.8	−19.8	−42.3	−13.7	−34.4	−17.5	−18.3	−21.2
Direct Investment, Net	−28.3	−16.5	−17.2	−16.4	−19.7	−7.5	−10.1	−10.0	−12.6	−14.7
Portfolio Investment, Net	3.2	14.2	−10.9	1.0	−0.5	8.2	−5.5	−3.8	0.9	−0.2
Financial Derivatives, Net	. . .	. . .	. . .	. . .	. . .	. . .	. . .	. . .	. . .	. . .
Other Investment, Net	0.7	−0.3	3.0	6.0	−0.8	−11.2	−7.5	−14.7	−13.1	−13.7
Change in Reserves	9.3	−9.3	13.5	−10.0	−23.1	−2.4	−10.5	11.6	7.0	7.7
Memorandum										
World										
Financial Account Balance	−135.1	75.7	51.5	72.0	42.1	295.9	407.0	461.1	593.3	477.3

Note: The estimates in this table are based on individual countries' national accounts and balance of payments statistics. Country group composites are calculated as the sum of the U.S. dollar values for the relevant individual countries. Some group aggregates for the financial derivatives are not shown because of incomplete data. Projections for the euro area are not available because of data constraints.

[1]Excludes the G7 (Canada, France, Germany, Italy, Japan, United Kingdom, United States) and euro area countries.

[2]Georgia, Turkmenistan, and Ukraine, which are not members of the Commonwealth of Independent States, are included in this group for reasons of geography and similarity in economic structure.

Table A14. Summary of Net Lending and Borrowing
(Percent of GDP)

| | Averages | | | | | | | | Projections | | |
	1998–2007	2002–09	2010	2011	2012	2013	2014	2015	2016	2017	Average 2018–21
Advanced Economies											
Net Lending and Borrowing	−0.7	−0.8	0.0	0.0	0.1	0.5	0.5	0.7	0.7	0.4	0.1
Current Account Balance	−0.7	−0.8	0.0	−0.1	0.0	0.5	0.5	0.7	0.7	0.4	0.1
Savings	22.5	21.5	20.3	20.8	21.2	21.4	21.7	21.9	21.4	21.5	21.6
Investment	22.9	22.2	20.4	20.8	20.8	20.6	20.8	20.7	20.8	21.1	21.5
Capital Account Balance	0.0	0.0	0.0	0.1	0.0	0.0	0.0	0.0	0.0	0.0	0.0
United States											
Net Lending and Borrowing	−4.3	−4.7	−3.0	−3.0	−2.7	−2.3	−2.2	−2.7	−2.9	−3.3	−3.7
Current Account Balance	−4.3	−4.7	−3.0	−3.0	−2.8	−2.3	−2.2	−2.7	−2.9	−3.3	−3.7
Savings	18.9	17.1	15.1	15.7	17.7	18.2	18.8	18.7	17.5	17.5	17.5
Investment	22.6	21.6	18.4	18.5	19.4	19.5	19.9	20.2	20.4	20.8	21.1
Capital Account Balance	0.0	0.0	0.0	0.0	0.0	0.0	0.0	0.0	0.0	0.0	0.0
Euro Area											
Net Lending and Borrowing	. . .	0.1	0.4	0.4	1.4	2.2	2.6	2.9	. . .	. . .	. . .
Current Account Balance	−0.4	0.0	0.3	0.2	1.3	2.0	2.4	3.0	3.5	3.2	2.8
Savings	23.3	22.9	21.5	22.3	22.3	22.4	22.6	23.2	23.5	23.6	23.7
Investment	22.6	22.4	21.0	21.6	20.1	19.6	19.5	19.6	19.6	20.0	20.6
Capital Account Balance	. . .	0.1	0.1	0.1	0.1	0.2	0.2	−0.1	. . .	. . .	. . .
Germany											
Net Lending and Borrowing	2.0	4.5	5.7	6.1	7.1	6.8	7.4	8.5	8.4	8.0	7.3
Current Account Balance	2.1	4.5	5.6	6.1	7.0	6.8	7.3	8.5	8.4	8.0	7.3
Savings	23.2	24.1	25.2	27.2	26.3	26.1	26.6	27.3	27.6	27.4	26.9
Investment	21.1	19.6	19.6	21.1	19.3	19.4	19.3	18.8	19.2	19.4	19.6
Capital Account Balance	0.0	0.0	0.0	0.1	0.1	0.0	0.1	0.0	0.0	0.0	0.0
France											
Net Lending and Borrowing	1.9	0.5	−0.8	−0.9	−1.2	−0.7	−0.8	0.0	0.7	0.3	0.1
Current Account Balance	1.9	0.5	−0.8	−1.0	−1.2	−0.8	−0.9	−0.1	0.6	0.3	0.0
Savings	23.9	22.9	21.1	22.2	21.5	21.5	21.2	21.4	21.0	21.0	21.4
Investment	22.0	22.4	21.9	23.2	22.6	22.3	22.2	21.5	20.4	20.8	21.4
Capital Account Balance	0.0	0.0	0.1	0.1	0.0	0.1	0.1	0.1	0.1	0.1	0.1
Italy											
Net Lending and Borrowing	0.0	−1.2	−3.5	−3.0	−0.2	0.9	2.1	2.3	2.4	2.1	1.4
Current Account Balance	−0.2	−1.3	−3.5	−3.1	−0.4	0.9	1.9	2.1	2.3	2.0	1.3
Savings	20.8	20.0	17.1	17.4	17.4	17.9	18.2	18.9	19.0	19.3	19.3
Investment	21.0	21.3	20.5	20.5	17.9	17.0	16.3	16.8	16.8	17.3	18.0
Capital Account Balance	0.1	0.1	0.0	0.1	0.2	0.0	0.2	0.1	0.1	0.1	0.1
Spain											
Net Lending and Borrowing	−4.5	−5.9	−3.5	−2.8	0.3	2.2	1.4	1.8	2.3	2.4	2.3
Current Account Balance	−5.3	−6.6	−3.9	−3.2	−0.2	1.5	1.0	1.4	1.9	2.0	1.9
Savings	22.5	22.2	19.6	18.7	20.0	20.7	20.8	22.0	22.8	23.1	23.2
Investment	27.8	28.8	23.5	21.9	20.2	19.1	19.8	20.7	20.9	21.1	21.3
Capital Account Balance	0.8	0.7	0.5	0.4	0.5	0.7	0.4	0.4	0.4	0.4	0.4
Japan											
Net Lending and Borrowing	3.1	3.4	3.9	2.2	1.0	0.7	0.5	3.3	3.7	3.6	3.6
Current Account Balance	3.3	3.5	4.0	2.2	1.0	0.8	0.5	3.3	3.8	3.7	3.6
Savings	26.8	25.8	23.8	22.4	21.9	22.1	22.3	25.3	25.6	25.8	26.0
Investment	23.6	22.3	19.8	20.2	20.9	21.2	21.8	22.0	21.8	22.1	22.4
Capital Account Balance	−0.2	−0.1	−0.1	0.0	0.0	−0.2	0.0	−0.1	−0.1	−0.1	−0.1
United Kingdom											
Net Lending and Borrowing	−1.9	−2.3	−2.8	−1.7	−3.3	−4.5	−5.1	−4.4	−4.3	−4.0	−3.5
Current Account Balance	−1.9	−2.3	−2.8	−1.7	−3.3	−4.5	−5.1	−4.3	−4.3	−4.0	−3.5
Savings	17.3	15.9	13.6	14.4	12.9	12.1	12.3	12.8	13.8	14.4	15.8
Investment	19.2	18.2	16.4	16.1	16.2	16.6	17.4	17.2	18.1	18.3	19.4
Capital Account Balance	0.0	0.0	0.0	0.0	0.0	0.0	0.0	0.0	0.0	0.0	0.0

Table A14. Summary of Net Lending and Borrowing *(continued)*
(Percent of GDP)

	Averages 1998–2007	Averages 2002–09	2010	2011	2012	2013	2014	2015	Projections 2016	Projections 2017	Projections Average 2018–21
Canada											
Net Lending and Borrowing	1.2	0.8	−3.6	−2.5	−3.6	−3.2	−2.3	−3.3	−3.5	−3.0	−2.5
Current Account Balance	1.2	0.8	−3.6	−2.8	−3.6	−3.2	−2.3	−3.3	−3.5	−3.0	−2.5
Savings	22.7	23.1	19.9	21.4	21.3	21.5	22.0	20.5	19.7	20.3	21.1
Investment	21.4	22.3	23.5	24.2	24.9	24.6	24.3	23.8	23.2	23.3	23.5
Capital Account Balance	0.0	0.0	0.0	0.3	0.0	0.0	0.0	0.0	0.0	0.0	0.0
Other Advanced Economies[1]											
Net Lending and Borrowing	3.8	4.1	5.0	4.2	4.3	5.3	5.2	5.8	5.7	5.4	5.0
Current Account Balance	3.9	4.1	5.0	4.1	4.3	5.3	5.4	6.0	5.9	5.5	5.2
Savings	29.7	29.9	31.0	30.7	30.4	30.5	30.6	30.7	30.2	30.0	29.9
Investment	25.7	25.6	25.6	26.3	26.1	25.2	25.2	24.5	24.2	24.4	24.6
Capital Account Balance	−0.1	−0.1	0.0	0.1	0.0	0.1	−0.1	−0.1	−0.2	−0.2	−0.1
Emerging Market and Developing Economies											
Net Lending and Borrowing	2.0	3.0	1.5	1.5	1.3	0.7	0.5	0.0	−0.4	−0.4	−0.5
Current Account Balance	2.0	2.9	1.2	1.4	1.3	0.6	0.5	−0.2	−0.6	−0.6	−0.7
Savings	27.1	30.1	32.1	32.9	32.8	32.1	32.2	31.4	31.1	30.8	30.5
Investment	25.5	27.5	31.0	31.5	31.7	31.5	31.7	31.5	31.5	31.2	31.0
Capital Account Balance	0.2	0.1	0.3	0.1	0.1	0.1	0.0	0.2	0.1	0.1	0.1
Regional Groups											
Commonwealth of Independent States[2]											
Net Lending and Borrowing	6.2	5.1	3.7	4.1	2.2	0.6	0.6	2.8	2.0	3.0	4.4
Current Account Balance	6.5	5.8	3.3	4.1	2.4	0.6	2.1	2.8	2.0	3.0	4.4
Savings	26.6	27.2	24.9	27.6	25.8	22.4	24.0	23.5	24.9	25.6	27.8
Investment	20.4	21.5	21.5	23.5	23.4	21.6	21.7	20.4	22.5	22.3	23.3
Capital Account Balance	−0.4	−0.7	0.4	0.0	−0.2	0.0	−1.5	0.0	0.0	0.0	0.0
Emerging and Developing Asia											
Net Lending and Borrowing	3.2	4.1	2.5	0.9	1.0	0.8	1.4	1.9	1.7	1.1	0.2
Current Account Balance	3.2	4.0	2.4	0.9	1.0	0.7	1.4	1.9	1.7	1.1	0.1
Savings	35.6	39.7	44.0	43.3	43.0	42.5	42.7	41.5	40.2	39.0	36.8
Investment	32.8	36.0	41.5	42.4	42.0	41.7	41.3	39.6	38.5	37.9	36.6
Capital Account Balance	0.1	0.1	0.1	0.1	0.1	0.1	0.0	0.0	0.0	0.0	0.0
Emerging and Developing Europe											
Net Lending and Borrowing	−4.2	−5.0	−4.4	−5.6	−3.6	−2.7	−1.7	−0.5	−1.1	−1.7	−2.6
Current Account Balance	−4.4	−5.3	−5.1	−6.5	−4.6	−3.8	−3.1	−1.9	−2.1	−2.6	−3.3
Savings	17.6	16.9	16.0	16.8	16.6	16.8	17.8	19.0	18.4	18.1	17.9
Investment	21.8	22.0	21.0	23.2	21.1	20.6	20.9	20.8	20.4	20.7	21.1
Capital Account Balance	0.2	0.3	0.7	0.8	1.0	1.2	1.3	1.4	1.0	0.8	0.7
Latin America and the Caribbean											
Net Lending and Borrowing	−0.7	0.3	−1.7	−1.9	−2.3	−2.6	−3.1	−3.5	−2.8	−2.4	−2.0
Current Account Balance	−0.8	0.2	−1.9	−1.9	−2.3	−2.6	−3.1	−3.6	−2.8	−2.4	−2.1
Savings	19.2	20.8	19.9	20.3	19.9	19.4	18.3	17.6	18.0	18.4	19.5
Investment	20.1	20.7	21.8	22.2	22.2	22.1	21.5	21.1	20.7	20.9	21.7
Capital Account Balance	0.1	0.1	0.2	0.0	0.0	0.0	0.0	0.1	0.0	0.0	0.0
Middle East, North Africa, Afghanistan, and Pakistan											
Net Lending and Borrowing	7.5	9.1	6.1	13.0	11.5	10.0	6.1	−2.9	−6.0	−4.5	−2.0
Current Account Balance	7.8	9.5	6.2	12.9	11.9	10.0	5.5	−3.6	−6.9	−5.2	−2.5
Savings	31.8	35.4	34.4	38.7	37.9	35.5	32.3	23.1	20.6	22.1	25.1
Investment	24.2	26.4	29.0	25.5	26.2	24.8	25.6	25.0	25.4	25.3	25.7
Capital Account Balance	0.2	0.2	0.3	0.0	0.0	0.0	0.1	0.2	0.3	0.2	0.2
Sub-Saharan Africa											
Net Lending and Borrowing	1.4	2.2	0.9	−0.1	−1.3	−2.0	−3.8	−5.6	−5.7	−5.1	−4.6
Current Account Balance	0.2	0.8	−0.8	−0.6	−1.8	−2.4	−4.1	−5.9	−6.2	−5.5	−5.0
Savings	18.8	20.1	19.8	19.2	18.5	17.7	16.4	13.7	13.3	13.8	14.8
Investment	19.1	19.7	20.3	19.9	20.5	20.3	20.6	19.7	19.4	19.2	19.7
Capital Account Balance	1.3	1.4	1.7	0.5	0.6	0.4	0.4	0.4	0.4	0.4	0.4

Table A14. Summary of Net Lending and Borrowing *(continued)*
(Percent of GDP)

	Averages 1998–2007	Averages 2002–09	2010	2011	2012	2013	2014	2015	Projections 2016	Projections 2017	Projections Average 2018–21
Analytical Groups											
By Source of Export Earnings											
Fuel											
Net Lending and Borrowing	8.3	9.2	6.2	10.0	8.5	6.8	4.0	−1.1	−3.6	−1.7	0.6
Current Account Balance	8.6	9.6	6.0	10.0	8.8	6.8	4.4	−1.5	−4.1	−2.1	0.3
Savings	30.8	32.8	30.4	34.1	33.3	30.1	28.6	22.5	21.1	22.3	24.8
Investment	22.7	23.7	24.7	24.1	24.6	22.9	23.5	22.7	23.5	23.0	23.3
Capital Account Balance	0.0	−0.1	0.3	0.0	−0.1	0.0	−0.7	0.1	0.1	0.1	0.1
Nonfuel											
Net Lending and Borrowing	0.4	1.1	0.1	−1.0	−0.9	−1.0	−0.4	0.2	0.3	−0.1	−0.7
Current Account Balance	0.2	0.9	−0.1	−1.2	−1.1	−1.1	−0.6	0.0	0.1	−0.3	−0.9
Savings	26.2	29.4	32.6	32.6	32.7	32.6	33.2	33.3	33.0	32.4	31.5
Investment	26.2	28.6	32.7	33.6	33.7	33.8	33.8	33.3	32.9	32.7	32.4
Capital Account Balance	0.2	0.2	0.3	0.2	0.2	0.2	0.2	0.2	0.2	0.1	0.1
By External Financing Source											
Net Debtor Economies											
Net Lending and Borrowing	−0.8	−0.8	−1.8	−2.5	−3.0	−2.6	−2.3	−2.1	−2.1	−2.2	−2.3
Current Account Balance	−1.1	−1.1	−2.2	−2.7	−3.2	−2.9	−2.6	−2.4	−2.3	−2.4	−2.5
Savings	21.0	22.4	22.9	23.0	22.2	21.8	21.8	21.9	22.1	22.3	23.3
Investment	22.4	23.6	25.0	25.6	25.4	24.6	24.4	24.4	24.5	24.8	25.8
Capital Account Balance	0.3	0.3	0.5	0.2	0.2	0.3	0.3	0.3	0.2	0.2	0.2
Net Debtor Economies by Debt-Servicing Experience											
Economies with Arrears and/or Rescheduling during 2010–14											
Net Lending and Borrowing	−0.1	−0.3	−2.1	−3.6	−5.4	−5.4	−3.2	−4.2	−4.8	−4.6	−3.7
Current Account Balance	−0.3	−0.5	−2.5	−3.9	−5.8	−5.5	−3.4	−4.4	−5.1	−4.8	−3.9
Savings	21.6	22.7	19.7	17.3	14.8	13.6	14.1	13.0	12.1	12.3	14.7
Investment	21.6	23.1	22.2	21.3	20.6	19.0	17.6	17.5	17.3	17.2	18.8
Capital Account Balance	0.2	0.2	0.4	0.4	0.4	0.1	0.2	0.2	0.3	0.1	0.1
Memorandum											
World											
Net Lending and Borrowing	0.0	0.2	0.5	0.6	0.6	0.6	0.5	0.4	0.3	0.1	−0.2
Current Account Balance	−0.1	0.2	0.4	0.5	0.5	0.5	0.5	0.3	0.2	0.0	−0.2
Savings	23.6	23.8	24.4	25.2	25.6	25.6	25.8	25.6	25.2	25.2	25.3
Investment	23.5	23.6	24.0	24.7	24.9	24.8	25.0	24.9	24.9	25.1	25.5
Capital Account Balance	0.0	0.1	0.1	0.1	0.1	0.1	0.0	0.1	0.1	0.1	0.0

Note: The estimates in this table are based on individual countries' national accounts and balance of payments statistics. Country group composites are calculated as the sum of the U.S. dollar values for the relevant individual countries. This differs from the calculations in the April 2005 and earlier issues of the *World Economic Outlook*, in which the composites were weighted by GDP valued at purchasing power parities as a share of total world GDP. The estimates of gross national savings and investment (or gross capital formation) are from individual countries' national accounts statistics. The estimates of the current account balance, the capital account balance, and the financial account balance (or net lending/net borrowing) are from the balance of payments statistics. The link between domestic transactions and transactions with the rest of the world can be expressed as accounting identities. Savings (S) minus investment (I) is equal to the current account balance (CAB) ($S − I = CAB$). Also, net lending/net borrowing (NLB) is the sum of the current account balance and the capital account balance (KAB) ($NLB = CAB + KAB$). In practice, these identities do not hold exactly; imbalances result from imperfections in source data and compilation as well as from asymmetries in group composition due to data availability.

[1]Excludes the G7 (Canada, France, Germany, Italy, Japan, United Kingdom, United States) and euro area countries.

[2]Georgia, Turkmenistan, and Ukraine, which are not members of the Commonwealth of Independent States, are included in this group for reasons of geography and similarity in economic structure.

Table A15. Summary of World Medium-Term Baseline Scenario

	Averages				Projections		Averages	
	1998–2007	2008–17	2014	2015	2016	2017	2014–17	2018–21
	Annual Percent Change							
World Real GDP	**4.2**	**3.2**	**3.4**	**3.1**	**3.2**	**3.5**	**3.3**	**3.8**
Advanced Economies	2.8	1.1	1.8	1.9	1.9	2.0	1.9	1.9
Emerging Market and Developing Economies	5.8	5.0	4.6	4.0	4.1	4.6	4.3	5.0
Memorandum								
Potential Output								
Major Advanced Economies	2.2	1.3	1.3	1.4	1.4	1.5	1.4	1.6
World Trade, Volume[1]	**6.7**	**3.0**	**3.5**	**2.8**	**3.1**	**3.8**	**3.3**	**4.3**
Imports								
Advanced Economies	6.2	2.2	3.5	4.3	3.4	4.1	3.8	4.3
Emerging Market and Developing Economies	8.8	4.6	3.7	0.5	3.0	3.7	2.7	4.6
Exports								
Advanced Economies	5.8	2.5	3.5	3.4	2.5	3.5	3.2	3.9
Emerging Market and Developing Economies	8.8	3.9	3.1	1.7	3.8	3.9	3.1	4.6
Terms of Trade								
Advanced Economies	−0.2	0.1	0.3	1.9	1.1	−0.3	0.7	0.0
Emerging Market and Developing Economies	1.8	−0.2	−0.4	−3.9	−2.3	−0.3	−1.7	−0.3
World Prices in U.S. Dollars								
Manufactures	1.5	0.1	−0.7	−4.0	−2.7	0.7	−1.7	0.5
Oil	14.0	−5.4	−7.5	−47.2	−31.6	17.9	−20.8	5.4
Nonfuel Primary Commodities	3.9	−1.5	−4.0	−17.5	−9.4	−0.7	−8.1	0.4
Consumer Prices								
Advanced Economies	2.0	1.5	1.4	0.3	0.7	1.5	0.9	1.9
Emerging Market and Developing Economies	7.9	5.6	4.7	4.7	4.5	4.2	4.5	4.0
Interest Rates				*Percent*				
Real Six-Month LIBOR[2]	1.8	−0.5	−1.3	−0.5	−0.4	−0.1	−0.6	0.8
World Real Long-Term Interest Rate[3]	2.3	1.0	0.5	1.4	1.0	0.4	0.8	0.5
Current Account Balances				*Percent of GDP*				
Advanced Economies	−0.7	0.1	0.5	0.7	0.7	0.4	0.6	0.1
Emerging Market and Developing Economies	2.0	0.8	0.5	−0.2	−0.6	−0.6	−0.2	−0.7
Total External Debt								
Emerging Market and Developing Economies	33.7	27.3	28.4	28.8	29.2	28.7	28.8	26.9
Debt Service								
Emerging Market and Developing Economies	9.5	9.8	11.4	12.4	10.9	9.8	11.1	9.3

[1]Data refer to trade in goods and services.
[2]London interbank offered rate on U.S. dollar deposits minus percent change in U.S. GDP deflator.
[3]GDP-weighted average of 10-year (or nearest-maturity) government bond rates for Canada, France, Germany, Italy, Japan, the United Kingdom, and the United States.

WORLD ECONOMIC OUTLOOK
SELECTED TOPICS

World Economic Outlook Archives

I. Methodology—Aggregation, Modeling, and Forecasting

II. Historical Surveys

III. Economic Growth—Sources and Patterns

IV. Inflation and Deflation and Commodity Markets

V. Fiscal Policy

VI. Monetary Policy, Financial Markets, and Flow of Funds

VII. Labor Markets, Poverty, and Inequality

VIII. Exchange Rate Issues

IX. External Payments, Trade, Capital Movements, and Foreign Debt

X. Regional Issues

XI. Country-Specific Analyses

XII. Special Topics

The following remarks were made by the Chair at the conclusion of the Executive Board's discussion of the Fiscal Monitor, Global Financial Stability Report, *and* World Economic Outlook *on March 28, 2016.*

Executive Directors broadly shared the assessment of global economic prospects and risks. They noted that while the global economy continues to expand modestly, prospects have weakened across a wide range of countries, and downside risks are rising. Risks to global financial stability have also increased amid volatility in global asset markets, weaker confidence, and geopolitical tensions. Directors agreed that the current conjuncture increases the urgency of a broad-based policy response, both individually and collectively, to raise growth, manage vulnerabilities, and boost confidence.

Directors observed that growth in advanced economies is projected to remain modest, in line with the 2015 outcomes. A stronger recovery continues to be restrained by weak external demand, low productivity growth, unfavorable demographic trends, growing income inequality, and legacies from the 2008–09 global financial crisis. Meanwhile, deflation risks remain a concern in Japan and several euro area countries.

Directors noted the generally weakening outlook for emerging market and developing economies, reflecting tighter global financial conditions and a weaker commodity market outlook. Growth prospects differ considerably across countries, and many have demonstrated more resilience to shocks given existing buffers and strengthened fundamentals and policy frameworks. China's transition toward more sustainable growth, backed by ample policy buffers, is a welcome development; however, given the increasingly prominent role of China in the world economy and financial markets, challenges and uncertainties in the process could have potential international implications.

Directors concurred that the outlook for global financial stability is clouded by downside risks. They noted in particular market pressures on banking systems and life insurance sectors in advanced economies. Emerging market economies face volatile capital flows and exchange rate pressures, as well as corporate sector vulnerabilities. A more balanced and potent policy mix that includes strong supervision, macroprudential frameworks, and implementation of the regulatory reform agenda is therefore vital.

Directors underscored that a combination of structural reforms and supportive monetary and fiscal policies is needed to raise actual and potential output. They generally endorsed the main policy recommendations in the reports, although the appropriate mix should be tailored to each country's circumstances. Directors also highlighted the importance of clear communication of policy intentions, especially by large economies. Commitment by policymakers to facilitate cross-border trade flows and global rebalancing remains crucial and must be followed through in order to achieve strong, sustainable, and balanced global growth. The fragile conjuncture calls for concerted efforts to identify potential responses to downside risks were they to materialize, to ensure strong, well-coordinated oversight and global financial safety nets and to ring-fence spillovers from noneconomic shocks.

Directors broadly agreed that, in advanced economies, securing higher sustainable growth requires a bold three-pronged approach consisting of mutually reinforcing (1) structural reforms, (2) continued monetary policy accommodation, and (3) prudent fiscal support. Recognizing the need to avoid overburdening monetary policy and preserve debt sustainability, Directors saw as a key element of this strategy a well-designed and -sequenced country-specific structural reform agenda that takes into account both the short- and medium-term impact of reforms. Reforms that entail fiscal support and reduce barriers to entry in product and services markets would best help strengthen near-term demand, while well-targeted tax and spending policies to encourage innovation and education investment could also play a useful role.

Directors stressed that accommodative monetary policy remains important, particularly in Japan and the euro area. Mindful of the side effects of extremely low—and, in some countries, negative—interest rates on domestic financial institutions, exchange rates, and other countries, they stressed the importance of complementary efforts to enhance policy transmission and accelerate balance sheet repair. The growing systemic importance of the insurance sector, in an environment of low interest rates, warrants a strong macroprudential approach to supervision and regulation.

Directors agreed that, where needed and where fiscal space is available, fiscal policy in advanced economies should be supportive of short- and medium-term growth—with a focus on boosting future productive capacity, in particular through infrastructure investment, and financing demand-friendly structural reforms. To preserve debt sustainability and anchor expectations, any fiscal relaxation should be based on a credible plan to return fiscal policy settings back toward targets over the medium term. Where fiscal space is limited, the emphasis should be placed on a more growth-friendly composition of the budget.

While recognizing the diverse challenges facing policymakers in emerging market and developing economies, Directors agreed that common policy priorities center on reducing macroeconomic and financial vulnerabilities and rebuilding resilience. They stressed that, in many countries, better fiscal and debt management frameworks that anchor longer-term plans will help mitigate procyclical policy and build resilience, while structural reforms are urgently needed to raise productivity and remove bottlenecks to production. Exchange rate flexibility, where feasible, can help cushion external shocks, although its effects on inflation and the balance sheets of the private and public sectors would need to be monitored closely.

Directors noted that the positive growth effects of the decline in commodity prices in commodity-importing economies have been less pronounced than expected. Commodity-exporting countries, on the other hand, have been hit hard and many have run down their policy buffers. Some of these countries need to adjust public spending to lower fiscal revenues. This adjustment should be complemented by further efforts to improve revenue diversification and phase out poorly targeted and wasteful spending, including fuel subsidies. For commodity importers, depending on their needs, part of the windfall gains from lower oil prices could be used to finance critical structural reforms or growth-enhancing spending.

Directors concurred that, in low-income countries, policies must respond to the heightened challenges and vulnerabilities stemming from the difficult external environment, taking account of domestic circumstances. For many commodity exporters whose fiscal and external balances are deteriorating, a tight macroeconomic policy stance is required to preserve hard-won macroeconomic stability. Directors also stressed the need to make further progress toward the Sustainable Development Goals, particularly through economic diversification, domestic revenue mobilization, and financial deepening. Appropriate policy advice and adequate financial assistance from the IMF and development partners remain important in that regard.